I0815369

"Chisholm's commentary strikes an ideal balance between technical proficiency and general accessibility. It does an excellent job of articulating the text in its context and exploring Zephaniah's place in the broader revelation of Scripture. The introductory comments on the book's literary unity, rhetorical strategy, and theological themes are particularly impressive. This will be a valuable resource for both pastors and scholars."

– Joel Barker,
Professor of Biblical Studies,
Heritage College & Seminary

ZEPHANIAH

CHRISTIAN STANDARD
COMMENTARY

ZEPHANIAH

—

Robert B. Chisholm, Jr.

Christian Standard Commentary: Zephaniah

ISBN: 978-1-0877-4195-6

Dewey Decimal Classification: 224.96

Subject Heading: BIBLE. OT. ZEPHANIAH-COMMENTARIES

1 2 3 4 5 6 • 28 27 26 25

Printed in China

RRD

Dedication

With love and affection to my grandsons, Frank Lawrence Stanesic IV *and* Robert Bruce Stanesic, *who bring me constant and immeasurable joy with their inquiring minds and passion for life. May they grow to appreciate fully the magnitude of Zephaniah's vision of God's coming kingdom, in which they, as followers of the Lord Jesus Christ, will someday live.*

Dedication

TABLE OF CONTENTS

SERIES INTRODUCTION

The Christian Standard Commentary (CSC) aims to embody an "ancient-modern" approach to each volume in the series. The following explanation will help us unpack this seemingly paradoxical practice that brings together old and new.

The *modern commentary* tradition arose and proliferated during and after the Protestant Reformation. The growth of the biblical commentary tradition largely is a result of three factors: (1) *The recovery of classical learning* in the fifteenth–sixteenth centuries. This retrieval led to a revival of interest in biblical languages (Greek, Hebrew, and Aramaic). Biblical interpreters, preachers, and teachers interpreted Scripture based on the original languages rather than the Latin Vulgate. The commentaries of Martin Luther and John Calvin are exemplary in this regard because they return to the sources themselves (*ad fontes*). (2) *The rise of reformation movements* and the splintering of the Catholic Church. The German Reformation (Martin Luther), Swiss Reformation (John Calvin), and English Reformation (Anglican), among others (e.g., Anabaptist), generated commentaries that helped these new churches and their leaders interpret and preach Scripture with clarity and relevance, often with the theological tenets of the movements present in the commentaries. (3) *The historical turn in biblical interpretation* in the seventeenth and eighteenth centuries. This turning point emphasized the historical situation from which biblical books arise and in which they are contextualized.

In light of these factors, the CSC affirms traditional features of a *modern commentary*, evident even in recent commentaries:

- Authors analyze Old and New Testament books in their original languages.
- Authors present and explain significant text-critical problems as appropriate.
- Authors address and define the historical situations that gave rise to the biblical text (including date of composition, authorship, audience, social location, geographical and historical context, etc.) as appropriate to each biblical book.
- Authors identify possible growth and development of a biblical text so as to understand the book as it stands (e.g., how the book of Psalms came into its final form or how the Minor Prophets might be understood as a "book").

The CSC also exhibits recent shifts in biblical interpretation in the past fifty years. The first is the literary turn in biblical interpretation. Literary analysis arose in biblical interpretation during the 1970s and 1980s, and this movement significantly influenced modern biblical commentaries. Literary analysis attends to the structure and style of each section in a biblical book as well as the shape of the book as a whole. Because of this influence, modern commentaries assess a biblical book's style and structure, major themes and motifs, and how style impacts meaning. Literary interpretation recognizes that biblical books are works of art, arranged and crafted with rhetorical structure and purpose. Literary interpretation discovers the unique stylistic and rhetorical strategies of each book. Similarly, the CSC explores the literary dimensions of Scripture:

- Authors explore each book as a work of art that is a combination of style and structure, form and meaning.
- Authors assess the structure of the whole book and its communicative intent.
- Authors identify and explain the literary styles, poetics, and rhetorical devices of the biblical books as appropriate.
- Authors expound the literary themes and motifs that advance the communicative strategies in the book.

As an *ancient commentary*, the CSC is marked by a theological bent with respect to biblical interpretation. This bent is a tacit recognition that the Bible is not only a historical or literary document but is fundamentally the Word of God. That is, it recognizes Scripture as fundamentally both historical *and* theological. God is the primary speaker in Scripture, and readers must deal with him. Theological interpretation affirms that although God enabled many authors to write the books of the Bible (Heb 1:1), he is the divine author, the subject matter of Scripture, and the One who gives the Old and New Testaments to the people of God to facilitate their growth for their good (2 Tim 3:16–17). Theological interpretation reads Scripture as God's address to his church because he gives it to his people to be heard and lived. Any other approach (whether historical, literary, or otherwise) that diminishes emphasis on the theological stands deficient before the demands of the text.

Common to Christian (patristic, medieval, reformation, or modern) biblical interpretation in the past two millennia is a sanctified vision of Scripture in which it is read with attention to divine agency, truth, and relevance to the people of God. The *ancient commentary* tradition interprets Scripture as a product of complex and rich divine action. God has given his Word to his people so that they may know and love him, glorify him, and proclaim his praises to all creation. Scripture provides the information and power of God that leads to spiritual and practical transformation.

The transformative potential of Scripture emerges in the *ancient commentary* tradition as it attends to the centrality of Jesus Christ. Jesus is the One whom God sent to the world in the fullness of time and whom the OT anticipates, testifies to, and witnesses to. Further, he is the One the NT presents as the fulfillment of the OT promise, in whom the church lives and moves and has her being, who the OT and NT testify will return to judge the living and the dead, and who will make all things new.

With Christ as the center of Scripture, the *ancient commentary* tradition reveals an implicit biblical theology. Old and New Testaments work together as they reveal Christ; thus, the tradition works within a whole-Bible theology in which each Testament is read in dialectic relationship, one with the other.

Finally, the *ancient commentary* tradition is committed to spiritual transformation. The Spirit of God illumines the hearts of readers so they might hear God's voice, see Christ in his glory, and live in and through the power of the Spirit. The transformational dimensions of Scripture emerge in *ancient commentary* so that God's voice might be heard anew in every generation and God's Word might be embodied among his people for the sake of the world.

The CSC embodies the *ancient commentary* tradition in the following ways:

- Authors expound the proper subject of Scripture in each biblical book, who is God; further, they explore how he relates to his world in the biblical books.
- Authors explain the centrality of Jesus appropriate to each biblical book and in the light of a whole-Bible theology.
- Authors interpret the biblical text spiritually so that the transformative potential of God's Word might be released for the church.

In this endeavor, the CSC is ruled by a Trinitarian reading of Scripture. God the Father has given his Word to his people at various times and in various ways (Heb 1:1), which necessitates a sustained attention to historical, philological, social, geographical, linguistic, and grammatical aspects of the biblical books that derive from different authors in the history of Israel and of the early church. Despite its diversity, the totality of Scripture reveals Christ, who has been revealed in the Old and New Testaments as the Word of God (Heb 1:2; John 1:1) and the One in whom "all things hold together" (Col 1:15–20) and through whom all things will be made new (1 Cor 15; Rev 21:5). God has deposited his Spirit in his church so that they might read spiritually, being addressed by the voice of God and receiving the life-giving Word that comes by Scripture (2 Tim 3:15–17; Heb 4:12). In this way, the CSC contributes to the building up of Christ's church and the Great Commission to which all believers are called.

AUTHOR'S PREFACE

The prophecy of Zephaniah is one of the least known and read books of the Bible. One can cover its 53 verses in a matter of minutes, perhaps leading some to the impression that the book is relatively insignificant. The fact that it is one of the so-called minor prophets tends to support this conclusion.

While one might be tempted to downplay Zephaniah's importance, to do so would be unwise, for the well-worn proverb "good things come in small packages" is certainly true of this book. It is a little gem God has hidden away in the heart of the Bible to give joy and confidence to those who read it as they seek to navigate troubling times. Having studied Zephaniah carefully over the past couple of years, I can promise you that a thoughtful, prayerful reading of the prophecy will comfort your spirit and draw you closer to the sovereign God who dominates the book's landscape through both judgment and salvation. In short, reading Zephaniah can be a spiritually enriching and transformative experience.

Within these 53 verses, God has given us a vision of his plan for this world. At first the vision is dark and frightening, but then the light of God's mercy dispels darkness and fear as we read how our sovereign God will fulfill his purposes for his covenant nation Israel and for all the nations of the earth. According to Zephaniah, God will someday bring to fruition the creation mandate as the nations of the world worship the one true God.

In this commentary I apply an historical-grammatical method, which takes seriously the historical and cultural context in which Zephaniah prophesied and pays careful attention to the words that he has written. I deal selectively with text-critical matters and Hebrew grammar, focusing on problematic and significant issues that are vital to understanding the book's message. For more exhaustive technical treatments of text-critical and grammatical matters, I recommend the commentaries by Thomas Renz and Marvin A. Sweeney. I deal with background matters where they are important, but avoid the temptation to try to be encyclopedic, which often causes one to wander down rabbit trails that are only tangential to the book's message and purpose. Furthermore, I prefer not to attempt to reconstruct Zephaniah's historical setting where evidence is lacking. Such speculative attempts are vestiges of an older form-critical approach that needs to be given a proper burial.

My presuppositions are decidedly and unashamedly evangelical. I affirm that all Scripture is the inspired Word of God, "profitable for teaching, for rebuking, for correcting, for training in righteousness" (2 Tim 3:16). Consequently, I assume and find that God has given us a coherent, unified message through Zephaniah that reveals his plan for the world. One of my goals is to demonstrate this. As I explain in the introduction to the commentary, I reject as fundamentally flawed diachronic approaches that rob the text of its unity as they seek to divide it up into its alleged developmental layers based on alleged contradictions. Though I find form-critical analysis of the text's structure useful, I repudiate as speculative its concern with oral tradition and reconstructing original life situations. I prefer a literary-rhetorical approach that examines the book's structure and style and how these features contribute to its rhetorical strategy and demonstrate its unity. As such, my approach is canonical, focusing on the text as we have it.

I agree with the vision of this commentary series as cast by the editorial team. Indeed, this is one of the reasons I agreed to accept their invitation to participate in the project. God's primary purpose in giving us the Bible is to reveal himself and his plan for his world. As we read and study Zephaniah, we want to learn more about God and discover what we should believe and how we should conduct our lives as we worship and serve him. As such, our study should be inherently theological in scope. For this reason, I have included a lengthy theological section prior to the commentary proper. In it I surface the book's themes and their development in the broader context of the Old Testament prophets and of the Bible as a completed canon. I place the theological section before the commentary proper because it is designed to give you the foundation and framework you need as you read through the text of Zephaniah with the commentary in hand. I also suggest that once you have read and studied the book with the aid of the commentary proper, you circle back and read the theological section a second time to solidify the book's message and significance.

Finally, I believe all preaching and teaching should lead to Jesus. Article 1 of the doctrinal statement of Dallas Theological Seminary, where I have taught since 1981, puts it this way: "We believe that all the Scriptures center about the Lord Jesus Christ in His person and work in His first and second coming, and hence that no portion, even of the Old Testament, is properly read or understood until it leads to Him." The book of Zephaniah poses a challenge to this Christotelic approach, since, as I explain in the introduction, there are no directly "messianic" passages in the book. Yet this does not mean that we should ignore Jesus when preaching and teaching Zephaniah. Good exposition always develops applications that are rooted in solid exegesis of the text, but it also correlates the principles of the text with other passages pertinent to the theme being developed as one moves from interpretation to application. In other words, sound biblical sermons and lessons combine accurate exegesis with insightful biblical theology and are canonical in scope. It is at the level of canonical correlation that one can legitimately introduce a Christotelic dimension to one's preaching and teaching of Zephaniah. In the introduction I discuss specific ways to do this.

Producing a commentary project of this nature takes a team effort. I want to thank Ray Clendenen for inviting me to write the commentary on Zephaniah for this series. Thanks as well to the editorial team for their wise direction, to Andrew King for his efficient guidance of the draft to publication, and to Andrew Steinmann for his helpful and encouraging comments and suggestions, all of which have improved the final product. We all stand on the shoulders of those who have gone before us. I am grateful to the many scholars who have written on Zephaniah. I have learned and benefited to varying degrees from their work, even when I disagreed with them. I am thankful for my many teachers over the years, especially my mentor and friend, the late Donald Glenn, who patiently taught me how to approach and execute the exegetical-theological task. I hope that this commentary, at least in some small way, rewards their efforts.

When I write academic works, my target audience is not the academic guild, but rather pastors and teachers who have the grave task of proclaiming the Bible's message to the people whom God has entrusted to them. I have tried to follow Peter's instruction: "If anyone speaks, let it be as one who speaks God's words" (1 Pet 4:7). My goal is to convey clearly and accurately God's message through Zephaniah. My prayer is that this commentary helps pastors and teachers to carry out their task of proclaiming the whole counsel of God. If that proves to be the case, all the hard labor that goes into producing a work of this nature will be well worth it.

All honor to King Jesus!
Robert Bruce Chisholm, Jr
August 12, 2024

ABBREVIATIONS

BIBLE BOOKS

Gen
Exod
Lev
Num
Deut
Josh
Judg
Ruth
1, 2 Sam
  1, 2 Kgdms (LXX)
1, 2 Kgs
  3, 4 Kgdms (LXX)
1, 2 Chr
Ezra
Neh
Esth
Job
Ps (pl. Pss)
Prov
Eccl
Song
Isa
Jer
Lam
Ezek
Dan
Hos
Joel
Amos
Obad
Jonah
Mic
Nah
Hab
Zeph
Hag
Zech
Mal
Matt
Mark
Luke
John
Acts
Rom
1, 2 Cor
Gal
Eph
Phil
Col
1, 2 Thess
1, 2 Tim
Titus
Phlm
Heb
Jas
1, 2 Pet
1, 2, 3 John
Jude
Rev

COMMONLY USED SOURCES FOR OLD TESTAMENT VOLUMES

AB	Anchor Bible
ABD	*Anchor Bible Dictionary*
ANET	*Ancient Near Eastern Texts Relating to the Old Testament*
AOTC	*Apollos Old Testament Commentary*
ARAB	*Ancient Records of Assyria and Babylonia*. Daniel David Luckenbill. Two volumes. Chicago: University of Chicago Press, 1926–27.
AUSS	*Andrews University Seminary Studies*
BA	*The Biblical Archaeologist*
BASOR	*Bulletin of the American Schools of Oriental Research*
BBR	*Bulletin for Biblical Research*
BDB	Francis Brown, S. R. Driver, and Charles A. Briggs, *A Hebrew and English Lexicon of the Old Testament*. Oxford: Clarendon, 1907.
BECNT	Baker Exegetical Commentary on the New Testament
BSac	*Bibliotheca Sacra*
BZAW	Beihefte zur Zeitschrift für die alttestamentliche Wissenschaft
CBQ	*Catholic Biblical Quarterly*
CAT	*Commentaire de l'Ancien Testament*
COS	*The Context of Scripture*. Edited by William W. Hallo and K. Lawson Younger Jr. Three volumes. Leiden: Brill, 2003.
CSB	Christian Standard Bible
DHS	A. B. Davidson, *Hebrew Syntax*. 3rd ed. Edinburgh: T & T Clark, 1901.
ESV	English Standard Version
FOTL	Forms of Old Testament Literature
GKC	*Gesenius' Hebrew Grammar.* Edited by E. Kautzsch. Translated by A. E. Cowley. 2nd English ed. Oxford: Clarendon, 1910.
HALOT	*The Hebrew and Aramaic Lexicon of the Old Testament*. Ludwig Koehler, Walter Baumgartner, and J. J. Stamm. Translated and edited under the supervision of M. E. J. Richardson. Two volumes. Leiden: Brill, 2001.
HUCA	*Hebrew Union College Annual*
IBHS	Introduction to Biblical Hebrew Syntax
JAOS	*Journal of the American Oriental Society*
JBL	*Journal of Biblical Literature*
JETS	*Journal of the Evangelical Theological Society*
JSOT	*Journal for the Study of the Old Testament*
JSOTSup	Journal for the Study of the Old Testament–Supplement Series
KJV	King James Version
MT	Masoretic Text
NAC	New American Commentary
NASB	New American Standard Bible
NCB	New Century Bible Commentary

NET	The NET Bible (New English Translation)
NICOT	New International Commentary on the Old Testament
NIDOTTE	*New International Dictionary of Old Testament Theology and Exegesis*
NIV11	*New International Version* (2011 edition)
NLT	New Living Translation
OTL	Old Testament Library
SBLDS	Society of Biblical Literature Dissertation Series
SHBC	Smyth & Helwys Bible Commentary
TDOT	*Theological Dictionary of the Old Testament*
TOTC	Tyndale Old Testament Commentaries
VT	*Vetus Testamentum*
VTSup	Vetus Testamentum, Supplements
WBC	Word Biblical Commentary
WTJ	*Westminster Theological Journal*
ZAW	*Zeitschrift für die alttestamentliche Wissenschaft*

ZEPHANIAH

INTRODUCTION OUTLINE

1 Introduction
  1.1 Author
  1.2 Date
    1.2.1 Historical Framework
    1.2.2 Josiah's Reign
  1.3 Zephaniah's Prophecy in Its Historical and Canonical Contexts
    1.3.1 Zephaniah's Prophecy within the Context of Josiah's Reign
    1.3.2 Zephaniah's Prophecy within Its Canonical Context
  1.4 Literary Structure and Rhetorical Strategy of Zephaniah
  1.5 Christotelic Proclamation of Zephaniah's Message
    1.5.1 Three Messages on Zephaniah
    1.5.2 Six Messages on Zephaniah
    1.5.3 Seven Messages on Zephaniah
  1.6 Challenges to Literary Unity
    1.6.1 Systemic Flaws
    1.6.2 A Response to Some Specific Redaction Critical Arguments
2 Theological Interpretation of Zephaniah
  2.1 God's Self-Revelation
    2.1.1 Name and Titles
    2.1.2 Kingship
      2.1.2.1 The Lord as Creator-King
      2.1.2.2 The Lord as Warrior-King
        2.1.2.2.1 The Day of the Lord
        2.1.2.2.2 The Lord's Anger
        2.1.2.2.3 God of War or God of Peace?
      2.1.2.3 The Lord as Shepherd-King
    2.1.3 The Relational God
      2.1.3.1 The Lord's Relationship with His Covenant People
        2.1.3.1.1 Sin
        2.1.3.1.2 Judgment

1 INTRODUCTION

1.1 Author

The book's heading identifies Zephaniah as the recipient of the word of the Lord that follows. The name, which means "the Lord has hidden," is attested in extrabiblical Hebrew, and three other individuals in the OT have this name.[1] Zephaniah the prophet is further identified as "son of Cushi, son of Gedaliah, son of Amariah, son of Hezekiah."[2] The structure is unique because it traces the prophet's ancestry back four generations.[3]

The uniqueness of the heading prompts one to seek a reason for extending Zephaniah's genealogical tree. Hezekiah, from whom Josiah descended and whose reign coincided with Zephaniah's ministry ends the list, prompting questions of Zephaniah's familial relationship to the king.[4] Such a family connection explains the lengthy family tree since the prophet's royal ancestry and familial connection to Josiah would be noteworthy.[5] There is no corroborating evidence for this

---

[1] See *HALOT*, 1049.

[2] The Syriac version reads "Hilkiah" instead of "Hezekiah." This may reflect a tradition that Zephaniah and Jeremiah, son of Hilkiah, were relatives. For discussion see Marvin A. Sweeney, *Zephaniah: A Commentary*, Hermeneia (Minneapolis: Fortress, 2003), 48.

[3] One other heading in the Latter Prophets goes back two generations (Zechariah son of Berechiah son of Iddo), six headings name only the prophet's father (Isaiah son of Amoz, Jeremiah son of Hilkiah, Ezekiel son of Buzi, Hosea son of Beeri, Joel son of Pethuel, Jonah son of Amittai), and seven give no genealogical information (Amos, Obadiah, Micah, Nahum, Habakkuk, Haggai, Malachi).

[4] For a discussion of the chronological issues involved, see Thomas Renz, *The Books of Nahum, Habakkuk, and Zephaniah*, NICOT (Grand Rapids: William B. Eerdmans, 2021), 455–56, and Gene Rice, "The African Roots of the Prophet Zephaniah," *The Journal of Religious Thought* 36, 1 (Spring–Summer 1979): 21–22.

[5] See Robert R. Wilson, *Prophecy and Society in Ancient Israel* (Minneapolis: Fortress, 1980), 279–80, as well as O. Palmer Robertson, *The Books of Nahum, Habakkuk, and Zephaniah,*

proposal in Scripture or in external sources; nevertheless, it remains the best explanation for the extended genealogy despite scholarly reservations and arguments to the contrary.[6]

The presence of the name Cushi (*kûšî*) in Zephaniah's genealogy has occasioned discussion. In a genealogical list following "son of," it must be understood as a proper name. The proper name Cushi also appears in the genealogy of a man named Jehudi in Jer 36:14.[7] More often *kûšî* is an ethnic term for a Cushite, a descendant of Cush (*kûš*), one of Ham's sons (cf. Gen 10:6). The Cushites settled in Ethiopia. Zephaniah mentions the Cushites (2:12) and the rivers of Cush (3:10).

Some theorize the Cushi mentioned in the genealogy was of African descent. Gene Rice points out the other four names in the heading's genealogy are compounded with the divine name Yahweh. Cushi stands out in this regard; and Rice, pointing to Buzi, the name of Ezekiel's father, suggests the ethnic name Cushi may have become a proper name.[8] Rice observes that "Ethiopians were scattered throughout the Near East and the Mediterranean world. This came about initially because of their being used as mercenaries by the principal powers of the ancient world: Egypt, Israel, Phoenicia, Greece, Persia."[9] Rice also draws attention to the close relationship between Judah and the Twenty-fifth Dynasty of Egypt, which was Ethiopian.[10] According to Rice, there were two individuals of Ethiopian descent in the royal court of Judah in the time of Jeremiah—the aforementioned Jehudi, a

---

NICOT (Grand Rapids: William B. Eerdmans, 1990), 253; Waylon Bailey, "Nahum, Habakkuk, Zephaniah," in Kenneth L. Barker and Waylon Bailey, *Micah, Nahum, Habakkuk, Zephaniah,* NAC 20 (Nashville: Broadman & Holman, 1998), 408; J. Alec Motyer, "Zephaniah," in J. Alec Motyer, Thomas E. McComiskey, and Douglas Stuart, *Zephaniah, Haggai, Zechariah, Malachi,* in Thomas Edward McComiskey, *The Minor Prophets: An Exegetical and Expository Commentary, Vol. III* (Grand Rapids: Baker Books, 1998), 898; and Rice, "African Roots of the Prophet Zephaniah," 21.

[6] For reservations regarding and objections to the proposal, see J. J. M. Roberts, *Nahum, Habakkuk, and Zephaniah: A Commentary,* OTL (Louisville: Westminster/John Knox, 1991), 166; Ehud Ben Zvi, *A Historical-Critical Study of the Book of Zephaniah,* BZAW 198 (Berlin: Walter de Gruyter, 1991), 46–47; Renz, *Zephaniah,* 456–57.

[7] An individual named Cush is identified as a Benjaminite in the heading of Psalm 7.

[8] Rice, "African Roots of the Prophet Zephaniah," 22.

[9] Rice, "African Roots of the Prophet Zephaniah," 24. See also Roger W. Anderson Jr., "Zephaniah Ben Cushi and Cush of Benjamin: Traces of Cushite Presence in Syria-Palestine," in Steven W. Holloway and Lowell K. Handy, eds., *The Pitcher is Broken: Memorial Essays for Gösta W. Ahlström,* JSOTSup 190 (Sheffield: Sheffield Academic, 1995), 45–70.

[10] Rice, "African Roots of the Prophet Zephaniah," 25.

descendant of Cushi (Jer 36:14), and Ebed-melech (Jer 38:7).[11] Rice theorizes:

> The incidental, chance references to Yehudi and Ebed-melech suggest the existence of a larger presence of which they are representative, a presence most naturally accounted for by the alliance between Judah and the Ethiopian dynasty of Egypt. At least, the presence of two men of Ethiopian ancestry with close ties to the royal house of Judah in the time of Jeremiah, which is virtually the same as that of Zephaniah, makes the existence of another such man, especially one with the name Cushi, completely credible.

He adds this:

> Since Zephaniah's ancestry is traced in an unbroken line on his father's side to Hezekiah, it is most natural to think of Cushi's mother (Gedaliah's wife) as an African. If this were the case, still it would have been Gedaliah who named his son Cushi, for it was the custom at this time for the father to name the children. That Gedaliah broke with the family tradition of names compounded with Yahweh, a significant departure for one related to the royal house of Judah, is most intelligible on the assumption that his son was of Ethiopian ancestry and that he affirmed this ancestry with pride."[12]

Finally, Rice argues Zephaniah's interest in Cush and the Cushites (2:12; 3:10) is consistent with the theory of the prophet's African descent.[13] While this proposal is certainly creative, several interpreters express reservations or reject it outright.[14]

The prophet Zephaniah appears in later Jewish and Christian tradition.[15] He is mentioned briefly in *The Lives of the Prophets,* which originated in the first century AD. There we read: "Zephaniah was of the tribe of Simeon, of the countryside of Sabaratha. He prophesied

---

[11] See also Gene Rice, "Two Black Contemporaries of Jeremiah," *The Journal of Religious Thought* 32, 1 (Spring–Summer 1975): 95–109.

[12] Rice, "African Roots of the Prophet Zephaniah," 28.

[13] Rice, "African Roots of the Prophet Zephaniah," 29–30.

[14] See, for example, Bailey, "Zephaniah," 384–85; Ben Zvi, *Zephaniah,* 45; Adele Berlin, *Zephaniah,* AB (New York: Doubleday, 1994), 67; Renz, *Zephaniah,* 455; Roberts, *Zephaniah,* 166; and Sweeney, *Zephaniah,* 48–49.

[15] For a summary of the evidence, see Sweeney, *Zephaniah,* 41.

concerning the city and about the end of the gentiles and the shaming of the impious. And he died and was buried in his field."[16] *The Apocalypse of Zephaniah*, which originated between 100 BC and 175 AD, purports to be a vision seen by Zephaniah when he was transported to the fifth heaven.[17]

1.2 Date

According to the heading, Zephaniah received his message from the Lord during the reign of Judah's King Josiah (641–609 BC), son of Amon (643–641 BC). This was an eventful time in the Near East and in the nation of Judah. To appreciate Josiah's reign fully, we must place it within its broader historical framework.

1.2.1 Historical Framework

Between 733 and 722 BC the Assyrian Empire reduced the territory of the northern kingdom Israel to provinces. This culminated in the conquest of Samaria in 722 BC. When Sargon II (721–705 BC) replaced Shalmaneser V as king of Assyria, the change in rule prompted rebellions in the south and in the west. Sargon, after solidifying his strength at home, had to stabilize his empire. In the south a coalition of Elamites and Chaldeans, led by Merodach-baladan (2 Kgs 20:12), beat back the Assyrians at Der in 720 BC. Sargon was not able to drive Merodach-baladan out of Babylon until 710. In the west Sargon encountered a Syro-Palestinian coalition that included rebel forces from Damascus, Samaria, and Gaza, among others. In 720 Sargon defeated the rebels at Qarqar, swept through Philistia, and went as far as the Egyptian border, forcing Judah, ruled by Ahaz (735–716 BC), to pay tribute. Sargon also brought the siege of Tyre, begun five years earlier by Shalmaneser, to a successful conclusion. After campaigning in the east for two years, Sargon was forced to put down another western rebellion in 717 BC. In 712 he sent a force to the west again, this time to put down a rebellion by the king of Ashdod (see Isa 20:1).

After Sargon's death in battle in 705 BC, Sennacherib (704–681 BC) rose to the throne of Assyria. Rebellions broke out in the empire

---

[16] James Charlesworth, ed., *The Old Testament Pseudepigrapha* 2 vols. (Garden City, NY: Doubleday & Company, 1983, 1985), 2:394. This passage associates him with Simeon, not Judah, suggesting it does not view him as a descendant of King Hezekiah.

[17] Charlesworth, *The Old Testament Pseudepigrapha*, 1:497–515.

shortly after this. In 703 BC Merodach-baladan tried unsuccessfully to regain the throne of Babylon. In 701 BC, in conjunction with his religious reforms and his attempt to revive the glory of the Davidic monarchy, Hezekiah of Judah (729–687 BC) allied with the kings of Sidon and Ashkelon, along with the leaders of Ekron, and attempted to overthrow Assyrian rule.[18] Sennacherib came west to put down the rebellion. The king of Sidon fled to Cyprus, the king of Ashkelon was carried away into exile, and the rebel leaders in Ekron were impaled, leaving Judah.

Sennacherib's invasion of Judah consisted of two forces. The first advanced through central Judah and established a line of approach and supply through the northern Shephelah. This force captured Azekah, Gath, and the cities of the Shephelah, including Lachish.[19] A second force moved from Lachish up to Jerusalem, destroying several towns along the way. In his annals Sennacherib describes his conquest of the land and his siege of Jerusalem (see *COS*, 2:303). He boasts that he captured forty-six walled cities, took over 200,000 captives, forced Hezekiah to pay a large amount of tribute, and trapped the Judahite king in his royal city "like a bird in a cage." The biblical account (see 2 Kgs 18:17–19:35; Isa 36–37) provides us with a more complete picture of what happened. Here we learn the Lord destroyed a large number of Assyrian soldiers, forcing Sennacherib to return to Assyria. Sennacherib does not record this disaster; this comes as no surprise, given his well-attested tendency to falsify history in his royal annals.[20] Most importantly, Sennacherib does not claim to have taken Jerusalem or to have deposed Hezekiah. His silence in this case speaks volumes!

For the remainder of his reign, Sennacherib was occupied with rebellions in the south. In 700 BC he defeated Merodach-baladan and his Elamite and Aramean allies. In 695–691 BC he campaigned against the Elamites, while in 689 he destroyed Babylon after besieging it for nine months. According to 2 Kgs 19:37 (see also Isa 37:38), two of Sennacherib's sons assassinated him while he worshipped in the temple

---

[18] On Hezekiah's reforms and anti-Assyrian policies, see Oded Borowski, "Hezekiah's Reforms and the Revolt against Assyria," *BA* 58 (1995), 148–55.

[19] See Nadav Na'aman, "Sennacherib's Campaign to Judah and the Date of the *lmlk* Stamps," *VT* 29 (1979), 61–86, and David Ussishkin, "The Destruction of Lachish by Sennacherib and the Dating of the Royal Judean Storage Jars," *Tel Aviv* 4 (1977), 28–60.

[20] Antti Laato, "Assyrian Propaganda and the Falsification of History in the Royal Inscriptions of Sennacherib," *VT* 45 (1995), 198–226.

of one of his gods. They escaped to Armenia, while Sennacherib's son Esarhaddon (681–669 BC) took the Assyrian throne.

Esarhaddon rebuilt Babylon, regaining the loyalty of the Babylonians, and solidifying his rule in the south. In the west Esarhaddon maintained control of the Assyrian provinces and vassals, including Judah, now ruled by Hezekiah's son Manasseh (697–643 BC), who is listed as one of Esarhaddon's subjects in one of the Assyrian king's inscriptions.[21] Esarhaddon also campaigned against the Egyptians and even forced the princes of Lower Egypt to acknowledge his sovereignty.

Esarhaddon's successor, his son Ashurbanipal (668–627 BC), attempted to strengthen Assyrian control over Egypt. Toward the end of his father's reign, the Egyptians had rebelled against Assyrian rule. After Ashurbanipal took the throne, he marched against Egypt and defeated the rebels. However, once the main army withdrew, the Egyptians did not cooperate with Assyrian occupational troops, which had to put down the uprising.

Sometime later, probably after 648 BC, Manasseh of Judah rebelled against Assyrian rule. He was taken to Babylon in humiliation but eventually was allowed to return to Jerusalem (2 Chr 33:11–13). Manasseh was succeeded by his son Amon (643–641 BC), who was in turn succeeded by Josiah (641–609 BC). During Josiah's reign major political changes occurred in the Near East, as the Assyrian Empire collapsed, and the Babylonians and Egyptians rushed to fill the vacuum.

Ashurbanipal was succeeded by his son, Ashur-etil-ilani, who had to suppress two internal uprisings during his brief reign. During these internal struggles (if not before in some cases) Babylon, Palestine, Phoenicia, and Media repudiated Assyrian rule. About 623 BC Sin-shar-ishkun seized the throne from his brother, Ashur-etil-ilani, with the help of the Chaldean Nabopolassar, who had already rebelled against Assyria in 626 BC. Sin-shar-ishkun then broke off relations with Nabopolassar; Assyria and Babylon remained hostile until the demise of the former a few years later. In 615 BC the Medes under Cyaxares invaded Assyria, capturing the city of Ashur. Cyaxares and Nabopolassar formed an alliance and defeated Nineveh in 612 BC, an event prophesied by Nahum and described in the Babylonian

---

[21] See *ANET*, 291, and Roy Gane, "The Role of Assyria in the Ancient Near East during the Reign of Manasseh," *AUSS* 35 (1997), 22–23.

Chronicle.[22] Assyrian forces under Ashur-uballit, an officer of the king, regrouped in Harran.

In 609 BC the Egyptians, under Neco (who was trying to maintain the balance of power in the Near East), marched northward to aid the Assyrians. Josiah of Judah challenged him at Megiddo and was killed in battle (2 Kgs 23:29–30). Judah became an Egyptian vassal. In 609 BC Josiah's son Jehoahaz became king of Judah. He apparently rebelled against Egyptian rule, for Necho quickly replaced him with his brother Jehoiakim (609–598 BC; see 2 Kgs 23:31–35).

In 605 BC the Egyptians and Babylonians, led by Nebuchadnezzar (605–562 BC), clashed at Carchemish (see Jer 46:2). The Babylonians emerged victorious, and Nebuchadnezzar marched southward into Palestine, making Jehoiakim his vassal. When Jehoiakim rebelled in 601 BC (2 Kgs 24:1), Nebuchadnezzar sent troops to the west, reestablished control of Judah, and claimed territory all the way to the Egyptian border (2 Kgs 24:2, 7). In 598 Jehoiachin (598–597) succeeded Jehoiakim to the throne of Judah. Apparently, Judah rebelled at this time, for Nebuchadnezzar besieged Jerusalem, replaced Jehoiachin with Zedekiah, and deported many people, including Jehoiachin, to Babylon (see 2 Kgs 24:10–17 and *ANET*, 305). Zedekiah (597–587) remained loyal for a time, but he, like his predecessors, rebelled against Babylonian rule. In 589 Nebuchadnezzar besieged Jerusalem, which eventually capitulated. The Babylonians sacked the city, burned the temple, and carried most of the people away into exile (2 Kgs 25). The Jews would not return to their homeland until almost fifty years later, when the Persians, led by Cyrus, conquered Babylon (see *ANET*, 306–7) and allowed them to go back.

1.2.2 Josiah's Reign

Following the assassination of Amon in 641 BC, the people of Judah made his son Josiah king (2 Kgs 21:24–26; 2 Chr 33:24–25). Josiah was only eight years old when he assumed the throne (2 Kgs 22:1; 2 Chr 34:1). The opening summary of his reign reads as follows: "He did what was right in the LORD's sight and walked in all the ways of his ancestor David; he did not turn to the right or the left" (2 Kgs 22:2)/"He did what was right in the LORD's sight and walked in the

---

[22] See *ANET*, 304–5, and Jean-Jacques Glassner, *Mesopotamian Chronicles*, SBL Writings from the Ancient World 19 (Atlanta, SBL, 2004), 222–23.

ways of his ancestor David; he did not turn aside to the right or the left" (2 Chr 34:2).

In Josiah's eighth year (fall 633–summer 632 BC, when he was sixteen years old), he had a spiritual awakening and "began to seek the God of his ancestor David" (2 Chr 34:3). Four years later (629 BC), when he was twenty, he began a spiritual cleansing of Judah and Jerusalem that lasted several years and gained momentum in his eighteenth year (623 BC) when the long-neglected book of the law was discovered during repairs on the temple. Seeking to eliminate idol worship, he targeted the high places, Asherah poles, and shrines to the god Baal. He desecrated the graves of those priests who had led the people in idol worship (2 Chr 34:3b–5). This purge extended into the north into former Israelite territory, including the tribal regions of Manasseh, Ephraim, Simeon, and even Naphtali (2 Chr 34:6–7). While this area was technically under Assyrian rule, the turmoil taking place in Mesopotamia (see above) enabled Josiah to extend his authority into the north.

As noted above, while Josiah had already launched a purge four years before, the discovery of the book of the law gave the revival its impetus. In fact, in 2 Kings a purge follows the discovery of the law, while in 2 Chronicles a purge precedes its discovery.

2 KINGS 22–23	2 CHRONICLES 34–35
Discovery of the Law (22:3–13)	**Purge of Idolatry (34:3–7)**
Huldah's Prophecy (22:14–20)	*Discovery of the Law (34:8–21)*
Covenant Renewal (23:1–3)	Huldah's Prophecy (34:22–28)
Purge of Idolatry (23:4–20)	Covenant Renewal (34:29–33)
Passover Observed (23:21–23)	Passover Observed (35:1–19)

When Josiah heard the law read, he tore his clothes as a sign of mourning because he realized the nation had been disregarding it, causing the Lord's wrath to come upon them (2 Kgs 22:8–13; 2 Chr 34:19–21). Huldah the prophetess confirmed his concern (2 Kgs 22:14–20; 2 Chr 34:22–28). She pronounced a judgment speech upon Jerusalem and its inhabitants in accordance with the curses contained in the law. The basis for this judgment was the people's rejection of the Lord and their idolatry. The Lord's unquenchable wrath, like fierce fire, would be kindled against them.

Nevertheless, the news was not all bad. The Lord promised Josiah because of his humility and repentant spirit, "I will indeed gather you to your ancestors, and you will be gathered to your grave in peace. Your eyes will not see all the disaster that I am bringing on this place" (2 Kgs 22:20; cf. 2 Chr 34:28).

In response to Huldah's message, Josiah gathered many people, including priests, prophets, and all the residents of Jerusalem, for a covenant renewal ceremony (2 Kgs 23:1–2a; cf. 2 Chr 34:29–30a). Josiah "read in their hearing all the words of the book of the covenant that had been found in the LORD's temple" (23:2; cf. 2 Chr 34:30b) and "made a covenant in the LORD's presence to follow the LORD and to keep his commands, his decrees, and his statutes with all his heart and with all his soul in order to carry out the words of this covenant that were written in this book; all the people agreed to the covenant" (23:3; cf. 2 Chr 34:31–32).

Second Kings 23:4–20 gives a lengthy account of how Josiah purged the land of idolatry in conjunction with this renewal of covenant. He removed from "the LORD's sanctuary all the articles made for Baal, Asherah, and all the stars in the sky" and "burned them outside Jerusalem in the fields of the Kidron and carried their ashes to Bethel" (23:4). He also removed the "idolatrous priests" who "burned incense to Baal, and to the sun, moon, constellations, and all the stars in the sky" (23:5). He moved an Asherah pole from the temple to the Kidron Valley, where he burned it and beat it to dust (23:6). He "also tore down the houses of the male cult prostitutes that were in the LORD's temple, in which the women were weaving tapestries for Asherah" (23:7). He purged Judah of its high places (23:8–9), defiled Topheth, where child sacrifices to Molech were offered (23:10), and eliminated worship of the sun (23:11–12). Throughout Jerusalem he purged the high places Solomon had built for Ashtoreth, Chemosh, and Milcom (23:13). He "broke the sacred pillars into pieces" and "cut down the Asherah poles" (23:14). Turning his attention northward, he destroyed the high place built by Jeroboam in Bethel (23:15–16) and "the high places that were in the cities of Samaria" (23:19). To top it off, "he slaughtered on the altars all the priests of those high places, and he burned human bones on the altars" (23:20).

Josiah commanded the people to observe the Passover, which had not been observed since the days of the judges (2 Kgs 23:21–23). He organized the Levites to offer the Passover sacrifices, and he and his officials donated a huge number of sacrificial animals (2 Chron 35:1–9). The ceremony, which the Chronicler describes in great detail (35:10–19), was unprecedented in the nation's history:

> No Passover had been observed like it in Israel since the days of the prophet Samuel. None of the kings of Israel ever observed a Passover like the one that Josiah observed with the priests, the Levites, all Judah, the Israelites who were present in Judah, and the inhabitants of Jerusalem" (35:18).

The closing summary of Josiah's reign provides further details concerning the purge of idolatry, stressing he was motivated by his desire to obey the newly discovered law: "In addition, Josiah eradicated the mediums, the spiritists, household idols, images, and all the abhorrent things that were seen in the land of Judah and in Jerusalem. He did this to carry out the words of the law that were written in the book that the priest Hilkiah found in the LORD's temple" (2 Kgs 23:24). The closing assessment exceeds the opening summary (cf. 22:2) in its praise of the king: "Before him there was no king like him who turned to the LORD with all his heart and with all his soul and with all his strength according to all the law of Moses, and no one like him arose after him" (23:25).

Unfortunately, Josiah's commendable efforts did not rescue Judah from judgment (2 Kgs 23:26–27). There was no mass repentance, and as a result of Manasseh's sins, the Lord's anger continued to burn against Judah. He determined to remove Judah from his presence as he had done to the northern kingdom of Israel. Even though he had chosen Jerusalem for his earthly dwelling place, he announced he would reject the city and the temple.

As for Josiah, he met a tragic end (2 Kgs 23:29–30). The prophetess Huldah, having announced the downfall of Jerusalem, commended Josiah and assured him he would die "in peace" and not have to "see the disaster" the Lord would bring upon the city (22:15–20). Nevertheless Josiah was killed in battle, seemingly contradicting what Huldah had promised about his dying in peace. Cogan and Tadmor conclude, "These words of Huldah remain a striking example of unfulfilled prophecy."[23] Indeed, dying a bloody death on a battlefield can hardly

[23] Mordechai Cogan and Hayim Tadmor, *II Kings*, AB (New York: Doubleday, 1988), 295.

be viewed as dying "in peace."[24] If, however, we view the prophecy as implicitly conditional to begin with and make room for human freedom, it becomes apparent Josiah's decision to intervene in international politics compromised God's antecedent will as expressed by Huldah. Nevertheless, the promise was fulfilled in its essence. As stated by Huldah, Josiah died without having to see Jerusalem's demise.[25]

1.3 Zephaniah's Prophecy in Its Historical and Canonical Contexts

1.3.1 Zephaniah's Prophecy within the Context of Josiah's Reign

As noted above in the description of Josiah's purge in 2 Kings 23:4–5, the author refers to Baal worship and describes how Josiah "did away with the idolatrous priests" (*kəmārîm*) who sacrificed to Baal. He speaks of astral worship and includes within Josiah's purge those who burned incense to the stars in the sky (*ṣəbāʾ haššāmāyim*, "the host of heaven"), as well as worshippers of Milcom and Molech (vv. 10, 13).

Zephaniah's description of Judah's idolatry fits well within the period of Josiah's reign. In the accusation in chapter 1, the prophet records the Lord's announcement that he would cut off "every vestige of Baal" (lit., "the remnant of Baal"), which included the priests (*kəmārîm*) who functioned within the Baal cult (v. 4). The Lord would eliminate those who worshipped "the stars in the sky" (*ṣəbāʾ haššāmāyim*, "the host of heaven") (v. 5). The coming judgment would also include those who made oaths in the name of "their king" (the

---

[24] In the Chronicler's version of Josiah's death, the king cries out, "I am severely wounded" (2 Chr 35:23). This is incongruous with Huldah's prophecy, for dying "in peace" is the antithesis of dying violently, as Jer 34:4–5 indicates.

[25] See Robert B. Chisholm, "When Prophecy Appears to Fail, Check Your Hermeneutic," *JETS* 53/3 (September 2010): 569–70. The 2 Kings and 2 Chronicles accounts of the king's death appear to differ in their chronology. According to 2 Kgs 23:29–30, Josiah was killed at Megiddo. His servants transported his corpse via chariot to Jerusalem, where he was buried. However, in 2 Chr 35:23–24 Josiah, having been wounded, commands his servants to remove him from the battlefield. They transfer him to another chariot and take him to Jerusalem. The text informs us that he died and was buried. NIV's "where he died" is overly interpretive. The text simply says, "and he died." This could be sequential to the preceding verb ("and brought him"), but it could be a concluding summary statement involving temporal overlay. The verbal combination "died and was buried" is common (see Gen 35:8, 19; Num 20:1; Deut 10:6; Judg 8:32; 10:2, 5; 12:7, 10, 12, 15; Ruth 1:17; 2 Sam 17:23; Jer 16:4; 20:6). Perhaps Josiah died at Megiddo after being taken from the battlefield, but the Chronicler delays stating that he died until he mentions his burial. See Robert B. Chisholm Jr., "History or Story? The Literary Dimension in Narrative Texts," in *Giving the Sense*, ed. D. Howard and M. Grisanti (Grand Rapids: Kregel, 2003), 69–70.

literal reading here, cf. NET) (v. 5). The referent is unclear. Options include Baal, the Ammonite god Milcom (cf. CSB, ESV, NASB), and Molech (NIV11), to whom children were sacrificed (see the commentary below).

In addition to his denunciation of idolatry, Zephaniah alludes to social oppression within Jerusalem. Many gained wealth through deceit and violence (1:9, 12–13; 3:1–3). Jeremiah, who also prophesied during Josiah's reign, speaks of such oppression (Jer 7:5–6; 22:3, 11–17). Since Josiah promoted "justice and righteousness" and championed the just cause of the "poor and needy" (Jer 22:15–16), it is likely Zephaniah's critique reflects the injustice characterizing the covenant community while Josiah was still young. Unfortunately, these oppressive practices were eventually perpetuated by Josiah's sons, making Zephaniah's denunciation of injustice relevant even after Josiah's death.

Zephaniah also alludes to foreign cultural influence compromising the integrity of the covenant community. This is unsurprising since Judah had suffered under Assyrian rule for decades by the time of Josiah's reign. According to Nathan Hays, astral worship "was especially prominent in Assyria and material evidence for astral worship in the Levant increases considerably with greater contact with Assyria."[26] This explains in part the Lord's denunciation of astral worship in 1:5. In 1:8 the Lord announces he will "punish the officials, the king's sons, and all who are dressed in foreign clothing." According to Hays, there is "iconographic evidence for Assyrian-style dress in the Levant during the period of Assyrian domination." He explains: "Elites were attempting to gain prestige by aligning themselves with Assyria even on the level of their clothing."[27]

In 3:1–2, as Zephaniah moves from a judgment speech against Nineveh to a woe oracle against Jerusalem, he links the two cities rhetorically. It is not apparent he has shifted his focus until 3:2 when he says the rebellious, defiled, and oppressive city of 3:1 "has not trusted in the Lord" and "has not drawn near to her God." This rhetorical move serves to associate Nineveh and Jerusalem morally. Hays says, "The rapid and unmarked transition from the oracle against Assyria/Nineveh . . . to the condemnation of Jerusalem . . . rhetorically

---

[26] Nathan Hays, "Humility and Instruction in Zephaniah 3.1–7," *JSOT* 44, 3 (2020): 477–78.

[27] Hays, "Humility," 478.

underscores the deep and troubling continuity between Jerusalem and Assyria/Nineveh."[28] Several verbal links between the two oracles solidify the point that Jerusalem had become corrupted by pagan influences (see 3:15 below).

The judgment speeches against foreigners in 2:4–15 fit well in the context of the late seventh century BC when Josiah ruled Judah. Like Zephaniah, his contemporary Jeremiah prophesied judgment upon the Philistine cities (Jer 25:20; 47:1–7), as well as Moab and Ammon (Jer 25:21; 48:1–49:6). It is unsurprising that Zephaniah would describe Assyria's downfall since it was unfolding during the time of his prophetic ministry, and the prophet's rhetoric reflects this immediacy. In 2:13 he uses three jussives to call judgment down upon Assyria/Nineveh, and in verse 15 he uses a perfect verbal form to depict Nineveh as a heap of ruins. The perfect form of the verb syntactically functions to reflect imminent action, picturing Nineveh's ruin as certain to occur. However, it is also possible verse 15 depicts Nineveh's fall (612 BC) as accomplished, and Zephaniah appended this description of the aftermath of judgment to the original curse and prophecy (see 2:13–15 below).

As for Cush, its appearance in the oracles against the nations is surprising because its power had declined following the fall of Thebes in 664/663 BC.[29] Regardless, the prophet uses Cush as representative of distant nations to the south and as archetypal, much like Ezekiel does shortly after this (Ezek 30:4–5; 38:5). This makes sense when one understands the eschatological dimension of Zephaniah's prophecy, which encompasses distant nations (2:11) and foresees their reclamation in the reversal of the Babel judgment and dispersion (3:9–10). The brevity of the oracle against Cush (2:12) underscores its purely representative function.

1.3.2 Zephaniah's Prophecy within Its Canonical Context

Zephaniah is one of the so-called Minor Prophets, traditionally viewed as a unified collection called "The Twelve." Following Micah, three short prophetic books appear—Nahum, Habakkuk, and Zephaniah, each three chapters in length. All three date to the seventh century BC,

[28] Hays, "Humility," 472.

[29] See Renz, *Zephaniah,* 569.

an eventful time when Judah seemed to be at the mercy of the near Eastern megapowers Assyria and Babylon.

The three books share a common overarching theme: "The justice of God as exhibited in powerful judgment on an international scale."[30] All three make clear Judah's destiny is in the hands of the Lord, the God who is sovereign over the nations. In Nahum the Lord comes as the "avenging God" who "takes vengeance against his foes" and does not allow "the guilty" to go "unpunished" (Nah 1:2–3). The focal point of his judgment is Assyria. In Habakkuk the Lord uses the Chaldeans (Babylonians) as his instrument of judgment against those in Judah who are guilty of violence and injustice (Hab 1:2–11). He then turns on the Babylonians and punishes them for the injustice they have perpetrated among the nations (2:5–19; 3:1–15). In Zephaniah the Lord pours out his judgment on the world (1:2–3, 14–18). He targets Judah and Jerusalem (1:4–13), where injustice abounds (Zeph 3:1–4), even though the righteous and just Lord lives within the city (3:5).[31]

These three prophetic books share several subthemes:[32]

1. The sovereign God opposes the arrogant, whose hubris fuels their greed and imperialism and whose trust is in wealth and fortifications. Nahum compares Assyria to a ravaging lion eager to maul its prey (Nah 2:11–13) and a seductive prostitute greedy for economic gain (3:4). Babylon violently robbed other nations (Hab 2:5–17). Habakkuk compares her to a fisherman collecting fish in his net (1:15–16), a drunkard who, "like Death," is "never satisfied" (2:5), and a loan shark who exploits others (2:6). Even the leaders of Judah, convinced God does not hold people accountable for their actions (Zeph 2:12), viciously robbed others (1:9–13; 3:1–4). The Lord would plunder Assyria's great wealth (Nah 2:9) and destroy her fortified cities (3:8–13). Nineveh boasted, "I exist, and there is no one else" (Zeph 2:15), but the Lord would make it desolate. Death would overwhelm greedy Babylon (Hab 2:5–17), and the Lord would deprive the oppressive leaders of Jerusalem of their wealth (Zeph 1:9–13) and destroy the earth's fortifications (1:16). Wealth will be of no value in the face of his destructive wrath (1:18).

---

[30] Robert B. Chisholm Jr., "A Theology of the Minor Prophets," in R. B. Zuck, ed., *A Biblical Theology of the Old Testament* (Chicago: Moody, 1992), 413.

[31] Chisholm, "A Theology of the Minor Prophets," 413–14.

[32] Chisholm, "A Theology of the Minor Prophets," 414–17.

2. The Lord comes as an angry warrior whose arrival disturbs the cosmos, signaling the destructive judgment he unleashes. All three prophets call him the Lord of Armies (Nah 2:13; 3:5; Hab 2:13; Zeph 2:9) and describe him as angry and/or as seeking vengeance (Nah 1:2, 6; Hab 3:8, 12; Zeph 1:15, 18; 3:8). Nahum depicts him as coming in the "whirlwind and storm" with "clouds . . . beneath his feet" (1:3–4). "Mountains quake before him, and the hills melt; the earth trembles at his presence—the world and all who live in it. . . . Even rocks are shattered before him" (1:5–6). He brings a flood against Nineveh and chases his enemies into the darkness (1:8). Habakkuk pictures him coming in splendor accompanied by plague and pestilence (3:4–5). "[God] stands and shakes the earth. . . . The age-old mountains break apart; the ancient hills sink down" (3:6). Zephaniah describes his judgment as flood-like in its reversal of creation (1:2–3). The day of the Lord is a "day of wrath, . . . trouble and distress, . . . destruction and desolation, . . . darkness and gloom, . . . clouds and total darkness" (1:15).

3. The Lord demonstrates his superiority to the idol-gods of the nations. The Lord directly attacks the gods of the Assyrian king (Nah 1:14). When he unleashes his violent judgment upon Babylon (Hab 2:17), it becomes clear that carved idols and cast images are worthless (2:18). One might as well deliver a death chant (cf. "woe") over those who trust in lifeless idols (2:19). In contrast to them, the Lord "is in his holy temple" (2:20). He will someday defeat the gods of the earth, prompting the nations to "bow in worship to him" (Zeph 2:11).

4. On a more positive note, all three prophets declare the Lord protects and saves his faithful people. Nahum affirms, "The LORD is good, a stronghold in a day of distress; he cares for [lit., "knows"] those who take refuge in him" (1:7). By the end of his prophecy, Habakkuk's concerns have been addressed, and with robust faith he can assert: "I will rejoice in the God of my salvation! The LORD my Lord is my strength" (3:18–19). Zephaniah, speaking to personified Zion in the day of restoration beyond judgment, assures her: "The LORD your God is among you, a warrior who saves" (3:17).

1.4 Literary Structure and Rhetorical Strategy of Zephaniah

Heading (1:1)

I. The Day of the Lord: Worldwide Judgment Targeting Judah and Jerusalem (1:2–18)

On the day of the Lord, he will unleash judgment on a worldwide scale (cf. 1:2–3, 14–18) with Judah and Jerusalem being the focal point (1:4–13). There are two main literary units in chapter 1 (vv. 2–6 and 7–18). The functionally hortatory interjection "be silent" at the beginning of verse 7 marks the division between them. By the end of the chapter, the prophet circles back to where he began, with the worldwide judgment of the day of the Lord forming a framework for the judgment of Judah and Jerusalem.

A. Judgment Reverses Creation and Eliminates False Worship (1:2–6)

One of the most common forms in prophetic literature is the judgment speech, which typically consists of a formal accusation (the basis for judgment) and a formal announcement of judgment.[33] The latter may contain a notice of the Lord's intervention, often spoken in the first person, and a description of its outcome.

Zephaniah's prophecy begins with a judgment speech (1:2–6). There is no formal accusation in this speech, but the description of the objects of judgment in verses 3b–6 is functionally accusatory. They are wicked, promote false worship, turn from the Lord, and fail to seek him. The speech consists of a formal announcement of judgment expressed through six "I will" declarations in which the Lord states his intention to intervene, namely "I will stretch out my hand," "I will sweep away" (three times), and "I will cut off" (twice). While the guilt of the objects of judgment is apparent and described in detail, the prominence of the first-person verbs highlights the Lord's active involvement in the coming judgment.

---

[33] Claus Westermann, *Basic Forms of Prophetic Speech,* trans. H. C. White (Philadelphia: Westminster Press, 1967), 129–88.

1. The Reversal of Creation through Flood-like Judgment (1:2–3)

The coming judgment will be worldwide in scope. In flood-like fashion, it reverses the created order as the Lord "sweeps away everything from the face of the earth" (v. 2), including people and animals, the birds of the sky, the fish of the sea, and the "ruins along with the wicked" (v. 3). The twofold mention of human beings as the objects of judgment (note "people" [*ʾādām*] and "mankind" [*hāʾādām*]) suggests they are the focal point. But the judgment is discriminating; it targets the "wicked."

2. The Elimination of False Worship (1:4–6)

Within the framework of worldwide judgment, the Lord zeroes in on Judah and Jerusalem. He eliminates from the covenant community those who give mere lip service to him while worshipping other gods, including Baal and astral deities. He removes those who turn from him and fail to seek him.[34]

B. The Imminent Day of the Lord Brings Punishment and Devastation (1:7–18)

In verses 7–18 the day of the Lord becomes the primary judgment motif. This day is imminent and will bring destructive punishment. References to the nearness of the day (vv. 7a, 14a) introduce the two judgment speeches that comprise this literary unit. The first of these (vv. 7–13), like verses 4–6, focuses on Jerusalem, while the second (vv. 14–18), like verses 2–3, broadens the scope of the coming judgment to the world, paving the way for the oracles against the nations that appear in 2:4–15.

[34] It is worth noting that the Lord's removal of idols is not simply an act of judgment. It also expresses his mercy, for it seeks to protect his faithful remnant from the evil influence of idolatry.

1. A Day of Punishment for Jerusalem (1:7–13)

The coming judgment upon Jerusalem will be like a sacrifice, with the objects of judgment being the sacrificial animals.

a. A Call for Silence in Anticipation of a "Sacrifice" (1:7)

This judgment speech begins with an exhortation. This prophetic speech form typically contains an exhortation proper accompanied by reasons for heeding it. Here the interjection "be silent" (v. 7a) functions as the exhortation, and two *kî* clauses introduce the reasons for silence (v. 7b).[35] The approaching day of the Lord demands a response of silence, for the Lord will slaughter the objects of his judgment as if they were sacrificial animals.

b. Punishment as "Sacrifice" (1:8–13)

In the judgment speech proper, the Lord announces he will intervene to punish sinners (note the threefold "I will punish" in vv. 8–9, 12, accompanied by "I will search" in the third case). Verses 10–11, 13 describe the results of the Lord's intervention.[36] The Lord will punish the corrupt royal court, including those who steal from others, and bring economic activity to an end. He will punish all those who persist in sin and who believe he will not hold them accountable for their actions. He will deprive them of their ill-gotten wealth. As in verses 2–6 there is no formal accusation, but the description of the objects of judgment is functionally accusatory.

---

[35] CSB translates the first with "for" and second with "indeed," but see the commentary below.

[36] Embedded within the description of the results of judgment is a rhetorical call to lament that dramatically depicts what will happen when the Lord intervenes (v. 11). The exhortation ("wail") is supported (note "for") by reasons lamentation is appropriate. Merchants will be "silenced" and "cut off."

2. A Day of Devastation for the World (1:14–18)

The approaching day of the Lord will bring devastation and ruin on a widespread scale against those who have sinned against him. Their wealth will not protect them from his fiery wrath.

a. Devastation for the Proud (1:14–16)

This judgment speech begins with an announcement that the day of the Lord is near (v. 14, cf. v. 7a) accompanied by a detailed characterization of this day as one of warfare, wrath, destruction, and darkness directed against human pride (vv. 15–16).

b. Devastation for Sinners (1:17–18)

A formal announcement of the Lord's intervention follows ("I will bring distress"), accompanied by a description of the gory results of judgment (vv. 17–18a). Embedded within this description is the formal basis for judgment (note *kî*, "because"): "They have sinned against the LORD." The speech concludes with a reference to the Lord's intervention (in the third person, v. 18b) as the immediate cause of the devastation depicted so vividly prior to this. By the end of this speech, the judgment, while including Judah and Jerusalem, has broadened to include "the whole earth" and "all" its "inhabitants."

II. The Lord's Angry Judgment: Devastation Mixed with Glimpses of Hope (2:1–15)

Chapter 2 contains two main literary units (2:1–3, 4–15) that are logically connected (note *kî*, "for," at the beginning of v. 4). The prophet begins by exhorting an "undesirable nation" (Judah) to prepare for destruction (vv. 1–2) and the "humble of the earth" to seek the Lord by maintaining their quest for righteousness and humility (v. 3). Urgency is necessary because the coming judgment will devastate nations from west (Philistia, vv. 4–7) to east (Moab and Ammon, vv. 8–11) and south (Cush, v. 12) to north (Assyria, vv. 13–15).

While the inevitability of judgment dominates the landscape of the chapter, a rhetorical shift occurs as the prophet's message progresses. Initially, Judah is doomed, and there are no guarantees of deliverance, even for the humble who persist in obedience. Nevertheless, in the aftermath of this judgment, the Lord will reverse the situation of Judah's survivors (vv. 7, 9) and even make distant nations his genuine worshippers (v. 11). This marks a rhetorical turning point in the message of Zephaniah. What appears to be strictly a prophecy of Judah's and Jerusalem's ruin and of destruction on a worldwide scale becomes instead a message of hope. Chapter 3 describes how the Lord will reclaim the nations scattered at Babel and restore his covenant community.

A. Imminent Devastation Demands Preparation (2:1–3)

Irony pervades the two exhortations. The prophet commands the "undesirable nation" to gather as kindling for the fiery judgment that is coming. By transforming what is expected—a call to repent before judgment falls—to a sarcastic call to prepare to be burned, he emphasizes the inevitability of destruction. By urging the humble to persist in their obedience, but without a guarantee of deliverance (note "perhaps"), he emphasizes the Lord's sovereignty in judgment. Nevertheless, a glimpse of hope is offered for the obedient. The rhetorical technique paves the way for the display of divine mercy that follows. (For a fuller discussion of verses 1–3 from a speech act and rhetorical perspective, see the commentary below.)

B. Widespread Devastation Has a Surprising Aftermath (2:4–15)

The coming judgment will have a worldwide impact on nations. Given the historical situation at the time, one might have expected Egypt and Babylon to appear in this list, but the nations are strategically chosen as representatives of those located in all directions of the compass.

1. The Devastation of the Philistines to the West (2:4–7)

This oracle begins with a description of the results of judgment (v. 4). A woe (*hôy*) oracle follows, accompanied by a formal announcement of the Lord's intervention (v. 5, note "I will destroy") and an additional description of the results of judgment (v. 6). The oracle ends on a positive note with a salvation announcement. The "remnant of the house of Judah" will occupy Philistine territory as "the LORD their God" reverses their situation (v. 7).

As for the woe oracle, the interjection *hôy*, "woe," was used in funeral laments (see 1 Kgs 13:30; Jer 22:18–19; 34:5; Amos 5:16). When used in prophetic judgment speeches, it often carries the connotation of death. This speech form is a subcategory of the judgment speech. The pronouncement of woe (*hôy*) is typically accompanied by an accusation (sometimes implicit in the description of the addressee, cf. 3:1–5). However, in Zeph 2:5 there is no formal accusation accompanying the woe pronouncement, nor is there an embedded accusation in the vocative that merely identifies the addressee.

2. The Devastation of Moab and Ammon to the East (2:8–11)

This oracle begins with the Lord stating his accusation against Moab and Ammon (v. 8). Using an oath, he announces the coming judgment, focusing on its results without including a formal statement about his intervention (v. 9a). As in the preceding oracle (cf. v. 7), there is a statement about the remnant of Judah (note "my people") occupying the territory of the objects of judgment (v. 9b). In verse 10 the prophet correlates the description of the judgment (cf. v. 9a) with the accusation (v. 8). After affirming the Lord's awesome position (v. 11a^1), he puts the judgment of Moab and Ammon in broader, worldwide perspective (vv. 11a^2–11b). The Lord will weaken (CSB, "starve") the "gods of the earth," prompting the distant nations to worship him. Ironically, judgment becomes the first stage in the Lord's reclamation of the nations (cf. 3:9–10).

3. The Devastation of Cush to the South (2:12)

   This third oracle stands out due to its brevity: "You Cushites will also be slain by my sword." It consists of an announcement of the Lord's intervention (note "my sword").

4. The Devastation of Assyria to the North (2:13–15)

   The prophet begins this fourth oracle by calling a curse down upon Assyria and the city of Nineveh.[37] After the curse, which appeals for divine intervention, the prophet, confident his prayer will be answered, describes the results of judgment (v. 14). He then provides the accusation, or basis for judgment, Nineveh's arrogance, before further describing the results of judgment (v. 15).

III. Glimpses Become Reality: Judgment Gives Way to Salvation (3:1–20)

Chapter 3 contains two major literary units (3:1–10, 11–20). In the first unit the judgment theme continues as Zephaniah denounces Jerusalem's sins (vv. 1–5). The Lord expected the city to repent when it saw the devastating judgment he brought upon the nations, but her people persisted in disobedience (vv. 6–7). Consequently, those hoping for restoration of blessing must wait patiently (v. 8). A salvation announcement then appears (vv. 9–10) as the Lord expands the theme of 2:11, which foresees a time when the distant nations will worship the Lord.

The second unit, introduced by the formula "on that day" (v. 11), expands the salvation announcement to include Jerusalem and her people. It develops in much greater detail the salvation notices of 2:7, 9. Jerusalem will be populated by a faithful remnant that will celebrate the Lord's powerful presence and the security he provides (vv. 11–20).

---

[37] Note the three *weyiqtol* verb forms, the first and third of which are distinctly jussive; see the commentary below.

A. The Necessity of Judgment and Patience (3:1–10)

The first unit begins with a woe oracle in which the prophet denounces the city for its sins, which were committed despite the Lord's presence within the city (vv. 1–5). The Lord suddenly speaks, addressing the city (vv. 6–7; note "I have cut off" at the beginning of v. 6). He explains that, despite his expectations, the city and her people have not repented. He then addresses a group (probably the remnant mentioned in v. 12), urging them to wait patiently for judgment to run its course (v. 8). The message takes a positive turn, as the Lord describes the transformation of the nations to genuine worshippers (vv. 9–10). "Therefore" at the beginning of verse 8 formally links the exhortation with what precedes, but the switch from a feminine singular addressee in verse 7a to a masculine plural addressee in verse 8 marks the transition to a new subunit. Three causal clauses introduced by "for" (*kî*) follow (two in v. 8b and one at the beginning of v. 9).

1. The Necessity of Judgment upon Jerusalem (3:1–5)

This woe oracle is strictly accusatory, with no formal announcement of judgment, though impending doom is inherent in the "woe." The accusatory elements highlight the city's rebellion, defilement, and oppression (v. 1). More specifically, "She has not obeyed . . . accepted discipline . . . trusted in the LORD" or "drawn near to her God" (v. 2). Her princes, judges, prophets, and priests are corrupt (vv. 3–4), in contrast to "the righteous LORD" who dwells in the city. The fact that the leaders display their sin in his presence heightens their guilt (v. 5).

2. The Necessity of Judgment upon the Nations (3:6–7)

The Lord elaborates on the accusation by giving a detailed account of his attempt to bring his people to repentance. He expected his destructive judgment upon the nations to have a positive impact on his people. He anticipated the city would "fear" him and "accept correction." This would entail submitting to his sovereign authority and turning from evil. Despite his efforts, the people persisted in sin.

3. The Necessity of Waiting upon the Lord (3:8–10)

The appearance of "therefore" leads one to expect a formal announcement of judgment. Instead, an exhortation follows, instructing an unidentified group to wait patiently for judgment to run its course. The judgment will be worldwide in scope (note "nations" and "kingdoms"). The addressees are probably his obedient followers, whom he addressed in 2:3: "Seek the LORD, all you humble of the earth, who carry out what he commands." This group is also described in 3:12 as "meek and humble people" who "take refuge in the name of the LORD." "Wait for" has a positive connotation here, where it carries the nuance "wait in faith." Such hopeful expectation will sustain God's people through the difficult time to come when he pours out his anger on the nations.

Three reasons are given for waiting: (1) The Lord has decided to gather the nations for judgment; (2) this judgment will consume the whole earth; and (3) the nations will then unify in pure worship of the Lord. The positive turn is abrupt and perhaps surprising, but the salvation announcement in 2:11 has already signaled this development. The focus on salvation paves the way for a salvation announcement addressed to Zion in 3:11.

B. The Transformation of the Lord's People (3:11–20)

The transformation of the nations will be accompanied by a transformation of the Lord's covenant community. Jerusalem and her people will celebrate the Lord's powerful presence and the security he provides. This literary unit begins with "on that day" (v. 11), followed by a salvation announcement addressed to Jerusalem (vv. 11–19) and her people (v. 20) that describes her spiritual transformation and the restoration of blessing. The Lord speaks first (vv. 11–13), followed by an exhortation from the prophet (vv. 14–15). Another "on that day" formula marks the beginning of a new subunit in which the prophet speaks first (vv. 16–17), followed by the Lord (vv. 18–19). The final subunit begins with the formula "at that time" (v. 20) and contains a message from the Lord to the remnant (addressed with masculine plural forms).

1. Jerusalem's Joy (3:11–15)

   The Lord will purge Jerusalem, replacing the proud with a righteous remnant that is humble and meek (vv. 11–13). It will be a time of celebration for Jerusalem and all Israel (v. 14), for the Lord, their King, will turn away his judgment, dwell among them, and protect them (v. 15).

2. The Lord's Joy (3:16–19)

   In the concentric structure of verses 11–19, the themes of verses 11–15 are reiterated. In the day of restoration, there will be no need for fear because the Lord, the mighty Warrior, will be present in the city (vv. 16–17a, cf. v. 15). Just as Zion rejoices over the Lord (v. 14), so the Lord will rejoice over his people (v. 17b). He will restore a remnant and remove his people's shame (vv. 18–19, cf. vv. 11–13).

3. The Lord's Restoration of the Exiles (3:20)

   As the prophecy concludes, the Lord assures his people that he will gather them and give them honor among the nations. They will become famous and an object of praise among all the peoples of the earth when he restores their fortunes before their eyes. The prophecy ends by declaring: "The LORD has spoken," which corresponds nicely to the first words of the prophecy: "The word of the LORD" (1:1).

1.5 Christotelic Proclamation of Zephaniah's Message

In this section I discuss proclaiming the message of Zephaniah. In approaching the proclamation of any biblical book, one must decide how to divide the text into sermonic units. For Zephaniah, one could limit a series to three messages (one per chapter) or, digging a bit deeper, two messages per chapter (corresponding to the A and B subunits of each chapter in the outline above). In the section to follow, I will provide sermonic main ideas for each of these approaches. Not all literary units, however, carry the same freight. Some are denser than others and require more attention to detail, while others can be consolidated more readily. Consequently, I will also offer a third sermon series that takes these factors into consideration and divides the book into seven messages. This series divides chapter 1 differently for sermonic purposes as it gives attention to the concentric structuring within the chapter: (1) 1:2–3, 14–18; (2) 1:4–6, 7–13; (3) 2:1–3; (4) 2:4–15; (5) 3:1–8; (6) 3:9–10 (cf. 2:11); and (7) 3:11–20.

I believe all preaching/teaching should lead to Jesus. Article 1 of the doctrinal statement of Dallas Theological Seminary, where I have taught since 1981, puts it this way: "We believe that all the Scriptures center about the Lord Jesus Christ in His person and work in His first and second coming, and hence that no portion, even of the Old Testament, is properly read or understood until it leads to Him."

Nevertheless, the book of Zephaniah poses a challenge to this Christotelic approach. There are no messianic passages in the book. Indeed, there are only two references to a human king—Josiah is identified as the king of Judah at the time of Zephaniah's prophetic ministry (1:1), and the king's sons are mentioned as objects of God's judgment (1:8). The Lord is called the "King of Israel" (3:15), but there is no mention of a human mediator to whom he has delegated authority, let alone an ideal Davidic king.[38]

Some might object that Luke 24:27 demands that we find Jesus mentioned in every book of the OT: "Then beginning with Moses and all the Prophets, [Jesus] interpreted for them the things concerning himself in all the Scriptures." However, at the time Luke wrote this, the so-called twelve Minor Prophets were understood as one book, known today as "the Twelve." Indeed, writing in the first century AD, Josephus states the Jewish community recognized twenty-two books as those "justly believed in." These correspond to the thirty-nine books of the English OT, but the only way Josephus could have arrived at a figure of twenty-two is if he understood the Twelve as one book.

---

[38] In their study of messianism in the OT, Abernethy and Goswell offer no examples of messianic passages from Zephaniah. In fact, they cite Zephaniah just twice in their index (p. 283). The first citation (p. 137) makes the point that after Amos 1:1, prophetic headings (including Zeph 1:1) "mention only southern kings." The second citation (p. 170) lists Zeph 3:14–17 as an example of the "proclamation of arrival" literary form attested in Zech 2:10. See Andrew T. Abernethy and Gregory Goswell, *God's Messiah in the Old Testament: Expectations of a Coming King* (Grand Rapids: Baker Academic, 2020).

Though one is hard-pressed to find a messianic reference in Zephaniah, there are messianic passages elsewhere in the Twelve (see, for example, Micah 5 or Zechariah 9), so it is unnecessary to read Jesus into Zephaniah through strained exegesis (eisegesis?).

Nevertheless this does not mean one should ignore Jesus when preaching/teaching Zephaniah. Good preaching/teaching always develops applications rooted in solid exegesis of the text, but, when preaching/teaching, it is also essential to correlate the principles of the text with other passages pertinent to the theme being developed as one moves from exegesis to application. In other words, good sermons/lessons combine accurate exegesis with insightful biblical theology and are canonical in scope. At the level of canonical correlation, one can legitimately introduce a Christotelic dimension to one's preaching/teaching of Zephaniah.

For example, Zephaniah 2:11 and 3:9–10 picture a day when all nations will unify in worshipping the one true God. One can correlate this theme with Psalm 72, which envisions a day when the nations, in conjunction with their worship of the one true God (vv. 18–19), will recognize his chosen king as sovereign and bow before him and serve him (v. 11). In the progress of revelation, we discover that this king is, of course, Jesus. We can correlate the Zephaniah passages with Psalm 72 (and other passages, such as Phil 2:9–11) in depicting this future day of worldwide genuine worship. In a congregational setting it would be fitting to sing Isaac Watts's great hymn, "Jesus Shall Reign Where'er the Sun," at the conclusion of the message. As I develop preaching themes for Zephaniah, I will include a brief discussion of how I would include a Christotelic dimension in the preaching/teaching of each passage at the level of correlation/biblical theology. Perhaps Jesus was doing some of this on the Emmaus Road![39]

NOTE: To appreciate the following section, the reader will need to be familiar with the preceding section, "Literary Structure and Rhetorical Strategy," and, when pertinent, the commentary *per se* below.

---

[39] For helpful examples of how to proclaim the message of Zephaniah in a Christotelic manner, see Iain M. Duguid and Matthew P. Harmon, "Zephaniah: Hope through the Darkness," in *Zephaniah, Haggai, Malachi*, Reformed Expository Commentary (Phillipsburg: P & R Publishing, 2018).

1.5.1 *Three Messages on Zephaniah*

The three messages correspond to the book's three chapters, labeled as follows in the outline above:

I. The Day of the Lord: Worldwide Judgment Targeting Judah and Jerusalem (1:2–18)
II. The Lord's Angry Judgment: Devastation Mixed with Glimpses of Hope (2:1–15)
III. Glimpses Become Reality: Judgment Gives Way to Salvation (3:1–20)

The main ideas for each message may be stated this way:

Message 1: The Lord's judgment of Judah/Jerusalem for its idolatry and injustice foreshadows his future judgment of the world for its sinful pride (1:2–18).

Christotelic dimension: Jesus will be the one who executes judgment on the day of the Lord. Texts for correlation and development of an application: 1 Thess 5:1–11; 2 Thess 1:5–12; Rev 19:11–21.

Message 2: One wonders if anyone can escape the devastation of the coming worldwide judgment, but a glimpse beyond judgment reveals the Lord will preserve those who seek him and his righteousness. Furthermore, the Lord will reclaim the nations after he defeats all their gods (2:1–15).

Christotelic dimension: (1) Jesus assured the humble who desire righteousness will be satisfied and vindicated (Matt 5:3, 6). (2) Jesus, the servant of the Lord in Isaiah's Servant Songs, will mediate a covenant between God and the nations and take the light of salvation to them (Isa 42:1–7). The Lord will be glorified as he demonstrates his superiority to the idol-gods of the nations (Isa 41:21–29; 42:8–9), prompting the nations to worship him (Isa 42:10–12). See also Rev 21:23–24; 22:2.

Message 3: Judgment of the covenant community and the nations is necessary, but beyond judgment the Lord will reverse the Babel dispersion and unify the nations as his worshippers. He will also bring the Zion ideal to realization as he dwells among his people (3:1–20).

Christotelic dimension: (1) Psalm 72 envisions a day when the nations, in conjunction with their worship of the one true God (vv. 18–19; cf. Zeph 2:11; 3:9–10), will recognize his chosen king as sovereign and bow before him and serve him (v. 11; see also Rev 21:23–26). According to Phil 2:9–11, this king is Jesus, before whom "every knee will bow" and whose sovereignty "every tongue will confess." (2) As John described the realization of the Zion ideal (Rev 21:1–22:5), he pictured the new Jerusalem, populated by the godly of all ages (see especially Rev 21:12, 14), as the bride of the Lamb (Jesus).

1.5.2 Six Messages on Zephaniah

I. The Day of the Lord: Worldwide Judgment Targeting Judah and Jerusalem (1:2–18)

A. Judgment Reverses Creation and Eliminates False Worship (1:2–6)

Message 1: The Lord's judgment of Judah/Jerusalem for its idolatry foreshadows his future judgment of the world.

B. The Imminent Day of the Lord Brings Punishment and Devastation (1:7–18)

Message 2: The Lord's judgment of Judah/Jerusalem for its injustice foreshadows his future judgment of the world for its sinful pride.

Christotelic dimension (for messages 1 and 2): Jesus will execute judgment on the day of the Lord. Texts for correlation and development of an application: 1 Thess 5:1–11; 2 Thess 1:5–12; Rev 19:11–21.

II. The Lord's Angry Judgment: Devastation Mixed with Glimpses of Hope (2:1–15)

A. Imminent Devastation Demands Preparation (2:1–3)

Message 3: Certain doom awaits those who persist in sin, but there is hope for the humble who seek the Lord by seeking righteousness.

Christotelic dimension: Jesus assured the humble, who desire righteousness, that they will be satisfied and vindicated (Matt 5:3, 6).

B. Widespread Devastation Has a Surprising Aftermath (2:4–15)

Message 4: Judgment will overtake the nations, but the Lord will vindicate his people as he defeats all foreign gods and reclaims the worship of the nations (cf. 3:9–10).

Christotelic dimension: Jesus, the servant of the Lord in Isaiah's Servant Songs, will mediate a covenant between God and the nations and take the light of salvation to them (Isa 42:1–7). The Lord will be glorified as he demonstrates his superiority to the idol-gods of the nations (Isa 41:21–29; 42:8–9), prompting the nations to worship him (Isa 42:10–12). See also Rev 21:23–24; 22:2.

III. Glimpses Become Reality: Judgment Gives Way to Salvation (3:1–20)

A. The Necessity of Judgment and Patience (3:1–10)

Message 5: Judgment of the covenant community and the nations is necessary, but beyond judgment the Lord will reverse the Babel dispersion and unify the nations as his worshippers (cf. 2:11).

Christotelic dimension: Psalm 72 envisions a day when the nations, in conjunction with their worship of the one true God (vv. 18–19; cf. Zeph 2:11; 3:9–10), will recognize his chosen king as sovereign and bow before him and serve him (v. 11). According to Phil 2:9–11, this king is Jesus, before whom every knee will bow and whose sovereignty every tongue will confess.

B. The Transformation of the Lord's People (3:11–20)

Message 6: Beyond judgment, the Lord will bring the Zion ideal to realization as he dwells among his people, who celebrate his powerful presence and the security he provides. Just as Zion rejoices over the Lord, so he will rejoice over his people.

Christotelic dimension: As John described the realization of the Zion ideal (Rev 21:1–22:5), he pictured the new Jerusalem, populated by the godly of all ages (see especially Rev 21:12, 14), as the bride of the Lamb (Jesus).

1.5.3 Seven Messages on Zephaniah

I The Day of the Lord: Worldwide Judgment Targeting Judah and Jerusalem (1:2–18)

A. Judgment Reverses Creation and Eliminates False Worship (1:2–6)

B. The Imminent Day of the Lord Brings Punishment and Devastation (1:7–18)

Message 1: The Lord will judge the world for its sinful pride (1:2–3, 14–18).

Christotelic dimension: Jesus will be the one who executes judgment on the day of the Lord. Texts for correlation and development of an application: 1 Thess 5:1–11; 2 Thess 1:5–12; Rev 19:11–21.

Message 2: The Lord's judgment of Judah/Jerusalem for its idolatry and injustice foreshadows his future judgment of the world (1:4–6, 7–13).

Christotelic dimension: The idolatry and injustice of Judah/Jerusalem's sinners proved they did not love God and their neighbors. When asked, "Teacher, which command in the law is the greatest?" Jesus replied:

> Love the Lord your God with all your heart, with all your soul, and with all your mind. This is the greatest and most important command. The second is like it: Love your neighbor as yourself. All the Law and the Prophets depend on these two commands. (Matt 22:36–40)

II. The Lord's Angry Judgment: Devastation Mixed with Glimpses of Hope (2:1–15)

A. Imminent Devastation Demands Preparation (2:1–3)

Message 3: Certain doom awaits those who persist in sin, but there is hope for the humble who seek the Lord by seeking righteousness.

Christotelic dimension: Jesus assured the humble, who desire righteousness, that they will be satisfied and vindicated (Matt 5:3, 6).

B. Widespread Devastation Has a Surprising Aftermath (2:4–15)

Message 4: Judgment will overtake the nations, but the Lord will vindicate his people as he defeats all foreign gods and reclaims the worship of the nations (cf. 3:9–10).

Christotelic dimension: Jesus, the Servant of the Lord in Isaiah's Servant Songs, will mediate a covenant between God and the nations and take the light of salvation to them (Isa 42:1–7). The Lord will be glorified as he demonstrates his superiority to the idol-gods of the nations (Isa 41:21–29; 42:8–9), prompting the nations to worship him (Isa 42:10–12). See also Rev 21:23–24; 22:2.

III. Glimpses Become Reality: Judgment Gives Way to Salvation (3:1–20)

A. The Necessity of Judgment and Patience (3:1–10)

Message 5: Blatant disregard for the Lord and his just standards necessitates judgment 3:1–8).

Christotelic dimension: Jesus, the Servant of the Lord, is God's instrument in bringing justice to the earth (Isa 42:1–4; see also Isa 11:1–9).

Message 6: Beyond judgment the Lord will reverse the Babel dispersion and unify the nations as his worshippers (3:9–10; cf. 2:11).

Christotelic dimension: Psalm 72 envisions a day when the nations, in conjunction with their worship of the one true God (vv. 18–19; cf. Zeph 2:11; 3:9–10), will recognize his chosen king as sovereign and bow before him and serve him (v. 11). According to Phil 2:9–11, this king is Jesus, before whom every knee will bow and whose sovereignty every tongue will confess.

B. The Transformation of the Lord's People (3:11–20)

Message 7: Beyond judgment, the Lord will bring the Zion ideal to realization as he dwells among his people, who celebrate his powerful presence and the security he provides. Just as Zion rejoices over the Lord, so he will rejoice over his people.

Christotelic dimension: As John described the realization of the Zion ideal (Rev 21:1–22:5), he pictured the new Jerusalem, populated by the godly of all ages (see especially Rev 21:12, 14), as the bride of the Lamb (Jesus).

1.6 Challenges to Literary Unity

Some are convinced the book of Zephaniah is not a literary unity. For example, Anselm Hagedorn confidently asserts, "Even a cursory reading of Zephaniah reveals . . . the book cannot possibly be a literary unity or even written by just one author. Too diverse are the ideas put forward in the book."[40] Christoph Levin says,

[40] Anselm C. Hagedorn, "When Did Zephaniah Become a Supporter of Josiah's Reform?," *The Journal of Theological Studies*, NS 62, 2 (October 2011): 461.

> Though no more than fifty-three masoretic verses in length, the book reads as an extremely heterogeneous composition. Prophetic speech and divine speech change frequently, and with no obvious reason. There is also a sudden change of addressees, and the themes of the book vary greatly.[41]

Tchavdar Hadjiev remarks:

> There are a number of places in the book of Zephaniah that can be recognized as secondary in their present literary context. Analysis of their style and content shows that they are the result of three subsequent reworkings of the prophetic scroll: a 'restoration of the remnant' redaction (2:7, 9b–10 and 3:11–13 plus the phrase 'all the humble of the earth who do his justice' in 2:3); a 'salvation of the nations' redaction (2:11 and 3:9–10) and a 'salvation of Judah' redaction (3:14–20). These redactions focused exclusively on the issue of salvation beyond judgment but gave very different answers to the questions 'who is going to be saved?' (the remnant, all the nations, Judah) as well as 'what ushers the age of salvation?' (repentance or the grace of Yahweh).[42]

In a subsequent article, he elaborates on this three-step redactional process, beginning with a preexilic call for Judah to repent followed by an explanation for the disaster that overtook the nation, and, finally, a promise of salvation to the postexilic community.[43]

I will not interact individually with the various scholars who deny the unity of the book. Instead, I will limit myself to Levin's comments about changes in speakers and addressees, the remarks of Hagedorn and Levin regarding thematic diversity, and Hadjiev's arguments for a triple redaction based on thematic diversity.

Before getting into the specifics of Zephaniah, however, it is necessary to discuss two systemic flaws of the redactional critical method

---

[41] Christoph Levin, "Zephaniah: How This Book Became Prophecy," in *Constructs of Prophecy in the Former and Latter Prophets and Other Texts,* ed. Lester L. Grabbe and Martti Nissinen, Ancient Near East Monographs, 4 (Atlanta, SBL, 2011), 117. Levin cites several interpreters who see the book of Zephaniah as compositionally diverse (pp. 118–19).

[42] Tchavdar S. Hadjiev, "Survival, Conversion and Restoration: Reflections on the Redaction History of the Book of Zephaniah," *VT* 61 (2011): 570–81. The quote comes from the abstract on p. 570.

[43] Tchavdar S. Hadjiev, "The Theological Transformations of Zephaniah's Proclamation of Doom," *ZAW* 126 (4) (2014): 506–20.

that are often the basis for dividing material into various layers in prophetic literature, including Zephaniah. The proponents of this method engage in self-perpetuating groupthink that inevitably produces predictable results. Their pedestrian conclusions may seem creative and impressive to the members of their guild, but uninitiated skeptics are left asking, "Did the ancient prophets and prophetic guilds really operate as redaction critics assume they did?[44] Were the proposed redactors as inept as redaction critics imply, leaving us with a 'heterogeneous,' incoherent mess on our hands?"

1.6.1 Systemic Flaws

The redactional critical method has several systemic flaws, two of which are especially problematic and in need of exposure at the outset of this discussion:

1. Rigid commitment to uniformity of style and content. As the above quotations from Hagedorn and Levin illustrate, redaction critics have difficulty handling diversity of style and content, as if a single author is incapable of creatively blending stylistic devices and themes. This leads to statements such as these: "The book cannot possibly be a literary unity" and "Prophetic speech and divine speech change frequently, and with no obvious reason." In fact, the blending of prophetic and divine speech and the shift in addressees, which are troubling to Levin, are the product of a creative rhetorical strategy. Changes in speaker reflect the close relationship between the messenger and the one who has sent him, while shifts in addressee reflect diversity within the prophet's implied audience. Contrary to what redaction critics state or imply, these shifts are not haphazard, nor are they symptoms of inept redacting.

Redaction critics give little, if any, attention to rhetorical strategy in light of the prophet's implied audience. The critic's stance is etic (on the outside looking in). While claiming objectivity, this approach is invariably tainted by certain Western literary standards and quickly becomes coldly analytical. What is needed is an emic perspective that positions the interpreter within the prophet's rhetorical situation and understands his rhetoric as that of a preacher who uses often

[44] For an overview of the method and its assumptions, see Levin, "Zephaniah: How This Book Became Prophecy," 118–19.

customized communication devices that engage the audience for persuasive purposes.

A good example of such a rhetorical strategy can be found in Isaiah 40–55, which begins on an optimistic note as the Lord promises the restoration of Zion in seemingly unconditional terms (40:1–11). God's word, in contrast to human promises, is reliable and certain to be realized (40:6–8). The Lord urges his exiled people not to fear and assures them of his presence and their coming vindication (41:8–20). Nevertheless, the Lord tempers this optimism by reminding his people they are in exile because of their past covenant violations (42:18–25; 43:22–28) and by exposing their moral condition (48:1–22.) He singles out the wicked (48:22) and distinguishes them from the righteous (50:10–11). By the time we reach 55:1–7 and the invitation to covenant renewal, the realization of the promised salvation is contingent upon a positive response to the appeal that entails the repudiation of sin. The tone of certainty with which the section began is qualified, though the emphasis on the reliability of the divine promise persists (55:8–13; cf. 40:6–8), attesting to the essential unity of chapters 40–55.[45]

Antje Labahn's attempt to explain the shifts within Isaiah 40–55 is a prime example of a flawed redactional approach that overlooks the rhetorical dimension of the prophet's strategy. She states Deutero-Isaiah "formulated a new programme for Israel's future, expecting a new exodus in the form of liberation of the people and return to Zion." When this vision failed to materialize, "doubts about the reliability of the prophetic message arose." Consequently, statements like 46:13; 51:5, and 55:6 were added because "the people became doubtful about the announcements of salvation and had to be reassured more emphatically." As the promised salvation was delayed even longer, "a different ploy became necessary." An element of contingency was introduced as "the people are now accused of deviating from the ways of Yahweh (42:24; 48:18), described as obdurate and full of iniquity (43:24, 27–28; 48:4) and portrayed as refusing to listen to the words of Yahweh." Labahn proposes "this explanation of a delayed salvation" is rooted in Deuteronomistic theology.[46]

However, as I have observed elsewhere,

---

[45] Chisholm, "When Prophecy Appears to Fail, Check Your Hermeneutic," 568.

[46] Antje Labahn, "The Delay of Salvation within Deutero-Isaiah," *JSOT* 85 (1999): 72–76.

> this diachronic reconstruction is unnecessary once one recognizes the dynamic nature of the prophet's rhetoric. In fact, the variety in mood and theme is exactly what one expects when dynamic predictive discourse and expository-hortatory discourse are blended. Labahn has mistakenly assumed the prophet's announcement of salvation was unconditional. On the contrary, it was dynamic, designed to encourage and ultimately motivate the people to respond positively to the culminating appeal. By stressing from the outset God's intention to save his people, the prophet emphasized their sin was not a barrier to the future although they must acknowledge and abandon it. The prophet draws on the theology of Deuteronomy. In Deuteronomy 30:1–10 Moses anticipates the exile. He explains that repentance will be the catalyst for restoration from exile, spiritual transformation, and renewed prosperity.
>
> Likewise, Solomon foresees a time when the people will be exiled. At that time, they will repent, prompting God to restore them (1 Kgs 8:46–51). The prophet . . . reverses this order for rhetorical purposes. He begins with dynamic predictive discourse, highlighting what the future will look like. As he develops his message, he forces his audience to reflect upon the reason for their predicament and then calls them to repentance, which will activate the promised salvation. The dynamic predictive discourse paves the way for the prophet's expository-hortatory discourse, putting the latter in proper perspective. Dealing with one's sin need not be a depressing, discouraging experience. On the contrary it is the doorway to a bright future, characterized by divine blessing. The emphasis on the integrity and reliability of the divine word in both the prologue and the final exhortation highlights this.[47]

The blending of the themes of divine sovereignty and human responsibility is not unique. Indeed, it permeates all of Scripture.

Prophetic rhetorical strategy, as illustrated in Isaiah 40–55, typically blends theological themes and can even hold them in tension without implying they are contradictory. Attributing them to different sources or voices is essentially a form of protesting the text as it stands. However, like it or not, themes are blended in the text as we have it.

---

[47] Chisholm, "When Prophecy Appears to Fail, Check Your Hermeneutic," 569.

It does no good to complain that themes "vary greatly" and are "too diverse." On the contrary, it is only reasonable and fair to assume those doing the blending had a strategy and intended to produce a coherent message. Therefore, the interpreter's task is to take an emic stance and attempt to discern how themes are complementary and work together in the prophet's rhetoric. There is no inherent reason a prophet could not engage in such blending, especially when one considers the theological foundation upon which the prophets operate.

Redaction critics typically operate on the assumption that the themes of judgment and salvation are incompatible. Below, in the section "Theological Interpretation," under "God's Self-Revelation" and then in the subsection "The Relational God," I discuss at length how the themes of judgment and salvation, rather than being incompatible, are inextricably linked in the Latter Prophets and, more specifically, in Zephaniah.

2. Rigid commitment to a historical critical approach. For redaction critics the prophet's message addresses only immediate concerns of his time which are often viewed as political in nature. A corollary of this is a rigid distinction between prophecy (or historical prophecy) and apocalyptic (or eschatological prophecy) that makes them incompatible. Historical prophecy addresses specific nations, people groups, or individuals and warns of impending judgment or announces deliverance. Eschatological prophecy envisions a culminating judgment of the nations on a worldwide scale, followed by a radical transformation of the world as we know it, including both the Lord's covenant community and the nations. For redaction critics, any vision of a culminating reality with its radical transformations is assigned to a later source, as if a prophet would not look beyond his immediate situation. After all, prophecy must be relevant in the prophet's immediate context.

In this regard, Brevard Childs, who states, "Redactional study has been helpful in identifying different layers within the book" of Zephaniah, is nevertheless critical of redaction criticism's application of the historical critical method.[48] In his opinion, the "canonical process" has produced a "theological centre." The day of the Lord is a central theme that "includes a word of judgment and promise." There is an

[48] Brevard S. Childs, *Introduction to the Old Testament as Scripture* (Philadelphia: Fortress, 1979), 459.

"overriding eschatological perspective in the book" in which "temporal differences have been transcended." He makes this assessment:

> The misunderstanding in the usual application of the historical critical method arises from assuming that each prophetic passage must be interpreted from a specific historical setting. When the canonical process has disregarded historical differences and organized the material theologically, the effect of the critical approach is to fragment the book into various editions and thus misunderstand the total witness.[49]

He then proceeds to discuss the function of "post-exilic additions" in relation to "pre-exilic" material. While I disagree with his adherence to the conclusions of redaction critics regarding "additions," I find his critique of the historical critical approach telling. I would modify his words this way:

> The misunderstanding in the usual application of the historical critical method arises from assuming that each prophetic passage must be interpreted from a specific historical setting. *When the prophet has blended historical and eschatological dimensions* and organized the material theologically, the effect of the critical approach is to fragment the book into various editions and thus misunderstand the total witness.

The fact is that prophetic texts as we have them blend historical and eschatological prophecies. For example, in Isaiah 1:21–4:6 one finds an interweaving of the two: 1:21–31 (historical); 2:1–4 (eschatological), 2:6–21 (historical with a mixture of eschatological motifs); 3:1–4:1 (historical); 4:2–6 (eschatological). Practical applications (hortatory discourse) are drawn in 2:5 and 2:22. The first of these ("House of Jacob, come and let's walk in the LORD's light"), though joined formally to what follows (note "for" at the beginning of v. 6) comes on the heels of an eschatological vision, as if the vision had practical relevance for Isaiah's contemporary audience. The point seems to be this: if the nations will someday come all the way to Jerusalem to seek the Lord's instruction (see 2:2–4), then surely the Lord's covenant people (called here the "house," or family, of Jacob) should follow his

[49] Childs, *Introduction to the Old Testament as Scripture*, 460.

teaching in the present. This invitation to Israel to take advantage of what will be offered to the Gentiles in later eras is a prime example of how eschatological motifs could have relevance in the prophet's historical context and need not be relegated to alleged later redactional layers. Other examples of blending historical and eschatological prophecy occur in Isaiah 13; 18–19 (see the references to Cush and Assyria) and 34–35. For a fuller discussion see below in the section "Theological Interpretation," under "Prophecy and Fulfillment: Merging the Historical and Eschatological Dimensions," where I attempt to show that the two dimensions are inextricably linked in the Prophets, including Zephaniah.

1.6.2 A Response to Some Specific Redaction Critical Arguments

1. Levin contends that within Zephaniah "prophetic speech and divine speech change frequently, and with no obvious reason."[50] An analysis of the blending of speakers (the Lord and the prophet) is in order:

TEXT	SPEAKER	OBSERVATIONS
1:2–6	Lord	First-person verb + identifying formula + three first-person verbs + identifying formula + three first-person forms (two verbs) + three third-person references to Lord (vv. 5–6)[51]
1:7–8a	Prophet	Exhortation + immediate reference to *ʾădōnāy*[52] + four third-person references to Lord[53]
1:8b–13	Lord	Two first-person verbs + identifying formula (v. 10)[54] + two first-person verbs (v. 12) with third-person reference to Lord in embedded quotation (v. 12b)
1:14–16	Prophet	Two third-person references to Lord (v. 14)
1:17	Lord	First-person verb + third-person reference to Lord[55]

50 Levin, "Zephaniah," 119.

51 The Lord refers to himself in the third person in verses 5–6. This makes the accusation (vv. 4b-6) embedded within the announcement of judgment (v. 4a) more objective and formal in tone, whereas the first person would focus on personal offense and injury. By using the third person, the Lord speaks more as prosecutor than defendant and assumes the point of view of those hearing his case and his verdict against the guilty party.

52 The inclusion of אֲדֹנָי, "Master," signals the shift to the prophet as speaker.

53 It is not certain if the introductory words in verse 8, lit., "And it will be in the day of the sacrifice of the Lord," are spoken by the prophet or the Lord. For discussion, see the commentary.

54 The prophet may insert this formula.

55 The Lord refers to himself in the third person for rhetorical reasons. As noted above (vv. 5–6), the technique makes the Lord's accusation more objective and formal in tone. Using the first person would focus on personal offense and injury, but by using the third person, the

TEXT	SPEAKER	OBSERVATIONS
1:18	Prophet	Third-person reference to Lord[56]
2:1–3	Prophet	Exhortation + four third-person references to Lord
2:4–5a	Prophet	Third-person reference to Lord in identifying formula
2:5b	Lord	Embedded speech with first-person verb
2:6–7	Prophet	Third-person reference to Lord (v. 7b)
2:8–9	Lord	First-person verb + first-person pronoun (followed by embedded identifying formula containing third-person reference to Lord)
2:10–11	Prophet	Two third-person references to Lord
2:12	Lord	Note “my sword”
2:13–15	Prophet	Note jussives (prayer) in v. 13
3:1–5	Prophet	Two third-person references to Lord (vv. 2, 5) and one to “her God” (v. 2)
3:6–10	Lord	Sixteen first-person forms (five verbs) with embedded identifying formula (v. 8) and third-person reference to Lord (v. 9)[57]
3:11–13	Lord	Four first-person forms (two verbs) and a third-person reference to Lord (v. 12)[58]
3:14–17	Prophet	Three third-person references to Lord
3:18–20	Lord	Nine first-person forms (six verbs) and identifying formula (v. 20b)[59]

Lord speaks more as prosecutor than defendant and assumes the point of view of those hearing his case and his verdict against the guilty party.

[56] The prophet is the speaker in verse 18. The third-person reference to the Lord (note “the day of the Lord’s wrath”) by itself does not rule out the possibility that the Lord is still speaking (see vv. 5–6, 17, where the Lord uses his own name when speaking). However, there are two more third-person references that follow (note “*his* jealousy” and “*he* will make”). Furthermore, the clauses containing these third-person references are syntactically linked.

[57] The Lord refers to himself in the third person (cf. 1:5–6, 8, 17). In this case, he uses the idiom “call on *the name of the* Lord,” which is used eleven times and is more common than “call in *my name*,” which appears only two times (Isa 41:25; Zech 13:9).

[58] By using “name of the Lord,” the Lord draws attention to the character trait suggested by his personal name. The name Yahweh (translated Lord) means, “he is [with],” or, perhaps better, “he will be [with]” (cf. Exod 3:12–15). The name focuses on his protective presence with his people.

[59] Wendland sees the structure of the book as “antiphonal.” He arranges the speeches in three dialogues:
Dialogue 1: YHWH (1:2–6) // Zeph (1:7) / Y (1:8–10) // Z (1:11) / Y (1:12–13) // Z (1:14–16) / Y (1:17) // Z (1:18)
Dialogue 2: Z (2:1–5b) / Y (2:5c) // Z (2:6–7) /Y (2:8–9) // Z (2:10–11) / Y (2:12) // Z (2:13–15)
Dialogue 3: Z (3:1–5) / Y (3:6–7b) // Z (3:7c) / Y (3:8–13) // Z (3:14–17) / Y (3:18–20).

The presence of first-person forms and/or an identifying formula indicate the Lord is speaking, while third-person references to the Lord indicate the prophet is speaking. However, in some cases the Lord refers to himself in the third person (1:5–6, 8[?], 12, 17; 3:9, 12). In each case the reason for this is clear (see footnotes to chart above).

The mixing of speakers (Lord and prophet) is typical of prophetic style, and the reason for this is obvious, unless the interpreter's stance is so etic that he feels compelled to impose his own notion of what is proper on the ancient, rhetorically charged text. Blending the Lord's words with the prophet's establishes the prophet's authority. The prophet, who is the Lord's messenger, and the Lord who has sent him speak in tandem. In this regard, Adele Berlin, responding to House's view that the shifts in speaker are a dialogue that constitutes a drama, observes such shifts are "a normal aspect of prophetic writing." She explains:

> The prophet conveys the words of God but he also interjects his own thoughts and reactions. While the prophet fully identifies with God's message, he may step in and out of his role as God's mouthpiece. This actually strengthens the effect, because the prophet's own words confirm the words that he speaks in God's name.[60]

In the case of Zephaniah, a closer look reveals that the prophet assumes various roles, which explains why he inserts his own statements in strategic places:

a. As the Lord's messenger, the prophet's primary role is to proclaim the word of the Lord, which he does by quoting what the Lord has said. Except for the shortest quotations from the Lord (1:17; 2:5b, 12), the prophet includes a formula identifying the Lord as speaker.

b. Closely related to his role of proclamation is the task of being a herald. As the day of the Lord approaches, the prophet's job is to announce this important fact, which he does in 1:7 and 1:14–16, 18.

c. As a preacher, the prophet must also exhort. This hortatory role is evident in 1:7, where he indicates silence is the proper response to the preceding announcement of judgment, and in 2:1–3, where he tells

---

The patterning is evidence of design. See E. Wendland, "The Drama of Zephaniah. A Literary-Structural Analysis of a Proclamatory Prophetic Text," *Journal for Semitics* 16/1 (2007): 26–27.

[60] Berlin, *Zephaniah*, 12–13.

his audience to prepare for the coming judgment he has just described. In his final exhortation in 3:14–17, the prophet becomes a worship leader as he urges Zion to sing and rejoice in response to the Lord's salvation. In this case, the call to sing marks a radical reversal of the earlier "be silent" (1:7).

d. In relation to his hortatory role, the prophet serves as accuser or prosecutor on the Lord's behalf, providing the basis of judgment (see 3:1–5), making clear that judgment is necessary and unavoidable except perhaps through repentance.

e. As an aspect of his hortatory role, the prophet also describes the aftermath of the Lord's intervention in judgment (1:18). Judgment speeches have a dynamic function; they are designed to produce a response. In speech-act terms, words of judgment often have a perlocutionary dimension; they are intended to persuade. By forcing the objects of judgment to focus on their destiny, judgment speeches seek to motivate positive change.

f. As for the judgment speeches against the nations, the prophet's role is less obvious. Unless the prophet really did proclaim the Lord's word to the nations in view (which seems unlikely), the implied audience of these oracles is the covenant community and probably, more specifically, the obedient faithful ones (cf. 2:3). As such, the prophet's role is that of encourager. The announcement of judgment on the nation's enemies and the vision of a remnant that is vindicated would encourage the obedient faithful (cf. 2:4–7, 10, 13–15). In this regard, Zephaniah also has an intercessory role. On behalf of the covenant community, he calls upon the Lord to judge Assyria/Nineveh (2:13).

g. As an encourager of the Lord's people, the prophet also has a prophetic role, understood in a traditional, popular sense. He foresees the future when the distant nations will worship the one true God (2:11). Literarily, his vision sets the stage for the Lord's announcement in 3:9–10.

To summarize and conclude, the prophet strategically inserts his own words into his proclamation of the Lord's word. Following the opening announcement of judgment, he urges a proper response ("be silent") while heralding the day of the Lord (1:7). After the continuation of the Lord's announcement of judgment (1:8–13), he again heralds the fast-approaching day of the Lord (1:14–16). Inserting another announcement of judgment from the Lord (1:17), he supports its dynamic intent by describing the aftermath of the judgment (1:18).

Continuing in his hortatory role, he exhorts both sinners and the godly to respond properly to the coming judgment (2:1–3). He launches the oracles against the nations, connecting them logically to what precedes (note "for" at the beginning of 2:4). His description of the aftermath of judgment upon Philistia (2:4), coupled with a woe oracle (2:5a), anticipates the Lord's announcement of judgment (2:5b), which he supplements with a prophecy of the Lord's restoration of a remnant of the house of Judah (2:6–7). After the Lord's announcement of judgment on Moab and Ammon (2:8–9), the prophet again supplements the divine proclamation by giving the basis for the judgment and a surprising prophecy of the reclamation of the nations that signals a thematic turn (2:10–11).[61] As the oracles against the nations develop in 2:4–11, the prophet's words work in tandem with the Lord's proclamation. This is apparent once more in 2:12–15, where the prophet supplements a divine proclamation of judgment (on Cush, v. 12) with his prayer for judgment on Assyria/Nineveh (2:13) and his confident assertion that his prayer will be answered (2:14–15). In 3:1–5 the prophet creatively links arrogant Nineveh with rebellious Jerusalem as he takes up the role of prosecutor, paving the way for the Lord's proclamation (3:6–13). Finally, he again assumes a hortatory role and places himself rhetorically beyond the day of judgment. Speaking within the day of restoration, he calls upon restored Zion to celebrate the Lord's salvation (3:14–17).[62] He reverses his earlier pessimistic exhortations made in response to the realization the day of the Lord's judgment was approaching. As such, the prophet plays a key role in transforming the Lord's announcements of impending judgment into a promise of eschatological restoration and radical transformation.

In Isaiah 36 one can detect in Sennacherib's royal spokesman's speeches parallels to Zephaniah's blending of divine and prophetic speech. Sennacherib's royal spokesman begins by identifying his master and then quoting him verbatim. Note the first-person forms in verses 4–7. The spokesman then assumes a hortatory role, inserting his own appeal (vv. 8–9, note his reference to his master in v. 9) before abruptly returning to quoting Sennacherib's proclamation (v. 10). In

---

[61] For a detailed analysis of how verses 8–9 are linked with 10–11, see Wendland, "The Drama of Zephaniah," 44.

[62] Wendland ("The Drama of Zephaniah," 54) observes, "YHWH's oracle of salvation (vv. 8–13) is so awesome, so earth-shaking in its implications, that the prophet cannot, as it were, contain himself."

a second speech, the official gives a brief exhortation to listen (v. 13a) before again identifying and directly quoting his master (vv. 13b–15). He briefly inserts an exhortation of his own (v. 16a, the exhortation "don't listen" complements "listen" in v. 13a) before delivering the remainder of Sennacherib's proclamation, which he duly introduces with another formal identifying formula (vv. 16b–20).[63]

2. Levin also finds "a sudden change in addressees" problematic. However, such changes are expected, given the prophet's diverse implied audience and his rhetorical creativity. An analysis of the direct addressees is in order:

TEXT	ADDRESSEE	SPEAKER	OBSERVATIONS
1:7	Mankind/ Judah/ Jerusalem	Prophet	Though no addressee is specified, mankind and those living in Judah and Jerusalem are in view (cf. vv. 3–4).
1:11	Residents of "Hollow"	Lord	The Lord speaks as if the coming judgment has arrived, urging the "residents of the Hollow" to "wail."
2:1–2	Undesirable nation	Prophet	The addressees are the members of the sinful nation.
2:3	Godly obedient	Prophet	The addressees are a godly remnant within the sinful nation.
2:5a	Philistines	Prophet	The prophet uses the plural in addressing the residents of the seacoast.
2:5b	Philistines	Lord	Within the embedded quotation, the Lord uses the feminine singular in addressing the "land" (feminine noun) of the Philistines.
2:12	Cushites	Lord	
3:7	Rebellious city	Lord	The addressee is not specified, but the feminine singular verb form indicates that the personified rebellious city (cf. v. 1) (Jerusalem) is in view.

[63] The identity of the speaker in verse 10 is uncertain. The official could still be referring to himself since he does not introduce the words as Sennacherib's, as he does in vv. 4, 13, and 16. Yet the content of the statement sounds like something the king, not a mere official, would say. Perhaps the official, as a messenger, speaks as if he is Sennacherib at this point, much like we see the messenger of the Lord doing on occasion. See, for example, Gen 22:12.

TEXT	ADDRESSEE	SPEAKER	OBSERVATIONS
3:8	Godly obedient	Lord	The addressee is not specified, but the switch to the masculine plural suggests the addressees are the Lord's obedient followers (cf. 2:3). This group is also described in 3:12 as "meek and humble people" who "take refuge in the name of the LORD."
3:11–12	Personified Jerusalem	Lord	The addressee is not specified, but the feminine singular forms indicate the personified city (Jerusalem) is in view.
3:14–17	Personified Jerusalem and Israel	Prophet	Note the specified addressees.
3:18–19	Personified Jerusalem	Lord	Note the feminine singular forms.
3:20	Future exiles	Lord	Note the shift to masculine plural forms.

The various addressees reflect the diversity of the prophet's implied audience within his rhetorical situation. Creative rhetoric is frequently at work, often in combination with metaphor. Both the Lord and the prophet address the prophet's contemporaries in a straightforward manner (2:1–3, 5, 12; 3:8), but at times both also take a rhetorical stance in the future and address participants in those future events (1:11; 3:14–17, 20). Both also address metaphorically personified Jerusalem as a woman (3:7, 11–12, 14–17, 18–19).

The "sudden" shifts in addressee, which are limited in number, are hardly evidence of lack of unity. It makes sense that the prophet would address both evildoers and godly individuals within the covenant community (2:1–3; 3:7–8). In 3:18–20 the Lord first speaks to the personified city to which the exiles will return and then to the exiles themselves.

3. Hagedorn and Levin appeal to diversity of themes as proof Zephaniah is not a literary unity. For Hagedorn the ideas are "too diverse," and for Levin the "themes vary greatly." As noted above, in this regard redaction critics typically find the blending of judgment and salvation and the mixture of historical and eschatological prophecies problematic. Introductory remarks regarding alleged incoherence appear above, with much fuller discussion to follow. At this point I will specifically address Hadjiev's proposed evidence for redaction and

especially his argument that diversity regarding the remnant theme points to "three subsequent reworkings of the prophetic scroll."[64]

a. In developing his proposal, Hadjiev identifies the key addressee in 2:3 ("all you humble of the earth, who carry out what he commands") as a gloss because he thinks it creates incoherence with what precedes. He states,

> Within 2:1–3 there is certainly some amount of tension insofar as the opening imperatives are addressed to the whole nation which is moreover described as shameless, while in v. 3 the call is directed to a restricted group of righteous people from within the nation. It is possible to resolve this problem by taking the whole of v. 3 as a later addition but a better solution would be to regard only the phrase "all the humble of the earth who do his justice" as a gloss. The reason is that the tension is not just between vv. 1–2 and v. 3 but also within v. 3. As it now stands the text of v. 3 is somewhat strange: those who are already humble are encouraged to seek humility but are also told that even this does not guarantee them salvation. If we remove the gloss then the rest of v. 3 makes perfect sense as a call addressed to the same people who are referred to in v. 1.[65]

Granted it seems odd that this call to righteousness and humility is addressed to "all you humble of the earth who carry out what he commands," in other words, to people who are already humble and demonstrating obedience, the verb translated "carry out" (*pāʿal*, "do," understood in the sense of "practice, perform") is a perfect form, probably functioning here as present perfective ("have done"), indicating completed action with continuing results. This may help explain how obedient humble people can be commanded to do what they have already done. The prophet urges them to sustain their obedient spirit before the Lord. Obedience is always an ongoing responsibility, and one can never rest complacently on past performance. The prophet uses the verb "seek" three times in this verse, exhorting the obedient humble to "seek" first the Lord, then righteousness, and then humility.

---

[64] Hadjiev, "Survival, Conversion and Restoration," 570 (in abstract). I have chosen to focus on Hadjiev's work because it is recent, appears in a major journal, incorporates the arguments of previous redaction critics, and is representative of the method.

[65] Hadjiev, "Survival, Conversion and Restoration," 571–72.

One seeks the Lord by seeking righteousness and humility. In this case "seek" can be paraphrased "make every effort to put into practice."[66] This is consistent with the notion the exhortation pertains to sustaining the humility they have practiced to this point.

b. Hadjiev regards 2:7, 9–10 as likely "insertions." He argues,

> Logically they do not follow very well from the preceding material. The remnant of Judah are promised that they will inhabit the land of Philistia, Moab and Ammon after divine judgment has rendered that land uninhabitable. The problem is especially obvious in 2:9 where Judah is to inherit a land which like Sodom and Gomorrah has been turned into a 'desolation for ever.' Here we have a redaction, which picks up some of the language of the surrounding verses (this is especially clear in v. 10 with which compare v. 8).

He adds that the redaction "reinterprets" the oracles against the nations "as a proclamation of salvation for the remnant of Judah. This takes the oracles in a direction completely opposite to the intention of the initial composition where judgment on the nations is the context and guarantee for the judgment on Judah, not for her salvation."[67]

Hadjiev's analysis illustrates the point made earlier that redaction critics typically assume the themes of judgment and salvation are incompatible. He finds it incoherent that the remnant of Judah will inhabit an uninhabitable land (vv. 4–7) and take over a land that is reduced, like Sodom and Gomorrah, to a perpetual wasteland (vv. 8–10). However, if the text as it stands is so obviously incoherent when subjected to Hadjiev's analysis, why in the world would a redactor create such a monstrosity? Perhaps a hyperliteral reading of the prophet's words can miss the mark. Roberts warns against applying "hairsplitting logic to poetry that works with graphic and shifting imagery."[68] Indeed, the Lord mixes two sets of stereotypical judgment language here, destruction on the one hand and dispossession on the other, without being overly concerned with harmonizing them at the locutionary (surface) level. At a deeper illocutionary level, the images agree: Moab and Ammon will experience severe judgment through

---

[66] Note NET, "strive," both here and in Ps 34:14 [Hebrew v. 15]: "Strive for peace and promote it" (lit., as in CSB, "seek peace and pursue it"). Note also that BDB lists both Zeph 2:3 and Ps 34:15 under the gloss "aim at, practice" (p. 134, *piel*, category 2. b).

[67] Hadjiev, "Survival, Conversion and Restoration," 573–74.

[68] Roberts, *Zephaniah*, 201.

the instrumentality of the remnant of the Lord's people, while this remnant will be elevated to prominence over their defeated enemies. Roberts puts it this way: "The main thought . . . is that Israel will drive Moab and Ammon out of their territories and take everything of value that belonged to them. There is no contradiction between this imagery and the portrayal of these conquered territories, following such a conquest, as wasteland."[69]

A discussion of destruction language is in order.[70] In the ancient Near East, as well as in several prophetic judgment speeches, a speaker will sometimes use idiomatic, hyperbolic language to describe a disaster/conquest. If taken literally, one might think total annihilation is in view, leaving no hope of reversal and restoration. For example, Sennacherib's description of the destruction of Babylon (in 689 BC) says,

> I destroyed and tore down and burned with fire the city (and) its houses, from its foundations to its parapets. I tore out the inner and outer walls, temples, the ziggurat of brick and earth, as many as there were, and threw them into the Arahtu river. I dug canals through the city and flooded its place with water, destroying the structure of the foundation. I made its devastation greater than that of 'the Flood.' So that in future days, the site of the city, its temples and its gods, would not be identifiable, I completely destroyed it with water and annihilated it like inundated territory.[71]

A few years later, Esarhaddon rebuilt the city.[72]

One finds such destruction language in treaty curses. For example, in the Aramaic Sefîre treaty between Bir-Ga'yah and Matî'el, a portion

---

[69] Roberts, *Zephaniah*, 201.

[70] For a discussion of the prophets' hyperbolic use of stereotypical "destruction" language, see Homer Heater Jr., "Do the Prophets Teach that Babylonia Will Be Rebuilt in the *Eschaton*?" *JETS* 41 (1998): 23–43.

[71] *COS*, 2:305 ("Sennacherib: The Capture and Destruction of Babylon," translation by Mordechai Cogan).

[72] See *COS*, 2:306. See also Ashurbanipal's description of the destruction of Elam (*ARAB*, 2:310–11, para. 811). He "devastated the provinces of Elam," scattering salt over them. He carried off all the people and animals as plunder, as well as the "dust" of several cities. He boasts, "In a month of days I ravaged Elam to its farthest border. The noise of people, the tread of cattle and sheep, the glad shouts of rejoicing, I banished from its fields. Wild asses, gazelles and all kinds of beasts of the plain, I caused to lie down among them, as if at home." Despite the devastation, the Elamite king "returned from the mountains, the place of his refuge, and into Mandaktu, the city which I had destroyed, devastated and plundered at the command of Assur and Ishtar, he entered and took up his mournful abode (in that) place of desolation" (2:312, para. 815).

of a lengthy curse reads, "May his kingdom become like a kingdom of sand." Bir-Ga'yah asks the gods to overwhelm it with "every sort of evil (which exists) on earth and heaven and every sort of trouble" and to destroy it "unto desolation!" He also asks that Arpad would become a "mound" inhabited by desert animals, which he enumerates, and that it would "not be mentioned" again.[73]

Sometimes the idiom of perpetuity is included in destruction language, giving the impression there is no possibility of reversal and restoration (cf. Zeph 2:9). For example, Mesha, king of Moab, boasted his god Chemosh enabled him to defeat the king of Israel. He declared, "Israel has gone to ruin [*ʾbd*], yes, it has gone to ruin [*ʾbd*] for ever [*ʿlm*]."[74] Despite his rhetoric, Mesha's expectation failed to materialize. A useful biblical example of this idiom appears in Jer 25:9–11a, where the Lord announces he will bring Nebuchadnezzar against Judah and the surrounding nations as his instrument of judgment. He then declares,

> I will completely destroy them and make them an example of horror and scorn, and ruins forever [*ʿôlām*]. I will eliminate the sound of joy and gladness from them—the voice of the groom and the bride, the sound of the millstones and the light of the lamp. This whole land will become a desolate ruin.

Yet perpetuity (*ʿôlām*) proves to be in this case "seventy years," after which the Lord will bring restoration. He declares, "These nations will serve the king of Babylon for seventy years. When the seventy years are completed, I will punish the king of Babylon and that nation . . . the land of the Chaldeans, for their iniquity, and I will make it a ruin forever" (25:11–12).

Destruction language is prevalent in prophetic literature. Representative examples include these passages: (1) Isa 34:8–10:

> For the Lord has a day of vengeance, a time of paying back Edom for its hostility against Zion. Edom's streams will be turned into pitch, her soil into sulfur; her land will become burning pitch. It will never go out—day or night. Its smoke will go up forever. It

---

[73] Joseph A. Fitzmyer, *The Aramaic Inscriptions of Sefîre*, Biblica et Orientalia 19 (Rome: Pontifical Biblical Institute, 1967), 15. See also Fitzmyer's translation in *COS*, 2:214.

[74] *COS*, 2:137 ("The Inscription of King Mesha," translation by K. A. D. Smelik).

will be desolate, from generation to generation; no one will pass through it forever and ever.

(2) Jer 50:39–40:

Therefore, desert creatures will live with hyenas, and ostriches will also live in [Babylon]. It will never again be inhabited or lived in through all generations. Just as God demolished Sodom and Gomorrah and their neighboring towns—this is the LORD's declaration—so no one will live there; no human being will stay in it even temporarily as a temporary resident.

(3) Jer 51:37–40:

Babylon will become a heap of rubble, a jackals' den, a desolation and an object of scorn, without inhabitant. They will roar together like young lions; they will growl like lion cubs. While they are flushed with heat, I will serve them a feast, and I will make them drunk so that they celebrate. Then they will fall asleep forever and never wake up. This is the LORD's declaration. I will bring them down like lambs to the slaughter, like rams together with male goats.

Homer Heater lists eight motifs that characterize destruction language, amply illustrated from biblical and ancient Near Eastern texts. These include (1) object of horror [cf. Zeph 2:15], (2) haunt of animals [cf. Zeph 2:14], (3) overthrow as of Sodom and Gomorrah [cf. Zeph 2:9], (4) summons to attack, (5) desolation [cf. Zeph 2:9, 13, 15], (6) no one passes through or lives there [cf. Zeph 2:5; 3:6], (7) inhabitants scattered everywhere, and (8) removal of sounds of joy.[75]

When one takes an emic approach sensitive to biblical/ancient Near Eastern idiom, it becomes clear Zephaniah uses destruction language to emphasize the degree of devastation that will accompany the day of the Lord. Only one taking a flawed etic approach would read such language in a hyperliteral manner and then use such a reading to make a case for the presence of redaction.

In addition, one should not overlook the final statement in Zeph 2:7: "For the LORD their God will return to them and restore their

[75] Heater, "Do the Prophets Teach that Babylonia Will Be Rebuilt in the *Eschaton*?" *JETS* 41 (1998): 33–36.

fortunes." John Bracke concludes there is "a model of restoration" here.[76] The language points to a radical transformation that will occur, despite what a hyperliteral interpretation of verses 4–5 (or of v. 9) might suggest to one reading the text from the outside.

c. Tchavdar Hadjiev finds 2:11 especially problematic and labels it secondary. He says the verse is . . .

> completely isolated from its context both formally and thematically. In contrast to the oracle against Moab and Ammon, the first person divine speech gives way to third person references to Yahweh (like the preceding v. 10 which is secondary). More importantly, the idea of the nations' conversion to Yahweh comes unexpectedly and stands in tension with the surrounding oracles of doom which presuppose the complete destruction of the enumerated peoples. The opening words of v. 11 suggest that the verse is intended to serve as a proof of the inevitability of the divine punishment announced in vv. 9–10 because the only possible antecedent of the suffix in the preposition "against them" can be Moab and Ammon from the preceding oracle. The continuation, however, which speaks of all the coastlands of the nations and their gods, suggests that all the nations and not just Moab and Ammon are implied in the opening words. The effort to integrate the alien idea of v. 11 within the overall thrust of 2:8–10 is not altogether successful and the resulting tension speaks strongly in favor of its secondary character.[77]

Hadjiev sees as problematic the transition from first-person divine speech to third-person references to Yahweh, the mixture of judgment and salvation themes, and the blending of historical prophecy with an eschatological vision encompassing all nations. These are arguments I address above and below. I will focus on his statement that "the nations' conversion to Yahweh comes unexpectedly and stands in tension with the surrounding oracles of doom which presuppose the complete destruction of the enumerated peoples." The statement raises issues of stylistic and thematic coherence.

The introduction of a worldwide conversion theme is indeed abrupt and perhaps unexpected. However, there is no reason one

---

[76] John M. Bracke, "*šûb šəbût:* A Reappraisal," *ZAW* 97, 2 (1985): 243.

[77] Hadjiev, "Survival, Conversion and Restoration," 574.

should assume this stylistic technique is evidence of redaction. If, for the sake of argument, we assume a redactor would introduce a theme abruptly, we must ask, Why? Too often the unstated assumption of redaction critics is that alleged redactors were inept. It is more likely that such a stylistic technique has a purpose. Once we articulate what that is, we have no need for a redactor anymore because the prophet himself could have had that purpose. Such is the case here. From a rhetorical perspective, abrupt stylistic shifts grab one's attention and, in some cases, highlight contrasts. Against the backdrop of the worldwide judgment associated with the day of the Lord, one might not expect a reclamation of the nations. But the abruptness of 2:11 forces one to rethink the purpose of judgment, which is typically a prelude to God doing something new and transformative. This proves to be the case in Zephaniah. Actually, the reversal is not as abrupt as it might seem. There has already been a hint of a reversal in God's dealings with people (cf. 2:7, 9). The reversal is simply broadened here from Judah to the nations. If the statements in 2:7, 9 are comparable to a door opening just a crack, the announcement in 2:11 is the sudden push that opens it completely. This stylistic device is not limited to this passage. One finds it again in 3:8–10, where worldwide judgment is abruptly swallowed up by worldwide reclamation of the nations. Of course, in this case, it is not as arresting since 2:11 has prepared us for it. (For Hadjiev's treatment of 3:9–10 and my reply, see below).

As for the nations' conversion being in tension with the "complete destruction" depicted in the surrounding oracles, this is not an accurate observation. While desolation is the destiny of Philistia, Moab/Ammon, and Nineveh/Assyria, the prophet transitions in 2:11b from "them" (Moab/Ammon) to "the earth" and then to "all the distant coasts and islands of the nations," who "will bow in worship to him, each in its own place." At the surface level at least, the salvation described in 2:11 is broader in geographical scope than the oracles of 2:4–15.

But there might appear to be a problem when one compares 2:11 with the depiction of the day of the Lord in chapter 1. At the beginning of chapter 1, the Lord describes a devastating flood-like judgment that reverses creation and cuts off humankind from the face of the earth (1:2–3). At the end of the chapter, we read, "The whole earth will be consumed by the fire of his jealousy, for he will make a complete, yes, a horrifying end of all the inhabitants of the earth" (1:18). It sounds as if no one will remain, making a restoration of nations impossible.

It is important, however, to recall the nature and function of destruction language, discussed above regarding 2:4–10. Furthermore, there are signals that some might be spared. The specific targets of the judgment will be the "wicked" (1:3) and those who have sinned against the Lord (1:17). In 2:3 hope is held out for those who are godly. The allusion to the flood in 1:2–3 is instructive, for in the flood account God announces total judgment (Gen 6:7, 13, 17) but qualifies it by his promise to rescue Noah (6:9, 18). When a flood-like judgment is announced in 1:2–3, it is natural, based on the analogy to Genesis 6 to ask, Will anyone, like Noah, be spared? Initially it might not seem so, but, as the book unfolds, we discover there will be some who escape. The book's rhetorical strategy comes into sharper focus. It begins with devastating judgment to emphasize the extent of human corruption and to create tension: Will God's purpose in creation, which is about to be reversed, be realized? This sets us up for the reversal, which highlights God's commitment to his people and the world, as well as his sovereignty in overcoming their rebellion in order to achieve his purpose.

d. As in 2:11, Hadjiev finds incoherence in 3:8–10. He writes,

> The position of that oracle [referring to 3:9–10], following immediately the proclamation of total and universal judgment in 3:6–8, suggests that within the redactor's chronology world judgment would be succeeded by worldwide conversion. The transition between the two oracles, although fairly smooth from a syntactical point of view, is rough and sudden on the level of content. Conversion and judgment stand next to each other totally unrelated and it is not explained how and why there is going to be salvation after the fire of Yahweh's wrath or who is going to benefit from it after the whole earth has been consumed. The purification which initiates the new age is not achieved by the preceding punishment but by a new transforming action of God. This awkwardness would seem to argue in favor of the view that 3:9–10 were subsequently added after 3:8 since nothing in the preceding material prepares the reader for their appearance and message.[78]

[78] Hadjiev, "Survival, Conversion and Restoration," 575.

As for the "rough and sudden" transition "on the level of content," my comments regarding the abrupt transition in 2:11 also apply here. Hadjiev states "conversion and judgment" are simply juxtaposed without an explanation for

> how and why there is going to be salvation after the fire of Yahweh's wrath or who is going to benefit from it after the whole earth has been consumed. The purification which initiates the new age is not achieved by the preceding punishment but by a new transforming action of God.

As Hadjiev looks for methods and reasons, he misses the Lord's rhetoric and logic. As noted above, abruptness is a rhetorical attention-getting device that highlights the radical contrast between the coming judgment and its aftermath, which, to use Hadjiev's words, is "a new transforming action of God." There is an obvious connection between punishment and purification. Fiery judgment is the prelude to transformation. Again, Hadjiev is troubled by the logical problem of how anything can be saved or transformed if the whole earth is consumed by fiery judgment. I addressed this in my comments on the use of destruction language in 2:4–10 and on the relationship between 2:11 and the global judgment language of chapter 1. Roberts's comments regarding 2:4–10, cited above, are also pertinent here.

e. Hadjiev regards 3:11–13 as especially problematic for several reasons.[79] From Hadjiev's perspective, 3:11–13 "stands in tension with 2:1–3." He explains:

> The earlier passage assumes that judgment is universal and rescue is not guaranteed even for those who repent and seek Yahweh. The promise is formulated in the most careful and qualified manner: *perhaps* you will be hidden. The call is not directed to a righteous remnant but to the "shameless nation" as a whole. In contrast to that, 3:11–13 takes for granted that the poor and the lowly will be saved and consequently interprets judgment solely as a means of purification of the nation by removal of those who are arrogant and sinful. The tone and the thrust of both passages are very different. The urgency of the call in 2:3 stands in contrast to the somewhat more encouraging words of 3:12–13 which assume that

[79] Hadjiev, "Survival, Conversion and Restoration," 576–77.

> the poor and lowly will definitely survive the catastrophe and will live happily ever after.

Once again, it is important to consider rhetorical factors. In contrast to 3:11–13, where the Lord speaks, the exhortation in 2:3 reflects the prophet's perspective. It is his response to the preceding announcement of judgment (1:2–18) and complements the sarcastic exhortation that immediately precedes it (2:1–2).[80] The use of *ʾûlay*, "perhaps," coming on the heels of the description of the devastation that will accompany the day of the Lord, emphasizes the degree of destruction that judgment will bring. As the prophet stands in the shoes of those who have heard the announcement of 1:2–18, his words reflect what some might be thinking: Given the coming reversal of creation and unleashing of divine fury, does anyone have a chance to escape? At the same time, the prophet's words carry an important theological function. As Greg King states, the word "perhaps" reminds his audience of

> the absolute sovereignty and freedom of Yahweh. In other words, it depends entirely on Yahweh whether he wants to show mercy. Yahweh is not indebted to respond by saving a remnant. On the contrary, He reacts in His sovereignty and freedom, and salvation springs out of His grace and love.[81]

Hadjiev's identification of the addressees in 2:3 with the "shameless nation" of verses 1–2 is based on his decision to omit from verse 3 "all you humble of the earth, who carry out what he commands" (see the discussion above). If we retain these words, then 2:3 harmonizes nicely with 3:12, where the Lord tells Zion that he will leave "a meek and humble people" in the city who "will take refuge in the name of the Lord." There is no contradiction here when one grasps the prophet's rhetorical strategy. The prophet's qualifying, seemingly pessimistic, "perhaps" (2:3), though having an important rhetorical function to play by emphasizing the degree of devastation about to be unleashed, is not the final word. As the message progresses from judgment to salvation, one sees the hopeful, optimistic side of "perhaps" will be

[80] For a fuller discussion of 2:1–2, see the commentary below.

[81] Greg A. King, "The Remnant in Zephaniah," *BSac* 151 (1994): 421.

realized. Godly people will be preserved, a promise that prompts the prophet to call for celebration (3:14).[82]

Hadjiev detects lack of coherence between 3:11–13 and 3:3–4:

> Less significant but still worth noting is the fact that the sinners are described in very different ways. In 3:3–4 these are identifiable groups of people—judges and officials who are likened to predators, priests and prophets who profane the holy. In 3:11–13 these are generally identified as the "proud ones" and their sins are not social and religious evils but their pride and deceitful speech.[83]

There is no incoherence here. Verses 3–4 focus on the actions of leaders in the community, while verses 11–13 broaden the scope to include the people in general, viewed as residents of the city (identified as Zion in v. 14). Verse 11, addressed to the city, focuses on attitudes that underlie actions, namely obstinate pride. As such it correlates nicely with verse 2, which describes the obstinance of the personified city. Verse 13a alludes to the sinful actions that once characterized the people of the city, actions the future remnant, which is meek and humble, will reject.

Hadjiev also argues 1:2–3:8 is a self-contained unit highlighting judgment that needs no conclusion:

> Finally, 3.1–8 is a unit which serves admirably well as a conclusion to 1.2–3.8 and as such is complete in itself. It reaches its climax in v. 8 and neither demands, nor expects a continuation. The major thought which unites it is that lack of repentance (vv. 2 and 7) will lead to final punishment. This idea is closely intertwined with the conception of world judgment—Judah has refused to repent when confronted with the fact that God has destroyed other nations and will, therefore, be punished when God punishes the whole world. Thus the unit sums up the themes of repentance (2.1–3) and the punishment of the nations of the world (2.4–15; 1.2–3, 17–18). In contrast to that, the only passages to which 3.11–13 relates thematically are the secondary additions in the OAN (2.7, 9b) where the remnant motif comes up. It seems, therefore, best to take those

---

[82] For a fuller discussion of 2:1–3, see the commentary below, where I examine the text from a speech act perspective that accounts for rhetorical strategy and the message of the book as a whole.

[83] Hadjiev, "Survival, Conversion and Restoration," 576.

> sections together as part of a subsequent 'salvation of a remnant redaction.[84]

Once more the unwarranted notion that judgment and salvation are incompatible surfaces. Of course, as he admits, he must dismiss 2:7, 9b as redactional for the proposal to work. His proposal turns the book in its original form into an unmitigated tragedy. But the fact of the matter is that judgment and salvation are together in the only form of the text we have. The movement from judgment to salvation is typical in the Latter Prophets, in which God's reclamation of his people and the world is a dominant theme. Only rarely does God intend judgment to be "complete in itself."

f. Hadjiev suggests several reasons 3:14–20 should be seen as an addition:

> Unlike the preceding passage (3:11–13) as well as other places within the book (2:7, 9), salvation here is promised not to a remnant of survivors but to the whole people. Restoration is pictured as the removal of an enemy and an oppressor not referred to in the preceding material and as the ingathering of the people although their dispersion does not form a part of the descriptions of judgment in the book. The new age is depicted primarily in terms of the renewal of Zion's joy, restoration of her honor and granting the gift of God's presence. It is strange that there is no stress on the removal of the sins which occasioned the punishment in 1:2–18 and 3:1–8 and it is not affirmed that the people have in any way heeded the call to seek Yahweh which is so central a concern in the beginning of the book (2:3; cf 1:6). We have a promise of salvation and restoration whose focus, concerns and style are significantly different from the preceding material.[85]

However, verses 14–20 should not be divorced from verses 11–13. Taken as a unit, verses 11–19 display a concentric structure:[86]

A The Lord will remove **shame** (11a) (cf. *lōʾ tēbôšî*, "you will not be put to shame")

B The Lord will restore a remnant (11b-13) (**shepherd** motif)

---

[84] Hadjiev, "Survival, Conversion and Restoration," 577.

[85] Hadjiev, "Survival, Conversion and Restoration," 577.

[86] For a thorough discussion of this structure, see the commentary below.

C Jerusalem/Zion (= Israel) should **rejoice** (14) (cf. *ronnî*, "sing for joy," and *śimḥî*, "be glad")

D The Lord turned back the enemy (15a) (**warrior** motif)

E Jerusalem/Zion **need not fear because the Lord is present** (15b) (cf. *lōʾ tîrəʾî*, lit., "you will not fear," and *yhwh bəqirbēk*, "the LORD is among you")

E′ Jerusalem/Zion **need not fear because the Lord is present** (16–17a[1]) (cf. *ʾal-tîrəʾî*, "do not fear" and *yhwh . . . bəqirbēk*, "the LORD . . . is among you")

D′ The Lord is "a warrior who saves" (17a[2]) (**warrior** motif)

C′ The Lord will **rejoice** over Jerusalem/Zion (17b) (cf. *śimḥâ*, "gladness,"and *rinnâ*, "singing")

B′ The Lord will restore a remnant (18–19a) (**shepherd** motif [cf. Mic 4:6–8])

A′ The Lord will remove **shame** (19b) (cf. *boštām*, lit., "their shame")

The Lord speaks to Zion in verses 11–13 and again in verses 18–19, while the prophet addresses the city (seemingly equated with Israel in v. 14a) in verses 14–15 and 16–17. "On that day" introduces the speech (v. 11) and appears at the pivot point at the beginning of verse 16. Within this structure, making a distinction between "a remnant of survivors" and "the whole people" is a false dichotomy that betrays a lack of adequate attention to the text's rhetorical dimension. Verse 13 speaks of a future "remnant of Israel." Prior to this, "Israel" has been mentioned just once in Zephaniah (in 2:9 in the traditional title "God of Israel"), but now this righteous remnant of the future is viewed as what is left of the covenant community. In verses 14–15 they are called "Israel." For all intents and purposes, going forward they *are* the covenant community. In this regard, Floyd observes,

> The whole notion of the remnant is extended by referring to it as "Israel" (v. 13), indicating that the new existence of Yahweh's

> people will not be any mere reconstruction of the state of Judah but rather a re-creation in some new form of the ancient entity that predated the separation of the northern from the southern kingdom.[87]

There is a progression from "the remnant of the house of Judah" (2:7) to "the remnant of my people" (2:9) to "the remnant of Israel" (3:13) to "Israel" (3:14–15) that rhetorically depicts the full restoration of the covenant community to its ideal state in the eschaton. Once this movement is detected, one does not expect to see the word "remnant" in verses 14–20. However, the use of the shepherd motif links verse 19 with verse 13, where the phrase "remnant of Israel" appears, and perhaps also to Mic 4:6–8, where the Lord, as shepherd king, turns a remnant into a mighty nation that is, as here in Zephaniah 3, closely associated with restored Zion.

Hadjiev contends that the restoration described in verses 14–20 does not have an adequate backdrop earlier in the book. It is described "as the removal of an enemy and oppressor not referred to in the preceding material and as the ingathering of the people although their dispersion does not form a part of the descriptions of judgment in the book." Regarding the "enemy and oppressor," one might expect that Zephaniah's historical audience would think of Assyria, whose downfall was impending (cf. 2:15–17) and materialized in 609 BC.[88] However, the Babylonians quickly became the new enemy on the block and sacked Jerusalem in 587 BC. Trying to explain these verses strictly against the historical background of Zephaniah's time is inadequate. The prophet envisions events that are eschatological in scope. The enemy must be understood from the perspective of the prophet's implied audience, addressed in verse 14 as Daughter Zion/Israel of the future. The enemy is an eschatological one, defeated prior to the restoration of the city.[89] In this case one does not expect to see it mentioned before this culminating point in the book, though it has been foreshadowed by Nineveh/Assyria. As for the gathering of the dispersed, the covenant curses warned that rebellion would culminate

---

[87] Michael H. Floyd, *Minor Prophets, Part 2,* FOTL (Grand Rapids: William B. Eerdmans, 2000), 235.

[88] See Sweeney, *Zephaniah,* 199.

[89] One finds this motif elsewhere in the Latter Prophets (see, for example, Isa 17:12–14; Joel 3:9–16 [Hb. 4:9–16]; Mic 7:8–11; Zech 12:1–9). It is rooted in the Zion ideal, the fulfillment of which Zephaniah envisions (see Pss 46; 48; 76).

in exile (Deut 28:36–37, 63–68). Israel (2 Kgs 17:5–6) and Judah (to a significant degree)[90] had experienced exile in the late eighth century. Prophets prior to (see, for example, Isa 39:5–7; Mic 4:10) and contemporary with Zephaniah had predicted an exile to Babylon. Against this theological and historical-cultural background, was it necessary for the prophet to specify that the day of the Lord would culminate in exile? Nevertheless, exile may be hinted at in 1:13 and in 2:7 (if not dismissed as redactional), which (like 3:19–20) alludes to Deut 30:1–8, where Moses predicts exile and a return from it.[91]

Hadjiev finds it "strange that there is no stress on the removal of the sins which occasioned the punishment in 1:2–18 and 3:1–8." He also argues that "it is not affirmed that the people have in any way heeded the call to seek Yahweh which is so central a concern in the beginning of the book (2:3; cf 1:6)." However, his flawed division of 3:11–19 (separating vv. 11–13 from 14–20) creates the alleged problems. Verses 11–13 describe "the removal of sins" in the form of elimination of Zion's sinners, who are characterized as "jubilant, arrogant people." Furthermore, if we keep verses 11–19 together as a unified speech (which he fails to do) and do not eliminate the words "humble of the earth, who carry out what he commands" from 2:3 (as he does), there is a clear correlation between 2:3 and 3:12. As noted above, the rhetorical "perhaps" of 2:3 has become certainty because the godly have sustained their commitment to the Lord. So the final speech of the book (3:11–19, along with the addendum in v. 20) is not divorced thematically from what precedes.

Based on his redactional critical proposals, Hadjiev draws the following conclusions:

> To sum up, if we leave aside minor glosses there are four major stages of the evolution of the text of Zephaniah. First, there was the initial composition 1:1–3:8*, followed by three redactional reworkings: one addressed to the remnant of Judah (2:7, 9b, 10; 3:11–13); a second, focusing on the conversion of the nations

---

[90] See *COS*, 2:303. Sennacherib claimed to conquer forty-six walled cities in Judah and numerous smaller towns. He took many (200,150 according to his annals) into captivity.

[91] See below, under Theological Interpretation/The Relational God: The Lord's Relationship with His Covenant People: Salvation: The Remnant Theme.

(2:11 and 3:9–10); and a third proclaiming the restoration of Judah (3:14–20).[92]

In his view, there are three answers to the question, Who is going to be saved? The answers correspond to the "redactional reworkings": (1) "The first answer is that a purified remnant from the people of God will survive to take over what is left after the destruction." (2) "The second answer is that after the universal judgment all the nations of the world will turn to Yahweh because he will defeat their gods and purify their lips (2:11, 3:9–10)." (3) "The third answer is that neither a remnant, nor the nations in general but only the 'true Israel', i.e. the renewed nation of Judah centered on the restored city of Jerusalem, will be the beneficiaries of Yahweh's deliverance.[93]

In response, I have argued the remnant is the true Israel, and the salvation of the covenant community and the reclamation of the nations are complementary themes that need not be pitted against each other and then used as a basis for a redactional theory.

Finally, Hadjiev also argues that the redactors disagree as to "the moral prerequisites for redemption." He states this:

> The "salvation of the remnant" insertions stress very strongly the ethical character of the restoration. Those who survive are the "humble" (3:11–12) who have heeded the call of 2:3. The following two redactions regard the coming salvation as a free and unconditional act of Yahweh based solely on his forgiveness and transforming grace.[94]

Once again, as is typical of redaction criticism, he has created a false dichotomy, arguing that complementary themes are contradictory and incompatible. Zephaniah, like the Bible as a whole, holds the elements of human responsibility and divine sovereignty in balance, especially with respect to the theme of salvation. One sees this when one compares 2:11b with 3:9–10, and 2:3 with 3:12 (when viewed in its proper context of 3:11–19, not just 3:11–13).

---

[92] Hadjiev, "Survival, Conversion and Restoration," 580.
[93] Hadjiev, "Survival, Conversion and Restoration," 580–81.
[94] Hadjiev, "Survival, Conversion and Restoration," 581.

2 THEOLOGICAL INTERPRETATIONS OF ZEPHANIAH

When studying the Bible, it is important to remember that we are reading and reflecting on Scripture, the inspired revelation of the sovereign God. Scripture is designed to lead us to God in worship and devotion. This in turn should motivate us to obedient action as we become doers, not just hearers of the Word. For this reason, it is important to read and interpret the Bible theologically. As we read any given portion of Scripture, we should correlate it with the biblical canon, asking and seeking answers to basic, vital questions, such as these: What does this passage, when considered canonically, reveal about God? What does it reveal about God's relationship to the people he has created and, more specifically, to those who are in covenant relationship with him? In light of this passage, how does God expect us to relate to him and others? To this end, I have included the following section. Since it assumes knowledge of Zephaniah's message, you may want to read it after reading the commentary section that follows it. On the other hand, reading it now will provide a theological foundation and canonical framework for understanding Zephaniah's message.

2.1 God's Self-Revelation

2.1.1 Name and Titles

We can learn much about God from the name and titles he chooses to use of himself. When one encounters the divine name or a title, it is particularly important to ask, What is the significance of the name or title in this context?

In the OT God's personal name is Yahweh, typically translated "the Lord," which occurs approximately 6,828 times. In Zephaniah it appears 34 times,[95] for an average of 29.90 appearances per thousand words. This is a high density of use. In fact, only two other books have a higher rate of use—Haggai at 39.59 occurrences per thousand words

[95] It appears in Zephaniah 1:1, 2, 3, 5, 6 [twice], 7 [three times], 8, 10, 12, 14 [twice], 17, 18; 2:2 [twice], 3 [twice], 5, 7, 11; 3:2, 5, 8, 9 [twice], 10, 12, 15 [twice], 17, 20. In five of these instances it appears in combination with a title: Lord Yahweh (אֲדֹנָ֣י יְהוִ֑ה, "the Lord, Yahweh," CSB, "Lord God," reflecting the traditional Hebrew vocalization, "Adonai Elohim") in 1:7 (see the commentary on 1:7 for fuller discussion), Yahweh [CSB, "the Lord"] their/your God (2:7; 3:17, respectively), and Yahweh [CSB, "the Lord"] of Armies (2:9–10).

and Malachi at 35.49 per thousand words. The statistical evidence indicates that Yahweh plays a prominent role in Zephaniah.

While the pronunciation and meaning of the name are debated, it seems clear that it derives from the verbal root "to be" (original *hwy/hyy* = later *hāwāh/hāyāh*) and carries the connotation of presence. Exodus 6:2–3 seems to suggest the patriarchs did not know God by the name Yahweh: "I appeared to Abraham, Isaac, and Jacob as God Almighty [lit., El Shaddai], but I was not known to them by the name 'the LORD' [lit., Yahweh]." If this is true, then it appears that the name Yahweh was first revealed to Moses at the burning bush (Exod 3:14–16).[96]

When Moses asked God his name (Exod 3:13), the Lord responded by identifying himself as "I am" (Hebrew *ʾehyeh*, perhaps better understood to mean, "I will be") (v. 14), which he then converted to "Yahweh" (third person; "he is," or better, "he will be") to facilitate reference (v. 15). It is far less confusing to refer to God as "he is" than to call him "I am." On the other hand, it is much more natural for God to refer to himself as "I am" than to call himself "he is." The context suggests the name points to God's enabling and saving presence with his people, not to his mere existence. In verse 12, before revealing the name, God assures Moses "I will certainly be with you." So, when he calls himself "I am" in verse 14, one naturally understands this to refer to his ongoing presence with Moses as the ever-present protector. Traditionally, God's words to Moses in verse 14 are translated "I am who I am" (Hebrew *ʾehyeh ʾăšer ʾehyeh;* CSB capitalizes it), which sounds rather cryptic. Perhaps we should paraphrase God's words in verses 14–15 this way:

> [Call me] I WILL BE [THE EVER PRESENT PROTECTOR] because [indeed] I will be [the ever present protector].[97] So you

---

[96] However, some propose that "name" in Exodus 6:3 does not refer to the name *per se*, but to the significance of the name. God appeared to the patriarchs primarily in the role of El Shaddai, a name associated in Genesis with the promise of numerous offspring, not as Yahweh, the one who fulfills his promises. In other words, the patriarchs knew and used the name Yahweh but had not experienced its full significance.

[97] For a defense of this interpretation, see Tryggve N. D. Mettinger, *In Search of God: The Meaning and Message of the Everlasting Names* (trans. Frederick H. Cryer; Philadelphia: Fortress, 1988), 33–36. Rather than functioning as a relative pronoun ("who") here, Hb. אֲשֶׁר, is better understood in a causal sense ("because"), as in Gen 31:49, where Laban names a stone pile both Galeed (meaning "Mound of Witness," see CSB note) and Mizpah (meaning "Watchtower") "for (Hb. אֲשֶׁר) he said, 'May the LORD watch between you and me.'" אֲשֶׁר follows the proper name and introduces the reason for the name being given. For other examples of the causal use of

> should say to the Israelites: 'I WILL BE [THE EVER PRESENT PROTECTOR] has sent me to you.' . . . Say to the Israelites, 'HE [WHO] WILL BE [THE EVER PRESENT PROTECTOR], the God of your fathers, the God of Abraham, the God of Isaac, and the God of Jacob has sent me to you.' This will be my name forever, by which I will be remembered from generation to generation.

The fundamental connotation of the name Yahweh as protective presence is not evident at first in Zephaniah. Yahweh is the source of Zephaniah's prophetic message (1:1), which contains announcements of devastating judgment (1:2–3, 10; 2:5; 3:8). This judgment is associated with the "day of Yahweh," when he intervenes as conqueror and destroyer (1:7–8, 14, 18; 2:2–3, 11) against those who have sinned against him (1:17) and whose only hope is to seek him and his righteousness (2:3). Yahweh's covenant people offer him mere lip service (1:5) as they turn back from him, refuse to seek him (1:6), and deny his just character (1:12). Yahweh is present, but ironically his presence is ominous (1:7–8), especially when one contrasts his righteous character with Zion's failure to trust him (3:2, 5).

Nevertheless, as the message transitions from judgment to salvation (see the overview above), the positive connotation of the name Yahweh emerges. In conjunction with his judgment on the Philistines, Yahweh will restore the well-being of a remnant from Judah. In fact, the prophet refers to Yahweh as "their God" (2:7). The remnant will take refuge in Yahweh (3:12), the king of Israel, who will dwell in Zion (3:15) as her God (note "your [feminine singular] God") (3:17). Ironically, the book ends with a declaration that Yahweh has spoken, in this case an announcement of restoration that reverses the previously announced judgment (3:20).

Several divine titles appear in Zephaniah, all of which are closely associated with Yahweh:

1. Adonai (*ʾădōnāy*, "Lord") (1:7). This title is combined with Yahweh approximately 301 times, primarily in the Latter Prophets (Ezekiel 217 times, Isaiah 25, Jeremiah 14, and the Twelve 25, with 21 being in Amos). The title *ʾădōnāy*, "Master," used exclusively of God, depicts him as sovereign. The title is appropriate in 1:7, where the prophet urges silence in Yahweh's presence.

אֲשֶׁר, see *HALOT*, 99, which lists Gen 30:18; 34:13; Josh 4:23; 1 Sam 30:10; 1 Kgs 15:5; Eccl 4:9; 8:11.

2. Elohim (*ʾĕlōhîm*, "God"). This title is combined with a pronoun and is appositional to Yahweh in 2:7 ("the LORD their God") and 3:17 ("the LORD your God"). It is combined with a pronoun and is in poetic parallelism with Yahweh in 3:2 ("She has not trusted in the LORD; she has not drawn near to her God"). In 2:9 it is followed by "Israel" and is appositional to "the LORD of Armies" ("the LORD of Armies, the God of Israel"). In each case, Elohim is used relationally in connection with Yahweh; Yahweh is Israel's God, not merely "the God."

The title "God of Israel" in 2:9 is appropriate in this oracle, where the Lord identifies with his people: "my people" (vv. 8, 9), "my nation" (v. 9), "the people of the LORD of Armies" (v. 10). "Israel" is mentioned here, rather than Judah, because the title is rooted deeply in Israel's past and has become standardized by Zephaniah's time.[98] The title "God of Judah" never appears in the Old Testament.

Elohim is used approximately 2,601 times in the Hebrew Bible. The form is plural, the significance of which varies according to the context. In some cases, the plural is a true (numerical) plural, referring to foreign (non-Israelite) gods (see, e.g., Exod 12:12 ["the gods of Egypt"]; 20:3; 34:15; Josh 24:15). This is the case in Zeph 2:4 ("all the gods of the earth"). More often the form is a so-called plural of degree or respect, sometimes called an honorific plural.[99] The honorific plural Elohim can be used of individual foreign gods, reflecting the attitude of their worshippers: Chemosh of Moab (e.g., Judg 11:24; 1 Kgs 11:33), Baal (e.g., 1 Kgs 18:24), Dagon of the Philistines (e.g., 1 Sam 5:7), Ashtoreth of Sidon (e.g., 1 Kgs 11:33), and Milcom of Ammon (e.g., 1 Kgs 11:33). Nevertheless, in the great majority of cases the honorific plural refers to the one true God of Israel.

It is more accurate to regard the so-called honorific plural as an abstract plural, a well-attested use of the plural form.[100] More specifically, Burnett argues the plural form in this case should be understood as a . . .

> concretized abstract plural, according to which the nominal plural form expresses an abstraction in reference to an individual or thing that holds a particular status named by the abstract category

[98] The title occurs 198 times in the Old Testament, including 6 times in the Torah and 42 times in Joshua, Judges, and 1–2 Samuel.

[99] See *IBHS*, 122.

[100] See GKC, 397, par. 124d.

in question. Thus the plural of the noun 'god' occurs with the meaning "deity."[101]

He adds, "In connection with the concept of the patron deity" the title "designates the god who stands in special relationship to a particular individual, group, territory, or nation."[102] Burnett points out that concretized abstract plural forms "can be used in reference to a single individual or object that is exemplary of the quality named and to which a corresponding status applies."[103] This is surely the case when the Old Testament uses Elohim of Israel's God. He is deity in an ultimate and unique sense.

3. The LORD of Armies (*yhwh ṣəbāʾôt*, 2:9–10). This title occurs 260 times, primarily in the Latter Prophets (56 times in Isaiah, 77 in Jeremiah, and 91 in Haggai/Zechariah/Malachi). Fundamentally, it depicts Yahweh as the heavenly King surrounded by his assembly.[104] The numerous instances where the title depicts the Lord as sovereign King without any direct military connotation support this. However, many times the title is associated with God's royal function of warrior-judge and has a military connotation.[105] Zephaniah 2:9, which describes Yahweh's judgment against Moab and Ammon, is such a case.

The referent of the title *ṣəbāʾôt*, "Armies," is debated.[106] Does it refer to Yahweh's earthly armies (see 1 Sam 17:45, as well as Isa 13:4), to his heavenly assembly, functioning as an army when Yahweh does

---

[101] Joel S. Burnett, *A Reassessment of Biblical Elohim*, SBLDS 183 (Atlanta: Society of Biblical Literature, 2001), 53.

[102] Burnett, *Biblical Elohim*, 65–66.

[103] Burnett, *Biblical Elohim*, 21–22. An example of this is seen in Judg 16:23, where the Philistine rulers use a plural in describing Samson as their "enemy." If this is a so-called plural of degree, it would have the force of "enemy *par excellence*" or "archenemy." Applying Burnett's theory, we may understand the plural as carrying the nuance "the one who is to us hostility personified or the epitome of hostility." In either case, the use of the plural, as opposed to the singular, suggests some degree of rhetorical emphasis.

[104] Mettinger, *In Search of God*, 134–35. For fuller discussion, see the commentary below on 2:9.

[105] Note especially the use of the title in 1 Sam 17:45; Pss 24:10; 46:7, 11 [Hb. vv. 8, 12]; 48:8 [Hb. v. 9]; 59:5 [Hb. v. 6]; 89:8 [Hb. v. 9]; Isa 1:9; 2:12; 5:9, 16; 9:19; 10:16, 23, 26, 33; 13:4, 13; 14:22–27; 28:22; 31:4; Jer 5:14–17; 6:6, 9; 9:7–11; 35:17; 38:17–18; Amos 3:13; 4:13; 5:14–16, 27; 6:8, 14; 9:5; Nah 2:13; 3:5; Mal 4:1–3.

[106] Mettinger, *In Search of God*, 155.

battle,[107] or to both? A second problem pertains to the grammatical structure of the title, with numerous options being proposed.[108] The title may be an abbreviated form of the longer "Yahweh, God of Armies," that is, "Yahweh, the God who Leads Armies," a title that occurs twenty-two times, primarily in Jeremiah (five times), Amos (eight times), and Psalms (five times).

4."King of Israel." This title is used in apposition to Yahweh in 3:15. This well-attested phrase, used 132 times in the Old Testament, only twice (here and Isa 44:6) refers to God/Yahweh as Israel's King. However, the Lord's kingship over Israel is mentioned in several passages[109] and conceptually Yahweh's kingship is a dominant theme in the Old Testament (see below for fuller discussion).

2.1.2 Kingship

In Zephaniah the Lord is first and foremost King. He is specifically called "the King of Israel" in 3:15, pointing to his status as Israel's covenant King. The Lord's kingship extends beyond the covenant nation and encompasses all of creation and the nations of the earth. In his capacity of King, the Lord assumes the role of warrior as he judges his rebellious people and all nations. However, as judgment gives way to salvation, distant nations become worshippers of the Lord (2:11), and the nations dispersed at Babel bring him tribute (3:9–10). In relation to his covenant people, his role of warrior is transformed from judge to protector as he becomes the shepherd-king who gathers his exiled covenant people (3:18–20).

2.1.2.1 The Lord as Creator-King

Zephaniah does not mention the Lord's work of creation or directly depict him as Creator. However, the book begins with the Lord announcing he will bring worldwide judgment, which, like the flood, will encompass both people and animals as it reverses the created order.

---

[107] See Josh 5:13–15; Judg 5:20; 2 Sam 5:24; 1 Kgs 22:19; 2 Kgs 2:11–12; 6:17; Pss 89:5–8; 103:20–21; 148:2; Isa 6:3, 5; 40:26; 45:12; Dan 8:10–13.

[108] Mettinger, *In Search of God*, 155–56.

[109] Deut 33:5; 1 Sam 12:12; Pss 5:2 [Hb. v. 3]; 10:16; 29:10; 44:4 [Hb. v. 5]; 48:2 [Hb. v. 3]; 68:24 [Hebrew v. 25]; 74:12; 84:3 [Hb. v. 4]: 145:1; 149:2; Isa 41:21; 43:15; 44:6.

Intertextual linking indicates Zeph 1:2–3 depicts judgment that rivals the flood in magnitude. The triad humankind, livestock, and birds of the sky occurs in proximity in only five passages: Gen 1:26; 2:20; 6:7; 7:23; and Zeph 1:3. This cluster appears with "off the face of the earth" only in Gen 6:7 and Zeph 1:3. The judgment entails a reversal of creation, akin to a return to primordial chaos where deep darkness prevails (see Zeph 1:15). In Genesis 1:20–27 God creates the fish and birds together on day five (vv. 20–23), and then on day six the land animals, including livestock [*bəhēmâ*] (vv. 24–25) and humankind [*'ādām*] (vv. 26–27). The judgment of the flood wiped away these things in reverse order (humankind, livestock, birds), though fish, mentioned in Zeph 1:3, are omitted from the lists (Gen 6:7; 7:23). The judgment depicted in Zeph 1:3 also describes the Lord sweeping away these things in reverse order of how they were created, and even includes the fish (humankind, livestock, birds, fish). The implication is apparent. Only the Lord can reverse creation and reduce it to primordial chaos because only the Lord as King of the created order has the authority and power to do so.

The first creation account in Genesis 1:1–2:3 answers a basic question that ancient Israel would have asked: Who created (perhaps "ordered" is a better term) the world in which we live? The text's answer is crystal clear: God (Elohim) created the heavens and the earth. This theme is present in the first statement of the first verse of the first chapter: "In the beginning God created" (or "When God created"). The account ends with another reference to God creating the heavens and the earth (2:3), thus forming a thematic framework for the entire literary unit.

In addition to these bookends, the body of the account depicts God as the Creator of the ordered world. In 1:1—2:2a (where God completes his work), God is the subject of a verb thirty-six times. Thirty-two times Elohim, "God," appears as the stated subject. Only four times is God the implied subject of a verb and only when the verb has already been used at least once with God as stated subject (see the *italicized* verse numbers in the following chart):

STATED SUBJECT	TIMES	VERSES
Created	5	1:1, 21, 27, 27, (*27*)
Said	10	1:3, 6, 9, 11, 14, 20, 24, 26, 28, 29
Saw	7	1:4, 10, 12, 18, 21, 25, 31

Separated	2	1:4, (*7*)
Called	5	1:5, (*5*), 8, 10, (*10*)
Made	3	1:7, 16, 25
Placed	1	1:17
Blessed	2	1:22, 28
Completed	1	2:2

Like a constant drumbeat, the repetition of Elohim as stated subject of the verbs, especially in the main storyline (thirty times), drives home the main point of the narrative: Elohim (God) created the ordered world in which we live. In the second creation account we discover that Yahweh is one and the same with Elohim as the compound name Yahweh Elohim (LORD God) appears twenty times.

In an ancient Israelite context, to ask who created the world is to ask, "To whom are we subject?" The answer in the creation accounts is clear: Elohim, that is Yahweh! This in turn leads to a related question answered by the initial creation account: "Why do we worship our God alone and reject polytheism and idols?" The creation account lays the foundation for Israel's monotheistic worship of God. It provides the basis for the first two commandments of the Decalogue (Exod 20:2–6; Deut 5:7–10), which prohibit worshipping other gods and making idols.

Support for this assertion comes from at least three sources:

1. The Decalogue (Ten Commandments), in its Exodus form, is very much aware of the creation account and appeals to it in the motivation clause attached to the fourth commandment (Exod 20:8–11).

2. The creation account's counter-mythical character is consistent with the Decalogue's radical monotheism. Genesis 1 is notable for its nonmythological tone. There is no divine battle with the deep corresponding to God's victory over the sea in the poetic creation texts depicting God as warrior (Job 26:12–13; Pss 74:12–17; 89:9–12).[110] On the contrary, the primordial deep does God's bidding. He divides it into two parts and relegates the waters below the sky to one place and calls them "seas" (vv. 10, 22). The use of the plural contrasts with

[110] On God's battle with the sea in conjunction with creation in Psalms 74 and 89, see Robert B. Chisholm Jr., "Suppressing Myth: Yahweh and the Sea in the Praise Psalms," in Andrew J. Schmutzer and David M. Howard, eds., *The Psalms: Language for All Seasons of the Soul* (Chicago: Moody, 2013), 75–78.

the poetic warfare texts, where the sea is referred to in the singular. Only later in the chapter is the singular form "the sea" used, but only after "fish" (vv. 26, 28), where it has no mythological connotation. The primordial deep poses no threat to God. It has been incorporated into the created order, along with the dry land and the sky.[111] In fact, God later demonstrates complete control over the heavenly ocean and the deep when he unleashes their waters upon the earth in judgment (Gen 7:11). In verse 21 God creates the large "sea creatures." Here the term *tannîn*, which, on at least three occasions, is a title or name of a chaos monster opposed to God (Job 7:12; Ps 74:13; Isa 51:9), is used generically for marine creatures (cf. Ps 148:7) with no evident mythological overtones.[112] In short, Genesis 1 emasculates the sea. God simply gathers into one place the water below the sky (which originates in the primordial deep) and calls it "seas" (1:10, 22) or "the sea" (1:26, 28). Texts where God "makes" the sea (Exod 20:11; Pss 95:5; 146:6) are consistent with this in that the sea owes its existence to God.

For ancient Israelites familiar with the mythological symbolism of the sea current in the ancient Near East (and reflected in some biblical texts), Genesis 1 would have made a startling assertion about the scope and nature of God's kingship. Neither the primordial deep nor the sea poses any threat whatsoever to God's rule. On the contrary, the sea has its appointed place in the created order and is subject to God's sovereignty.

3. In Israel's hymnic tradition God created the world, establishing the basis for his royal authority. For example, Ps 24:1–2 states, "The earth and everything in it, the world and its inhabitants, belong to the LORD; for he laid its foundation on the seas and established it on the rivers." Likewise, Ps 33:6–9 affirms,

---

[111] The primordial "deep" (NIV) of 1:2 is distinct from "the sea" of 1:26, 28. But there is a connection between them. The deep is equated with the "water" in 1:2. This water (that is, the deep) is then divided so that some is above the sky and the rest below the sky (1:6–7). The water below the sky is gathered to one place (1:9) and called "seas" (1:10). This water (= the seas) teems with fish (1:20) and other marine animals (1:21–22). Finally, the habitat of the fish is called "the sea" in 1:26, 28. So we see that the waters below the sky are the same as the "seas" of 1:10, 22 and "the sea" of 1:26, 28. The water of the sea(s) is derived from the primordial deep, but not in its entirety, for part of the primordial deep is located above the sky. See Paul H. Seely, "The Geographical Meaning of 'Earth' and 'Seas' in Genesis 1:10," *WTJ* 59 (1997): 247.

[112] See Jon D. Levenson, *Creation and the Persistence of Evil* (San Francisco: Harper & Row, 1988), 54–55.

> The heavens were made by the word of the LORD, and all the stars, by the breath of his mouth. He gathers the water of the sea into a heap; he puts the depths into storehouses. Let the whole earth fear the LORD; let all the inhabitants of the world stand in awe of him. For he spoke, and it came into being; he commanded, and it came into existence.

The relationship between kingship and creation is perhaps most clearly seen in Ps 95:3–5: "For the LORD is a great God, a great King above all gods. The depths of the earth are in his hand, and the mountain peaks are his. The sea is his; he made it. His hands formed the dry land." For this reason, he alone is worthy of worship (Pss 33:8; 95:6–7).

When Zephaniah depicts the Lord reversing creation, he assumes the Lord's status as King of the created order. This implies the Lord alone is worthy of worship, from his covenant people and from the nations. Consequently, it comes as no surprise the prophet denounces Judah's worship of pagan gods in the verses that follow and announces the Lord's judgment will target the worshippers of Baal and astral deities (1:4–6). Nor is it surprising to read in 2:11 that the Lord will defeat "all the gods of the earth" as a prelude to reclaiming the distant nations so that they may worship him in unison (3:9–10).

2.1.2.2 The Lord as Warrior-King

In Zeph 3:17 the prophet describes the Lord as "a warrior [*gibbôr*] who saves." In this context the Lord the warrior is in the midst of Zion, protecting a "humble and meek" remnant (v. 12) from the enemy (v. 15). The divine warrior's presence dispels fear (vv. 15–16), ensures safety (vv. 12–13), and produces joy and confidence (v. 14).

This description stands in marked contrast to the depiction of the Lord earlier in the book, where he comes as a warrior to judge and destroy.[113] He is called LORD of Armies [*yhwh ṣəbāʾôt*, see the discussion of this title above] as he reduces arrogant Moab and Ammon to a "perpetual wasteland" for what they have done to his people (2:9–10). His judgment is characterized as "a day of ram's horn and

[113] The referent of גִּבּוֹר, "warrior," in 1:14 is unclear. CSB translates: "Listen, the day of the LORD—then the warrior's cry is bitter." The warrior described here may be a human combatant issuing a battle cry or a lament of defeat, or the word could refer to the Lord whose battle cry has a negative impact on the objects of his judgment. For a fuller discussion, see the commentary below on 1:14.

battle cry," language that alludes to the sounds of battle and connotes destruction (1:16).

2.1.2.2.1 The Day of the Lord

The Lord's intervention as warrior takes place within the context of the day of the Lord, an important theme in the prophetic literature. The phrase *yôm yhwh*, "day of the LORD," occurs sixteen times, always in the Latter Prophets:

Isa 13:6	(preceded by *qārôb*, "near")
Isa 13:9	
Ezek 13:5	
Joel 1:15	(preceded by *qārôb*, "near")
Joel 2:1	(followed by *kî qārôb*, "for it is near")
Joel 2:11	
Joel 2:31	[Hb. 3:4]
Joel 3:14	[Hb. 4:14] (preceded by *qārôb*, "near")
Amos 5:18	(twice)
Amos 5:20	
Obad 15	(preceded by *qārôb*, "near")
Zeph 1:7	(preceded by *kî qārôb*, "for near is")
Zeph 1:14	(twice; preceded by *qārôb*, "near," in first use)
Mal 4:5	[Hb. 3:23]

A similar phrase, *yôm lyhwh*, "a day belonging to the LORD," appears in Isa 2:12 and Ezek 30:3 (preceded by *qārôb*, "near"). In Zech 1:14 we read *yôm bāʾ lyhwh*, literally, "a day comes belonging to the LORD" (cf. Ezek 39:8). Jeremiah 46:10 says, "That day [that is, the day of judgment announced in the preceding verses] belongs to the LORD. . . . a day of vengeance to avenge himself."

In several places a noun appears between "day" and "the LORD":

1. "day of the fury/anger/wrath of the LORD" (Lam 1:12; 2:1, 22; Ezek 7:19; Zeph 1:18; 2:2–3)
2. "day of the sacrifice of the LORD" (Zeph 1:8)
3 "day of vengeance for the LORD" (Isa 34:8; cf. Isa 61:2; Jer 46:10).

Interpreters have expended much energy in an effort to identify the background of the expression "day of the LORD." Chronologically, the earliest appearance of "day of the LORD" is in Amos 5:18, 20 (c. 760 BC),[114] where the prophet announces "the day of the LORD," contrary to Israel's expectation, will be a day of darkness symbolizing judgment, not a day of light symbolizing salvation. This raises the question of the origin of the concept. Did Amos draw on a concept that was already known, or did the prophet himself coin the expression?[115]

Gerhard von Rad's influential study argues the concept is rooted in Israel's holy war tradition.[116] According to von Rad, Amos 5:18 indicates the people were already longing for "the day of the LORD," implying that the concept was known before Amos mentioned it.[117] That may be the case, but there is no mention of "the day of the LORD" in any historical accounts of Israel's wars preserved in the OT outside the prophetic texts (and Lam 1–2) cited above.

Meir Weiss challenges von Rad's proposal, observing there are no references to "the day of the LORD" in "extra-prophetic literature."[118] He argues one need not assume from Amos 5:18 the prophet's audience was already familiar with the concept of "the day of the LORD."[119] He proposes Amos coined the expression, and it is rooted "in the ancient motif-complex concept of the theophany-descriptions."[120]

---

[114] I am assuming, based on internal evidence, that Joel dates to the early postexilic period, and that Obadiah was written in the exilic period.

[115] For an overview with critique of numerous theories regarding the origin and development of the "day of the LORD" concept, see Michael S. Moore, "Yahweh's Day," *Restoration Quarterly* 29 (1987): 193–208. For a survey of scholarly opinion on the subject, see Michael Ufok Udoekpo, *Re-thinking the Day of YHWH and Restoration of Fortunes in the Prophet Zephaniah: An Exegetical and Theological Study of 1:14–18; 3:14–20* (Bern: Peter Lang, 2010), 43–108.

[116] Gerhard von Rad, "The Origin of the Concept of the Day of Yahweh," *Journal of Semitic Studies* 4 (1959): 97–108.

[117] von Rad, "The Origin of the Concept of the Day of Yahweh," 107.

[118] Meir Weiss, "The Origin of the 'Day of the Lord' Reconsidered," *HUCA* 37 (1966): 41.

[119] Weiss, "The Origin of the 'Day of the Lord' Reconsidered," 45. For a critique of his position on this point, see Yair Hoffman, "The Day of the Lord as a Concept and a Term in the Prophetic Literature," *ZAW* 93 (1981): 41.

[120] Weiss, "The Origin of the 'Day of the Lord' Reconsidered," 46, 60.

Douglas Stuart proposes the expression is derived from the idea, broadly attested in the ancient Near East, that a mighty warrior king could consummate a military campaign in a single day.[121] Stuart's thirteen examples from the ancient Near East come from Sumerian, Assyrian, Syrian, Hittite, Canaanite, Egyptian, and Moabite texts, and span a time period from roughly 2000 BC to 830 BC. The motif appears to be a common one, not restricted to a particular time or place. Given this background, "the day of the LORD" is an idiom emphasizing the swift and decisive nature of his victory over his enemies on any given occasion. In this regard, it is noteworthy that Isaiah three times describes the Lord's judgment as occurring suddenly "in a single day/in one day" (*bəyôm ʾeḥād*; Isa 9:14 [Hb. 13]; 10:17; 47:9; cf. Zech 14:7).

Perhaps it is best to blend the views of von Rad, Weiss, and Stuart. If Stuart is correct, Amos's audience could have been familiar with the idiom and concept of a sovereign's "day" of conquest. Exploiting this familiarity with the concept, the prophet coined the expression "the day of the LORD" to depict Israel's God as a warrior king who suddenly and thoroughly defeats his enemies through holy war depicted poetically in theophanic terms.[122]

In the OT "the day of the LORD" often refers to a particular historical judgment on a specific nation.[123] Sometimes it is a day of judgment against the Lord's own people, including the northern kingdom of Israel (at the hands of the Assyrians, Amos 5:18, 20), Judah (at the hands of the Babylonians, Lam 1:12; 2:1, 21–22; Ezek 7:19; 13:5; Zeph 1:7–13; 2:2–3), and the postexilic community (Joel 1:15; 2:1–2, 11).[124] Sometimes the judgment of God's people appears in a cosmic framework (Zeph 1:18). This judgment will bring both intense suffering (Zech 14:1–3) and restoration (Mal 4:5; cf. Isa 61:2–11) for Israel.

---

[121] Douglas Stuart, "The Sovereign's Day of Conquest," *BASOR* 220/221 (1975–76): 159–64. Citing Stuart's work favorably, Aster argues that this motif of the sovereign's day of conquest "provides the most appropriate comparative context with which to analyze" Isa 2:5–22. See Shawn Zelig Aster, "The Image of Assyria in Isaiah 2:5–22: The Campaign Motif Reversed," *JAOS* 127 (2007): 259.

[122] Though not interacting with Stuart's proposal, Hoffman's statement is noteworthy: "I assume that though Am 5:18–20 does not indicate that יום יהוה was a current *term*, it does indicate that there was a common well-known *concept*, which, on this occasion, was called by Amos יום יהוה" ("The Day of the Lord," 41).

[123] See A. Joseph Everson, "The Days of Yahweh," *JBL* 93 (1974): 329–37.

[124] The judgment of which Joel warned was averted when God had compassion on his people (Joel 2:18).

At other times "the day of the LORD" involves judgment on foreign nations (Joel 3:14), including Babylon (at the hands of the Medes, Isa 13:17–19; cf. vv. 6, 9), Egypt (at the hands of the Babylonians, Jer 46:10; Ezek 30:3), Edom (Isa 34:8–9; Obad 15), and a northern coalition headed by Gog (Ezek 39:8). In some cases, these historical nations appear to be archetypes of the Lord's eschatological foes, as the cosmic elements in Isa 13 and Obadiah suggest. Indeed, Zeph 3:8 (cf. Zech 14:3) envisions a culminating eschatological battle against the nations on the day when the Lord attacks.[125]

The day of the Lord encompasses several specific historical "days" or events, including among others the defeat of the northern kingdom, the Babylonian exile, Babylon's conquest of Egypt, and the fall of Babylon. These examples of the Lord's intervention in history foreshadow and preview a culminating time, or "day," when he will annihilate his enemies on a cosmic scale. Zephaniah's references to "the day of the LORD" play an important role in the development of the eschatological dimension of the concept.[126]

A variety of motifs appear in the passages that mention and describe the day of the Lord:

	MOTIF	ISA	JER	LAM	EZEK	JOEL	AMOS	OBAD	ZEPH	ZECH
1	Nearness (*qārôb*)	**13**:6			**30**:3	**1**:15 **2**:1 **3**:14		15	**1**:7, 14	
2	Gathering of armies; battle	**13**:2–4, 17	**46**:3–4, 9		**13**:5	**2**:2–9 **3**:9–14				**14**:2
3	Destruction; slaughter	**13**:5–6, 9, 12, 15–22 **34**:3–17	**46**:8, 10	**2**:5–9	**7**:15 **30**:4–7	**1**:15–18			**1**:15, 17	**14**:2
4	Sacrificial imagery	**34**:6–7	**46**:10						**1**:7–8	
5	Outpouring of anger	**13**:9, 13		**1**:12 **2**:1–4	**7**:14, 19				**1**:15, 18 **2**:2–3	

[125] See Craig A. Blaising, "The Day of the Lord: Theme and Pattern in Biblical Theology," *BSac* 169 (2012): 15–17.

[126] For further discussion of this point, see below under "Prophecy and Fulfillment: Zephaniah's Eschatological Vision."

	MOTIF	ISA	JER	LAM	EZEK	JOEL	AMOS	OBAD	ZEPH	ZECH
6	Fire			**1**:13	**30**:8	**1**:19–20 **2**:3, 5, 30		18	**1**:18	
7	Thunder, roaring					**2**:11 **3**:16				
8	Cosmic quaking	**13**:13				**2**:10 **3**:16				
9	Darkening of luminaries	**13**:10 **34**:4				**2**:10, 31 **3**:15				
10	Darkness, clouds				**30**:3	**2**:2	**5**:18, 20		**1**:15	
11	Panic, flight	**2**:10, 19, 21 **13**:7–8, 14	**46**:5–6		**7**:16–17	**2**:6				

The densest clustering of motifs occurs in Joel (nine of eleven) and Isaiah 13 (seven). Zephaniah contains six, including the nearness of the day (number 1), its destructive character (number 3), sacrificial imagery (number 4), the outpouring of divine anger (number 5), fire (number 6), and darkness (number 10). Typical theophanic motifs (numbers 6–10) permeate Joel's description of the day, with just two of these (fire and darkness) occurring in Zephaniah. However, despite this limited use of theophanic imagery, the theme of divine intervention is prominent in Zephaniah's depiction of the day of the Lord:[127]

1:2 "I will completely sweep away everything"
1:3 "I will sweep away" (twice)
"I will cut off"
1:4 "I will stretch out my hand"
"I will cut off"
1:8 "I will punish"
1:9 "I will punish"
1:12 "I will search"
"and [I will] punish"
1:17 "I will bring distress"
1:18 "he will make a complete, yes, a horrifying end."

[127] Greg A. King, "The Day of the Lord in Zephaniah," *BSac* 152 (1995): 19.

2.1.2.2.2 The Lord's Anger

The Lord's anger is a prominent theme in Zephaniah's depiction of the divine warrior. The following words and phrases appear:

1. *ʿebrâ*, "wrath" (1:15, 18)
2. *ʾēš qinʾâ*, "fire of jealousy" (1:18; 3:8)
3. *ḥărôn ʾap*, "burning anger" (2:2; 3:8)
4. *ʾap*, "anger" (2:2–3)
5. *zaʿam*, "indignation" (3:8)

The term *ʿebrâ*, "wrath," is used thirty-four times in the Old Testament. On nine occasions it refers to human wrath,[128] viewed negatively in seven of the nine cases. Otherwise, it refers to God's wrath directed against sinners (Isa 13:9; cf. Prov 11:23) and is associated with retributive justice (Ezek 22:31). The use of "fire" with reference to the Lord's "jealousy" (or, "zeal") draws attention to the intensity of his irresistible anger and its destructive capacity. The expression "burning anger" (*ḥărôn ʾap*), which combines synonyms to emphasize the intensity of the Lord's anger, occurs thirty-three times, always of God's fury against sinners. The noun *zaʿam*, "indignation," appears twenty-two times, always of God's wrath.[129]

Proponents of the notion of divine impassibility are inclined to view these numerous references to divine anger as anthropomorphic (or, more accurately, anthropopathic), indicating God's opposition to sinners and his resolve to judge them. However, this position runs counter to the strong current of the biblical data and encounters a major obstacle in Hos 11:9, which reads, "I will not vent the full fury of my anger [cf. *ḥărôn ʾappî*]; I will not turn back to destroy Ephraim. For I am God and not man, the Holy One among you; I will not come in rage." As I have stated elsewhere,

> This promise not to annihilate his people, rooted in God's response to the prospect of such destruction (v. 8), is reliable because of his divine essence, when contrasted to human nature . . . After asserting that he will not carry out his anger and destroy his people, he

[128] Gen 49:7; Job 40:11; Prov 14:35; 21:24; 22:8; Isa 14:6; 16:6; Jer 48:30; Amos 1:11.

[129] Hos 7:16 is the lone possible exception, where the word may refer to human "insolence" (cf. CSB).

explains that this promise is guaranteed by the fact that he is "God and not man."[130]

In the context of the declaration, how exactly is God different from man? There are at least four explanations.[131] (1) The distinction between God and man may pertain to the expression of anger (note "I will not vent the full fury of my anger"). God, in contrast to men, releases his anger in proper measure and can relent from destroying the object of his judgment (cf. Jonah 3:9).[132] Stuart remarks, "He is not one of the Israelites ('a man in your midst') whose emotions might reflect arbitrary passions and whose wrath might be vindictive rather than equitable." On the contrary, God's "holiness embodies all that makes him different from humans, and especially the qualities that elevate his thinking and moral behavior above their usually petty standards."[133] Joy Kakkanattu states, "He is not a man, who lets himself/herself be overpowered by wrath, but he displays his divine character precisely in his ability to surpass his anger through love."[134] (2) The statement "I am God and not man" may encompass God's compassion, described in verse 8: "I have had a change of heart; my compassion is stirred!" In this case God, unlike man, possesses a level of compassion that prompts him to put proper restraints upon his anger. (3) Still another option is that "I am God and not man" pertains to verses 8–9a and presupposes the entire context of the speech, especially verse 1: "When Israel was a child, I loved him, and out of Egypt I called my son." In contrast to humans, whose faithfulness is short-lived, God's enduring covenantal commitment to his "son" Israel prompts him to compassionately restrain his anger. Kakkanattu speaks of God not repenting of "his election of Israel to be his own," adding, "He will not execute his wrath to nullify the election."[135] (4) God may differ from man in

---

[130] Robert B. Chisholm Jr., "God's Covenantal Suffering in Hosea 11," in *Divine Suffering: Theology, History, and Church Mission*, ed. Andrew J. Schmutzer (Eugene, OR: Pickwick, 2023), 111.

[131] Chisholm, "Hosea 11," 112–13.

[132] See Ps 85:4; Hos 14:5; Mic 7:18. However, God's capacity to relent is no guarantee he will always do so (Lam 4:11).

[133] Douglas Stuart, *Hosea-Jonah,* WBC (Waco, TX: Word, 1987), 181–82.

[134] Joy Philip Kakkanattu, *God's Enduring Love in the Book of Hosea: A Synchronic and Diachronic Analysis of Hosea 11:1–11* (Tübingen: Mohr Siebeck, 2006), 92.

[135] Kakkanattu, *God's Enduring Love,* 89. Graham I. Davies speaks of divine faithfulness and observes that God "rises above the human responses of anger and vengeance, and shows mercy instead." See his *Hosea*, NCB (Grand Rapids: Eerdmans, 1992), 263–64.

that his word is reliable (cf. Num 23:19; Isa 40:6–8). Consequently, he will keep his promise and "not turn back to destroy Ephraim." His faithfulness to his word tempers his anger and predisposes him to show compassion.

The four options outlined here are best understood as complementary, not as mutually exclusive. If we combine them, as I have stated elsewhere,

> Hos 11:9 affirms that God's promise not to destroy his people will prove true because he, unlike human beings, expresses his anger in perfect measure as he tempers it with his compassion, which is an outgrowth of his commitment to his people. This compassionate commitment makes his promise reliable.[136]

After affirming he is "God not man," God declares his holiness, calling himself "the Holy One among you" (v. 9).[137] He is distinct from his people, yet at the same time living "among" them (lit., in their "midst"). As argued above, the focus of God's holiness (distinctiveness) in this context is his capacity to temper his anger with compassion rooted in his covenantal commitment and reliable promise. As I have stated elsewhere,

> It is noteworthy that God does not distinguish himself from humans by stating he is devoid of emotions while they are driven by them. On the contrary, he has emotions, but he is able to express both anger and compassion in perfect balance because he, unlike humans, is faithful and reliable.[138]

There is no dramatic statement in Zephaniah comparable to God's declaration in Hos 11:8b-9a, where he describes how his compassion is stirred up and tempers his anger: "I have had a change of heart; my compassion is stirred! I will not vent the full fury of my anger; I will not turn back to destroy Ephraim." Nevertheless, the abrupt shift that occurs in Zephaniah 3, as one moves from verse 8 to verse 9, is startling. Verse 8 contains a cluster of terms for God's anger: "For my decision is to gather nations, to assemble kingdoms, in order to pour out

---

[136] Chisholm, "Hosea 11," 113.

[137] For a discussion of the syntactical structure of this statement, see Chisholm, "Hosea 11," 106, n. 30.

[138] Chisholm, "Hosea 11," 116.

my indignation [*zaʿmî*] on them, all my burning anger [*ḥărôn ʾappî*]; for the whole earth will be consumed by the fire of my jealousy [*ʾēš qinʾātî*].” Suddenly, the Lord envisions the reclamation of the nations (vv. 9–10) and speaks of a “day” (vv. 11, 16) when he will purify Zion and dispel fear, reversing the effects of the “day” of judgment described so vividly earlier in the book (cf. 1:7–10, 14–16, 18; 2:2–3). The same God who poured out angry judgment (1:15, 18; 2:2–3) will express his delight in his people and renew them with his love (3:17).

2.1.2.2.3 God of War or God of Peace?

Portrayals of the Lord as warrior, like the one painted by Zephaniah, prompt some to ask this: Is the Lord fundamentally a God of war, like so many of the deities worshipped in the ancient Near East? For example, the Ugaritic myths describe the storm god Baal as a mighty warrior-king who uses the elements of the storm as weapons. He is called “mightiest of warriors,” “lord of the storm cloud,” and “rider of the clouds.” One text depicts him this way: “Seven lightning bolts he casts, eight magazines of thunder, he brandishes a spear of lightning.”[139] The myths portray the goddess Anat as particularly violent:

> She smites the peoples (dwelling) on the seashore, wreaks destruction on the humans (dwelling) to the east. Under her are heads like balls, above her are hands like locusts, heaps of fighters’ hands are like (heaps of) grasshoppers. She attaches heads around her neck, ties hands at her waist. Up to her knees she wades in the blood of soldiers, to her neck in the gore of fighters (*COS*, 1:250).

Human warrior-kings in the ancient Near East were no strangers to violence. For example, the Moabite king Mesha tells how his god Kemosh enabled him to defeat Israel. Mesha “killed all the people” in the city of Ataroth and put the “whole population” of Nebo under “the ban for Ashtar Kemosh,” including “seven thousand male citizens,” “female citizens,” and “servant girls” (*COS*, 2:137–38). The Assyrian king Sennacherib boasts of his exploits this way:

---

[139] See Marvin H. Pope and Jeffrey H. Tigay, “A Description of Baal,” *Ugarit-Forschungen* 3 (1971):118, and Frank M. Cross, *Canaanite Myth and Hebrew Epic* (Cambridge: Harvard University, 1973), 147–48.

I put on my coat of mail. My helmet, emblem of victory battle, I placed upon my head. My great battle chariot, which brings low the foe, I hurriedly mounted in the anger of my heart. The mighty bow which Assur has given me, I seized in my hands; the javelin, piercing to the life, I grasped . . . speedily I cut them down and established their defeat. I cut their throats like lambs [cf. Isa. 34:5]. I cut off their precious lives as one cuts a string. Like the many waters of a storm, I made the contents of their gullets and entrails run down upon the wide earth. My prancing steeds harnessed for my riding, plunged into the streams of their blood as into a river. The wheels of my war chariot, which brings low the wicked and evil, were bespattered with blood and filth. With the bodies of their warriors I filled the plain, like grass (*ARAB*, 2: para. 253–54).[140]

Similar portraits of the Lord as warrior appear in the OT. At the Lord's command, Joshua put Jericho under the ban:

But keep yourselves from the things set apart, or you will be set apart for destruction. If you take any of those things, you will set apart the camp of Israel for destruction and make trouble for it. For all the silver and gold, and the articles of bronze and iron, are dedicated to the LORD and must go into the LORD's treasury" (Josh 6:18–19).

Isaiah describes the Lord's destruction of Edom like this:

When my sword has drunk its fill in the heavens, it will then come down on Edom and on the people I have set apart for destruction. The LORD's sword is covered with blood. It drips with fat, with the blood of lambs and goats, with the fat of the kidneys of rams . . . . Their land will be soaked with blood, and their soil will be saturated with fat" (34:5–7).

Later in Isaiah the Lord describes his slaughter of Edom in this way:

I trampled the winepress alone, and no one from the nations was with me. I trampled them in my anger and ground them underfoot

[140] For a similar account from Egyptian literature, see Ramses II's description of his victory over the Hittites, whom he killed without mercy, leaving them "slain in heaps in their blood." Miriam Lichtheim, *Ancient Egyptian Literature* 3 vols. (Berkeley: University of California, 1975–80), 2:70.

> in my fury; their blood spattered my garments, and all my clothes were stained. . . . I crushed nations in my anger; I made them drunk with my wrath and poured out their blood on the ground" (63:3, 6).

In Habakkuk 3 the Lord rides a horse-drawn chariot (vv. 8, 15), employs arrows and a spear (v. 11), rips open the enemy's body (v. 13b, which I translate, "laying him open from the lower extremities to the neck"), and pierces the heads of the enemy troops (v. 14). Zephaniah 1:17–18 contains such a bloody portrait as the Lord declares, "I will bring distress on mankind, and they will walk like the blind because they have sinned against the LORD. Their blood will be poured out like dust and their flesh like dung" (v. 17). The prophet then states, "The whole earth will be consumed by the fire of his jealousy, for he will make a complete, yes, a horrifying end of all the inhabitants of the earth" (v. 18).

Some troubled by such texts have opted for a monistic approach, arguing the Lord has a dark, or demonic, side. For example, Penchansky, after developing an OT portrait of a "monster god," concludes,

> In some sense . . . the theological claim of a monster God addresses the questions of theodicy. How can there be evil and suffering in the world? Answer: because God causes it. God is not reliably 'good' or 'benevolent,' in any human sense of the word. This provides an explanation for individual suffering in the world.[141]

Others, like Seibert, opt for a modified neo-Marcionite approach, arguing the OT portraits of the Lord as warrior reflect Israel's distorted view of God, not God as he really is.[142] In this model, to know what God is really like, one must apply a Christocentric hermeneutic. When the description of the God of the OT corresponds to the divine portrait revealed in Jesus, we know we are looking at the real God. Jesus reveals a God who is kind to the wicked, is nonviolent, does not judge people through disasters or infirmities, and is characterized by love. Of course, for this model to work, one must pick and choose texts,

---

[141] David Penchansky, *What Rough Beast? Images of God in the Hebrew Bible* (Louisville: John Knox, 1991), 93.

[142] Eric A. Seibert, *Disturbing Divine Behavior: Troubling Old Testament Images of God* (Minneapolis: Fortress, 2009).

for Jesus is depicted as a warrior in the NT (see, for example, 2 Thess 1:5–10), sometimes as graphically as in the OT (Rev 19:11–21).

Still others, preferring to maintain an orthodox view of biblical inspiration and a robust view of God's goodness, have sought to provide more satisfactory explanations for the OT portrait of the Lord as warrior.[143] Summarizing their arguments is beyond the scope of this discussion. Suffice it to say that God is a realist and confronts the realities of a fallen world. The earth has been contaminated by sin, and sinful, obstinate men can be removed from power only by raw force and violence. God knew his decision to accomplish his purposes through ancient Israel would be challenged by hostile nations and warfare would be necessary to preserve his people from those who desired their land. Sometimes he even had to engage in the "unexpected work" and "unfamiliar task" of coming as a warrior against his own people (Isa 28:21). God's warfare against sinners and enemies of the theocracy was a manifestation of his just character and decisions, an affirmation of his holiness and sovereignty, and the means of establishing his kingship on earth. By purifying the earth of sinners and rebels, God's wars become, ironically, the avenue to his peaceful ideal.

Despite the numerous references to the Lord as warrior in the OT, he is fundamentally a God of peace. God's ideal is that people multiply and rule the world on his behalf (Gen 1:28; 9:1, 7). Murder is antithetical to God's ideal and an attack on his image in human beings; therefore, it is outlawed (Gen 9:5–6). God's eschatological kingdom will be characterized by the cessation of oppression (Isa 11:1–9) and by peace among the once warring nations (Isa 2:2–4; 19:23–25; Mic 4:1–4; Zeph 3:9–10).

One sees God's ideal reflected in his choice of Solomon to be the builder of his temple. The Lord said to David,

> You have shed much blood and waged great wars. You are not to build a house for my name because you have shed so much blood on the ground before me. But a son will be born to you; he will be a man of rest. I will give him rest from all his surrounding enemies, for his name will be Solomon, and I will give peace and quiet to

---

[143] Two helpful volumes in this regard are (1) William J. Webb and Gordon K. Oeste, *Bloody Brutal and Barbaric? Wrestling with Troubling War Texts* (Downers Grove, IL: IVP Academic, 2019), and (2) Heath A. Thomas, Jeremy Evans, and Paul Copan, ed., *Holy War in the Bible: Christian Morality and an Old Testament Problem* (Downers Grove, IL: IVP Academic, 2013).

> Israel during his reign. He is the one who will build a house for my name. He will be my son, and I will be his father. I will establish the throne of his kingdom over Israel forever" (1 Chr 22:8–10; cf. 28:3).

While David fought the wars of the Lord with divine authorization and enablement, war was not God's ideal.

Humankind has failed to live up to the divine ideal. In a world characterized by arrogance and greed, nations fight against nations. As far as God is concerned, this carnage violates his mandate to Noah (called the "permanent covenant" in Isa 24:5) and prompts him to bring judgment upon the defiled earth (Isa 24:5–6; 26:21). The atrocities of humankind's imperialistic wars violate God's covenantal standards and result in his judgment (see Amos 1:3–2:3, where the nations' crimes in the context of war are viewed as covenantal violations). Zephaniah portrays the realization of God's ideal in 3:9–10: "For I will then restore pure speech to the peoples so that all of them may call on the name of the LORD and serve him with a single purpose. From beyond the rivers of Cush my supplicants, my dispersed people, will bring an offering to me."

2.1.2.3 The Lord as Shepherd-King

As Zephaniah's message turns from judgment to restoration, his vision of the Lord's kingship focuses on the Lord as the protector of his covenant people. Although the prophet does not specifically call the Lord the shepherd of his people, he pictures him in that role. Already in 2:6–7 the remnant of Judah finds pasture in the territory once occupied by the defeated Philistines:

> The seacoast will become pasturelands with caves for shepherds and pens for sheep. The coastland will belong to the remnant of the house of Judah; they will find pasture there. They will lie down in the evening among the houses of Ashkelon, for the LORD their God will return to them and restore their fortunes.

The grazing remnant are compared to sheep, suggesting that the Lord is their shepherd.

The shepherd motif is more fully developed as the prophecy moves toward a conclusion:

The Lord declares, "I will leave a meek and humble people among you, and they will take refuge in the name of the LORD. The remnant of Israel . . . will pasture and lie down, with nothing to make them afraid" (3:12, 13b). He concludes,

> I will gather those who have been driven from the appointed festivals. . . . I will save the lame and gather the outcasts; I will make those who were disgraced throughout the earth receive praise and fame. At that time I will bring you back, yes, at the time I will gather you . . . when I restore your fortunes before your eyes. The LORD has spoken (3:18–20).

The shepherding image is a kingship motif. In the ancient Near East kings were viewed as divinely appointed shepherds of their people.[144] The royal metaphor of a shepherd was an apt one because a king, like a shepherd, was responsible for the safety and security of those entrusted to him. As the shepherd-king of his people, the Lord provides such protection. In particular, the shepherd is concerned about the "lame" and the "outcasts" among the flock. The Lord will gather his needy sheep, his exiled people, removing their shame and bestowing them with honor.

We see this metaphor of the Lord as a concerned shepherd elsewhere in the OT. Like a shepherd he protects and cares for his vulnerable people. Jacob spoke of God as his personal shepherd (Gen 48:15; 49:24) and David declared the Lord was his shepherd (Ps 23:1). Nevertheless it is more common for the Lord to be depicted as the shepherd of Israel, his covenant people:

Ps 28:8–9	"The LORD is the strength of his people; he is a stronghold of salvation for his anointed. Save your people, bless your possession, shepherd them, and carry them forever."

---

[144] See the commentary below on 3:15. For numerous examples of the shepherd-king motif from Egypt and Mesopotamia, see Jeffrey J. Niehaus, *Ancient Near Eastern Themes in Biblical Theology* (Grand Rapids: Kregel, 2008), 34–50. See also Othmar Keel, *The Symbolism of the Biblical World: Ancient Near Eastern Iconography and the Book of Psalms* (Winona Lake, IN: Eisenbrauns, 1997), 229–30.

Ps 77:19–20	"Your way went through the sea and your path through the vast water, but your footprints were unseen. You led your people like a flock by the hand of Moses and Aaron."
Ps 78:52–53	"He led his people out like sheep and guided them like a flock in the wilderness. He led them safely, and they were not afraid; but the sea covered their enemies."
Ps 80:1–3	"Listen, Shepherd of Israel, who leads Joseph like a flock; you who sit enthroned between the cherubim, shine on Ephraim, Benjamin, and Manasseh. Rally your power and come to save us. Restore us, God; make your face shine on us, so that we may be saved."
Ps 95:6–7	"Come, let's worship and bow down; let's kneel before the LORD our Maker. For he is our God, and we are the people of his pasture, the sheep under his care."
Ps 100:3	"Acknowledge that the LORD is God. He made us, and we are his—his people, the sheep of his pasture."
Isa 40:10–11	"See, the Lord GOD comes with strength, and his power establishes his rule. His wages are with him, and his reward accompanies him. He protects his flock like a shepherd; he gathers the lambs in his arms and carries them in the fold of his garment. He gently leads those that are nursing."
Mic 7:14	"Shepherd your people with your staff, the flock that is your possession."

The motif of Yahweh as caring shepherd is most fully developed in Ezek 34:11–16:

> For this is what the Lord GOD says: See, I myself will search for my flock and look for them. As a shepherd looks for his sheep on the day he is among his scattered flock, so I will look for my flock. I will rescue them from all the places where they have been scattered on a day of clouds and total darkness. I will bring them out from the peoples, gather them from the countries, and bring

> them to their own soil. I will shepherd them on the mountains of Israel, in the ravines, and in all the inhabited places of the land. I will tend them in good pasture, and their grazing place will be on Israel's lofty mountains. There they will lie down in a good grazing place; they will feed in rich pasture on the mountains of Israel. I will tend my flock and let them lie down. This is the declaration of the Lord God. I will seek the lost, bring back the strays, bandage the injured, and strengthen the weak, but I will destroy the fat and the strong. I will shepherd them with justice.

2.1.3 The Relational God

The OT consistently portrays the Lord, the God of Israel, as relational. He is the sovereign God who rules the world from his heavenly throne, yet he is not remote and detached. On the contrary, he is involved in his world and promises to dwell with those who are needy: "For the High and Exalted One, who lives forever, whose name is holy, says this: 'I live in a high and holy place, and with the oppressed and lowly of spirit, to revive the spirit of the lowly and revive the heart of the oppressed'" (Isa 57:15). The OT prophets, including Zephaniah, provide insight into God's relationships with his covenant people Israel and with the nations.

2.1.3.1 The Lord's Relationship with His Covenant People

Zephaniah calls the Lord the "King of Israel" (3:15) and the "God of Israel" (2:9). The Lord is the God of Judah's remnant (2:7, "their God") and Zion's God (3:2, "her God," 3:17, "your [feminine singular] God"). The Lord calls Israel "my people" (2:8, 9) and "my nation" (2:9). They are "the people of the Lord of Armies" (2:10).

The foundation of the Lord's relationship with Israel is covenantal. The Lord instituted a covenant with Israel whereby he promised to be their God and they agreed to obey his commandments. If Israel obeyed the stipulations of this covenant (the Mosaic law), the Lord promised to bless them with security and agricultural prosperity in the land he was about to give them. If, however, they rebelled against his authority, he would judge them, depriving them of crops and allowing enemies to invade their land and carry them away into exile (see Lev 26; Deut 28).

2.1.3.1.1 Sin

The preexilic prophets came as messengers of Israel's God to warn the nation of impending judgment for breaking the covenant commandments. When a Pharisee, "an expert in the law," asked Jesus which of the commandments is the greatest, the Lord replied: "Love the Lord your God with all your heart, with all your soul, and with all your mind. This is the greatest and most important command. The second is like it: Love your neighbor as yourself. All the Law and the Prophets depend on these two commands" (Matt 22:35, 37–40). The message of the prophets is consistent with Jesus's understanding of the law. The two primary accusations leveled by the prophets against Israel pertained to their worship of other gods (a failure to love God) and their unjust treatment of others (a failure to love their neighbor).

We see this in Zephaniah. The prophet announces judgment against Judah and the people of Jerusalem for rejecting the Lord (1:6) by worshipping Baal, bowing in worship to the stars in the sky, and for taking oaths in the name of "their king" (1:4–5), the precise identity of whom is debated (see the commentary on 1:5). When the law was given, the Lord commanded the people not to worship other gods and not to "bow in worship" to idols made "in the shape of anything in the heavens above" (Exod 20:3–5; cf. Deut 5:7–9) or to the gods of the Canaanites (Exod 23:23–24). Later Moses told Israel, "When you look to the heavens and see the sun, moon, and stars—all the stars in the sky—do not be led astray to bow in worship to them and serve them" (Deut 4:19; cf. 17:3).

The prophet also accuses members of the elite royal bureaucracy of committing acts of injustice, specifically mentioning "officials" (*śārîm*) who worked within the royal administration and were responsible for promoting and maintaining justice (1:8). According to 3:3, "The princes (*śārîm*) within [Jerusalem] are roaring lions, her judges are wolves of the night, which leave nothing for the morning." The imagery portrays them as violent. Injustice is in view as indicated in the immediate context which mentions "oppression" (3:1) in contrast to the Lord's commitment to justice (3:5). Such violence is most likely the focus in 1:9, which denounces "all who skip over the threshold, who fill their master's house with violence and deceit." While most understand this as describing a cultic practice borrowed from the Philistines (1 Sam 5:5), the second half of the verse with its reference to "violence and deceit" suggests a correlation with 3:3 is more likely, and that social oppression is in view. If this is correct, 1:9a pictures the accused as violently breaking into houses and leaping over the thresholds in their haste to steal (see the commentary for a more detailed discussion).[145] The Lord refers to their eagerness to sin in 3:7b, which reads literally, "They arose early and corrupted all their actions." The *hiphil* of the verb *šākam*, "to do (something) early," is often combined with another verb to indicate that an action (in this case, acting corruptly) was committed early, or more figuratively, with eagerness.

Elsewhere in the Prophets, we read of Judah's officials (*śārîm*) perpetrating injustice against the vulnerable of society and corrupting the legal system by taking bribes. Isaiah and Micah denounced royal bureaucratic injustice in the late eighth century BC[146] and, as we see in Zephaniah, such oppressive actions continued right through Judah's final days.[147]

The Lord's presence in Jerusalem made this injustice and oppression especially reprehensible. Speaking of Jerusalem, the "rebellious and defiled . . . oppressive city," Zephaniah declared, "The righteous LORD is in her; he does no wrong. He applies his justice morning by morning; he does not fail at dawn, yet the one who does wrong knows no shame" (3:1, 5). Underlying their wrongdoing was a rebellious spirit, arrogantly displayed on the Lord's "holy mountain" (3:11).

Zephaniah's contrast between the Lord's commitment to justice (v. 5a) and the wrongdoers' shameless commitment to injustice and covenant rebellion (vv. 1–4, 5b) provides insight into how the Lord operates in the world. His commitment to justice does not prevent or cancel out evildoers' unjust behavior. However, it does guarantee

---

145 If royal officials are in view in 1:8–9, then the likely referent of "master" would be the king. It is unlikely this refers to godly Josiah, but it could describe practices occurring early in Josiah's reign, when he was still a boy (see Ben Zvi, *Zephaniah,* 280–81). Officials in the royal court may have been perpetuating the sins of Josiah's predecessors Manasseh (cf. 2 Kgs 21:16) and Amon (2 Kgs 21:20).

146 See, for example, (1) Isa 1:23: "Your rulers are rebels, friends of thieves. They all love graft and chase after bribes. They do not defend the rights of the fatherless, and the widow's case never comes before them." (2) Isa 3:14–15a: "The LORD brings this charge against the elders and leaders of his people: 'You have devastated the vineyard. The plunder from the poor is in your houses. Why do you crush my people and grind the faces of the poor?'" (3) Mic 7:3: "The official and the judge demand a bribe; when the powerful man communicates his evil desire, they plot it together."

147 See, for example, (1) Jer 34:8–11, which tells how the people of Jerusalem reenslaved individuals whom they had set free. (2) Ezek 22:27: "Her officials within her are like wolves tearing their prey, shedding blood, and destroying lives in order to make profit dishonestly."

that unjust behavior will be punished and that the perpetrators will be dealt with justly (v. 11).

The arrogant rebels failed to understand this. Their rebellion was fueled by a seriously flawed view of the Lord's character. Indeed, the Lord quotes them as saying to themselves, "The LORD will do nothing—good or bad" (1:12). The statement reads literally, "The Lord does not do good, and he does not do bad."[148] Both verb forms are in the *hiphil* stem (Hb. *yāṭab*, "be good," and *rāʿaʿ*, "be bad"). This pair of verbs appears in the *hiphil* stem elsewhere six times, used three times of humans (Lev 5:4; Jer 4:22; 13:23), twice of pagan gods (Isa 41:23; Jer 10:5), and once of the Lord in Joshua 24:20: "If you abandon the LORD and worship foreign gods, he will turn against you, harm [*hiphil* of *rāʿaʿ*, "be bad"] you, and completely destroy you, after he has been good [*hiphil* of *yāṭab*, "be good,"] to you." Doing bad refers to punishment, while doing good refers to blessing/reward. In other words, Joshua refers to the Lord's just character and actions. In verse 19 Joshua indicates that the Lord's justice is rooted in his holy nature (cf. "he is a holy God"). In short, the people described in Zeph 1:12 denied the Lord's holiness and its chief corollary, his justice.[149]

2.1.3.1.2 Judgment

The coming judgment would demonstrate just how flawed their theology was, for the Lord would put his holiness and justice on full display. Judgment would be appropriate and fitting. Those who had become wealthy at the expense of others (1:9), while denying the Lord's justice (1:12), would see their ill-gotten gain plundered (1:13a). They would build houses but not live in them and plant vineyards but not enjoy the fruit of their labors (1:13b). The covenantal curses would materialize, just as Moses had warned (Deut 28:30, 39).[150]

In addition to being just and appropriate, the coming judgment would be thorough and inescapable. The Lord would "search

---

[148] The imperfect verbal forms, whether translated as present or future, refer to typical behavior. Both verbs are in the *hiphil* stem, which has an exhibitive function here: "The Lord does not act well, and he does not act badly."

[149] One finds a similar attitude among the postexilic community in the time of the prophet Malachi. For fuller discussion see below.

[150] (1) Deut 28:30: "You will build a house but not live in it. You will plant a vineyard but not enjoy its fruit." (2) Deut 28:39: "You will plant and cultivate vineyards but not drink the wine or gather the grapes, because worms will eat them."

Jerusalem with lamps," punishing every culprit (1:12). There would be no place to flee, for the judgment would extend beyond Jerusalem: "The whole earth will be consumed by the fire of his jealousy, for he will make a complete, yes, a horrifying end of all the inhabitants of the earth" (1:18b). The Lord would accept no bribes from the wealthy: "Their silver and their gold will be unable to rescue them on the day of the LORD's wrath" (1:18). Even the "humble" who "carry out what" the Lord commands would have no guarantee of protection (2:3).

The severity of the judgment is apparent from the terms used to describe it: "trouble and distress . . . destruction and desolation . . . darkness and gloom . . . clouds and total darkness" (1:15). Its intensity is vividly evident in the sounds and sights that accompany it. The wealthy wail as they come to economic ruin (1:10–13), the blast of the ram's horn and the warriors' cries signal battle (1:16a), blood is poured out (1:17), and fire rages (1:18).

Perhaps the harshness of the judgment is most clearly seen in the metaphor of sacrifice used to depict it (1:7). The Lord would slaughter the objects of his judgment as if they were sacrificial animals. Ironically, in this case those invited to the sacrifice (identified in the verses that follow) are the sacrifice! (See 1:7.) While Zephaniah does not provide a gory description, three other prophets who compare divine judgment to sacrifice spare us no details regarding the reality behind the image: (1) Isa 34:6: "The LORD's sword is covered with blood. It drips with fat, with the blood of lambs and goats, with the fat of the kidneys of rams. For the LORD has a sacrifice in Bozrah, a great slaughter in the land of Edom." (2) Jer 46:10:

> That day belongs to the Lord, the GOD of Armies, a day of vengeance to avenge himself against his adversaries. The sword will devour and be satisfied; it will drink its fill of their blood, because it will be a sacrifice to the Lord, the GOD of Armies, in the northern land by the Euphrates River.

(3) Ezek 39:17, 19:

> Son of man, this is what the Lord GOD says: Tell every kind of bird and all the wild animals, "Assemble and come! Gather from all around to my sacrificial feast that I am slaughtering for you, a great feast on the mountains of Israel; you will eat flesh and drink blood. . . . You will eat fat until you are satisfied and drink blood

> until you are drunk, at my sacrificial feast that I have prepared for you.[151]

While judgment is just, thorough, inescapable, and severe, it also has a positive goal. Judgment not only destroys; it purifies. The coming judgment upon Jerusalem would purify the community by removing the proud and preserving a godly remnant.[152]

2.1.3.1.3 Salvation: The Remnant Theme

The remnant theme is central to Zephaniah's portrait of salvation beyond judgment. The Lord's judgment is discriminating and preserves the godly, through whom the Lord brings to realization his ideal for his people and for Zion. As noted above, the first mention of godly people among the sinners of Jerusalem is a bit disconcerting. The prophet, after urging the "humble . . . who carry out" the Lord's "commands" to "seek righteousness" and "humility," can only tentatively offer them some hope of escaping judgment: "Perhaps you will be concealed on the day of the Lord's anger" (2:3). King is likely correct when he suggests that *ʾûlay*, "perhaps,"

> preserves the absolute sovereignty and freedom of the Lord. In other words, it depends entirely on the Lord whether he wants to show mercy. The Lord is not indebted to respond by saving a remnant. On the contrary, He reacts in His sovereignty and freedom, and salvation springs out of His grace and love.[153]

In short, the Lord's salvation is grounded in his grace, not human effort (see Titus 3:5). (For a fuller discussion see Zeph 2:3).

Nevertheless, any concern for the destiny of the godly is quickly alleviated in 2:7, where we hear of "the remnant of the house of Judah" (*šəʾērît bêt yəhûdâ*) occupying Philistine territory as the Lord their God restores their fortunes. In verse 9 the Lord identifies himself as the God of Israel and refers to "the remnant of my people" (*šəʾērît ʿammî*) and "the remainder of my nation" (*yeter gôyî* [*qere*]). Any doubt raised by the appearance of *ʾûlay*, "perhaps," in 2:3 has been erased.

---

151 *HALOT*, 263.

152 Greg A. King, "The Message of Zephaniah: An Urgent Echo," *AUSS* 32, 2 (1996): 216–17; King, "The Remnant in Zephaniah," 416–17.

153 King, "The Remnant in Zephaniah," *BSac* 151 (1994): 421.

By the end of the book, the remnant occupies center stage. Speaking to the personified city, Zephaniah describes it this way:

> On that day you will not be put to shame because of everything you have done in rebelling against me. For then I will remove from among you your jubilant, arrogant people, and you will never again be haughty on my holy mountain. I will leave a meek and humble people among you, and they will take refuge in the name of the LORD" (3:11–12).

This righteous remnant would model godliness in their deeds, words, and motives. Consequently, they would experience the security of God's protection: "The remnant of Israel [*šəʾērît yisrāʾēl*] will no longer do wrong or tell lies; a deceitful tongue will not be found in their mouths. They will pasture and lie down, with nothing to make them afraid" (3:13). The pastoral imagery picks up on the Lord's earlier description of the remnant as his flock (cf. 2:7).

The remnant concept is prominent throughout the OT, which teaches God preserves the faithful through judgment and does not sweep them away with the wicked. When the smoke of judgment clears, the faithful are left standing and form the nucleus for a restored covenant community. The preservation of the righteous is a corollary of God's discriminating justice.

Perhaps the clearest illustration of this is Noah. Though the entire antediluvian civilization was corrupt and deserving of punishment (Gen 6:5), Noah "found favor with the LORD" (v. 8). This raises the question, Why? The beginning of the next literary unit tells us: "Noah was a righteous man, blameless among his contemporaries; Noah walked with God" (v. 9).[154] God warned Noah of the coming flood and gave him a means of preserving himself and his family through the deluge. When the flood had inundated the earth, God "remembered" Noah (8:1) and caused the flood to recede.

---

[154] The idiom used in verse 8, "find favor in the eyes of," often describes one's positive response to another's behavior. This is the case in Gen 6:8–9, where the description of Noah's righteous character disambiguates the meaning of verse 8. For other examples where one's behavior prompts favor from another, see Gen 33:8–9 (Jacob seeks Esau's favor with a gift); 39:3–4 (Joseph's God-given success prompts Potiphar's favor); Ruth 2:10–13 (Ruth's devotion to Naomi prompts Boaz's favor); 1 Sam 16:21–22 (David's effective service in Saul's royal court prompts the king's favor); 25:7–8 (David seeks Nabal's favor by appealing to his proper treatment of Nabal's servants).

The theme of discriminating divine judgment is present in several psalms. For example, after comparing the godly to a fruitful tree, the author of Ps 1 says,

> The wicked are not like this; instead, they are like chaff that the wind blows away. Therefore the wicked will not stand up in the judgment, nor sinners in the assembly of the righteous. For the LORD watches over the way of the righteous, but the way of the wicked leads to ruin" (vv. 4–6).

Psalm 11:4–5 states, "The LORD is in his holy temple; the LORD—his throne is in heaven. His eyes watch; his gaze examines everyone. The LORD examines the righteous, but he hates the wicked and those who love violence." Psalm 37 contrasts the respective destinies of the righteous and wicked in no uncertain terms. The wicked will wither away like grass in the face of God's judgment (vv. 2, 9–10, 20), but the righteous will survive this judgment and inherit the promised land: "For the LORD loves justice and will not abandon his faithful ones. They are kept safe forever, but the children of the wicked will be destroyed. The righteous will inherit the land and dwell in it permanently" (vv. 28–29; cf. vv. 11, 18–19).

We also find the related themes of discriminating divine judgment and the preservation of a godly remnant in the Prophets. Ezekiel 9:4–6 pictures the Lord instructing one of his servants to put a special mark (the Hb. letter *taw*, which looked like an X in Ezekiel's day) on the foreheads of the repentant so that they might be spared by God's executioners. In chapter 18 the Lord explains that he judges individuals according to their behavior and character. The righteous live, while the wicked perish.[155]

Habakkuk learned of God's discriminating judgment. When he expressed his concern about injustice, the Lord reminded him the righteous would be preserved because of their faithfulness to God (2:4b).

---

[155] Ezek 21:4, where the Lord announces that he will "cut off" both "the righteous and the wicked," seems to contradict what Ezekiel says about the preservation of a remnant. Interpreters have struggled to harmonize these apparently contradictory passages but have failed to propose a totally satisfying solution. (Obviously perplexed by the problem, the translator of the Septuagint, the ancient Greek version of the OT, changed "righteous" to "unrighteous" in 21:3–4. That proposal cuts, rather than unties, the knot!) Perhaps the statement reflects the perspective of the people, who would have categorized many individuals as "righteous" who did not deserve the label.

In the context of Habakkuk's prophecy, the righteous are those, like Habakkuk, who had remained faithful to the Lord but were being oppressed by the wicked (cf. 1:4). In due time the Lord's judgment would sweep away all oppressors in their proper turn (cf. 1:5–11; 2:6–20; 3:3–15). Armed with this assuring word, Habakkuk was able to affirm his confidence in God's ability to preserve his own through even the most trying times (3:16–19).

In Malachi's day, one finds an attitude among the postexilic community like what we see in Zephaniah's time. Some of Zephaniah's contemporaries denied the Lord's justice (see 1:12). Likewise, some of Malachi's contemporaries said,

> It is useless to serve God. What have we gained by keeping his requirements and walking mournfully before the LORD of Armies? So now we consider the arrogant to be fortunate. Not only do those who commit wickedness prosper, they even test God and escape" (Mal 3:14–15).

However, others feared the Lord, who took notice of them. He assured the righteous that his judgment would separate the righteous from the wicked:

> I will have compassion on them as a man has compassion on his son who serves him. So you will again see the difference between the righteous and the wicked, between one who serves God and one who does not serve him. For look, the day is coming, burning like a furnace, when all the arrogant and everyone who commits wickedness will become stubble. . . . But for you who fear my name, the sun of righteousness will rise with healing in its wings, and you will go out and playfully jump like calves from the stall. You will trample the wicked, for they will be ashes under the soles of your feet on the day I am preparing (3:17b–4:3).

The preservation of a remnant is grounded in the Lord's covenantal relationship with Israel. The covenant inaugurated at Sinai and renewed in Moab made demands on Israel. If these demands were not met, there would be severe consequences, as described in the covenant curses. Nevertheless the implementation of the curses would not mean the Lord's relationship with Israel was irreparably severed. Though the prophets warned Israel of the consequences of disobedience, they also prophesied a future deliverance of the nation from exile and the realization of the covenant blessings. In so doing, they followed the lead of Moses, who envisioned a time when the exiled people would "come to" their "senses . . . return to the LORD . . . and obey him" wholeheartedly (Deut 30:1–2). Moses promised the people this:

> Then he will restore your fortunes, have compassion on you, and gather you again from all the peoples where the LORD your God has scattered you. Even if your exiles are at the farthest horizon, he will gather you and bring you back from there. The LORD your God will bring you into the land your ancestors possessed, and you will take possession of it. He will cause you to prosper and multiply you more than he did your ancestors (vv. 3–5).

The Lord would then transform them spiritually: "The LORD your God will circumcise your heart and the hearts of your descendants, and you will love him with all your heart and all your soul so that you will live" (v. 6). The Lord would punish the hostile nations (v. 7), and Israel's renewed obedience would bring prosperity and abundance (vv. 8–10).

Intertextual links between Deuteronomy 30 and Zephaniah, especially the closing verses (3:19–20), are apparent:[156]

1. Moses's promise that the Lord would restore the people (note "he will restore your fortunes" in Deut 30:3) appears twice in Zephaniah. It occurs the first time in 2:7 where the remnant is also initially mentioned: "The coastland will belong to the remnant of the house of Judah; they will find pasture there. They will lie down in the evening among the houses of Ashkelon, for the LORD their God will return to them and restore their fortunes." It appears the second time in 3:20, in conjunction with the promise the Lord would deliver his outcast people from their disgrace (v. 19): "At that time I will bring you back, yes, at the time I will gather you. I will give you fame and praise among all the peoples of the earth, when I restore your fortunes before your eyes." It is noteworthy that the promise to "restore your fortunes" is the last thing the Lord says before the concluding speech formula, "The LORD has spoken."

[156] In this regard, see King, "The Day of the Lord in Zephaniah," 29.

2. Moses's promise that the Lord would "gather" them (30:4–5) is featured in the last two verses of Zephaniah: "Yes, at that time I will deal with all who oppress you. I will save the lame and gather the outcasts; I will make those who were disgraced throughout the earth receive praise and fame. At that time I will bring you back, yes, at the time I will gather you" (3:19–20).
3. The reference to the "outcasts" (feminine singular *niphal* participle [*niddāḥāḥ*] from *nādaḥ*, "be scattered") in 3:19 is an echo of Moses's statement in 30:1, where he speaks of the exiled people being "in all the nations where the Lord your God has driven you (*hiphil* of *nādaḥ*)." In 30:4 he calls them "your exiles" (lit., "your scattered ones," *niphal* participle [*niddaḥ*] from *nādaḥ*).
4. Moses promised, "The Lord your God will bring [*hiphil* of *bôʾ*] you into the land your ancestors possessed, and you will take possession of it" (v. 5). Zephaniah 3:20 begins with the statement, "At that time I will bring [*hiphil* of *bôʾ*] you back."

Moses's optimistic view of Israel's future mirrored in Zephaniah is rooted in the Lord's irrevocable covenantal promise to Abraham and the patriarchs. Indeed, Moses concludes his address in Deut 30:19–20 with this exhortation and promise:

> I call heaven and earth as witnesses against you today that I have set before you life and death, blessing and curse. Choose life so that you and your descendants may live, love the Lord your God, obey him, and remain faithful to him. For he is your life, and he will prolong your days as you live in the land the Lord swore to give to your ancestors Abraham, Isaac, and Jacob.

Earlier in this covenant renewal ceremony he told the people,

> All of you are standing today before the Lord your God . . . so that you may enter into the covenant of the Lord your God, which he is making with you today, so that you may enter into his oath and so that he may establish you today as his people and he may be your God as he promised you and as he swore to your ancestors Abraham, Isaac, and Jacob" (Deut 29:10a, 12–13).

In response to Abram's faith, the Lord made a covenant with him and promised to give his descendants a land (Gen 15:6, 18–20). When the patriarch, now named Abraham, demonstrated his faith through his willingness to sacrifice Isaac, the son of promise, Yahweh ratified the expanded form of the promise, which included numerous descendants and permanent title to the land (cf. Gen 17:3–8):[157]

> Because you have done this thing and have not withheld your only son, I will indeed bless you and make your offspring as numerous as the stars of the sky and the sand on the seashore. Your offspring will possess the city gates of their enemies. And all the nations of the earth will be blessed by your offspring because you have obeyed my command" (Gen 22:16–18).[158]

Abraham's descendants through Isaac (Gen 26:3–5, 24) and Jacob (Gen 28:3–4, 13–15; 35:11–2; 50:24) inherited this promise (cf. Jer 33:26; Hos 1:10; Mic 7:18–20).

Zephaniah does not mention the Abrahamic promise, but it stands in the background of his description of Israel's restoration. The intertextual links to Moses's speech in Deuteronomy 30 clustered at the conclusion of the book suggest the Lord (the speaker in Zeph 3:19–20) is describing the realization of what Moses promised. If this is correct, one may legitimately correlate the Lord's speech at the end of Zephaniah with his promise to Abraham because, as pointed out above, Moses's speech is rooted in that promise. The Lord's closing words are proof of his commitment to keep his promise to the patriarchs. When the curses have played out and the Lord's people find themselves scattered among the nations like lame and scattered sheep, the Shepherd-King, the one who was their ancestor Jacob's shepherd

[157] On the basic and expanded forms of the Abrahamic promise, see Robert B. Chisholm Jr. "Evidence from Genesis," in *A Case for Premillennialism*, ed. D. Campbell and J. Townsend (Chicago: Moody, 1992), 35–54.

[158] Permanent title to the land is not specifically mentioned here, but it is implied. Elsewhere the promise of permanent title to the land never appears in isolation, but, when mentioned, is attached to the promise of numerous descendants (see Gen 13:14–17; 17:6–8). Though it is absent in Gen 26:3–5, 24; 28:3–4, 13–15; and 35:11–12, later texts understand title to the land as part of the Lord's ratified promise to Abraham: (1) Exod 32:13: "Remember your servants Abraham, Isaac, and Israel—you swore to them by yourself and declared, 'I will make your offspring as numerous as the stars of the sky and will give your offspring all this land that I have promised, and they will inherit it forever.'" (2) Ps 105:8–11 [cf. 1 Chron 16:15–18]: "He remembers his covenant forever, the promise he ordained for a thousand generations—the covenant he made with Abraham, swore to Isaac, and confirmed to Jacob as a decree and to Israel as a permanent covenant: 'I will give the land of Canaan to you as your inherited portion.'"

(Gen 48:15), will not abandon them. He will seek them out, gather them, and lead them home (cf. Ezek 34:12–16a).

Nevertheless, there is a spiritual prerequisite for the Abrahamic promise to be realized in full. Genesis 18:17–19 makes clear that the irrevocable promise would be fulfilled when Abraham's descendants kept the way of the Lord, who said,

> Should I hide what I am about to do from Abraham? Abraham is to become a great and powerful nation, and all the nations of the earth will be blessed through him. For I have chosen him so that he will command his children and his house after him to keep the way of the LORD by doing what is right and just. This is how the LORD will fulfill to Abraham what he promised him.

The Mosaic covenant provided Israel with the opportunity to keep the way of the Lord through right and just behavior. However, the Former Prophets record the sad history of how the nation failed. In the judges period, when "there was no king," "everyone did whatever seemed right to him" (lit., "what was right in his eyes;" Judg 17:6; 21:25), instead of "doing what is right and just" (Gen 18:19). They needed a godly king to lead them, as described in Deut 17:14–20. Instead, they asked for a king like all the nations (1 Samuel 8). The Lord gave them a king, but through the prophet Samuel made clear they and their king were still subject to his authority and must keep his commands:

> If you fear the LORD, worship and obey him, and if you don't rebel against the LORD's command, then both you and the king who reigns over you will follow the LORD your God. However, if you disobey the LORD and rebel against his command, the LORD's hand will be against you as it was against your ancestors. . . . Above all, fear the LORD and worship him faithfully with all your heart; consider the great things he has done for you. However, if you continue to do what is evil, both you and your king will be swept away (1 Sam 12:14–15, 24–25).

Unfortunately, their first king, Saul, failed miserably and forfeited his dynasty and throne (1 Sam 13–15). The Lord chose David as his successor and promised him, "I will make a great name for you like that of the greatest on the earth" (2 Sam 7:9). The promise had important ramifications for Israel:

> I will designate a place for my people Israel and plant them, so that they may live there and not be disturbed again. Evildoers will not continue to oppress them as they have done ever since the day I ordered judges to be over my people Israel. I will give you rest from all your enemies" (2 Sam 7:10–11).

Despite the Lord's irrevocable covenant with the house of David (cf. Ps 89), the Davidic dynasty failed. The Former Prophets end with Jerusalem destroyed, the temple ransacked, and the Davidic king in exile in Babylon (2 Kings 25).

Nevertheless, the Lord's promise remained irrevocable. Isaiah, who prophesied the Babylonian exile and addressed the future exiles as if present with them, described the work of the Lord's special servant, an ideal Israel, who would be instrumental in reconciling the covenant nation to the Lord through his suffering (Isa 49:1–13; 52:13–53:12). God promised to make "a permanent covenant" with them in accordance with his irrevocable promise to David (55:3). However, the people must turn to the Lord: "Seek the LORD while he may be found; call to him while he is near. Let the wicked one abandon his way and the sinful one his thoughts; let him return to the LORD, so he may have compassion on him, and to our God, for he will freely forgive" (55:6–7). This appeal and promise draw on key terms from Deut 4:25–31; 30:1–10; and 1 Kgs 8:46–53. Both Moses and Solomon made clear that the exiled nation must seek (*dāraš*, Deut 4:29) the Lord and repent (*šûb*, Deut 4:30; 30:2, 10; 1 Kgs 8:47–48) of their rebellion (1 Kgs 8:47, cf. *rāšāʿnû*, "we have been wicked," with Isa 55:7, "Let the wicked one [*rāšāʿ*] abandon his way"). Then the Lord would compassionately (Deut 4:31; 30:3; 1 Kgs 8:50) forgive (1 Kgs 8:50) them.

Through Jeremiah, the Lord promises a new covenant:

> I will make a new covenant with the house of Israel and with the house of Judah. This one will not be like the covenant I made with their ancestors . . . that they broke. . . . Instead, this is the covenant I will make with the house of Israel after those days. . . . I will put my teaching within them and write it on their hearts. I will be their God, and they will be my people. No longer will one teach his neighbor or his brother, saying, 'Know the LORD,' for they will all know me, from the least to the greatest of them. . . . For I will forgive their iniquity and never again remember their sin" (31:31–35).

The Lord describes through Ezekiel's prophecies in greater detail the spiritual transformation of the covenant community when they are gathered from exile:

> For I will take you from the nations and gather you from all the countries, and will bring you into your own land. I will also sprinkle clean water on you, and you will be clean. I will cleanse you from all your impurities and all your idols. I will give you a new heart and put a new spirit within you; I will remove your heart of stone and give you a heart of flesh. I will place my Spirit within you and cause you to follow my statutes and carefully observe my ordinances. You will live in the land that I gave your ancestors; you will be my people, and I will be your God. I will save you from all your uncleanness (36:24–29).

Zephaniah does not explicitly refer to a new covenant or use the language of cleansing, but Zeph 3:11–20, like Jeremiah 31 and Ezekiel 36, describes the physical and spiritual restoration of the Lord's exiled people. In addition to the thematic/conceptual parallels, several intertextual links justify correlating the three passages theologically and understanding the promises of Zeph 3 within the framework of the new covenant.

In Jer 31, the Lord declares his commitment to the exiled northern tribes of Israel (vv. 1–7). It is noteworthy that the watchmen will urge the survivors of the north: "Come, let's go up to Zion, to the LORD our God!" (v. 6). The Lord promises to restore the survivors to their land (vv. 8–22). He then focuses on Judah and promises to restore the land and its towns (vv. 23–30). He will establish "a new covenant with the house of Israel and with the house of Judah," transform his people spiritually, and forgive their sins (vv. 31–37). Jerusalem will be rebuilt and "be holy to the LORD," never to "be uprooted or demolished again" (vv. 38–40).

Since the focus in Zeph 3:11–20 is Jerusalem, one might be inclined to correlate the Lord's promise there with Jer 31:23–40. However, as noted above, the survivors of Israel are urged in Jer 31:6 to "go up to Zion, to the LORD our God!" Then in Jer 31:12 we read, "They will come and shout for joy on the heights of Zion; they will be radiant with joy because of the LORD's goodness." Yahweh calls the future citizens of his "holy hill" the "remnant of Israel" (v. 13). Prior to this, "Israel" has been mentioned just once in Zephaniah (in 2:9, cf. "God of Israel"), but now the future righteous remnant is viewed as what is left of the covenant community. In verse 14 they are addressed as "Israel" (parallel to "Daughter Zion") and verse 15 refers to the Lord as "the King of Israel." Floyd observes:

> The whole notion of the remnant is extended by referring to it as "Israel" (v. 13), indicating that the new existence of Yahweh's people will not be any mere reconstruction of the state of Judah but rather a re-creation in some new form of the ancient entity that predated the separation of the northern from the southern kingdom.[159]

The remnant, centered in Zion (Jerusalem), is now the covenant community and heir to the Lord's promises.

In the light of this fusion of Zion and Israel, it is not surprising that the intertextual links between Zephaniah 3 and Jeremiah 31 come primarily from Jer 31:1–22:

1. *The Removal of Shame*: In Zeph 3:11 the Lord tells Zion, "You will not be put to shame," in contrast to Israel (Ephraim), who once said, "I was ashamed and humiliated" (Jer 31:19).
2. *Holiness of Zion*: In Zeph 3:11 the Lord declares that he will remove all arrogance from his "holy mountain." When the Lord, "the God of Israel," restores "the land of Judah" and "its cities," people will bless the "holy mountain" (Jer 31:23) and Jerusalem "will be holy to the Lord" (Jer 31:40). (Also note the emphasis on the Lord's holiness in Ezek 36:20–22.)
3. *Remnant of Israel*: In the day of restoration, "the remnant of Israel will no longer do wrong or tell lies" (Zeph 3:13). The Lord will say, "Sing with joy for Jacob; shout for the foremost of the nations! Proclaim, praise, and say, "Lord, save your people, the remnant of Israel!" (Jer 31:7).
4. *Shepherd/sheep*: According to Zeph 3:13, the remnant of Israel "will pasture and lie down, with nothing to make them afraid." In verse 19 the Lord declares his intention to "save the lame and . . . the outcasts," comparing the people to sheep (see the commentary). In Jer 31:10–11 the nations are urged to say, "The one who scattered Israel will gather him. He will watch

[159] Floyd, 235.

over him as a shepherd guards his flock, for the LORD has ransomed Jacob and redeemed him from the power of one stronger than he."

5. *Joy*: In Zeph 3:14 Daughter Zion/Jerusalem is urged to "sing for joy . . . Be glad and celebrate with all [her] heart," while Israel is told to "shout loudly." According to Jeremiah 31, when the Lord restores the remnant of Israel, gathering them like sheep (vv. 1–11), "they will come and shout for joy on the heights of Zion; they will be radiant with joy because of the LORD's goodness. . . . Then the young women will rejoice with dancing, while young and old men rejoice together." He "will turn their mourning into joy, give them consolation, and bring happiness out of grief" (vv. 12–13).
6. *Love*: In Zeph 3:17 the Lord renews (see commentary below) Zion "in his love." In Jer 31:3 he assures the survivors of Israel: "I have loved you with an everlasting love; therefore, I have continued to extend faithful love to you."
7. *Salvation*: In Zeph 3:19 the Lord declares, "I will save the lame." In Jer 31:7 he says, "Sing with joy for Jacob; shout for the foremost of the nations! Proclaim, praise, and say, 'LORD, save your people, the remnant of Israel!'"
8. *Gathering and Bringing Back*: In Zeph 3:19–20 the Lord says, "I will . . . gather the outcasts" and "I will bring you back, yes, at that time I will gather you." In Jer 31:8 he says, "I am going to bring them from the northern land. I will gather them from remote regions of the earth." The nations will say, "The one who scattered Israel will gather him" (v. 10).
9. *Restoration*: In Zeph 3:20 the Lord concludes his message with these words: "I will give you fame and praise among all the peoples of the earth, when I restore your fortunes before your eyes." In Jer 31:23 the Lord, "the God of Israel," says Judah will be repopulated "when I restore their fortunes."

Intertextual links between Zeph 3:19–20 and Ezek 36:24–36 include the following:

1. *Salvation*: In Zeph 3:19 the Lord declares, "I will save the lame." In Ezek 36:29, he says, "I will save you from all your uncleanness."

2. *Gathering and Bringing Back*: In Zeph 3:19–20 the Lord says, "I will . . . gather the outcasts" and "I will bring you back, yes, at that time I will gather you." In Ezek 36:24 he promises, "For I will take you from the nations and gather you from all the countries, and will bring you into your own land."

2.1.3.1.4 Salvation: The Zion Theme

The theme of Zion's restoration is prominent in Zephaniah's portrait of salvation beyond judgment. Zion/Jerusalem is the addressee in 3:11–19 and her people in 3:20 (note the switch from the second-person feminine singular forms in vv. 11–19 to the second-person masculine plural forms in v. 20). Once David centralized worship in Jerusalem (Zion), the city became the earthly dwelling place of the Lord, King of Israel, who lived within her (Zeph 3:5, 15, 17). Several psalms exalt Jerusalem (Zion) as the Lord's dwelling place and depict him as King, ruling from the city. For example, we read, (1) "His tent is in Salem [short form of Jerusalem], his dwelling place in Zion" (Ps 76:2 [Hb. v. 3]). (2) "For the Lord has chosen Zion; he has desired it for his home: 'This is my resting place forever; I will make my home here because I have desired it'" (Ps 132:13–14). (3) "The Lord reigns forever; Zion, your God reigns for all generations" (Ps 146:10). (4) "Let Israel celebrate its Maker; let the children of Zion rejoice in their King" (Ps 149:2).

The city enjoyed God's protection and blessing because the Lord lived in and ruled from it. His presence "within her" (Ps 46:5 [Hb. v. 6]: *qirbâ*; cf. Zeph 3:5, 15, 17, where suffixed *qereb*, "within" also occurs) made her safe from the raging nations outside her walls (46:6 [Hb. v. 7]). When they advanced against the city, they would be swiftly destroyed by his devastating power (Pss 48:3–8 [Hb. vv. 4–9]; 76:3–6 [Hb. vv. 4–7]). Zion would endure forever, unshaken by its foes (Ps 125:1). Eventually the nations would be forced to recognize Zion's greatness and the privileged position of its residents (Ps 87:3–7).

These psalms express an ideal, a portrait of what Jerusalem should and could have been had its leaders and people remained loyal to the God who lived among them. As the prophetic books make clear, however, the people's rebellion caused the Lord to abandon his city (Ezekiel 10–11), leaving it wide open to enemy invaders. This shattered the false, theologically incorrect optimism and presumption of the city's sinful people and deluded false prophets (cf. Jer 7,4; 8:19; 21:13) who had transformed an ideal into a dogma. The Zion ideal was not an unconditional guarantee of continual divine protection and blessing; it would only be realized if the people were loyal to God. Zephaniah does not depict the Lord leaving Jerusalem, though it is apparent that judgment was coming (cf. 1:4, 10–13; 3:11), as well as exile (cf. 3:19–20).

Nevertheless, judgment did not mean the cancellation of the Zion ideal. The voices of the prophets continued to ring out through Jerusalem's ruins. They prophesied the city's downfall, but they also anticipated its restoration when the Zion ideal would come to full realization.[160] Zephaniah makes a significant contribution to this prophetic vision. The Lord dwells within the city among a godly remnant, protecting it by driving back its enemies (3:15–17). Beyond judgment, even the nations will recognize the Lord's sovereignty (2:11) and send tribute to him (3:9–10).

It is noteworthy that a distinction between the Lord's covenant community (Israel) and the nations is assumed in Zephaniah's vision of the time of restoration. One sees this same distinction in Isa 40–55, where the Lord's Servant, the ideal Israel (49:3), mediates a covenant on behalf of "people" (*ʿām*) (49:8) and is a "light to the nations" (49:6). The "people" of 49:8 are prisoners that are released and led back to their homeland (49:9–12). The exiled covenant community is in view, for 49:13 says the Lord "has comforted his people" and extended "compassion" to "his afflicted ones." Furthermore, subsequently the prophet speaks of the Lord making a covenant with Israel (55:3; 59:21; 61:8), but not with nations.[161]

This distinction is preserved in the NT. When Simeon, guided by the Holy Spirit, saw the infant Jesus, he praised God: "My eyes have seen your salvation. You have prepared it in the presence of all peoples—a light for revelation to the Gentiles and glory to your people Israel" (Luke 2:30–32). As I have stated elsewhere,[162]

---

[160] See, among other texts, Isa 1:21–28; 2:2–4; 4:5–6; 14:32; 25:1–5; 27:2–6; 33:5; 54:11–17; 60:4–22; 61:4–6; 62:1–2; 65:17–18; Jer 30:17–20; 31:38–40; Ezek 43:1–5; Joel 2:32 [Hb. 3:5]; 3:17–21 [Hb. 4:17–21]; Obadiah 17; Mic 4:1–3; Hag 2:17–19; Zech 1:14; 8:3.

[161] See Robert B. Chisholm Jr., "The Servant of the Lord: Covenant Mediator and Light to the Nations," in *The Future Restoration of Israel: A Response to Supersessionism*, McMaster Biblical Studies Series 10, ed. S. E. Porter and A. E. Kurschner (Eugene, OR: McMaster Divinity College Press and Pickwick/Wipf and Stock, 2023), 29–30.

[162] Chisholm, "The Servant of the Lord," 33–34.

Simeon's declaration brings together several thematically related texts from Isaiah. His reference to "a light . . . to the Gentiles" recalls the servant songs (42:6; 49:6), especially the second song, where the Lord specifically mentions his "salvation" in conjunction with the servant's role as "light to the nations." The juxtaposition of "light" and "glory" recalls Isa 58:8 and 60:1.[163] Isa 58:8 occurs within a judgment speech, where the Lord is confronting his covenant people with their rebellion and sin (cf. v. 1). He urges them to promote justice and promises them, "Then your light will break forth like the dawn . . . and the glory of the LORD will be your rear guard" (v. 8, NIV11). In Isa 60:1 the Lord, after promising the gift of his Spirit (59:21), urges his people: "Arise, shine, for your light has come, and the glory of the LORD rises upon you" (60:1, NIV11). In verse 3, the prophet declares, "Nations will come to your light, and kings to the brightness of your dawn" (NIV11). The Lord himself is this light (vv. 1–2) and Israel's deliverance becomes the catalyst for the reclamation of the nations. The complex of passages merged by Simeon envisions salvation for both Israel and the nations. While both are beneficiaries of the Lord's salvation, Isaiah and Simeon keep them distinct.[164] In fact, there is no salvation for the nations apart from the Lord's deliverance of Israel.

Speaking after the resurrection of Jesus and the establishment of the church, Paul also preserves the distinction between the covenant community Israel and the Gentiles. He told Agrippa, "I stand and testify to both small and great, saying nothing other than what the prophets and Moses said would take place—that the Messiah would suffer, and that, as the first to rise from the dead, he would proclaim light to our people and to the Gentiles" (Acts 26:22–23). Both Israel and the Gentiles experience the light of salvation, but Paul keeps them distinct.[165] He does as well in Romans 11, where he explains that Isra-

[163] The terms "light" (אוֹר) and "glory" (כָּבוֹד) appear in poetic parallelism only in these two passages in the Old Testament. In Isa 58:8 "light" appears in the first line of the quatrain, while "glory" occurs in the fourth line.

[164] Speaking of Simeon's words in 2:32, Juraj Fenik and Robert Lapko observe, "Differentiating between two groups (nations and Israel) without the implication of replacement or opposition, these expressions bespeak the worldwide significance of the salvation coming in Jesus." See their "Annunciations to Mary in Luke 1–2," *Biblica* 96.4 (2015): 513.

[165] Chisholm, "The Servant of the Lord," 34.

el's hardening has facilitated the salvation of the Gentiles (v. 11). As if Isa 60:1–3 is in his thoughts, he then says, "Now if their transgression brings riches for the world, and their failure riches for the Gentiles, how much more will their fullness bring!" (v. 12, cf. v. 15). He makes the point that the rejection of Israel is only temporary and that they will be grafted back into the olive tree symbolizing the people of God (vv. 17–24). He says "a partial hardening has come upon Israel until the fullness of the Gentiles has come in. And in this way all Israel will be saved" (v. 25) and then quotes from Isa 27:9 (and possibly Jer 31:33–34) and 59:20–21: "The Deliverer will come from Zion; he will turn godlessness away from Jacob. And this will be my covenant with them when I take away their sins" (vv. 26–27).[166]

The distinction between Israel and the Gentiles in these texts makes it reasonable to assume there will be an essential fulfillment of Isaiah's prophecy—and Zephaniah's—in a kingdom envisioned by several OT prophets, Gabriel (Luke 2:32–33), and Zechariah, the father of John the Baptist (Luke 2:68–79), in which the ideal Davidic King reigns on earth over Israel and the nations in fulfillment of God's promise to Abraham (2:54–55, 72–73). The immediate context of each of the passages in Paul's composite quotation in Rom 11:26–27 associates Israel's salvation with their return to the land (Isa 27:6, 12–13; 60:9; Jer 31:33) and/or the rebuilding and glorification of Zion/Jerusalem (Isa 60:1–22; Jer 31:38–40).[167] This is unsurprising since the covenants belong to Israel (Rom 9:3–5).

However, there is more. Fundamentally, the Zion ideal envisions God dwelling among his people as their savior and protector. The NT extends the ideal to include realities beyond the earthly restoration of Jerusalem. Speaking to early, primarily Jewish Christians, the author of Hebrews contrasts Sinai with Mount Zion:

> Instead, you have come to Mount Zion, to the city of the living God (the heavenly Jerusalem), to myriads of angels, a festive gathering, to the assembly of the firstborn whose names have been written in heaven, to a Judge, who is God of all, to the spirits of righteous people made perfect, and to Jesus, the mediator of a

---

[166] On the meaning of Rom 11:25–27, see S. Louis Johnson Jr., "Evidence from Romans 9–11," in *A Case for Premillennialism*, ed. D. Campbell and J. Townsend (Chicago: Moody, 1992), 199–223.

[167] Chisholm, "Evidence from Genesis," 54.

> new covenant, and to the sprinkled blood, which says better things than the blood of Abel (Heb 12:22–24).

The Zion ideal is being realized now through the church (cf. Heb 13:14; Gal 4:26). The Zion ideal is central to the apostle John's vision of the culmination of history. Having described the final judgment (Rev 20:11–15), John envisioned "the holy city, the new Jerusalem, coming down out of heaven from God, prepared like a bride adorned for her husband" (Rev 21:2; cf. 3:12). This city, called "the bride, the wife of the Lamb" (21:9) is inhabited by the people of God from all ages (21:12–14). According to John, "the names of the twelve tribes of Israel's sons were inscribed on the gates" (v. 12) and "the city wall had twelve foundations, and the twelve names of the twelve apostles of the Lamb were on the foundations" (v. 14). A day will come when all God's people from all ages will collectively experience his glorious presence in the new Jerusalem.

2.1.3.2 The Lord's Relationship with the Nations

The Lord's relationship with the nations is an important theme in Zephaniah. On the day of the Lord, "the **whole earth** will be consumed" and "all the inhabitants of **the earth**" will meet a "horrifying end" (1:18). The Lord brought judgment upon "the **nations**" (3:6). He declares that another culminating round of judgment will take place: "For my decision is to gather **nations**, to assemble **kingdoms**, in order to pour out my indignation on them, all my burning anger; for the **whole earth** will be consumed by the fire of my jealousy" (3:8–9). Nevertheless, judgment will not be the end of the story. Once the Lord defeats "all the gods of **the earth** . . . all the distant coasts and islands of the **nations** will bow in worship to him, each in its own place" (2:11). The Lord "will then restore pure speech to the **peoples** so that all of them may call on the name of the Lord and serve him with a single purpose" (3:9). When he gathers his exiled people, he will grant them "fame and praise among **all the peoples of the earth**" (3:20) (emphasis added). In addition to these general references to the nations and peoples of the earth, Zephaniah singles out specific nations, namely Philistia, Moab and Ammon, Cush, and Assyria (2:4–15), as objects of the Lord's judgment.

2.1.3.2.1 A Broken Covenant

The Lord's relationship with the nations of the earth is covenantal in nature. This is apparent in Isa 24:5–6, where the prophet says,

> The earth is polluted by its inhabitants, for they have transgressed teachings, overstepped decrees, and broken the permanent covenant. Therefore a curse has consumed the earth, and its inhabitants have become guilty; the earth's inhabitants have been burned, and only a few survive.

What is the background for this reference to a permanent covenant? Some identify it with a supposed creation covenant or the Mosaic covenant. Since the expression "permanent covenant" (*bərît ʿôlām*) is used in Gen 9:16 of God's promise to Noah, the Noahic mandate (9:1–7) could be in view, where God commissions Noah and his descendants: "Be fruitful and multiply and fill the earth" (v. 1). He warns them not to violate his image in humankind: "And I will require a penalty for your lifeblood; I will require it from any animal and from any human; if someone murders a fellow human, I will require that person's life. Whoever sheds human blood, by humans his blood will be shed, for God made humans in his image" (vv. 5–6). He then repeats the mandate: "But you, be fruitful and multiply; spread out over the earth and multiply on it" (v. 7). The allusion to the Noahic flood in Isa 24:18 supports this. However, Gen 9:16 does not use the phrase "permanent covenant" of the Noahic mandate per se but rather of the promise not to destroy the world by water again (see vv. 11, 15). Isaiah 24:5 speaks of the permanent covenant being *broken*. How can a unilateral promise by God be broken by human beings?

Steven Mason proposes the Noahic covenant is comprised of both the Noahic mandate and the promise. According to Mason, the juxtaposition of "but you" (Gen 9:7) and "as for me, behold I," (literal translation, Gen 9:9) links the mandate with the promise. If so, the promise may well be conditional. The fulfillment of the promise depends on obedience to the mandate. The mandate requires human beings to be fruitful and multiply. Consequently, they are not to kill one another since murder violates the image of God possessed by all humanity and is contrary to the purpose of the mandate.[168]

---

[168] Steven D. Mason, "Another Flood? Genesis 9 and Isaiah's Broken Eternal Covenant," *JSOT* 32 (2207): 177–98.

In this case, one may see the verb "defile" (NIV) in Isa 24:5 as referring to bloodshed. It is used elsewhere of defilement caused by bloodshed (Num 35:33–34; Ps 106:38). In this context this makes good sense. Isaiah 26:21 announces the Lord is coming to judge the world for its sins; the earth will expose the blood shed on its surface, suggesting murder on a mass scale is in view. According to Num 35:33–34, bloodshed defiles the land; atonement can be made for the land only by shedding the blood of the murderer. Isaiah pictures such a scenario on a cosmic level. Mass slaughter of human life has polluted the earth (24:5; 26:21); the Lord comes to make atonement for the earth by judging those who have perpetrated the crime.

Isaiah 54:9–10 is a potential obstacle to seeing the "permanent covenant" as the Noahic mandate. It appears to view the Noahic promise as irrevocable with no conditions present. However, it is possible there is implicit contingency here and that this passage is speaking of the Lord's commitment to his side of the bargain, as it were.[169]

The coming judgment prophesied by Isaiah will be cosmic in scope, like Noah's flood, to which allusion is made in Isa 24:18. The windows (*ʾărubbôt*) in the sky have opened and poured out water from the heavenly ocean upon the earth, as in the days of Noah (Gen 7:11; cf. 8:2). This precise collocation ("the floodgates on high," lit., "the floodgates from the height") occurs only here, but it is synonymous with "the floodgates of the sky" (Gen 7:11; 8:2; 2 Kgs 7:2, 19; Mal 3:10). In several texts "height" (*mārôm*) is a synonym for *šāmayim,* "sky, heavens." In ancient Near Eastern and Israelite pre-scientific cosmology there was a heavenly ocean or reservoir of water

---

[169] I have proposed elsewhere that the "permanent covenant" of Isa 24:5 has a dual referent. See Robert B. Chisholm Jr., *Handbook on the Prophets* (Grand Rapids: Baker Academic, 2002), 65–66, and Robert B. Chisholm Jr., "The 'Everlasting Covenant' and the 'City of Chaos': Intentional Ambiguity and Irony in Isaiah 24," *Criswell Theological Review* 6 (1993): 245–49. For the nations, the "permanent covenant" cannot be the Mosaic covenant, which was made with Israel. However, the nations can and did violate the Noahic mandate to respect human life. For Israel and Judah, both of whom are included in the previous judgment oracles against the nations (see Isaiah chapters 17 and 22), the "permanent covenant" is the Mosaic covenant. Though the Mosaic covenant in its entirely is never called "permanent," its prohibitions against murder and bloodshed (Exod 20:13; Num 35:6–34) are an extension of the Noahic mandate specifically applied to Israel/Judah (cf. 1:16–17, 21; 4:4; see Chisholm, "Intentional Ambiguity and Irony in Isaiah 24," 248). Amos's oracles against the nations in chapters 1–2 may provide a parallel. The nations' rebellious deeds (פֶּשַׁע is used) can be viewed as covenantal violations. For the nations, their lack of respect for their fellow humans violates the Noahic mandate, at least in spirit, while Israel and Judah have broken the stipulations of the Mosaic covenant (Chisholm, *Handbook on the Prophets,* 381).

(cf. Gen 1:6–7; Pss 104:13; 148:4). To bring abundant rainfall, God released water from the heavenly reservoir by opening the windows or floodgates of the heavens (cf. 2 Kgs 7:2, 19; Mal 3:10). In the time of Noah, he inundated the earth with water from above to wipe out the sinful inhabitants of the world (Gen 7:11; 8:2).

It is noteworthy that Zeph 1:2–3 also depicts cosmic divine judgment in flood-like terms (cf. Zeph 1:2–3 with Gen 6:7; 7:4, 23). The conceptual parallel with Isa 24:18 suggests an intertextual relationship although Zeph 1:2–3 does not mention mass bloodshed as a basis for the coming judgment. In fact, there is no formal reason given in Zephaniah for the reversal of creation and the flood-like judgment.

2.1.3.2.2 Arrogance and Idolatry

In 2:4–15 the Lord's judgment targets four nations. No specific reason is given for Philistia's judgment (vv. 4–7) or for Cush's (v. 12) (but see below), while arrogance is the primary reason for the judgment of Moab/Ammon and Assyria. The Lord will punish Moab and Ammon because of their taunting of his covenant people (v. 8), which was an expression of their pride and arrogance (v. 10). More specifically, their taunts were "against the people *of the* Lord *of Armies*" (emphasis added). The Lord identifies with his people (note "my people" and "God of Israel" in vv. 8–9), so the taunts are ultimately against him. This is obviously unwise because he has "armies" at his disposal and is fully capable of reducing Moab and Ammon to ruins (v. 9). The Hebrew word translated "pride" (*gāʾôn*) has a negative connotation here. It is associated with human strength[170] and characterizes the evil people of the earth,[171] including various nations and cities.[172] The Lord abhors human pride (Prov 8:13; Amos 6:8), which prompts his judgment (Isa 13:11; 23:9). This is why pride goes before destruction (Prov 16:18).

As for Assyria, Nineveh's hubris is the basis for judgment.[173] The city is called "jubilant" (v. 15, *ʿallîzâ*). The word describes joyful celebration, referring in this case to boastful arrogance. Nineveh lived in "security," seemingly insulated from threat, harm, or invasion. This

---

[170] Lev 26:19; Ezek 7:24; 24:21; 30:6, 18; 33:28.

[171] Isa 13:11; 23:9.

[172] Isa 14:11; 16:6; Jer 13:9; 48:29; Ezek 16:56; 32:12; Hos 5:5; 7:10; Zech 9:6; 10:1.1

[173] Daniel Hojoon Ryou, *Zephaniah's Oracles against the Nations: A Synchronic and Diachronic Study of Zephaniah 2:1–3:8*, Biblical Interpretation 13 (Leiden: Brill, 1995), 251.

made her self-confident, as evidenced by her statement, spoken "to herself" (lit., "in her heart"): "I exist, and there is no one else" (lit., "I, and there is none besides"). The grammatical structure of the statement makes it a declaration of incomparability and an affirmation of uniqueness and superiority. Nineveh was in a class all by herself, or so she thought.

In addition to arrogance, verse 11a hints at another reason for the judgment of the nations, including the ones specifically mentioned in vv. 4–15. I translate v. 11a, "The LORD will be terrifying over them [that is, more terrifying than they are] when he weakens all the gods of the earth."[174] This is an affirmation of the Lord's sovereignty. The *niphal* participle *nôrāʾ* describes him as worthy of fear or awe-inspiring, and in this context "terrifying" using metonymy. When used with *nôrāʾ*, the preposition *ʿal*, while possibly adversative, "against," more likely carries the sense of "above, over," with the connotation "superior to."[175] The prophet affirms the Lord will, through his judgment upon Moab and Ammon, prove himself to be more worthy of fear than these two defeated nations despite all their threatening, insulting taunts against his people and, as his people's God, against him. Furthermore, standing behind Moab and Ammon are their gods, Chemosh and Milcom. By implication, the assertion of the Lord's superiority to Moab and Ammon is also an assertion of his preeminence over their gods. Verse 11, with its reference to weakening "all the gods of the earth," indicates a time is coming when the Lord defeats the pagan gods on a worldwide scale. The verb, translated "starves" by CSB, probably means "weakens," in the sense of leaving them emaciated and gaunt. One can paraphrase verse 11a this way: Through his judgment on Moab and Ammon (v. 10), the Lord will prove himself more worthy of fear than these boastful nations, for his judgment upon Moab and Ammon, as part of the day of the Lord, will encompass all nations. In

---

[174] CSB: "The LORD will be terrifying to them, when he starves all the gods of the earth." For a discussion of the meaning of this statement, see the commentary below on 2:11.

[175] BDB, 755, category II. 3; *HALOT*, 826, category 1. f. In the few texts where the *niphal* participle *nôrāʾ* combines with the preposition *ʿal*, the combination three times means "worthy of fear above," in a comparative sense ("more worthy of fear than") (1 Chr 16:25; Pss 89:7 [Hb. v. 8]; 96:4). In Ps 66:5 it is used of God's work (note the parallel line, "wonders of God"), and may have the nuance "toward" when combined with "the sons of man." However, the comparative nuance is possible, "more worthy of fear than (the work of) the sons of man." Renz, *Zephaniah,* 542, note hh, prefers the comparative view.

defeating them he will weaken their gods to the point where they are incapable of functioning with any kind of effectiveness or strength.

The Lord takes the hostility of the surrounding nations seriously because their taunts against his people are ultimately insults against him. A taunting diatribe against Israel is a verbal attack against the Lord himself, as the Philistine champion Goliath discovered. The Philistine defied the army of Israel (1 Sam 17:10), but David viewed this army as belonging to the "living God" (17:26, 36). Israel's God was inextricably linked with Israel's army; to defy his army was to defy the Lord. While the Philistine's focus was his personal honor and prowess (17:43–44), David focused attention on the Lord and would act to bring glory to the Lord, Israel's God, not himself. David identified with the Lord and viewed himself as the Lord's instrument in silencing this Philistine blasphemer.

The Lord also takes statements of self-reliance seriously. When Nineveh said, "I, and there is none besides," she made an insulting claim that only the Lord, the one true God, can legitimately make. Consequently, judgment upon such hubris was appropriate. From the Lord's perspective, the gods of Moab, Ammon, Nineveh, and all nations stand behind their worshippers. The clash is not simply between him and the human worshippers of the pagan gods. He regards the human speakers as representatives of their gods. This is why his judgment upon the human speakers entails "weakening" these gods.

This implies that idolatry, in addition to arrogance and self-reliance, is a basis for his judgment upon the nations. Consequently, although no specific accusation appears in the judgment speeches against the Philistines and Cushites (see 2:4–7, 12), one can assume based on 2:11a that their idolatry is a basis for the Lord's judgment. His attack on them is an attack on the gods they worship.

2.1.3.2.3 Reclamation: Worldwide Worship

The prophets make clear the Lord has not abandoned the nations. For example, in Isaiah's first Servant Song we read,

> This is what God, the Lord, says—who created the heavens and stretched them out, who spread out the earth and what comes from it, who gives breath to the people on it and spirit to those who walk on it—"I am the Lord. I have called you for a righteous purpose, and I will hold you by your hand. I will watch over you,

> and I will appoint you to be a covenant for the people and a light to the nations, in order to open blind eyes, to bring out prisoners from the dungeon, and those sitting in darkness from the prison house. I am the LORD. That is my name, and I will not give my glory to another or my praise to idols" (42:5–8).

The referent of "people" in verse 6 (cf. "covenant for the people") is debated. The immediate context suggests the earth's inhabitants are in view. The following phrase, "light to the nations," favors the translation "people" (rather than, "a people" or "[the] people"), as does verse 5 which uses "people" for humankind in general.[176] The second Servant Song also describes the servant as a covenant mediator for "people" (49:8), as well as "a light for nations" (49:6). In this case, "people" refers to the Lord's exiled rebellious servant, the people of the covenant community Israel/Jacob (see especially 49:6, 9–12). Correlating the second song with the first, some equate "people" in 42:6 with "people" in 49:8 and understand both texts as referring to Israel.[177] Nevertheless, the immediate context of 42:6 must receive priority. The contextual indicators in 42:6 point to a broader referent here.

The servant mediates a covenant with the nations to whom he is a light. Light is a metaphor for deliverance. In Isa 42:7 the servant delivers prisoners from bondage.[178] This deliverance is associated with opening blind eyes. The deliverance has two dimensions. In 42:8 the Lord says, "I am the LORD. That is my name, and I will not give my glory to another or my praise to idols." This suggests that the nations will be delivered spiritually from the bondage of their idolatry as they experience the light of the Lord's salvation. Elsewhere the imagery of opening blind eyes (see Ps 146:8–9; Isa 29:18–21; 35:4–5) and freeing prisoners (Pss 69:34; 79:11; 102:21; 107:10; 146:7; Isa 49:9; 61:1)

---

[176] See J. Alec Motyer, *The Prophecy of Isaiah: An Introduction & Commentary* (Downers Grove, IL: InterVarsity, 1993), 322; Christopher R. North, *The Second Isaiah* (Oxford: Clarendon, 1964), 112; R. N. Whybray, *Isaiah 40–66*, NCB (Grand Rapids, William B. Eerdmans, 1981), 74–75.

[177] For example, Oswalt understands Israel as being the "people" in view in 42:6, based on the parallel with 49:5–8. John N. Oswalt, *The Book of Isaiah, Chapters 40–66*, NICOT (Grand Rapids: William B. Eerdmans, 1998), 118. See also J. L. Koole, *Isaiah, Part 3, Vol. 2: Isaiah 49–55*, Historical Commentary on the Old Testament, trans. A. P. Runia (Leuven: Peeters, 1998), 230.

[178] One also sees this connection between light and deliverance in two other texts in this section of Isaiah: (1) In 49:6, the phrase "light of nations" appears again and is immediately followed by "to be my salvation to the ends of the earth." (2) In 51:4–5 the Lord makes his justice a "light to the nations."

depicts the just treatment of the afflicted. This suggests that the nations will be delivered from the bondage of injustice and oppression.

A look at Isa 11:1–10 helps us appreciate more fully this aspect of the servant's deliverance of the nations. Here the Lord establishes justice on earth through an ideal king who sprouts forth from Jesse's root stock (v. 1). The Lord's spirit rests upon this king, who is a new David (cf. 1 Sam 16:13; 2 Sam 23:2). The king will promote justice by defending the just cause of the needy and eliminating the wicked from his kingdom because he fears the Lord (vv. 3–5):

> His delight will be in the fear of the LORD. He will not judge by what he sees with his eyes, he will not execute justice by what he hears with his ears, but he will judge the poor righteously and execute justice for the oppressed of the land. He will strike the land with a scepter from his mouth, and he will kill the wicked with a command from his lips. Righteousness will be a belt around his hips; faithfulness will be a belt around his waist.

The radical change in human society will be mirrored by a radical transformation of the animal kingdom (vv. 6–8), where predators (representing the oppressors of human society) will no longer attack their prey (representing the oppressed of human society). Peace will prevail on earth:

> They will not harm or destroy each other on my entire holy mountain, for the land will be as full of the knowledge of the LORD as the sea is filled with water. On that day the root of Jesse will stand as a banner for the peoples. The nations will look to him for guidance, and his resting place will be glorious" (vv. 9–10).

Zephaniah makes an important contribution to this theme of the reclamation of the nations. When the Lord weakens "all the gods of the earth . . . all the distant coasts and islands of the nations will bow in worship to him, each in its own place" (2:11). After the nations have experienced the Lord's "indignation," "burning anger," and the "fire" of his zeal, the Lord "will restore pure speech to the peoples so all of them may call on the name of the LORD and serve him with a single purpose" (3:8–9). This is a reversal of the Babel judgment, when God confused the people's language and scattered them, ironically forcing them to fill the earth in accordance with the creation and Noahic mandates. At that time his "supplicants," further identified as his "dispersed people" will bring tribute to him (3:10). One tends to think of "dispersed people" as being the exiles of Israel.[179] They may be included, since Moses foresaw Israel being dispersed among the peoples in distant places (cf. Deut 4:27; 28:64), but one would expect the exiles to return to the land of Israel to live (Isa 11:12), not simply bring an offering/tribute. It is more likely the tribute bearing suppli-cants/dispersed ones of verse 10 are primarily the peoples mentioned in verse 9 (cf. 2:11). This is an additional allusion to the Babel event described in Genesis 11, where the verb used here (*pûṣ*) appears three times to describe how the Lord "dispersed" the people of the earth (11:4, 8–9).[180] At Babel the rebellious people joined forces to build a tower as a monument to their greatness and refused to fill the earth, as Adam and Noah had been commanded to do. They were punished by having their language confused and by being forced to disperse. In the future age they will serve the Lord in the lands where they were dispersed (cf. 2:11), invoke his name, serve him, pray to him, and bring him tribute. The creation mandate and God's ideal for the peoples of the world will finally be realized.

Zephaniah alludes to the two major cosmic judgments of God that occur in Genesis 1–11. The first, the flood, destroys humankind, except for Noah and his family, and reduces the world to its primordial watery state. The second, the Babel dispersion, prevents humankind from unifying in defiance of the creation and Noahic mandates and scatters them over the earth.[181] According to Zephaniah, the coming cosmic judgment will, like the flood, be devastating in its effects, so much so that the judgment can be compared to a reversal of creation (cf. 1:2–3, 18; 3:8). It is a third cosmic judgment. By alluding to the second judgment, Zephaniah develops a contrast not a comparison. The coming judgment will reverse the created order, but there will be no subsequent (fourth) cosmic judgment corresponding to the Babel dispersion. In fact, just the opposite will occur as the effects of the Babel dispersion are reversed. The Lord's ideal—humanity, spread throughout the world, worshipping him in unity—will be realized.

---

[179] See, among many other passages, Deut 4:27; 28:64; Isa 11:12; Jer 9:16 [Hb. v. 15]; Ezek 28:25.

[180] See Sweeney, *Zephaniah,* 183.

[181] On the scattering at Babel as fundamentally an act of judgment, not blessing, see Carol M. Kaminski, *From Noah to Israel: Realization of the Primaeval Blessing after the Flood,* JSOTSup 413 (London: T & T Clark International, 2004), 30–42.

Excursus 1: The Backstory of Zephaniah 3:9–10

BABEL AND THE DISPERSION OF HUMANITY (GEN 11:1–9): THE LORD THWARTS HUBRIS

In the creation mandate God told the man and woman, "Be fruitful, multiply, fill the earth" (Gen 1:28). Following the flood, he repeated the mandate to Noah and his sons (Gen 9:1).

Later in chapter 9 we read that from the three sons of Noah, "the whole earth was dispersed" (9:19, literal translation).[182] The Table of Nations in chapter 10 gives a detailed account of the various people groups that descended from Noah's three sons. Verse 18 speaks of the Canaanite families (or tribes/clans) being dispersed (the verb is a passive form of *pûṣ*). Verse 25 mentions the fact that Peleg was so named (the name means "half" or "separation") because during his days the earth was "divided" (the verb is a passive form of *pālag*). Verse 32 informs us that from the tribes/clans of Noah, "the nations were separated [the verb is a passive form of *pārad*, "to separate"] in the earth after the flood" (literal translation). In each of these cases, the wording (a passive verb form) is peculiar. One might expect to read that Noah's offspring, in response to the creation mandate, "filled the earth." The use of passive verbs suggests that they were acted upon by someone and were forced to disperse, rather than being proactive in obedience to the mandate by filling the earth. That leads us to the Babel account (11:1–9), which tells us how this dispersion occurred. Indeed, our suspicions prove correct. Humanity did not willingly carry out the mandate.

According to verse 1, the whole earth had one language. The text reads lit., "And all the earth was one lip and unified words." In other words, they shared a common language, which would have been conducive to communication and a sense of unity. This might seem like a good thing, but, as the following account reveals, this shared language proved to be a hindrance to the fulfillment of God's will, as expressed in the mandate. That humans would take something potentially good and pervert it into something evil is not surprising, given the Lord's assessment of the human race that descended from the survivors of the flood. In 8:21 the Lord states regarding humanity, "The inclination of the human heart is evil from youth onward." The account in 11:1–9 corroborates this, and, unfortunately, their unified language facilitated their evil inclinations.

---

[182] The Hebrew verb used here (vocalized נָפְצָה, from נָפַץ) appears to be a rare biform of the more common Hebrew verb פּוּץ, "to scatter, disperse," which is used in the Babel account (Gen 11:4, 8–9). Apart from Gen 9:19, it appears only two other times (1 Sam 13:11; Isa 33:3). However, in all three instances a slight change in vowels would yield a passive form (*niphal* pattern) of the verb פּוּץ. In Gen 9:19 the form would be vocalized נָפוֹצָה.

Noah's offspring moved eastward (actually, southeast from the location of Eden, cf. Gen 2:10–14) to Shinar in southern Mesopotamia. It was the region in which Babylon was located (Gen 10:10; Dan 1:2). The text does not indicate that every single descendant of Noah was part of this movement, but most of them must have been involved. Verse 2 reads lit.: "And it was, when they moved off east, they found a plain in the land of Shinar and settled there." There is no grammatical antecedent for the three uses of "they" in verse 2. This suggests that "all the earth" in verse 1, understood collectively as referring to all the people in the earth, is in view. Later (v. 4) "they" express their fear of being "scattered across the face of the whole earth" (lit. translation), suggesting this had not yet happened. In verse 4, "the whole earth" is used geographically, as indicated by "across the face of."

Once in Shinar, the people decided to embark on a building project involving bricks and bitumen (v. 3). They proposed building a city (v. 4). Prior to this, city building has been mentioned just twice. After being reduced to the lifestyle of a wandering vagabond by the Lord, Cain circumvented his sentence by building a city (Gen 4:17). In 10:11–12 we read of Nimrod, who was a powerful warrior-king in Shinar, extending his rule northward. He went to Assyria and built cities, including Nineveh. The reference to Assyria and Nineveh would have negative connotations for later Hebrew readers.

They also decided to build a high tower (*migdāl*), with its top reaching into the heavens (or, sky). The only other place in the Old Testament where the top of a structure reaches the sky is the stairway seen by Jacob in his dream upon which angelic beings were ascending and descending (Gen 28:12). In that case, the structure is called a *sullām*, "stepped ramp," not a tower. Since ziggurats became popular in Mesopotamia, some identify the tower of Babel as one of these. Ziggurats were built in a temple complex. They were high pyramid-like structures with terraces and stepped ramps. In Mesopotamian texts they are described as having their tops in the heavens. Because of the Mesopotamian setting of Gen 11:1–9, some conclude that building the tower was an attempt to connect heaven with earth and to facilitate God's descent to meet worshippers. However, this is highly speculative, especially since the text uses the word *migdāl*, "tower," and specifically reveals their motivation in building it. Elsewhere in the Old Testament the word refers to a tower, often a watchtower or defensive tower in a city, not a cultic structure for worship. Towers symbolized security and immunity to being defeated by an attack and, as such, could be a source of pride (see, for example, Isa 2:15).[183] The people of Shinar specifically stated

---

[183] In this regard, see David Smith, "What Hope after Babel? Diversity and Community in Gen 11:1–9; Exod 1:1–14; Zeph 3:1–13; and Acts 2:1–3," *Horizons in Biblical Theology* 18, 2 (1996): 174–75.

that their purpose in building this city and tower was to "make a name for" themselves, an expression referring to building a reputation.

In addition, their motive was to prevent themselves from dispersing across the face of the whole earth. Perhaps anticipating that population growth might lead to people dispersing, they proposed to build a city with a tower symbolizing their strength and solidarity as a people. No one would want to venture too far from a place that is impregnable to attack and a testimony to human greatness. This was hubris and a blatant attempt to circumvent the creation mandate to fill the earth and to serve as God's vice-regents over his world, including the animal kingdom. Rather than serving the King, they wanted to make a name for *themselves*. Perhaps their tower, reaching into the heavens, revealed their desire to usurp God's authority, for he is the one who looks down on the earth from his heavenly throne (see, for example, Ps 11:4). Ironically, the God who dwells in heaven is willing to descend and dwell among people, but only with the humble and downtrodden, not the arrogant (Isa 57:15).

The Lord descended to look upon the city and tower construction project (v. 5). He concluded that their ability to communicate through a common language was problematic (v. 6). If it facilitated this building project, then it would also enable them to concoct other plans even more morally reprehensible. Nothing would be beyond their evil, calculating minds. Perhaps we could say, not even the sky would be their limit! Using the first-person plural, the Lord issued a call to action, declaring the time had arrived to confuse (the verb is *bālal*) their unified language (lit., "lip"), making it difficult for them to understand (lit., "hear") one another (v. 7). The language barrier that characterizes the post-Babel world is more conducive to disunity than unity and, from the Lord's perspective, that is advantageous, at least until the day when the Lord himself rectifies the situation (Zeph 3:9).

The Lord did what he proposed (vv. 8–9). He confused the language of the "whole earth" (that is, the mass of humanity congregated there in Shinar) and scattered (the verb is the causative form of *pûṣ*) them over the face of the whole earth geographically. Their building project came to a halt, at least temporarily. In time a city did arise there. The Babylonians named it *bab-ili*, "gate of God" (that is, Babylon). However, for readers of the biblical account, the name Babel is a reminder that this was a place of sin and judgment, not worship, for the Lord "confused" (*bālal*, note the "b" and "l" sounds in *babel* and *bālal*) the unified human language there and thwarted human hubris. No wonder Babylon becomes in the Bible a symbol of proud opposition to God that is destined for destruction (see especially Revelation 17–18).

2.2 Prophecy and Fulfillment

2.2.1 Prophetic Speech and Discourse Types

Prophetic speech combines different discourse types. As the Lord addresses his people through the prophets, we hear a blend of expository and hortatory discourse (traditionally referred to as "forth telling").[184] The prophets accuse their audience of breaking their covenant with the Lord and exhort them to repent and change their ways. This expository-hortatory discourse blend has evaluative and dynamic speech functions. According to Macky, evaluative speech expresses the speaker's "judgment on the quality of something," while dynamic speech is "intended to change hearers personally."[185]

Predictive discourse (traditionally called "foretelling") is also prominent in prophetic speech. It can be performative or dynamic in function.[186] According to Macky, performative language "performs some non-linguistic act, such as a judge decreeing, 'The defendant is acquitted.'"[187] Prophecies are performative when they announce God's purposes unconditionally. In such cases, they set in motion a series of events leading to their fulfillment. Dynamic predictive discourse announces God's purposes conditionally with the intent of motivating a positive response to the accompanying expository-hortatory discourse with which it is joined. In such cases the purpose of the predictive element is to prevent (if an announcement of judgment) or facilitate (if an announcement of salvation) the realization of the prophecy.

In terms of its scope, predictive discourse can be historical and eschatological. Historical predictive discourse addresses specific nations, people groups, or individuals in the prophet's context. It warns of impending judgment or announces deliverance. It is typically dynamic in nature and supports the hortatory discourse which it accompanies. Clendenen observes that in such cases . . .

> the most prominent element is naturally the behavioral change or changes being advocated. All the other elements in the discourse

---

[184] Chisholm, "When Prophecy Appears to Fail, Check Your Hermeneutic," 562.

[185] Peter W. Macky, *The Centrality of Metaphors to Biblical Thought: A Method for Interpreting the Bible* (Lewiston, NY: Edwin Mellen, 1990), 16.

[186] Chisholm, "When Prophecy Appears to Fail, Check Your Hermeneutic," 562–63.

[187] Macky, *The Centrality of Metaphors to Biblical Thought*, 16.

must relate to one or more of the commands or exhortations, and it would be a misuse of Scripture to listen to only one of the supplementary elements, such as predictive prophecy, without relating it to the central message of the book.[188]

Eschatological predictive discourse envisions a culminating judgment of the nations on a worldwide scale, followed by a radical transformation of the world as we know it, including both the Lord's covenant community and the nations. The transformation of the covenant community entails repentance, return from exile, and spiritual renewal (Deut 30:1–10). As for the nations, they will recognize the Lord as the one true God and worship him as such (Zech 14:9). Often the historical and eschatological dimensions are blended, with the historical dimension set within a larger eschatological frame. Eschatological predictive prophecy tends to be more performative. More immediate historical situations addressed by the prophet occasion visions of culminating events in God's plan for his covenant people and for the nations.

Eschatological prophecy is especially prominent in Isaiah. For example, Isa 13:1–16 describes the destructive judgment of the day of the Lord that will devastate the "world" and its "wicked people" (v. 11). Isaiah 24 gives a more detailed description of this judgment that encompasses the "world" (v. 4). The noun *tēbēl*, "world," appears here, parallel to *ʾereṣ*, "earth." This word pair clearly refers to the earth/world, as opposed to a specific land, in several texts.[189] In other contexts a broader worldwide scope is not as obvious but still makes adequate, if not excellent sense.[190] Used apart from *ʾereṣ*, *tēbēl* refers to the world in several passages.[191] According to Stadelmann, *tēbēl* designates "the habitable part of the world."[192] When the Lord unleashes this worldwide judgment, he will defeat a heavenly-earthly coalition (v. 21) as he establishes his rule from Zion (v. 23). He will prepare a great feast and eliminate death "once and for all" (25:6–8). The

---

[188] E. Ray Clendenen, "Textlinguistics and Prophecy in the Book of the Twelve," *JETS* 46 (2003): 390.

[189] 1 Sam 2:8; 1 Chr 16:30; Job 37:12; Pss 19:4; 24:1; 33:8; 89:11; 90:2; 96:13; 98:9; Prov 8:26, 31; Isa 14:16–17; 34:1; Jer 10:12; 51:15; Lam 4:12.

[190] Job 18:17–18; 34:13; Pss 77:18; 97:4; Isa 14:21; 18:3; 26:9, 18; Nah 1:5.

[191] Pss 9:8; 18:15; 50:12; 93:1; 96:10; 98:7; Isa 13:11; 27:6.

[192] Luis I. J. Stadelmann, *The Hebrew Conception of the World*, Analecta Biblica 39 (Rome: Biblical Institute, 1970), 130.

dead will rise (26:19), Yahweh will destroy the sea monster Leviathan (27:1), symbolizing opposition to his reign, and the Israelite exiles will come to Jerusalem to worship the Lord (27:12–13). Isaiah 2:2–4 (see Mic 4:1–4) envisions a time when the Lord will rule over the world from Zion and ensure justice and peace among the nations. They will come to Jerusalem for him to adjudicate any disputes they may have with one another.[193] Similarly, Isa 11:1–10 looks forward to an ideal king (called the "root of Jesse") ruling the nations justly. He establishes justice within his realm, eliminating oppression. This transformation of human society will be mirrored in the animal kingdom, where predators will coexist with animals that once served as their prey. Wolves, leopards, lions, and bears will pose no danger to livestock or to little children.

Zephaniah, like Isaiah, contains its share of eschatological prophecy. The book begins with a bang, as the Lord announces he will come in a flood-like judgment to reverse creation (1:2–3). The day of the Lord will overtake the earth (1:14–18). The language is not merely hyperbolic, for the Lord later says,

> Therefore, wait for me—this is the LORD's declaration—until the day I rise up for plunder. For my decision is to gather nations, to assemble kingdoms, in order to pour out my indignation on them, all my burning anger; for the whole earth will be consumed by the fire of my jealousy (3:8).

The judgment will impact negatively "all the gods of the earth" (2:11). Nevertheless, it will have a positive impact on "all the distant coasts and islands of the nations" who "will bow in worship to [the Lord], each in its own place" (2:11). The Lord will reverse the Babel judgment: "For I will then restore pure speech to the peoples so that all of them may call on the name of the LORD and serve him with a single

[193] The passage (see also Mic 4:1) begins with the phrase "in the last days" (*bə'aḥărît hayyāmîm*). The phrase (lit., "in the end of days") occurs thirteen times in the OT. It often refers to the future in a general way (see Gen 49:1; Num 24:14; Deut 31:29; Jer 23:20; 30:24; 48:47; 49:39). On other occasions, it appears to refer more specifically to the culminating period in Israel's history when God destroys his enemies and vindicates his people (see Deut 4:30; Ezek 38:16; Dan 10:14; Hos 3:5; Isa 2:2 = Mic 4:1). Several translations, like CSB, see a reference to an eschatological period in Isa 2:2 (cf. KJV, NIV, NASB, NLT, ESV ["in the latter days"]), while others understand it as referring to an indeterminate future (NET ["in future days"], NRSV ["in days to come"]).

purpose. From beyond the rivers of Cush my supplicants, my dispersed people, will bring an offering to me" (3:9–10).

In Isaiah 13–27 and Zephaniah, the judgment of specific nations (Isa 13:17–23:13; Zeph 1:4–13; 2:4–15), which has a historical dimension, is set within a broader worldwide, eschatological frame, making interpretation challenging at times. When such a blending of the historical and eschatological occurs, historical fulfillment can foreshadow and preview the eschatological dimension.[194]

2.2.2 Historical Fulfillment of Zephaniah's Prophecies

Interpreters attempt to understand the prophets' messages in the historical-cultural contexts in which they were spoken. After all, the headings of the books locate the prophets in specific historical contexts. Within the prophets' messages are numerous references to places, people, and events contemporary with each prophet. Their messages contain a great deal of expository and hortatory discourse as the prophets speak to their contemporary generations, confronting them with their sins and urging them to repent and obey the Lord. When one moves to the predictive discourse of their messages, it is natural to look for fulfillment of their warnings within their historical contexts. The fact that they often address and prophesy concerning nations of their times justifies this approach. One often finds historical evidence of a prophecy's fulfillment.

Zephaniah illustrates this well. The book's heading dates the prophecy to the late seventh century BC when Josiah ruled Judah. The Lord directly addresses Judah/Jerusalem (cf. 1:4) and the Cushites (2:12) and speaks of the destiny of Moab and Ammon (2:8–9). The prophet addresses the Philistines (2:5) and delivers messages pertaining to Philistine cities (2:4–7), Moab/Ammon (2:10–11), and Assyria/Nineveh (2:13–15).[195] It is unsurprising Zephaniah describes Assyria's downfall since this historical development was unfolding during the time he prophesied.

There is historical evidence that illuminates the fulfillment of some of Zephaniah's oracles. Second Kings 24–25 provides a detailed

---

[194] On the merging of historical and eschatological dimensions in Zephaniah's portrait of the day of the Lord, see King, "The Day of the Lord in Zephaniah," 31–32.

[195] Zephaniah's contemporary, Jeremiah, also prophesied judgment upon the Philistine cities (Jer 25:20; 47:1–7), as well as Moab and Ammon (Jer 25:21; 48:1–49:6).

account of Babylon's conquest of Judah,[196] and Babylonian Chronicle 22 tells of the conquest of Nineveh and the Assyrian Empire.[197] In Babylonian Chronicle 24 we read of Nebuchadnezzar's destruction of Ashkelon in 604 BC. He and his troops marched against Hatti and were victorious. He received "massive tribute" from "all the kings" of Hatti. As for Ashkelon, "he seized its king, pillaged and [plu]ndered it. He reduced the city to a heap of rubble" (cf. Zeph 2:4).[198]

Beaulieu writes:

> Excavations at Ashkelon have confirmed that the city was completely destroyed and began to recover only in the Persian period. The find of Egyptian artefacts in the destruction level suggests close contacts between Egypt and Ashkelon at that time and probably the presence of an Egyptian garrison. Also, the appearance of Greek wares at a number of harbors along the coast at the end of the seventh century suggests an influx of Greek mercenaries employed by the Egyptians in towns that had become subservient to them. Barely one year after crushing the Egyptians at Carchemish, Nebuchadnezzar made sure to expel them from the Syro-Palestinian corridor for good. This probably explains his systematic and planned destruction of Ashkelon, a fortified harbor that could be used again by the Egyptians as a base for military operations.[199]

Master comments:

> Perhaps it was the increased level of Egyptian involvement that caused Nebuchadnezzar to respond so harshly. Perhaps he realized that the tensions of the Assyrian policy were untenable. Perhaps it was a fear of the new economic order brought on by new Mediterranean trade routes running through ports he did not control.

---

[196] See also Babylonian Chronicle 25; Glassner, *Mesopotamian Chronicles*, 231. For a summary of the Babylonian conquest of Judah, see John W. Betlyon, "Neo-Babylonian Military Operations Other Than War in Judah and Jerusalem," in Oded Lipschits and Joseph Blenkinsopp, ed., *Judah and the Judeans* (Winona Lake, IN: Eisenbrauns, 2003), 265–68. For a fuller account, see Oded Lipschits, *The Fall and Rise of Jerusalem: Judah under Babylonian Rule* (Winona Lake, IN: Eisenbrauns, 2005).

[197] Glassner, *Mesopotamian Chronicles*, 218–25.

[198] Glassner, *Mesopotamian Chronicles*, 229. See also Lawrence E. Stager, "Ashkelon and the Archaeology of Destruction: Kislev 604 B.C.E.," *Eretz-Israel* 25 (1996): 61*–74*.

[199] Jean-Alain Beaulieu, "Judah in the Shadow of Babylon," *Hebrew Bible and Ancient Israel* 9 (2020): 8.

> Or, perhaps, this was just Nebuchadnezzar making an example of a border town in Hatti-land at the outset of his reign. For the people of Ashkelon, it mattered little. Nebuchadnezzar's arrival was a death sentence. No alliance or trading network could thwart him. Ashkelonians were caught in the streets and the shops, left under the collapsing, burning wreckage. . . . The boundaries of the Babylonian empire were pushed all the way to the border of Egypt. But this was not just more of the same. In the midst of a dynamic moment in the Mediterranean, a world of new routes and new rivalries, Nebuchadnezzar destroyed Ashkelon, depopulated the coast, and cut off this region from the West for almost a century. The march of Ionian trade was stopped, and, when Ashkelon reappeared decades later, it was as a distinctively Phoenician foundation.[200]

Lipschits concludes that the destruction of Ashkelon was "singular and exceptional and that the Babylonians quickly and easily took control of all Hatti-land."[201] Nebuchadnezzar campaigned regularly in the west after taking the throne.[202] He marched on Hatti in his accession year and years one through four and six through eight. During year five he remained home and "strengthened his numerous chariotry and cavalry." He took "massive tribute" home in his accession year and year one, destroyed Ashkelon in year one, marched unsuccessfully on Egypt in year four,[203] looted the Arabs in year six, took Jerusalem in year seven, but, otherwise, significant details are lacking.[204] We do not know to what degree the Babylonian invasion impacted the other Philistine towns, Moab, and Ammon in relation to the judgment language used by Zephaniah in 2:4–11.[205] As Watai says, "Unlike the preceding Neo-Assyrian kings, the Neo-Babylonian rulers left little

---

200 Daniel M. Master, "Nebuchadnezzar at Ashkelon," *Hebrew Bible and Ancient Israel* 7 (2018): 92.

201 Lipschits, *The Fall and Rise of Jerusalem*, 41.

202 See the discussion in David Vanderhooft, "Babylonian Strategies for Imperial Control in the West: Royal Practice and Rhetoric," in Oded Lipschits and Joseph Blenkinsopp, ed., *Judah and the Judeans* (Winona Lake, IN: Eisenbrauns, 2003), 240–42.

203 For a summary of "the relations between Mesopotamia (Assyria and Babylonia) and Egypt from the time of the Assyrian withdrawal from the Levant in the early 630s until the Babylonian attempt to conquer Egypt in 567," see Dan'el Kahn, "Nebuchadnezzar and Egypt: An Update on the Egyptian Monuments," *Hebrew Bible and Ancient Israel* 7 (2018): 65–78.

204 Glassner, *Mesopotamian Chronicles*, 228–31.

205 For discussion of Moab and Ammon, see Renz, *Zephaniah,* 550–51.

documentation of their actions, policies, and administrative structures in the western territories of their empire, especially the region on the Mediterranean, which they called *Eber-nāri*."[206] Nevertheless, Kahn states, "The remaining Philistine cities were conquered and destroyed in less than 40 years" after 604 BC.[207]

2.2.3 Zephaniah's Eschatological Vision

The judgment against Judah/Jerusalem (1:4–13) and against the nations listed in the speeches of 2:4–15 grounds the book of Zephaniah in its historical context and gives it immediate relevance to those living in Judah at the time of Zephaniah. Yet the list contains an important anomaly, namely, the appearance of *kûšîm* in 2:12. One wonders why the Cushites are included in the list if the discourse type is predictive as the immediate context indicates it is and the referent is the Cushites of Ethiopia/Nubia, the most likely of the proposals for their identity (see 2:12). Cush's power declined following the fall of Thebes in 664/663 BC.[208] In the historical context of the late seventh century, one does not expect the Cushites to appear in a relatively abbreviated list of four nations.[209] Indeed, why is the list limited to four nations, and why are more obvious candidates for inclusion, such as Egypt and Babylon, omitted?

To answer this question, one must examine the structure and purpose of the list in light of Zephaniah's rhetorical strategy. More specifically, one must come to grips with how the judgments pronounced on nations of Zephaniah's time relate to his vision of judgment on

[206] Yoko Watai, "The Monuments of the Neo-Babylonian Kings as an Indication for Their Presence in the Western Territories of Their Empire," in Shuichi Hasegawa and Karen Radner, eds., *The Reach of the Assyrian and Babylonian Empires: Case Studies in Eastern and Western Peripheries,* Studia Chaburensia 8 (Wiesbaden: Harrassowitz, 2020), 149. For a summary of what we do know about Babylonian involvement in the west from the available evidence, see Watai's entire chapter (pp. 149–65).

[207] Dan'el Kahn, "The Historical Setting of Zephaniah's Oracles against the Nations (Zeph 2:4–15)," in G. Galil, M. Keller, and A. Millard, eds., *Homeland and Exile,* VTSup 130 (Leiden: Brill, 2009), 441.

[208] See Renz, *Zephaniah,* 569.

[209] For attempts to explain how the inclusion of Cush would be relevant in Josiah's time, see Christensen, "Zephaniah 2:4–15," 681, and Sweeney, "Form Criticism of Zephaniah," 405. Kahn ("Zephaniah's Oracles," 447–50) postulates a historical setting where Cushites may have come in conflict with Judean soldiers serving under the Egyptian king Psammetichus I during the time of Josiah. See also Dan'el Kahn, "Judean Auxiliaries in Egypt's Wars against Kush," *JAOS* 127 (2008): 507–16.

a broader, worldwide scale, described above (cf. 1:2–3, 14–18; 2:11; 3:8–10).

In Zeph 2:4–15, the arrangement of nations is not random. It has a geographical orientation in relation to Judah. The list begins with the Philistine cities to the west of Judah (cf. Isa 11:14), moves across to the east (Moab/Ammon located in trans-Jordan, cf. Isa 11:14), swings down to the distant south (the Cushites) and then finishes in the far north (Assyria/Nineveh).[210] The list's geographical orientation, with the four points of the compass represented, suggests the all-encompassing extent of the judgment. This is consistent with the reversal of creation theme that begins the book (1:2–3), the language used in 1:14–18 and 3:8 to describe the worldwide scope of the judgment, and the references to the reclamation of distant nations in 2:11 and 3:10. The coming day of the Lord would impact nations in all directions, both near (for example, those located to the west and east) and far (for example, those located to the south and north),[211] and suggests the specific nations mentioned are not chosen just because of their historical significance but as representatives and archetypes of the surrounding nations.

Within the broad framework of the "nations" and "kingdoms" of the "whole earth" (3:8), Cush represents the nations to the south all the way to its distant borders and beyond. The Philistines to the west also have a representative function, much like Cush. One can easily overlook this if one ignores the reference to the Philistines as "nation of the Cherethites" (*gôy kerētîm*, 2:5). The Cherethites were an ethnic group (called here a "nation") that originated in Crete, settled on the coast west of Judah, and were identified with the Philistines (cf. Ezek 25:16). Mentioning their ethnicity and thereby alluding to their origins across the sea facilitates their representative function.

Moab/Ammon and Assyria, in addition to occupying the eastern and northern points of the compass, respectively, function in a representative role in another way. They also epitomize and serve as archetypes of the arrogant nations of the world, including Babylon.

---

[210] Zephaniah views Assyria as north of Judah (see Zeph 2:13).

[211] Hagedorn ("When Did Zephaniah Become a Supporter of Josiah's Reform?," 465, note 47) speaks of 2:12–15 "transforming a local perspective into a global one. As such Cush and the North signify the farthest ends of the known world." He subsequently comments: "Where Nineveh and Assur are mentioned (Zeph. 2:12–15), they represent the universal expansion of the divine judgement over all the earth and Cush and Assur serve as cipher for the ends of the earth" (p. 475).

They are denounced for taunting the Lord's people. The key descriptive word in the oracle is *gāʾôn*, "pride" (2:10; see also Isa 16:6 and Jer 48:29, where it is used of Moab). Such arrogance characterizes the wicked, arrogant people of the world, whom the Lord will punish when he unleashes his angry judgment upon them on the day of the Lord (Isa 13:11). In Isa 13:19 the Lord uses the term to describe Babylon, whose destiny is compared to that of Sodom and Gomorrah (cf. Jer 50:40), just like Moab/Ammon in Zeph 2:9. Zephaniah's oracle against Assyria also highlights arrogance as a basis for judgment. Nineveh had the audacity to say (lit.): "I, and there is no one else" (2:15). In so doing, she is like Babylon, who uses these identical words (*ʾănî wəʾaphsî ʿôd*) in Isa 47:8, 10.

Zephaniah's oracles against the nations in 2:4–15 are far more than prophecies of the impending Babylonian invasion and the fall of Assyria. The four nations have a representative function as they occupy the four points of the compass, pointing to the totality of the Lord's coming judgment on "nations" and "kingdoms" of "the whole earth" (3:8). Additionally, Moab/Ammon and Assyria represent all the proud nations that will experience the destructive effects of the day of the the Lord (Zeph 1:14–18; cf. Isa 13:6–11). Babylon and Egypt are not included in the list, but when one understands the archetypal value of Moab/Ammon and Assyria, they are lurking in the shadows, for they epitomize such pride as well (for Babylon, see Isa 13:19; 47:8, 10; for Egypt, see Ezek 30:6, 18; 32:10, where *gāʾôn*, "pride" appears). The implication is clear: proud Babylon and Egypt, despite their emerging power, will end up like boastful but puny Moab and Ammon, destined to go up in smoke. They will meet the same destiny as Assyria, the great empire before them that was then on life support and destined for devastation. In fact, this is the destiny of all proud nations on the day of the Lord.

2.2.4 Merging the Historical and Eschatological Dimensions

Zephaniah's use of a list of nations within a broader framework of worldwide judgment on the day of the Lord demonstrates a parallel with Isa 13–27. This section of Isaiah begins with an oracle against Babylon. Nevertheless, before focusing on Babylon, the speech opens with a vision of worldwide judgment on the day of the Lord (13:2–16). The Lord summons and assembles his army (vv. 2–5). The prophet urges his audience to wail, for the day of the Lord is near, when everyone will be overcome by fear as the heavenly lights turn dark (vv. 6–10). The Lord will intervene against the wicked and proud with devastating consequences (vv. 11–16). The oracle then becomes more specific as the Lord announces he will stir up the Medes as his instrument of judgment (13:17–18). The primary target of divine judgment will be proud Babylon, which will be reduced to ruins (vv. 19–22).

There are thirteen distinct oracles in these chapters, arranged as follows:

A	Oracle concerning Babylon	13:1–14:27
B	Oracles concerning nearby states (west & east)	14:28–16:14
C	Oracle concerning Damascus (Aram) (and ally Israel)	17:1–11
	+ Woe Oracle against hostile nations	17:12–14
D	Oracles concerning Cush and Egypt	18:1–20:6
A	Oracle concerning Babylon	21:1–10
B	Oracles concerning desert peoples (east)	21:11–17
C	Oracle concerning Jerusalem	22:1–25
D	Oracle concerning Tyre (Egypt's trade partner)	23:1–18

The opening set of four oracles begins with Babylon (to the distant east) and then moves closer to home (from Judah's perspective), focusing on relatively weak neighboring peoples to the west (Philistines) and east (Moab). The fourth oracle concerns Damascus to the northeast, but it includes judgment pronouncements against Israel (17:3, 10), which was an ally of the Arameans of Damascus (chap. 7). The woe oracle against "many peoples" (17:12–14), with its lack of geopolitical specificity, keeps the cosmic framework of the larger unit in view. Three messages concerning Cush and Egypt follow. They combine with the oracle concerning Tyre, Egypt's trade partner (23:3, 5), to form a frame (inclusio) around chapters 18–23. The structure of chapters 21–22 mirrors to some degree the pattern of 13:1–17:11. An oracle concerning Babylon (to the distant east) is followed by messages concerning relatively weak peoples living in Arabia to the east. An oracle concerning Judah follows, corresponding to the Damascus oracle of 17:1–11 where the Lord's covenant community is also in view (cf. 17:3, 10).

In chapters 24–27 the focus broadens from individual nations to the "earth/world." In chapter 24 the prophet picks up the theme of worldwide judgment that highlights the preface to the oracle against Babylon (13:2–16) and surfaces briefly in 17:12–14 (cf. also 14:26–27). In so doing he creates a frame (inclusio) for chapters 13–23. In chapters 25–27 the focus becomes the vindication and restoration of the Lord's covenant people, as well as the reclamation of the nations (cf. 25:6–8).

There are conceptual and structural parallels between Isaiah 13–27 and the paneled arrangement within Zephaniah:

WORLDWIDE JUDGMENT	JUDGMENT OF SPECIFIC NATIONS	WORLDWIDE JUDGMENT	RESTORATION
Isa 13:2–16	Isa 13:17–23:18	Isa 24	Isaiah 25–27
Zeph 1:2–3	Zeph 1:4–13	Zeph 1:14–18	—
Zeph 1:14–18	Zeph 2:1–3:7	Zeph 3:8	Zeph 3:9–20

In the paneling within Zephaniah, the day of the Lord section in 1:14–18 does double duty. It provides the concluding frame for chapter 1, linking with the introductory frame of 1:2–3. At the same time, it is pivotal and supplies an introductory frame for what follows, linking with 3:8 to form a frame around 2:1–3:7. The theme of restoration, while briefly mentioned in chapter 2, is not fully developed until the two judgment panels are completed. The relatively brief reference to worldwide judgment in 3:8 is a signal of a major thematic shift, which comes in 3:9–20. Restoration displaces the devastating effects of judgment.

In Isaiah 13–27 and Zephaniah the judgment of specific nations, which has a historical dimension, is set within a broader worldwide frame. The historical dimension of the prophecies foreshadows and previews an eschatological dimension. Worldwide judgment is coming, to be followed by a radical transformation of the world as we know it, which is the distinguishing and dominant feature of prophetic eschatology.[212]

---

[212] Christensen, in contrasting the day of the Lord in Amos and Zephaniah, observes, "For Zephaniah, on the other hand, *the day of Yhwh is trans-historical*. The 'gods of the earth' are opposed by Yhwh who will defeat them (Zeph 2:11). The fire of Yhwh's wrath will consume 'all the earth' (3:9). The focus of attention in Zephaniah is not the judgment of Israel per se, but the vindication of Yhwh and the restoration of a righteous remnant as the true people of Yhwh (3:12–13). *Zephaniah has moved beyond the events of history, in the sense of the here and now, to eschatology.* The Divine Warrior and suzerain of all nations will accomplish his purposes through 'a people humble and lowly, who seek refuge in the name of Yhwh' (3:12). Yhwh is again king in Jerusalem (3:15–16), and he will change Israel's shame into praise such that she is again 'renowned and praised among all the peoples of the earth' (3:20)" (emphasis added). See Duane L. Christensen, "Zephaniah 2:4–15: A Theological Basis for Josiah's Program of Political Expansion," *CBQ* 46 (1984): 682.

Isaiah's prophecy regarding Cush, which plays a representative role in Zeph 2:12 (see above), illustrates this. Isaiah prophesies the historical defeat of Cush (18:1–6; 20:1–6), but 18:7 looks ahead to another development: "At that time a gift will be brought to the LORD of Armies from a people tall and smooth-skinned, a people feared far and near, a powerful nation with a strange language, whose land is divided by rivers—to Mount Zion, the place of the name of the LORD of Armies." The prophet envisions a time when the Cushites (described once more as they were in 18:2) will bring their tribute to Zion, the city which the Lord has chosen as his capital (cf. Isa 24:23).[213]

The pattern of this oracle—judgment followed by recognition of the Lord's sovereignty—is repeated in the next oracle, which pertains to Cush's neighbor Egypt. Egypt's judgment (19:1–15) will result in submission to the Lord (19:16–25). Verses 23–25 look beyond any historical fulfillment in Isaiah's time and describe a radical change that will occur:

> On that day there will be a highway from Egypt to Assyria. Assyria will go to Egypt, Egypt to Assyria, and Egypt will worship with Assyria. On that day Israel will form a triple alliance with Egypt and Assyria—a blessing within the land. The LORD of Armies will bless them, saying, "Egypt my people, Assyria my handiwork, and Israel my inheritance are blessed."[214]

---

[213] Wildberger assigns 18:7 to a later redactor because of the phrase "at that time" and the verse's prose style. Hans Wildberger, *Isaiah 13–27: A Commentary,* Continental Commentary, trans. Thomas H. Trapp (Minneapolis: Fortress, 1997), 209. He also claims that verse 7 "directly contradicts what has just been said." However, the phrase "at that time" is not an indication of redactional activity unless one has arbitrarily predetermined it to be so, and the quasi-prose style (which duplicates much of v. 2) may be a simple case of terminal stylistic deviation. The remark about verse 7 contradicting the previous verses is particularly unfortunate, for it fails to take seriously the goal of divine judgment, which, oddly enough, Wildberger articulates nicely, though within the framework of his redactional model (p. 226). See Childs, who states, "Verse 7 is not a late scribal gloss, but integral to the editor's intention in shaping the entire passage as a testimony to God's future rule over the nations of the world." Brevard S. Childs, *Isaiah*, OTL (Louisville: Westminster John Knox, 2001), 139.

[214] Some interpreters see a fulfillment of this prophecy in the late eighth century BC, when Sargon promoted trade with Egypt, but this approach is unconvincing. See J. J. M. Roberts, *First Isaiah: A Commentary*, Hermeneia (Minneapolis: Fortress, 2015), 264; John H. Hayes, and Stuart A. Irvine, *Isaiah the Eighth Century Prophet: His Times and His Preaching* (Nashville: Abingdon, 1987), 266; and Alviero Niccacci, "Isaiah XVIII–XX from an Egyptological Perspective," *VT* 48 (1998): 217–24. Sargon's gesture of peace was short-lived. Sennacherib, Sargon's successor, was in conflict with Egypt, as were subsequent Assyrian kings. Furthermore, Egypt and Assyria never joined with Israel in the worship of the one true God (see vv. 24–25). The prophet's vision

When chapter 18 is paired with chapter 19, it becomes apparent the Cushite pilgrimage to Zion described in 18:7 is part of this worldwide recognition of the Lord's sovereignty that will characterize the eschatological age.[215]

The use of Cush in Isaiah and Zephaniah is instructive for understanding how oracles against nations function in prophetic eschatology. Beyond the historical dimension, there is, when the context dictates, a merger of the near (historical) and far (eschatological) with historical nations assuming a representative archetypal function.

Ezekiel 38 provides another example of this involving Cush. The previous chapters envision a time when a miraculously reunified Israel would enjoy prosperity and security. Chapter 38 assumes this development. Israel is restored from exile (v. 8; cf. 36:8–12, 34–35) and is living safely under God's protective care (vv. 11, 14; cf. 34:27). However, a coalition of hostile nations, misinterpreting Israel's sense of security for vulnerability (see the reference to unwalled towns in v. 11), decides to invade Israel with the intent to destroy them. The leader of the coalition is "Gog, of the land of Magog, the chief prince of Meshech and Tubal" (v. 2). This is a region north of Assyria; the names occur in Assyrian inscriptions (see also Gen 10:2–3). Cush is part of the coalition that includes nations from the east (Persia), south (Put [Libya], in addition to Cush), and north (Gomer and Beth-togarmah (vv. 5–6). As appears to be the case in Zeph 2:4–15, Cush, along with Put, is used to represent nations from the distant south.

Additional examples of nations from the prophets' times functioning as archetypes in eschatological predictive discourse include Edom and Assyria. Isaiah 34, like Zephaniah 1, begins with a description of cosmic, worldwide judgment in which the Lord pours out his anger on all nations (vv. 1–4). But then, like Zeph 1:4–6, the judgment becomes focused on a particular target, Edom, which represents all

---

is utopian and eschatological. There was no historical fulfillment of this prophetic vision. Its realization lies in the future. Since the Assyrian and the ancient Egyptian empires have long since passed into history, one should expect an essential, not hyperliteral, fulfillment of Isaiah's utopian vision. Someday the powerful, Assyria-like and Egypt-like nations of the world will join in worshipping the one true God in his kingdom of peace (cf. Isa 2:2–4). For a fuller discussion of essential fulfillment of historically contextualized prophecy, see Robert B. Chisholm Jr., "Israel according to the Prophets," in *The People, the Land, and the Future of Israel: Israel and the Jewish People in the Plan of God*, ed. D. Bock and M. Glaser (Grand Rapids: Kregel, 2014), 53–69.

[215] Gary V. Smith, *Isaiah 1–39*, NAC 15A (Nashville: B & H Publishing, 2007), 352; cf. Isa 2:2–4; 11:10; 14:2.

the hostile nations (vv. 5–17). One finds the same technique in Isa 63:1–6, where the Lord marches from Edom in blood-stained garments, having crushed the nations. As for Assyria, the historical judgment of Nineveh/Assyria is announced in the book of Nahum, but in other places Assyria has become archetypal, as in Isa 19:23–25, discussed above. One sees this as well in Micah 5, which describes how the ideal Davidic king of the future will defeat the Assyrians when they seek to invade his land and exercise his sovereignty over Assyria (vv. 5–6 [4–5]). Long after the Assyrian Empire had fallen, Zechariah uses proud Assyria as archetypal for the nations (10:11).

2.2.5 The Eschatological Day of the Lord in the New Testament

The NT develops the eschatological dimension of the day of the Lord theme, which is so prominent in Zephaniah. The phrase "the day of the Lord" occurs several times:

1. *Acts 2:20*: Peter uses the phrase when quoting from Joel 2:28–32 (Acts 2:17–21), which describes events that would take place "in the last days" before the coming of the day of the Lord. According to Peter, the prophecy of the outpouring of the Spirit was fulfilled, at least in part, on the day of Pentecost, when the Spirit of the Lord came upon a large crowd of Christ-following Jews and supernaturally enabled them to speak in other languages (Acts 2:1–21). The events described in Joel 2:30–32 did not occur at Pentecost. Peter correctly saw the outpouring of the Spirit as initiating the fulfillment of the prophecy. He urged the people to repent so that the promise might be fully realized (Acts 2:33, 38–39) and the "times of refreshing," culminating in the return of Jesus, might arrive (3:19–21). But the Jewish leadership rejected God's offer (Acts 4). Eventually, Peter came to realize that Jewish unbelief would delay Jesus's return and that Gentiles would also receive the gift of the Spirit (Acts 10:44–48).

In the light of these later developments, we could say the fulfillment of Joel's prophecy was suspended (the prophetic videotape is on "pause," as it were). Nevertheless, since Jesus gives his Spirit to each new believer during the present era, it is probably better to view Joel 2:28–29 as being gradually fulfilled during this age, with verses 30–32 awaiting realization at the end of the age. Joel envisioned the outpouring of the Spirit as being confined to Jews, but in the progress of revelation and history, we discover Gentiles are included as well, for they too are incorporated into the new covenant community.

2. *1 Thess 5:2; 2 Thess 2:2*. See also "the day" (1 Thess 5:4) and "that day" (2 Thess 1:10). The day of the Lord will come like a thief in the night. Jesus will judge the world; but before that day comes, the lawless one will arrive and oppose God (2 Thess 2:3–4).

The day of the Lord will be one of divine "wrath" (*orgē*, 1 Thess 5:9). In this context "wrath" is not used generically for damnation,[216] nor does it refer to the "wrath" being revealed in Paul's day (cf. 2:16, if one interprets it as referring to a manifestation of present wrath). In conjunction with the day of the Lord, "wrath" in 5:9 is "the future punishment to be meted out at Christ's second coming."[217] Likewise, the "salvation" in view is not generic for deliverance from damnation, but rather deliverance from the "end-time judgment" in conjunction with Jesus's return.[218] In support of this interpretation, one can point to the following texts: (1) 1 Thess 1:10: "To wait for his Son from heaven [a reference to Jesus's second coming] . . . Jesus, who rescues us from the coming wrath." (2) 1 Thess 5:3: "Sudden destruction will come upon them, . . . and they will not escape." (3) Passages in Revelation that associate "wrath" with end-time judgment (6:16–17; 11:18; 14:10; 16:19; 19:15).[219] The characterization of the day of the Lord as one of wrath is rooted in the OT—especially Zeph 1:15, 18; 2:2–3, where the Septuagint uses *orgē* to describe divine anger/wrath on the day of the Lord. This text may have influenced Paul's view of the coming judgment (see also Isa 13:9, 13; Lam 1:12; Ezek 7:19).

3. *1 Cor 1:8; 5:5; 2 Cor 1:14*. The day of the Lord is associated with Jesus's second coming (cf. 1 Cor 1:7). See also "the day of Christ Jesus" (Phil 1:6), "the day of Christ" (Phil 1:10; 2:16), and "the day" (Rom 13:12; 1 Cor 3:13; Heb 10:25).

4. *2 Pet 3:10*. The day of the Lord (also called the "day of God" in v. 12; cf. Rev 16:14) will come like a thief and bring cosmic destruction.

---

[216] See possibly Rom 2:5; 5:9; Eph 5:6; Col 3:6.

[217] Jeffrey A. D. Weima, *1–2 Thessalonians*, BECNT (Grand Rapids: Baker Academic, 2014), 366.

[218] F. F. Bruce, *1 & 2 Thessalonians*, WBC (Waco, TX: Word Books, 1982), 112.

[219] Matt 3:7; Luke 3:7; 21:23 probably refer to the destruction of Jerusalem in AD 70, which foreshadows the end-time judgment.

COMMENTARY

SECTION OUTLINE

Heading (1:1)
1 The Day of the Lord: Worldwide Judgment Targeting Judah and Jerusalem (1:2–18)
  1.1 Judgment Reverses Creation and Eliminates False Worship (1:2–6)
    1.1.1 The Reversal of Creation through Flood-like Judgment (1:2–3)
    Excursus 2: The Hebrew Text of 1:2–3
    1.1.2 The Elimination of False Worship (1:4–6)
  1.2 The Imminent Day of the Lord Brings Punishment and Devastation (1:7–18)
    1.2.1 A Day of Punishment for Jerusalem (1:7–13)
      1.2.1.1 A Call for Silence in Anticipation of "Sacrifice" (1:7)
      1.2.1.2 Punishment as "Sacrifice" (1:8–13)
    1.2.2 A Day of Devastation for the World (1:14–18)
      1.2.2.1 Devastation for the Proud (1:14–16)
      1.2.2.2 Devastation for Sinners (1:17–18)

1 THE DAY OF THE LORD: WORLDWIDE JUDGMENT TARGETING JUDAH AND JERUSALEM (1:2–18)

1 The word of the LORD that came to Zephaniah son of Cushi, son of Gedaliah, son of Amariah, son of Hezekiah, in the days of Josiah son of Amon, king of Judah.

2 *I will completely sweep away everything*
from the face of the earth—this is the LORD's declaration.
3 *I will sweep away people and animals;*
I will sweep away the birds of the sky
and the fish of the sea,
and the ruins along with the wicked.
I will cut off mankind
from the face of the earth.
This is the LORD's declaration.

4 *I will stretch out my hand against Judah*
and against all the residents of Jerusalem.
I will cut off every vestige of Baal
from this place,
the names of the pagan priests
along with the priests;
5 *those who bow in worship on the rooftops*
to the stars in the sky;
those who bow and pledge loyalty to the LORD
but also pledge loyalty to Milcom;
6 *and those who turn back from following the LORD,*
who do not seek the LORD or inquire of him.

7 *Be silent in the presence of the Lord GOD,*
for the day of the LORD is near.
Indeed, the LORD has prepared a sacrifice;
he has consecrated his guests.
8 *On the day of the LORD's sacrifice*
I will punish the officials, the king's sons,
and all who are dressed in foreign clothing.
9 *On that day I will punish*
all who skip over the threshold,

who fill their master's house
with violence and deceit.

10 *On that day—this is the* Lord*'s declaration—there will be*
an outcry from the Fish Gate,
a wailing from the Second District,
and a loud crashing from the hills.
11 *Wail, you residents of the Hollow,*
for all the merchants will be silenced;
all those loaded with silver will be cut off.

12 *And at that time I will search Jerusalem with lamps*
and punish those who settle down comfortably,
who say to themselves:
The Lord *will do nothing—good or bad.*
13 *Their wealth will become plunder*
and their houses a ruin.
They will build houses but never live in them,
plant vineyards but never drink their wine.

14 *The great day of the* Lord *is near,*
near and rapidly approaching.
Listen, the day of the Lord*—then the warrior's cry is bitter.*
15 *That day is a day of wrath,*
a day of trouble and distress,
a day of destruction and desolation,
a day of darkness and gloom,
a day of clouds and total darkness,
16 *a day of ram's horn and battle cry*
against the fortified cities,
and against the high corner towers.
17 *I will bring distress on mankind,*
and they will walk like the blind
because they have sinned against the Lord*.*
Their blood will be poured out like dust
and their flesh like dung.
18 *Their silver and their gold*
will be unable to rescue them
on the day of the Lord*'s wrath.*

The whole earth will be consumed
by the fire of his jealousy,
for he will make a complete,
yes, a horrifying end
of all the inhabitants of the earth.

Heading (1:1): See Introduction

On the day of the Lord, he will unleash judgment on a cosmic scale (cf. 1:2–3, 14–18) with Judah and Jerusalem serving as the focal point (1:4–13). Chapter 1 divides into two main literary units (vv. 2–6 and 7–18), displaying a concentric arrangement at the thematic level. The functionally hortatory interjection "be silent" at the beginning of verse 7 marks the division.[1]

A Cosmic judgment (vv. 2–3)
  B Localized judgment (vv. 4–6)
  B Localized judgment (vv. 7–13)
A Cosmic judgment (vv. 14–18)

1.1 Judgment Reverses Creation and Eliminates False Worship (1:2–6)

In this opening judgment speech, the Lord announces he will bring worldwide judgment, which like the flood will disrupt the created order. It will encompass all creatures but specifically targets the wicked. While cosmic in scope, it will fall upon Judah and Jerusalem and remove those who turn from the Lord and fail to seek him. The Lord will eliminate from the covenant community those who worship other gods such as Baal and astral deities while giving mere lip service to the Lord.

The backbone of the speech is the formal announcement of judgment expressed through predictive discourse, specifically a series of six "I will" declarations in which the Lord states his intention to intervene.[2] The verb translated "I will stretch out my hand" draws attention to the Lord's active role in the judgment and the other verbs ("I will

---

[1] See, among others, Marvin A. Sweeney, "A Form-Critical Reassessment of the Book of Zephaniah," *CBQ* 53 (1991): 393–94.

[2] There are three first-person singular *yiqtol* [imperfect] verb forms in verses 2–3a and three first-person singular *weqatal* [perfect with *waw* consecutive] verb forms in verses 3b–4.

sweep away" three times and "I will cut off" twice) depict judgment as the removal of sinners "from the face of the earth" (used twice).

There is no formal accusation introduced, for example, by *kî*, "because," but the object of judgment in verse 3a ("the wicked") and the lengthy list of objects in verses 4b-6 are functionally accusatory since they describe the character of those whom the Lord is about to eliminate. The basis of judgment is apparent. The Lord will remove the wicked, including those who promote false worship, turn from the Lord, and fail to seek him.

The speech has two parts. In the first (vv. 2–3) the perspective is cosmic ("everything," "people and animals"); in the second (vv. 4–6) it is local (Judah, Jerusalem). Verses 2–3 are linked by the formula "this is the Lord's declaration," which concludes both verses. Repetition of key terms also binds them together ("I will sweep away," "from the face of the earth"). In fact, the latter appears in the first clause of verse 2 and in the last clause of verse 3, forming a bracket (inclusio) for the verses.[3] The appearance of two first-person *weqatal* verb forms ("I will stretch out," "I will cut off") in verse 4 establishes continuity with part 1. The transition to negated third-person verbs in verse 6b, necessitating the use of the relative pronoun, signals closure for the unit through terminal stylistic deviation.

1.1.1 The Reversal of Creation through Flood-like Judgment (1:2–3)

1:2–3 The opening two words of the Hebrew text of verse 2 (*ʾāsōph ʾāsēph*) have puzzled interpreters. While the similarity in sound between the two forms grabs one's attention, the meaning is debated. There are two main options for a literal translation based on how one understands the second form in the sequence: (1) "sweeping away, I will bring to an end," or (2) "sweeping away, I will sweep away." In the first case, the verbs are complementary. One could paraphrase: "by sweeping away, I will put an end to."[4] In the second case, the combination is a typical Hebrew emphatic construction where one verb is repeated in different grammatical forms. One can translate, "I will surely sweep away," or "I will completely sweep away" (see CSB). [For

---

[3] Michael DeRoche, "Contra Creation, Covenant and Conquest (Jer. viii 13)," *VT* 30 (1980): 282.

[4] Motyer, "Zephaniah," 911.

a more detailed and technical discussion of the issue for those trained in Hebrew, see the following excursus.]

Excursus 2: The Hebrew Text of 1:2–3

Verse 2 opens with an infinitive absolute (*ʾāsōp*) from the verbal root *ʾāsap*, "to gather, remove."[5] The form that follows (*ʾāsēp*) has occasioned much debate among interpreters. It appears to be a causative form (*hiphil* imperfect 1cs) from the verbal root *sûp*, "I will bring to an end" (cf. Jer 8:13). In this case one may lit. translate the two opening forms, "removing, I will bring to an end."[6]

However, understanding *ʾāsēp* as a causative form (*hiphil*) of *sûph* is problematic for two reasons: (1) The theme vowel *tsere* in *ʾāsēp* is peculiar; one expects a *hiriq yod*, as in Jer 8:13. (2) When an infinitive absolute precedes a verb, one expects it to be from the same verbal root. Other apparent examples of the use of two different verbs are rare and, in some cases, dismissed as textually corrupt.[7] They include (1) Isa 28:28: *ʾādôš yədûšennû*, which appears to combine an infinitive absolute of an otherwise unattested root *ʾādaš* with an imperfect of *dûš*, " he will thresh it";[8] (2) Jer 8:13: *ʾāsōp ʾăsîpēm,* which combines a *qal* infinitive absolute of *ʾāsap* with a *hiphil* imperfect of *sûp*, "removing, I will bring them to an end"; (3) Jer 42:10: *šôb tēšəbû*, which appears to combine an infinitive absolute of *šûb* with an imperfect of *yāšab*, "returning, you will live,"[9] (4) Jer 48:9: *nāṣōʾ tēṣēʾ*, which appears to combine a *niphal* infinitive absolute of an otherwise unattested root *nāṣāʾ*[10] with a *qal* imperfect of *yāṣāʾ*, "you will go out."

---

[5] Liudger Sabottka emends אָסֹף to a form of יָסַף, "to add," which, when combined with another verb, can indicate the repetition or continuation of an action. He understands this as referring to a repetition of the flood. See *Zephanja* (Rome: Pontifical Biblical Institute, 1972), 6–7. For a critique of the proposed emendation, see Roberts, *Zephaniah,* 169.

[6] Renz, following the MT vocalization and assuming two different roots (*Zephaniah,* 466), translates "make a sweeping end" (460). Others who understand a combination of two different verbs, אָסַף and סוּף, include Berlin (*Zephaniah,* 72), Sweeney (*Zephaniah,* 61), and Richard D. Patterson, *Nahum, Habakkuk, Zephaniah,* Wycliffe Exegetical Commentary (Chicago: Moody, 1991), 300.

[7] See GKC §113w, note 3; DHS, §86, Rem 2.

[8] See the discussion in Sweeney, *Zephaniah,* 59.

[9] In this case, some prefer to read יָשׁוֹב for שׁוֹב, understanding aphaeresis (DHS, §86, Rem 3) or a textual error (GKC, §19i). The MT reading, if retained, "returning, you dwell" would seem to make no sense in this context because the prophet is urging the people to stay in the land and not go to Egypt. However, in verse 12, the verb שׁוּב is used, referring to the Babylonian king allowing them to return to their land/property. Apparently, they had left their property and were in prerefugee status, ready to depart to Egypt. Jeremiah promises them that the Babylonian king will let them return to their property and live there.

[10] *HALOT*, 714, prefers to read נָצֹה, a *qal* infinitive absolute from נָצָה II, "go to ruin" (715).

Due to these problems, some prefer to understand the second word as deriving from *ʾāsap*, like the preceding infinitive absolute.[11] In this case, the form could be vocalized *ʾōsēp* and be understood as a *qal* imperfect 1cs[12] with the preceding infinitive absolute providing emphasis, "I will indeed remove" (= CSB "I will completely sweep away").[13] In this case, the vocalization *ʾōsēp* is also understood in verse 3, where *ʾāsēp* appears twice. DeRouchie proposes to retain the form *ʾāsēp* and to understand it as a *hiphil* imperfect 1cs of *ʾāsap*. He understands *ʾăsîpēm* in Jer 8:13 as also being a *hiphil* form from *ʾāsap*. He admits, however, that the *hiphil* of this root, apart from his proposal for Jer 8:13 and Zeph 1:2–3, is unattested elsewhere.[14]

Whether one understands the second verb in the sequence (*ʾāsēp* or *ʾōsēp*) as "I will sweep away" (derived from *ʾāsap*, "to gather, remove") or "I will bring to an end" (derived from *sûp*, "come to an end"), the interpretive consensus is that the verbal combination at the beginning of verse 2 refers to judgment, as do the two uses of this verb (*ʾāsēp* or *ʾōsēp*) in verse 3. If derived from *sûp*, "come to an end," the verb (*ʾāsēp*) would in its causative (*hiphil*) form mean "bring to an end," as in Jer 8:13.[15] If derived from *ʾāsaph*, "to gather, remove," then it would in this context refer to "removing" in the sense of eliminating or destroying (cf. CSB "sweep away").[16] The verb is used in this sense in 1 Sam 15:6, where Saul warns the Kenites to distance themselves from the Amalekites so that they will not be eliminated/destroyed when he attacks Amalek (cf. "Get away from the Amalekites, or I'll sweep you

[11] However, there are only two clear cases of the infinitive absolute of אָסַף appearing before a finite form of the verb: (1) 2 Sam 17:11: הֵאָסֹף [*niphal* infinitive absolute] יֵאָסֵף [*niphal* jussive], lit., "surely, let [all Israel] be gathered," (2) Mic 2:12: אָסֹף [*qal* infinitive absolute] אֶאֱסֹף [*qal* imperfect], lit., "I will surely gather."

[12] GKC (§72aa) emends the form to אֹסֵף on analogy with אֹמַר. This is possible with the verb אָסַף (see GKC, §68g), though it does not occur in the only clear case where the *qal* infinitive absolute precedes the imperfect (Mic 2:12). It is unlikely that the emended form אֹסֵף is a *qal* active participle (a suggestion listed by Berlin, *Zephaniah,* 72, and Renz, *Zephaniah,* 460), since a stated subject would be needed and there are no examples elsewhere of an infinitive absolute preceding an active participle of the same root and stem. In Ps 126:6 an infinitive absolute precedes an active participle, but the forms are from different roots and the participle is substantival.

[13] For discussion and critique of attempts to read אָסֵף as a *qal* imperfect 1cs of אָסַף, see Jason S. DeRouchie, "YHWH's Future Ingathering in Zephaniah 1:2: Interpreting אָסֹף אָסֵף," *Hebrew Studies* 59 (2018): 177.

[14] DeRouchie, "YHWH's Future Ingathering," 177.

[15] In this case, the preceding infinitive absolute is adverbial and complementary, lit., "(as I) sweep away, I will bring to an end."

[16] In this case, the preceding infinitive absolute is adverbial and emphatic (due to repetition), lit., "(as I) sweep away, I will sweep away" (= CSB, "I will completely sweep away").

away with them"). In Hos 4:3 the passive (*niphal*) form of the verb is used of fish being eliminated/destroyed in judgment (cf. "even the fish of the sea disappear").[17]

Three lines of contextual and intertextual evidence support the interpretive consensus:

(1) The use of the prepositional phrase "from the face of the earth" (*mēʿal pənê hāʾădāmâ*, lit., "from upon the face of the ground/earth") strongly suggests the preceding verb (*ʾāsēp* or *ʾōsēp*) refers to an aggressive act directed against the object of the verb ("everything").[18] This is the case in each of the eleven other texts where this precise prepositional phrase is combined with a transitive verb (a verb that takes an object).

Gen 4:14	("you are banishing [*piel* of *gāraš*] me today from the face of the earth")
Gen 6:7	("I will wipe [*māḥâ*] mankind . . . off the face of the earth")-
Gen 7:4	("every living thing . . . I will wipe off [*māḥâ*] the face of the earth")
Exod 32:12	("to kill them . . . and eliminate [*piel* of *kālâ*] them from the face of the earth")
Deut 6:15	("will . . . obliterate [*hiphil* of *šāmad*] you from the face of the earth")
1 Sam 20:15	("when the Lord cuts off [*hiphil* of *kārat*] . . . David's enemies from the face of the earth")
1 Kgs 9:7	("I will cut off [*hiphil* of *kārat*] Israel from the land [lit., "from upon the face of the land"]
1 Kgs 13:34	("to be cut off and obliterated [*hiphil* of *šāmad*] from the face of the earth")
Jer 28:16	("I am about to send you off [*piel* of *šālâ*] the face of the earth")

[17] See Michael DeRoche, "The Reversal of Creation in Hosea," *VT* 31 (1981): 403. Other examples of the passive form (*niphal*) with this meaning include Isa 16:10; 57:1; and Jer 48:33 (see BDB, 62, *niphal*, category 3).

[18] As Ben Zvi (*Zephaniah*, 54) observes, except for Gen 8:8, "the occurrences of" the phrase "in the OT are related to destruction." See also Ivan J. Ball, *A Rhetorical Study of Zephaniah* (BIBAL Press, 1988), 46.

Amos 9:8 (“I will obliterate [*hiphil* of *šāmad*] it from the face of the earth”)

Zeph 1:3 (“I will cut off [*hiphil* of *kārat*] mankind from the face of the earth”)

In every case God/the Lord is the subject of the aggressive action (the subject is implied in 1 Kgs 13:34), suggesting this prepositional phrase when combined with a transitive verb is a divine judgment idiom.[19]

Of course, there are no other cases of the verb “sweep away” (*ʾāsap*) or “bring to an end” (*sûp*) being used with the prepositional phrase. However, in Zeph 1:2–3 the phrase occurs in the first clause of verse 2 and in the last clause of verse 3, where the causative form (*hiphil*) of the verb “cut off” appears, forming a bracket (sometimes called an “inclusio”) for verses 2–3.[20] In each case the prophetic speech formula “this is the Lord’s declaration” (*nəʾūm yhwh*) follows the phrase.[21] This makes it likely that *ʾāsap*, “sweep away,” and *kārat*, “cut off,” are parallel and synonymous in the chiastic (ABBA) structure of verses 2–3, which can be outlined:

A I will completely sweep away everything from the face of the earth—this is the Lord’s declaration.

B I will sweep away people and animals;

B[1] I will sweep away the birds of the sky and the fish of the sea, and the ruins along with the wicked.[22]

A[1] [And, cf. Hb.] I will cut off mankind from the face of the earth. This is the Lord’s declaration.

The central B units, by repeating the verb “I will sweep away” (*ʾāsēp* or *ʾōsēp*), unpack “everything” in A, while “cut off” in A[1] clarifies what is

---

[19] The prepositional phrase occurs with an intransitive verb (no object) just once, in Gen 8:8: “to see whether *the* water on the earth’s surface had gone down” (lit., “to see whether the water had receded [*qal* of קָלַל] from upon the face of the ground”). This unique use of an intransitive verb with the idiomatic prepositional phrase of judgment grabs one’s attention because it reminds us that the judgment (cf. 6:7, “I will wipe [מָחָה] mankind . . . off the face of the earth,” and 7:4, “every living thing . . . I will wipe off [מָחָה] the face of the earth”) has ceased.

[20] See DeRoche, “Contra Creation, Covenant and Conquest (Jer. viii 13),” 282.

[21] The causative form (*hiphil*) of “cut off” (כָּרַת) is also used with the prepositional phrase in 1 Sam 20:15 and 1 Kgs 9:7.

[22] Note that the verb “I will sweep away” in both B1 and B2 is asyndetic (no prefixed conjunction “and”). This has a twofold function: (1) It facilitates recognizing the parallelism between the two statements, and (2) it indicates that the two statements are clarifying what was meant in A1 (“I will completely sweep away everything”), not describing additional/sequential actions.

meant by "sweep away," although the use of the idiomatic "from [upon] the face of the earth" in A already anticipates aggressive judgment.

(2) The appearance of "and I will stretch out" (a *weqatal* verb form *wənāṭîtî*) at the beginning of verse 4 indicates what follows is a continuation of the preceding announcement of the Lord's intervention in judgment. (It is the fifth first-person singular verb form in the verbal sequence of verses 2–4.) The repetition of "[and] I will cut off" (*wəhikrattî*) (cf. v. 3), the sixth first-person singular verb form in the sequence, suggests there is a concurrent structure at work here.[23] In addition to the chiastic pattern in verses 2–3 (ABBA), there is a paneled (ABAB) structure extending through verses 2–4, which can be outlined this way:[24]

A I will sweep away from the face of the earth . . . I will sweep away . . . I will sweep away (1:2–3)
B [and] I will cut off . . . from the face of the earth (1:3)
A[1] [and] I will stretch out my hand against Judah (1:4)
B[1] [and] I will cut off (1:4)

In this concurrent paneled structure, "I will sweep away from the face of the earth" corresponds to "I will stretch out my hand against" in the parallelism of the A units.

The combination of the verb "stretch out" (*nāṭâ*) with "hand" (*yād*,) as object followed by the preposition "upon" (*ʿal*) is used in the Exodus plague narratives of stretching out the hand over water or toward the sky.[25] In two texts in the plague narrative, the object of the preposition is Egypt (7:5) or the land of Egypt (10:12). In these cases, the preposition is better translated "against" since Egypt is the object of the Lord's hostile actions. In the prophets the expression is consistently used of aggressive action directed toward an object[26]:

---

[23] On concurrent structuring in texts, see H. van Dyke Parunak, "Some Axioms for Literary Architecture," *Semitics* 8 (1982): 10–12.

[24] DeRouchie, "YHWH's Future Ingathering," 180, proposes this structure, though he interprets its significance differently. For a summary and critique of his view, see below.

[25] BDB, 639, *qal*, 1.a. Passages include Exod 7:19 (over the waters of Egypt, etc.); 8:5 [Hb. 1] (over the rivers, etc.), 6 [Hb. 2] (over the waters of Egypt); 9:22 (toward the sky); 10:21–22 (toward the sky); 14:16, 21, 26–27 (over the sea). However, in 7:19 and 8:5–6, the nuance "against" may be preferable, since the water sources are turned to blood.

[26] See BDB, 640, *qal*, 1.a; Roberts, *Zephaniah*, 170; Renz, *Zephaniah*, 470.

Isa 5:25	("he raised his hand against them")
Isa 14:26	("this is the hand stretched out against all the nations")[27]
Jer 6:12	("I will stretch out my hand against the inhabitants of the land")
Jer 15:6	("I have stretched out my hand against you" [Jerusalem])
Jer 51:25	("I will stretch out my hand against you" [Babylon])
Ezek 6:14	("I will stretch out my hand against them" [people of Jerusalem])
Ezek 14:9	("I will stretch out my hand against him" [false prophet])
Ezek 14:13	("I will stretch out my hand against it" [a sinful country])
Ezek 16:27	("I stretched out my hand against you" [God's adulterous people])
Ezek 25:7	("I am about to stretch out my hand against you" [Ammon])
Ezek 25:13	("I will stretch out my hand against Edom")
Ezek 25:16	("I am about to stretch out my hand against the Philistines")
Ezek 35:3	("I will stretch out my hand against you" [Edom])
Zeph 2:13	("he will also stretch out [better: "may he stretch out"] his hand against the north")

In all fourteen prophetic passages the Lord is the one who stretches out his hand, while the object of the preposition is the recipient of judgment, namely, a city or nation and its residents, with one exception, Ezek 14:9, where the recipient is a false prophet.

The action of stretching out the hand is not isolated. It initiates an attack and is accompanied by other hostile actions (cf. Isa 5:25, "He raised his hand against them and *struck them*"). When God stretches out his hand, severe judgment follows, bringing destruction, famine, and death. In Jer 51:25 God stretches out his hand against Babylon and then rolls them off a cliff and makes them like a burned-out

[27] The combination is a bit different here, with the passive participle ("stretched out") modifying "hand" as an attributive adjective.

mountain. Three consecutive verb forms (all *weqatal*: "I will stretch out . . . [and] roll you down . . . and turn you into") describe related actions as an outworking of God's judgment. God sets the judgment in motion by stretching out his hand. In Zeph 2:13 the prophet asks the Lord to stretch out his hand against the north and destroy Assyria, turning Nineveh into a "desolate ruin, dry as a desert." Three successive verb forms (all *weyiqtol* jussives "may he stretch out . . . and destroy . . . and make") describe related actions that comprise God's judgment. Once again, when God stretches out his hand, it activates the judgment.

Based on the evidence, it is apparent the expression "stretch out the hand against" is a divine judgment idiom. The pattern exemplified in the passages discussed above is evident in Zeph 1:4, where (1) the Lord is the one who stretches out his hand, (2) a nation (Judah) and the residents of a city (Jerusalem) are the recipients of judgment, and (3) the action of stretching out the hand sets in motion judgment that cuts off idolaters (1:4b–6) and activates the day of the Lord (1:7–18). One could paraphrase the expression, "launch an attack against."

As verse 3 unpacks verse 2, it specifies what is meant by everything: "people and animals. . . the birds of the sky and the fish of the sea, and the ruins along with the wicked." Patterson sees an allusion here to the flood account.[28] For support he points to the clustering of terms from Genesis 6–8: "from the face of the earth" (6:7; 7:4; 8:8), "everything" (6:17; 7:4; 8:19), "ground/land" (*ʾădāmâ*) (6:7, 20; 7:4, 8, 23; 8:8, 13, 21). One can add to the list the references to "people/mankind" ([*hā*]*ʾādām*, 6:7; 7:21, 23, among others), "animals/livestock" (*bəhēmâ*, 6:7; 7:21, 23, among others), and "birds/birds of the sky" (6:7; 7:3, 23). The intertextual links with Gen 6:7; 7:4, 21, 23 are particularly noteworthy:

Zephaniah 1:2–3
"I will completely sweep away **everything from the face of the earth**—this is the LORD's declaration. I will sweep away **people** [*ʾādam*] and **animals** [*bəhēmâ*]; I will sweep away the **birds of the sky** and the fish of the sea, and the ruins along with the wicked. [And] I will cut off

[28] Patterson, *Zephaniah*, 301.

mankind [*haʾādām*][29] **from the face of the earth.** This is the LORD's declaration."

Genesis 6:7
"I will wipe **mankind** [*hāʾādām*], whom I created, **off the face of the earth,** together with the **animals** [*bəhēmâ*], creatures that crawl, and **birds of the sky.**"

Genesis 7:4
"**Every** living thing I have made I will wipe **off the face of the earth.**"

Genesis 7:21
"**Every** creature perished—those that crawl on the earth, **birds, livestock** [*bəhēmâ*], wildlife, and those that swarm on the earth, as well as **all mankind** [*hāʾādām*]."

Genesis 7:23
"He wiped out **every** living thing that was on **the face of the earth,** from **mankind** [*ʾādām*] to **livestock** [*bəhēmâ*], to creatures that crawl, to **the birds of the sky,** and they were wiped **off the earth.**"

The extensive intertextual linking strongly suggests Zeph 1:2–3 is depicting a judgment that rivals the flood in its magnitude. The triad "mankind, livestock, and birds of the sky" occurs in only five passages: Gen 1:26; 2:20; 6:7; 7:23; Zeph 1:3. The triad appears with "from upon the face of the earth" only in Gen 6:7 and Zeph 1:3. All five key words/phrases highlighted above occur only in Gen 6:7/7:4 and Zeph 1:2–3.

While the Lord does not mention the creatures that swarm and crawl, he includes the "fish of the sea," which are not mentioned in the flood account. The reason for this addition is not certain, but it may depict the coming judgment as even "more inclusive than" the flood.[30] Including the fish in the list also suggests the coming judgment, like the flood in some respects, entails a reversal of creation (see also Hos 4:3), similar to a return to primordial chaos where deep

---

[29] The article on הָאָדָם indicates previous reference, pointing back to the anarthrous אָדָם, "people," earlier in the verse.

[30] Roberts, *Zephaniah,* 170. There may be an echo of the plague of blood, which killed the fish in the Nile (Exod 7:18, 21).

darkness prevails (see Zeph 1:15).[31] In Gen 1:20–27 God creates the fish and birds together on day five (vv. 20–23), and then on day six the land animals, including livestock [*bəhēmâ*](vv. 24–25), and mankind [*ʾādām*] (vv. 26–27). The judgment of the flood wiped away these things in reverse order (mankind, livestock, birds), though the fish are omitted from the lists (Gen 6:7; 7:23). Likewise, the judgment depicted in Zeph 1:3 describes the Lord sweeping away these things in reverse order of how they were created but includes the fish (mankind, livestock, birds, fish).[32]

Zephaniah 1:2–3 depicts overwhelming judgment of a cosmic dimension. Two idiomatic judgment expressions, "from upon the face of the ground/earth" and "stretch out the hand against," appear, and numerous intertextual links to the flood account point to the scope and severity of the coming judgment. Furthermore, intertextual links to Gen 1:20–27 indicate this judgment will disrupt and even reverse the created order as it paves the way for the day of the Lord, which will bring a return to the darkness of primordial chaos (cf. 1:15).[33]

---

[31] See Michael DeRoche, "Zephaniah i 2–3: The 'Sweeping' of Creation," *VT* 30 (1980): 104–9. In Hos 4:3 wild animals, birds, and fish are mentioned in that order.

[32] Berlin, *Zephaniah,* 81. Ben Zvi (*Zephaniah,* 55–58) objects to seeing allusions to the flood and creation in Zeph 1:2–3. He argues that the shared language is too common and idiomatic to establish an intertextual connection. However, his method of assessment misses the point. It is the *clustering* of five key words/expressions in these two thematically congruous passages that establishes the intertextual link. For a critique of Ben Zvi's method, see James D. Nogalski, "Zephaniah's Use of Genesis 1–11," *Hebrew Bible and Ancient Israel* 2 (2013): 354–55, and Nicholas R. Werse, "Realigning the Cosmos: The Intertextual Image of Judgment and Restoration in Zephaniah," *JSOT* 45 (1) (2020): 115.

[33] DeRouchie has proposed a different explanation of Zeph 1:2–3 that counters the interpretive consensus ("YHWH's Future Ingathering," 173–91). He understands both forms in the opening verb combination as derived from the verbal root אָסַף, "to gather." It describes a "future ingathering . . . when YHWH will assemble all the earth for judicial assessment, distinguishing in that single event the righteous and wicked, the former whom he will save and the latter whom he will punish" (190). For support he points to Zeph 3:8, where the Lord gathers (אָסַף)/ assembles (קָבַץ) the nations/kingdoms for the outpouring of his judgment, and to the cryptic Zeph 3:18, which he interprets as referring to an ingathering of a righteous remnant to experience salvation (cf. 180–81, 190). He sees 1:2–3 as differentiating "the 'ingathering' of the world . . . from the act of 'cutting off' humanity . . . just as Zeph 1:4 distinguishes the 'stretching out' of YHWH's hand against Judah . . . from his act of 'cutting off' its inhabitants." He concludes that the opening verb combination "speaks only of YHWH's future ingathering of the world for judicial assessment and does not by itself insinuate a global destruction like the flood" (190). But herein lies the fundamental problem with DeRouchie's proposal. The verb combination is not "by itself." It is joined with "from upon the face of the ground/earth," which is idiomatic divine judgment language. When used with a transitive verb, this phrase consistently accompanies an aggressive action by the Lord directed toward the object of judgment. The verb אָסַף, while

In the second clause in 1:3a some question the originality of the words translated "and the ruins along with the wicked" (*wəhammakšēlôt ʾet-hārəšāʿîm*). These words are not accounted for in the Septuagint.[34] Omitting them produces better symmetry in the parallelism of 1:3a:

I will sweep away people and animals;
I will sweep away the birds of the sky and the fish of the sea.

The verb "I will sweep away" (*ʾāsēp* or *ʾōsēp*) has two objects in each case. The additional words make the second line look unduly long. Furthermore, the reference to "ruins" and "the wicked" seems incompatible with the preceding objects of the verb, "birds and fish."

However, the longer MT is the more difficult reading, making it more likely that a scribe would delete the words because of the reasons stated above rather than adding them.[35] A closer look reveals the additional words, although awkward structurally and conceptually, fit here.

Before developing this point further, we need to discuss the meaning of the form translated "and the ruins" (*wəehammakšēlôt*). The noun is the feminine plural form of *makšēlâ*, which appears to be related to the verbal root (*kāšal*) meaning "to stumble."[36] It appears in only one

carrying the primary meaning "gather," can also refer to such an aggressive action and have the nuance "remove, eliminate." Furthermore, the expression "stretch out the hand against" is also idiomatic divine judgment language that consistently sets in motion a severe attack by God. Additionally, the clustering of intertextual links between Zeph 1:2–3 and the flood account (6:7; 7:4, 21, 23) points to the implementation of a flood-like judgment which, given intertextual links with Gen 1:20–27, entails a reversal of creation. This explains the preponderance of cosmic language in 1:2–3 ("everything," "face of the earth," "people and animals," "birds of the sky and fish of the sea," "mankind").

[34] For a discussion of the Greek textual evidence, see Renz, *Zephaniah,* 461.

[35] Another possibility is that the shorter reading is due to an accidental error involving homoioteleuton ("same ending"). If we focus on the consonantal text, the two letters before the extra words are *yod-mem* (note **h*ym*** [הַיָּם]) and the final two letters in the last extra word are also *yod-mem* (note *hrš*ʿ***ym*** [הָרְשָׁעִים]). In an unvocalized consonantal text a scribe's eye could have jumped from the first *yod-mem* sequence to the second, leaving out the letters in between, along with the second *yod-mem* combination: ***hym****.whmkšlwt.ʾt.hršʿ****ym****.whkrty.* It is also noteworthy that *waw-he* follows *yod-mem* in both cases, giving us another option as to how the deletion occurred: ***hym.wh****mkšlwt.ʾt.hršʿ****ym.wh****krty.* Having written *ymwh*, he could have jumped to the next four-letter sequence *ymwh* at any point in the sequence, leaving out the intervening letters as well as the repeated letters prior to the point where his eye landed.

[36] Patterson (*Zephaniah,* 302) revocalizes the consonantal text as a causative (*hiphil*) participial form of כָּשַׁל, "to stumble," understands "the wicked" as the object, and translates (299), "the things that cause the wicked to stumble," referring to "every false religious practice" (cf.

other text, Isa 3:6, where it is typically understood to refer to a "heap of ruins"[37] (CSB says "heap of rubble.") Another noun, *mikšôl*, also related to the verb "to stumble," refers to something over which one stumbles or a stumbling block.[38] Since Zeph 1:4–5 describes idolatry, perhaps idols, viewed as stumbling blocks, are in view.[39] On the other hand, CSB may be on the right track with its translation "ruins" (cf. ESV, NASB), which reflects the assumed meaning of the term in Isa 3:6. In this case, the ruins of judgment are in view, just as the houses in 1:13 are reduced to ruins. The Lord will sweep the ruins away along with the wicked ones whose idolatry (vv. 4b–5) prompted such devastating judgment.

Returning to our previous discussion, we must ask, But how does a reference to the Lord sweeping away idols or ruins along with the wicked fit conceptually with the preceding reference to birds and fish? In general, the insertion of a reference to the wicked highlights that "sinful humanity" disrupts the created order.[40] However, there may be more involved. In verses 4–5 the idolatry of the people is described, particularly Baal and astral worship. Berlin points out that Deut 4:19 condemns astral worship and immediately preceding this, Moses warns Israel not to make images of any animal (*bəhēmâ*), bird, or fish (vv. 17–18). Berlin sees a possible double meaning in Zeph 1:3. In addition to contributing to the reversal of creation theme (see above), the references to animals, birds, and fish "may also be the elements of idolatry," especially if one understands the noun *makšēlôt* as referring to idolatrous "stumbling blocks."[41]

As for the asymmetrical style created by the additional words, perhaps the awkwardness of the longer text serves to focus the listener's attention and highlight the point. In this case, rhetoric engenders priority over formal stylistic precision.

While divine judgment is directed against "everything" (including "people and animals," "the birds of the sky," "the fish of the sea," and

---

NIV11, "the idols that cause the wicked to stumble"). See also Ball, *Zephaniah,* 22; Renz, *Zephaniah,* 460–61, who discusses various possible referents (468); and Sweeney's assessment (*Zephaniah,* 64).

[37] *HALOT*, 582.

[38] *HALOT*, 582; BDB, 506.

[39] See NIV11*;* cf. Ezek 7:19–20; 14:3, 7, where *mikšôl*, "stumbling block," refers to idols.

[40] Roberts, *Zephaniah,* 170.

[41] Berlin, *Zephaniah,* 73–74. See also Robertson, *Zephaniah,* 259. Sweeney, *Zephaniah,* 64, calls Berlin's proposal "attractive" but concludes that it "must remain speculative."

"mankind"), the "wicked" (*hārəšāʿîm*) are singled out in verse 3.[42] Similarly, in Isaiah's description of the day of the Lord, the Lord comes to punish the "world" (*tēbēl*) and, more specifically, "the wicked" (13:11).

This is the only place where the Hebrew word translated "wicked" appears in Zephaniah. The immediately following context suggests idolatry is in view. Perhaps the best character profile of the "wicked" occurs in Ezekiel 18, where a wicked person is contrasted with a righteous one. The actions that characterize the wicked (see vv. 10–18) are primarily deeds of injustice and violence, but idolatrous practices are also included (vv. 11–12, 15).

The prophetic speech formula "This is the LORD's declaration" (*nəʾūm yhwh*, lit. "oracle of YHWH) appears at the end of both verses 2 and 3. The formula appears 239 times in the OT, all but nine of which occur in the Latter Prophets. It appears four times in Zephaniah (see also 1:10; 3:8). In 2:9 "declaration" (*nəʾūm*) appears before "LORD of Armies, the God of Israel." The repetition of the formula at the beginning of Zephaniah's message emphasizes the fact that the Lord was speaking through him.[43]

1.1.2 The Elimination of False Worship (1:4–6)

The Lord's judgment will encompass Judah and Jerusalem. The Lord will eliminate from the covenant community those who give mere lip service to the Lord while worshipping other gods such as Baal and astral deities. He will remove those who turn from him and fail to seek him.

As noted earlier, "and I will stretch out" at the beginning of verse 4 continues the announcement of the Lord's intervention in judgment. The expression "stretch out the hand against" is idiomatic judgment language. The action sets in motion the Lord's judgment. We could paraphrase: "I will launch an attack against."

The Lord begins to particularize the worldwide judgment described in verses 2–3.[44] The object of judgment moves from "everything" in

---

[42] Ball, *Zephaniah,* 49.

[43] Ball, *Zephaniah,* 50–51. The formula also appears at or near the beginning of Jeremiah (1:8, 15, 19), Obadiah (4, 8), Haggai (1:9, 13), Zechariah (1:3–4), and Malachi (1:2). Thus, it appears to be a stylistic device used by late preexilic or postexilic prophets.

[44] This technique is common in prophetic literature. See Paul R. Raabe, "The Particularizing of Universal Judgment in Prophetic Discourse," *CBQ* 64 (2002): 652–74. Raabe discusses the following texts: Isa 2–3; 3:13–15; 10:22–23; 13:1–22; 14:4–27; 23:8–9; 28:14–22; 30:27–33;

verse 2 to humans, beasts, birds, fish, and the "wicked" (and perhaps their idols) in verse 3.[45] In verse 4a judgment zeroes in on Judah and the residents of Jerusalem. The Lord then gets more specific as he announces he will cut off "from this place" (Judah and Jerusalem)[46] every vestige of Baal, pagan priests, priests, those who bow in worship on the rooftops, and those who bow and pledge loyalty to the Lord while also pledging loyalty to a false god (vv. 4b–5). Judgment culminates with those who turn their backs on the Lord and do not seek or inquire of him (v. 6).[47]

1:4–6 There are only two clauses in verses 4–6: (1) "[And] I will stretch out my hand against Judah and against all the residents of Jerusalem" (v. 4a), and (2) "I will cut off . . ." (vv. 4b–6). In the second clause "I will cut off" is followed by five objects, each of which is introduced by the accusative sign *ʾet*. Each of these gets longer and more syntactically complex than the preceding one:

1. "every vestige of Baal" (lit., "the remnant of Baal," cf. ESV) (1:4)

The phrase "remnant of Baal" occurs only here in the OT. The noun *šəʾār*, "remnant," carries the primary meaning, "remainder, what is left."[48] It can refer to a remnant/a few (cf. Isa 10:22; 16:14; 21:17), but this is not always the case and must be determined on a contextual basis. The use of the phrase in this judgment context indicates totality of destruction, translated in CSB as "every vestige of Baal."

Modified by "Baal," *šəʾār* must refer to what was left of the formal cultic system worshipping Baal (cf. NIV11, "every remnant of Baal worship," NET, "every trace of Baal worship"), including images and priests. The following object, "the names of the pagan priests along

---

34:1–17; Jer 12:7–13; 25:15–29; Ezek 7:1–27; 30:1–9; Hos 4:1–6; Joel 3:1–8 [Hb. 4:1–8]; Amos 1–2; Obadiah; Micah 1; Zephaniah 1; Nahum 1–3. In some cases, the movement is from the universal to the particular, but in others the movement goes in the opposite direction (672). According to Raabe, this "particularizing of universal judgment is a convention of prophetic discourse—more precisely, a conventional type of argument. The convention operates, as it were, with a wide-angle lens and a zoom lens. It includes within itself both a worldwide perspective and a local perspective, both a big picture and a small picture, both a general judgment facing all nations and a specific judgment facing a particular nation. By particularizing universal judgment, the prophets grounded the fate of one place or of one group of people in a more all-inclusive phenomenon" (671).

[45] Ball, *Zephaniah,* 52–53.

[46] Ball, *Zephaniah,* 59.

[47] Raabe, "Particularizing of Universal Judgment," 669–70.

[48] BDB, 984; *HALOT*, 1378.

with the priests," is introduced by an object sign (*ʾet*) without a prefixed conjunction ("and"),[49] in contrast to the following three objects (vv. 5–6), all of which have prefixed conjunctions to the sign (Hb. *waw*, "and"). When two object signs appear in succession and the second has no prefixed conjunction, it often indicates apposition,[50] in which the second object is identified with the first in some way.[51] In this context, this would indicate the "remnant of Baal" is identified with the priests.[52]

Baal worship had long been a problem in Israel (Jer 2:8; 23:27) and had persisted into the seventh century BC (2 Kgs 21:3) right down to the time of Zephaniah as Jeremiah's message makes abundantly clear (Jer 2:23; 7:9; 9:14 [13]; 11:13, 17; 12:16; 19:5). King Josiah tried to purge Judah of Baal worship (2 Kgs 23:4–5), but the people continued to worship Baal (Jer 32:29, 35) in the tenth year of Zedekiah's reign (fall 588–summer 587 BC; cf. Jer 32:1).[53] Perhaps the "remnant of Baal" refers to the priests along with their idols that remained or resurfaced following Josiah's purge.

2. "the names of the pagan priests along with the priests" (1:4)

As noted above, the absence of the conjunction with the accusative sign may indicate these priests are identified with "the remnant of Baal." If *kəmārîm* is appositional to "remnant of Baal," then Baal's priests are in view (cf. 2 Kgs 10:19; 11:18; 2 Chr 34:4–5). If not, then the priests mentioned here could include those serving the astral deities mentioned in verse 5 (cf. 2 Kgs 23:5).

The "names" (the Hebrew is singular) of the priests refers to all memory of them (cf. NET).[54] The point is that the worship system they promote will cease.

---

[49] Of course, as one might expect, the conjunction is included in some Hebrew manuscripts and is represented in several textual witnesses. This is almost certainly an addition designed to create symmetry with what follows. However, if original, it is difficult to see in this graphic environment how the *waw* would have been accidentally omitted.

[50] See Patterson, *Zephaniah,* 305.

[51] See Isa 29:10; Jer 7:15; 12:14; 23:13; 27:8; 31:7; 32:11, 21; Ezek 24:2; 30:22; 39:14; Zech 10:3; 11:10. However, this is not always the case (see Jer 24:10; 27:5; 29:17).

[52] Ball, *Zephaniah,* 55. For a discussion of the terms used for priests, see below.

[53] For an attempt to explain Judah's Baal worship as syncretism, where worship of Yahweh took the form of the Baal cult, see Renz, *Zephaniah,* 471.

[54] Roberts, *Zephaniah,* 171; Renz, *Zephaniah,* 471.

Two different terms are used for "priests."[55] The first (*kemārîm*, "pagan priests") appears in only two other passages. As here, it refers to priests serving pagan gods. In 2 Kgs 23:5 it refers to priests appointed by the kings of Judah to burn incense to Baal and astral deities on the high places. In Hos 10:5 it refers to priests who served the calf idol of "Beth-aven," meaning, "house of sin," a derogatory substitute name for Bethel, "house of God."

After a thorough study of the term, Radine concludes the *kəmārîm* "were priests of an Aramean rite who served a specifically royal function, serving at the behest of the king. They were probably not foreigners but practiced a ritual tradition of Aramean origin." He adds that although these priests "seem to have been royally appointed, the deities they worshipped were probably not personal deities of the Judahite kings and their families, but more likely a part of state policy."[56] As such, these priests "may have had a partly diplomatic function, serving as a royal acknowledgement of a general Aramean cult for better relations with Assyria or any potentate approaching Israel or Judah from the northern direction."[57]

The second word for "priests" is the common designation used 740 times in the OT.[58] It can refer to priests of various types, including legitimate and illegitimate ones.[59] In this context, coupled with "pagan priests," it obviously has a negative connotation and refers to priests who, though distinct from the *kəmārîm*, served pagan deities.[60]

3. "[and] those who bow in worship on the rooftops to the stars in the sky" (1:5)

"Stars in the sky" translates Hebrew *ṣəbāʾ haššāmāyim*, traditionally, "host of heaven" (cf. KJV, ESV). The phrase, which occurs

[55] The Septuagint has only one reference to "priests" here. For discussion of the Greek reading, see Berlin, *Zephaniah,* 75, and Renz, *Zephaniah,* 461–62.

[56] Jason Radine, "The 'Idolatrous Priests' in the Book of Zephaniah," in Lena-Sofia Tiemeyer, ed., *Priests and Cults in the Book of the Twelve.* ANE Monographs 14 (Atlanta: SBL, 2016), 138.

[57] Radine, "The 'Idolatrous Priests'," 138.

[58] *HALOT*, 461.

[59] Renz, *Zephaniah,* 472; BDB, 463–64.

[60] Berlin, *Zephaniah,* 75, prefers to read, "the idolatrous priests *among* the priests." In her view, "there are not two types of priests slated for destruction, but rather those among the legitimate priests who have become idolatrous." Roberts, *Zephaniah*, 172, takes the second word as a gloss.

eighteen times, usually refers to the stars as objects of worship (1:5).[61] The participle *mištaḥăwîm* is a *hishtaphel* form from the verbal root *ḥāwāh*, which expressed the idea of "bow down." It is used generally of an inferior party bowing before a superior. When a deity is the object of the accompanying preposition, the expression refers to a gesture of worship. According to Nathan Hays, astral worship "was especially prominent in Assyria and material evidence for astral worship in the Levant increases considerably with greater contact with Assyria."[62]

4. "[and] those who bow[63] and pledge loyalty to the Lord but also pledge loyalty to Milcom" (CSB; 1:5)

The accusative sign appears only before the first word ("those who bow"). There is no conjunction ("and") in the Hebrew text before "[those who] pledge loyalty to the Lord." This suggests the two words are in apposition; one group is described in two ways: "[and] those who bow, [that is] those who pledge loyalty to the Lord." Bowing refers to a worship posture. While in this posture, they take oaths (cf. "pledge loyalty").

It may seem surprising the Lord refers to himself in the third person here and in verse 6. However, in this case it is rhetorically effective. It makes the accusation (vv. 4b–6) embedded within the announcement of judgment (v. 4a) more objective and formal in tone, whereas the first person would focus on personal offense and injury. By using the third person, the Lord speaks more as prosecutor than defendant and assumes the point of view of those hearing his case and his verdict against the guilty party.

The *niphal* participle (*nišbāʿîm*, "those who swear," from *šābaʿ*) is repeated with a connecting conjunction prefixed to the second participle. Theoretically, this could refer to two different groups, but this would make no sense in this case, since "those who pledge loyalty to the Lord" would not be the object of judgment. In this case, the second participle refers to the same group. In other words, as they assume

---

[61] The comparison of the stars to a "host" in the sky perhaps depicts them as regimented like an army in its battle lines: Deut 4:19; 17:3; 2 Kgs 17:16; 21:3, 5; 23:4–5; Neh 9:6; 2 Chr 33:3, 5; Isa 34:4; Jer 8:2; 19:13; 33:22; Dan 8:10. In 1 Kgs 22:19 (= 2 Chr 18:18) the phrase is used of the Lord's heavenly assembly standing at his right and left.

[62] Hays, "Humility and Instruction in Zephaniah 3.1–7," 477–78.

[63] The Septuagint omits "those who bow," and reads simply, "and those who swear by the Lord" (NET).

a worship posture, they "pledge loyalty to the LORD" but also "pledge loyalty to Milcom" [MT, "their king"]. The translations attempt to reflect this in various ways: "but also" (CSB), "and yet" (ESV), "and who also" (NIV11), "while taking" (NET).

The use of different prepositional phrases following the participles supports this understanding.[64] The first uses the preposition *lə-*, "to," while the second uses *bə-*, "by."[65] When the *niphal* of *šābaʿ* is used with *lə-*, "to," it can mean "swear to," or make an oath of allegiance to someone.[66] When used with *bə-*, "by," it can mean "swear by," or formulate an oath using the object of the preposition in the oath formula as the guarantor of the oath.[67] The subjects pledge allegiance to the Lord, but when committing themselves to a course of action, they appeal to Milcom/their king, demonstrating where their confidence lies. Renz cites the following examples where "both prepositions are used with persons for the same oath":[68]

Gen 21:23	"swear *to* me *by* God"
Exod 32:13	"you swore *to* them *by* yourself"
Josh 2:12	"swear *to* me *by* the LORD"
Josh 9:18–19	"sworn an oath *to* them *by* the LORD"
1 Sam 24:21	"swear *to* me *by* the LORD" [Hb. v. 22]
1 Sam 28:10	"swore *to* her *by* the LORD"
1 Sam 30:15	"swear *to* me *by* God"
1 Kgs 1:17	"you swore *to* your servant *by* the LORD" (lit., "you swore *by* the LORD . . . to your servant")
1 Kgs 1:30	"I swore *to* you *by* the LORD"
1 Kgs 2:8	"I swore *to* him *by* the LORD"

[64] Ball, *Zephaniah*, 26–28; Renz, *Zephaniah*, 474.

[65] For a list of passages where the constructions appear, see Heath D. Dewrell, "'Swearing to Yahweh, but Swearing by *Mōlek*-Sacrifices': Zephaniah 1:5b," *VT* 69 (2019): 741, notes 15–16.

[66] See BDB, 989. Only three other passages refer to "swearing to Yahweh" (2 Chr 15:14; Ps 132:3; Isa 19:18).

[67] Renz, *Zephaniah*, 474; Berlin, *Zephaniah*, 75; Patterson, *Zephaniah*, 306 (citing Keil).

[68] Renz, *Zephaniah*, 474, n. 83.

The key point here is that swearing to "their king" in contrast to the Lord, they violated Deut 6:13 in which Moses commands Israel: "Fear the LORD your God, worship him, and take your oaths in his name."[69] In Hebrew the third command reads literally, "*By* his name you must swear" (*ûbišmô tiššābeaʿ*).

There is some uncertainty regarding the referent of the final word of verse 5. MT has *malkām*, "their king." However, many interpreters prefer to emend the text to the name of a deity, either Molech (*mōlek*; NIV11) or the Ammonite god Milcom (*milkōm*; ESV, NASB).[70] The context speaks of judgment against idolatry, and a specific god (Baal) is named in verse 4. If we retain MT, "their king," it is not clear who the referent would be. It seems unlikely a human king is in view in this context[71] where idolatry is the focus.[72] The notion that Yahweh, viewed in a corrupted, syncretistic manner[73] is the referent seems overly subtle.[74] "Their king" is more likely an individual deity, perhaps Baal (cf. v. 4),[75] Molech, given the derivation of his name, or Milcom as CSB says. Renz prefers to see "their king" as vague enough to accommodate different royal deities worshipped by different people.[76] In any case, the use of "their king" for a rival master would be ironic and would

---

[69] Renz, *Zephaniah*, 475–76.

[70] On the textual evidence, see Nicholas R. Werse, "Of Gods and Kings: The Case for Reading 'Milcom' in Zephaniah 1:5bb," *VT* 68 (2018): 505–13. The Septuagint understands Hebrew מַלְכָּם, "their king," as Milcom in 2 Sam 12:30; Jer 49:1, 3 [LXX 30:17, 19] (see CSB) and as "Molchol" (= Molech?) in 1 Chr 20:2. However, in each of these texts, it is preferable to understand "their king" as the human king of Ammon. To further complicate matters, 1 Kgs 11:7 identifies Molech as the god of Ammon, in contrast to verses 5 and 33, which speak of Milcom.

[71] See the proposal of Sweeney, *Zephaniah,* 70–71.

[72] For a critique of the notion that a human king is in view, see Berlin, *Zephaniah,* 76; Werse, "Of Gods and Kings," 506.

[73] See Ben Zvi, *Zephaniah*, 77–78.

[74] Taylor understands "their king" as referring to Yahweh, identified with the sun, as king of the host of heaven. See J. Glen Taylor, *Yahweh and the Sun: Biblical and Archaeological Evidence for Sun Worship in Ancient Israel*, JSOTSup 111 (Sheffield: Sheffield Academic, 1993), 200–6. For a critique of Taylor's position, see Steve A. Wiggins, "Yahweh: The God of Sun?" *JSOT* 71 (1996):89–106. For Taylor's response see his "A Response to Steve A. Wiggins, 'Yahweh: The God of Sun?'," *JSOT* 71 (1996):107–19. For an overview and assessment of the debate over Yahweh's relationship with the sun, see John Day, *Yahweh and the Gods and Goddesses of Canaan,* JSOTSup, 265 (Sheffield: Sheffield Academic, 2000), 156–61.

[75] See Sabottka, *Zephanja,* 24; Patterson, *Zephaniah,* 306; Bailey, "Zephaniah," 421. Jeremiah 12:16 speaks of the surrounding nations swearing oaths "by Baal" and teaching Judah to do the same. This is the only place where a false god is mentioned as guarantor of the oath in an oath formula. Consequently, this suggests Baal may be the referent of "their king" in Zeph 1:5.

[76] Renz, *Zephaniah*, 475.

contribute to the Lord's accusation, for Zeph 3:15 speaks of *the Lord* as "Israel's king."[77] However, there is no other case in the OT of "king" being used for a deity other than the Lord, with the possible exception of Amos 5:26.[78] This suggests the form should be emended to a proper name, with Milcom and Molech serving as the prime candidates. Yet these proposals are not without problems.

Milcom was the god of the Ammonites (1 Kgs 11:33).[79] Solomon worshipped this god, who is called "the abhorrent idol of the Ammonites" (*šiqquṣ ʿammōnîm*, 1 Kgs 11:5) and "the detestable idol of the Ammonites" (*tôʿăbat bənê-ʿammôn*, 2 Kgs 23:13). This god was still being worshiped in Judah in the time of Josiah, who destroyed the high places of Milcom and several other gods (2 Kgs 23:13). However, in the other clear references to Milcom, he is always included in a list with Ashtoreth of the Sidonians (1 Kgs 11:5, 33; 2 Kgs 23:13) and Chemosh of the Moabites (1 Kgs 11:33; 2 Kgs 23:13; cf. 1 Kgs 11:7, where Milcom, not Molech, is the more likely reading). No such list appears in Zeph 1:5.

Molech was a Canaanite underworld god (cf. Isa 57:9) to whom his worshippers offered child sacrifices (Lev 18:21; 20:2–5; 2 Kgs 23:10; Jer 32:35).[80] Solomon built a high place for this god, who was still being worshipped in the time of Zephaniah, when Josiah ended Molech worship and its child sacrifices in the Ben Hinnom Valley (2 Kgs 23:10). The name of this deity was probably vocalized *mōlēk*, "king, ruler" (= Malik in extrabiblical texts) and altered to *mōlek* to mimic the vowels of the word *bōšet*, "shame."[81] A reference to Molech would fit the historical context of Zephaniah's time.[82] However, as Werse points out, this reading faces two difficulties: (1) Elsewhere child sacrifice is mentioned in conjunction with references to Molech, but Zeph 1:5 lacks any mention of this practice. (2) The final *mem* is problematic since names of deities do not take pronominal suffixes.[83]

---

[77] Motyer, "Zephaniah," 913. See Isa 6:5; 33:22; 41:21; 43:15; 44:6; Jer 8:19; 10:10; 46:18; 48:15; 51:57.

[78] See Werse, "Of Gods and Kings," 507–8.

[79] For a defense of reading Milcom, see Werse, "Of Gods and Kings," 505–13.

[80] See Day, *Yahweh and the Gods and Goddesses of Canaan*, 210–15; Richard S. Hess, *Israelite Religions: An Archaeological and Biblical Survey* (Grand Rapids: Baker Academic, 2007), 101–2. The extrabiblical evidence for Molech being an underworld deity is substantial (Day, 214–15).

[81] Day, *Yahweh and the Gods and Goddesses of Canaan*, 213–14. However, see George C. Heider, "Molech," in *ABD*, 4:896.

[82] Berlin, *Zephaniah*, 76–77.

[83] Werse, "Of Gods and Kings," 509–10. Berlin, *Zephaniah*, 77, argues that Molek "is not a proper noun," but a title and can, therefore, take a pronominal suffix.

Ball circumvents these difficulties by understanding consonantal *mlkm* as a reference to a *mulk* sacrifice offered to Molech.[84] He shows that Zeph 1:4–6 displays several points of contact with texts mentioning such a sacrifice, namely 2 Kgs 17:16–17; 21:1–7; 23:4–14; and Jer 19:1–15. Common elements include:

Baal worship:	Zeph 1:4	2 Kgs 17:16	2 Kgs 21:3	2 Kgs 23:4–5	Jer 19:5
Host of heaven:	Zeph 1:5a	2 Kgs 17:16	2 Kgs 21:3	2 Kgs 23:4–5	Jer 19:13
Mulk sacrifice:	Zeph 1:5b	2 Kgs 17:17	2 Kgs 21:6	2 Kgs 23:10	Jer 19:4
Divination:	Zeph 1:6[85]	2 Kgs 17:17	2 Kgs 21:6		
Priests (*kəmārîm*):	Zeph 1:4			2 Kgs 23:5	
Worship on roofs:	Zeph 1:5a			2 Kgs 23:12	Jer 19:13

Nevertheless, Day argues against taking Hebrew *mōlek* as a sacrificial term. He cites Lev 20:5, which refers to people "playing the harlot after *mōlek*," and points out parallel uses of "play the harlot" indicate a deity, not a sacrifice, is in view.[86] Additionally, the expression "swear by" (with the preposition *bə*-), when used elsewhere of human oaths, invariably invokes a deity (usually the Lord/God; see Jer 5:7 and Amos 8:14 for exceptions) and never a sacrifice.

What is described in verse 5 is not syncretism of the type where the Lord is fused with another deity. Instead, we have a form of polytheism, where the Lord and another deity are being worshipped simultaneously. Greenspahn (who regards the latter as a form of syncretism) describes this as an attempt "to follow two (or more) separate traditions simultaneously (syncretism) rather than the total abandonment of YHWH in favor of some other tradition."[87] First Kings 18:21, where Elijah accuses the people of wavering between the Lord and Baal, may be another example of this.

5. "and those who turn back from following the Lord, who do not seek the Lord or inquire of him" (1:6)

---

[84] Ball, *Zephaniah*, 32–33. See also Dewrell, "'Swearing to Yahweh," 737–41.

[85] However, see the discussion of verse 6 below.

[86] Day, *Yahweh and the Gods and Goddesses of Canaan*, 209–10.

[87] Frederick E. Greenspahn, "Syncretism and Idolatry in the Bible," *VT* 54 (2004): 492.

The relationship between the two poetic lines is complementary. The first half of the verse describes what the objects of God's judgment do, while the second half of the verse speaks of what they fail to do, "seek" and "inquire of" the Lord.[88]

Only here is the *niphal* form of the verb *sûg*, "turn," followed by *mēʾaḥărê*, "from after."[89] It occurs with *mēʾaḥar*, "from after," in Isa 59:13. In both passages the expression refers to turning back from following Israel's God (the Lord in Zeph 1:6, and "our God" in Isa 59:13).[90]

In verse 6b the synonyms *biqqēš* and *dāraš*, both of which mean "to seek," appear. The first of these (*biqqēš*) is also used with the Lord as object in Zeph 2:3. In that context the Lord announces judgment (vv. 1–2), urging the obedient humble to seek him. They are to do so by continuing to seek (*biqqēš*) righteousness (cf. Isa 51:1) and humility, with the hope that they will be protected from the Lord's anger. Elsewhere seeking the Lord can refer to seeking him in repentance and/or obedience[91] or through sacrifice.[92] On several occasions "seeking the Lord" means seeking his favor[93] or enablement.[94] In at least one case the expression may refer to seeking a reliable message from the Lord, though this is uncertain (Isa 45:19).

As for the verb *dāraš*, when it is used with the Lord as object, it often refers to seeking the Lord's will through a message.[95] Seeking the Lord can also mean seeking him in repentance[96] and/or obedience.[97] The expression can also be used of seeking the Lord for protection and/or enablement.[98]

---

[88] The relative pronoun in verse 6b is parallel to the substantival participle in verse 6a and refers to the same group. With the verb being negated in verse 6b, the relative pronoun is necessary.

[89] It most often appears with אָחוֹר, with the meaning "turn back."

[90] *HALOT* (744) uses the gloss "become disloyal."

[91] Deut 4:29; 2 Chr 15:4; Jer 29:13; 50:4; Hos 3:5; 7:6 [the verb is negated as in Zeph 1:6].

[92] Hos 5:6.

[93] 2 Chr 11:16; 15:15; 20:4; Zech 8:22–23.

[94] 1 Chr 16:10–11; Ps 105:3–4.

[95] Gen 25:22; 1 Kgs 22:8; 2 Kgs 3:11; 8:8; 22:13, 18; 1 Chr 15:13; 2 Chr 1:5; 16:12; 18:7; 2 Chr 20:3 [cf. vv. 5–17]; 34:21; Jer 10:21; Ezek 20:1, 3.

[96] Deut 4:29; Isa 9:13 [Hb. 12]; 55:6; Jer 29:13; Hos 10:12; Amos 5:4, 6 [by doing what is right, v. 14]).

[97] 2 Chr 12:14; 14:4 [Heb 3], 7; 15:2, 12–13; 22:9; 26:5; 30:19.

[98] Pss 9:10 [Hb. 11]; 22:26 [Hb. 27]; 24:6; 34:5 [Hb. 5], 10 [Hb. 11]; 105:4; Isa 31:1; Jer 21:2; Lam 3:25; 1 Chr 16:11.

Several translations use "inquire" to translate this verb in Zeph 1:6 (see, for example, CSB, NIV11, NASB, ESV) since *dāraš* is so often used of seeking the Lord's will through a message. However, the accompanying verb *biqqēš* is not used of seeking the Lord in this way, with the possible exception of Isa 45:19. The two verbs could have slightly different nuances here (e.g., NET, "do not want the LORD's help or guidance").[99] Nevertheless , they are often used together with the same nuance:

Deut 4:29	"You will *search* [*biqqēš*] for the LORD your God, and you will find him when you *seek* [*dāraš*] him with all your heart and all your soul."
1 Chr 16:11	"*Seek* [*dāraš*] the LORD and his strength; *seek* [*biqqēš*] his face always."
Ps 24:6	"Such is the generation of those who *seek* [*dāraš*] him, who *seek* [*biqqēš*] the face of the God of Jacob" (ESV). (CSB: "Such is the generation of those who *inquire* of him, who *seek* the face of the God of Jacob.")
Ps 105:4	"*Seek* [*dāraš*] the LORD and his strength; *seek* [*biqqēš*] his face always."
Jer 29:13	"You will *seek* [*biqqēš*] me and find me when you *search* [*dāraš*] for me with all your heart."

Deuteronomy 4:29 and Jer 29:13 refer to seeking the Lord in repentance. The passages that mention seeking the Lord's face refer to prayer, and in all three cases a prayer for the Lord's help and enablement is in view (Note "and his strength" in 1 Chr 16:11 and Ps 105:4 and the reference to the Lord's deliverance in Ps 24:5). To seek the Lord's face can refer to seeking his will through a message ("inquiring" of him, cf. 2 Sam 21:1), but the expression more often refers to seeking him in repentance (2 Chr 7:14; Hos 5:15) or trust (Ps 27:8).

The two clauses in Zeph 1:6b are best understood as synonymous since both state those who have turned back from following the Lord (v. 6a) have not sought[100] the Lord. Considering usage of the two words for "seek" when they appear together, it is likely they have failed to seek the Lord in repentance for their idolatry and misplaced

[99] So *NIDOTTE*, 1:721.

[100] I understand the *qatal* (perfect) verb forms in verse 6b as perfective.

allegiance and/or have not looked to him for help, enablement, and protection but instead have turned to other gods (vv. 4–5). Of course, seeking his help and protection could include seeking from him an oracle of deliverance (cf. 2 Chr 20:3–17).

1.2 The Imminent Day of the Lord Brings Punishment and Devastation (1:7–18)

In verses 7–18 the day of the Lord becomes the primary judgment motif.[101] This day is near and will bring widespread destruction. A basic paneled structure is apparent, if we view the references to the nearness of the day as introductory to subunits that give a detailed description of this day:

A The nearness of the day of the Lord (v. 7a)
B Detailed description of the day of the Lord (vv. 7b–13)
A The nearness of the day of the Lord (v. 14a)
B Detailed description of the day of the Lord (vv. 14b–18)

However, concurrent with this is a more complex, concentric structure, for which verse 7 lays the thematic foundation.[102] Silence before the Lord is appropriate because (1) the day of the Lord is near and (2) the Lord has prepared a sacrificial slaughter in which, ironically, the guests are the sacrifice. Verses 8–13 expand upon the second motif, while verses 14–18 expand upon the first:

"Be silent . . ." (v. 7a)
A "for the day of the LORD is near" (v. 7b¹)
B "[for] the LORD has prepared a sacrifice . . ." (v. 7b²)
B "On the day of the LORD's sacrifice . . ." (vv. 8–13)
A "The great day of the LORD is near . . ." (vv. 14–18)

Verses 8–13 provide a detailed description of "the day of the LORD's sacrifice" (v. 8). References to this day provide the backbone of the unit: "and it will be in that day" (v. 10), "and it will be in that time" (v. 12). Throughout verses 8–13 the events of the day of sacrifice are the focus. In verse 14a the focus shifts back to the nearness of the day

---

[101] For a discussion of the day of the Lord theme in the Old Testament, see the section above "Theological Themes," more specifically "God's Self-Revelation: Status and Roles: Yahweh as Warrior-King."

[102] On concurrent structures in Hebrew literature, see Parunak, "Some Axioms for Literary Architecture," 1–16.

of the Lord. Verses 14b–18 then give a detailed description of this impending day of judgment. "Day" appears ten times in verses 14–18, denoting further emphasis.

1.2.1 *A Day of Punishment for Jerusalem* (1:7–13)

The approaching day of the Lord demands a response of silence, for the Lord will slaughter the objects of his judgment as if they were sacrificial animals. He will punish the corrupt royal court, including those who steal from others, and bring economic activity to an end. He will judge all those who persist in sin and believe he will not hold them accountable for their actions, depriving them of their ill-gotten wealth.

This subunit begins with an exhortation to be silent (v. 7a) accompanied by two reasons silence is appropriate (v. 7b). An introductory formula (lit., "and it will be in the day of the LORD's sacrifice") marks the transition to the next portion of the subunit, which announces the Lord's intervention against the objects of judgment (vv. 8–9). There is no formal accusation (introduced, for example, by *kî*, "because"), but the description of the corrupt royal court is functionally accusatory. Another introductory formula (lit., "and it will be in that day"), combined with the formula "this is the LORD's declaration," marks the transition to the next section of the subunit, which describes the results of the Lord's intervention (vv. 10–11). Embedded within this section is an exhortation to the victims of judgment. Another introductory formula (lit., "and it will be in that time") appears in verse 12, marking the transition to the final section of the subunit. The Lord announces his intervention in judgment and describes the results of judgment (vv. 12–13). While there is no formal accusation, the description of the sinners as those who are complacent in their corruption and who think God will not hold them accountable for their behavior is functionally accusatory.

1.2.1.1 *A Call for Silence in Anticipation of "Sacrifice"* (1:7)

The approaching day of the Lord demands a response of silence, for the Lord will slaughter the objects of his judgment as if they were sacrificial animals.

1:7 The opening word (*has*) is an interjection, typically translated "be silent."[103] It is followed by the prepositional phrase *mippənê*, "from the face of, from before." In this context silence as an expression of submission to the sovereign God is in view, as the following *ʾădōnāy yhwh*, literally, "the Master, Yahweh" indicates.[104] The prepositional phrase sometimes has the sense "because of, for fear of," which is likely the case here.[105] Submissive silence before the Lord is also in view in the two other cases where *has* combines with *mippənê*. In Hab 2:20 "the whole earth" is told to "be silent" before the Lord, who "is in his holy temple," figurative for his palace set apart from the earth. In Zech 2:13 [Hb. v. 17] "all humanity" (lit., "all flesh") is urged to "be silent" before him for he has roused himself from "his holy dwelling." There is no addressee specified in Zeph 1:7, but the preceding context suggests humankind and particularly those living in Judah and Jerusalem are the addressees.

The prophet offers two reasons (note *kî*, "for," used twice) silence is appropriate.[106] When successive *kî* clauses occur after an exhortation (*has* is functionally, if not morphologically, imperatival), the second clause, if asyndetic (no prefixed conjunction) as here, can be causal in relation to the preceding *kî* clause. For example, in Isa 40:2 one can detect a causal relationship in the sequence: the Lord announces Jerusalem's warfare is over, *because* her punishment has been accepted, *because* it was adequate to pay for her sins.[107] At other times, the two

---

[103] Its usage in Judg 3:19 and Amos 6:10; 8:3 favors this. See BDB, 245. One could understand the form as a *piel* imperative masculine singular from a verbal root הָסָה, which is attested in two texts: Num 13:30 (*hiphil wayyiqtol*) and Neh 8:11 (*piel* imperative, masculine plural). The verb is usually understood as denominative in relation to the interjection (*HALOT*, 253). Ben Zvi (*Zephaniah*, 79) prefers to understand the form as a *qal* imperative from a root הָסַס.

[104] CSB's translation "the Lord God" reflects the traditional pronunciation of this combination: אֲדֹנָי אֱלֹהִים. Normally, אֲדֹנָי is read when the divine name Yahweh appears, but when the divine name follows אֲדֹנָי, it is vocalized אֱלֹהִים. The combination אֲדֹנָי יְהוִה occurs often, especially in Ezekiel (217 times). It appears 25 times in the Minor Prophets (the Twelve), 21 of these being in Amos. This is its only occurrence in Zephaniah.

[105] See BDB, 818, category II. 6 under פָּנֶה, "face."

[106] Note KJV, NASB. CSB understands the first כִּי as causal ("for") but takes the second as emphatic ("indeed"). Some do not translate the second כִּי (cf. ESV, NIV11, NLT, NET).

[107] See also (1) Jer 33:11, where the Lord's faithfulness is the basis for the preceding affirmation that he is good; (2) Hos 4:1, where the Lord has a case against the people of the land because there is no truth, faithful love, or knowledge of God; (3) Hos 5:1, where judgment is impending because the people have been a snare and net; (4) 1 Sam 9:12, where Samuel's arrival was due to the scheduled sacrifice; and (5) 1 Sam 25:28, where the Lord's promise to David is grounded in the fact that he has fought the Lord's wars.

kî clauses are parallel in relation to the exhortation, with the second, asyndetic clause reiterating, complementing, or specifying the first. For example, in Joel 2:1 the people should tremble (note the jussive) because (1) the day of the Lord has arrived and (2) is near.[108] In Zeph 1:7 the latter is more likely.[109] Silence is appropriate because (1) the day of the Lord is near and (2) more specifically, the Lord has prepared a sacrifice in conjunction with this day. In other words, as verse 8 indicates, the day of the Lord *is* a day of sacrifice.

The first reason for a response of silence is that "the day of the LORD is near." The following context clearly specifies a time of judgment and devastation (vv. 8–18) in which the Lord will reveal his sovereign power in full force. So submissive silence before him is appropriate.

The second reason for a response of silence is the Lord "has prepared a sacrifice" and "has consecrated his guests." The expression "prepared a sacrifice" [*hiphil* of *kûn*, "be prepared," followed by *zebaḥ*, "sacrifice"] occurs only here in the OT. The verb in this form is often used with the meaning "prepare, make ready," while the term for "sacrifice" refers to a "communal sacrifice . . . of slaughtered sheep, goat or cattle to create communion between the god to whom the sacrifice is made and the partners of the sacrifice, and communion between the partners themselves."[110] The participants in the sacrifice are referred to in the next line: "he has consecrated his guests." Once again, the language [*hiphil* of *qādaš*, "be holy," followed by a *qal* passive participle from *qārāʾ*, "to call"] is unique to this passage. The verb in this form (*hiphil*, lit., "make holy") is used here of consecrating the object, identified as "his guests" (lit.,"his called ones"). This refers to those whom the Lord has summoned to the sacrifice.[111]

In this context a literal sacrifice is not in view, for verse 8 describes "the day of the LORD's sacrifice" as one of punishment, and the

[108] See also (1) Ps 12:1 [Hb. v. 2], where the psalmist prays for deliverance because (a) no faithful one remains and (b) the loyal have disappeared, (2) Ps 147:1, where praise is fitting because (a) it is good to sing to God and (b) such praise is pleasant and lovely, (3) 1 Sam 8:7, where Samuel should listen to the people because (a) they have not rejected him, (b) but rather have rejected God.

[109] For a contrary opinion, see Motyer, "Zephaniah," 918. He argues that the day of the Lord is imminent "because . . . the Lord has already prepared the sacrificial meal and invited his guests."

[110] *HALOT*, 465; 262.

[111] *HALOT*, 1129; cf. 1 Sam 9:13, 22; 2 Sam 15:11; 1 Kgs 1:41, 49.

following verses elaborate on this judgment. The slaughter characterizing the coming judgment is viewed metaphorically as a sacrifice where blood is poured out (cf. v. 17). Within the sacrificial metaphor of Zeph 1:7 the victims of this judgment mentioned in the following verses correspond to the sacrificial animals that are slaughtered.[112] But who are the consecrated invitees?

Typically, the consecration mentioned here is understood to involve ritually purifying the object for participation in the meal.[113] Within this metaphor of judgment, the sinful people of Judah and Jerusalem are the sacrifice, while the invitees are identified as enemies summoned by the Lord as his instruments of destruction (cf. vv. 14–18),[114] and perhaps even wild animals summoned to devour the flesh of the corpses (cf. Ezek 39:17–20).[115]

However, John de Jong argues one expects the *piel* or *hithpael* stem of the verb *qādaš* to be used for this type of purification. After contrasting the use of *qādaš* in the *piel/hithpael* and *hiphil* stems, he concludes the *hiphil* "never expresses the idea of bringing someone or something into a temporary state of holiness in order to participate in cultic activity. Rather, it describes the causing of an object to become holy and therefore the property of Yahweh."[116] By using the *hiphil* rather than the *piel*, Zephaniah ironically subverts "the sacrificial meal scene." de Jong explains the implications of this:

> It is already highly irregular in that Yahweh himself prepares rather than receives the sacrifice, and now the guests, rather than being brought into a temporary state of holiness in order to participate in the cultic feast, are irrevocably dedicated to Yahweh. This is what happens to the sacrifice, not the guests. . . . In the context of Zephaniah 1, the guests are those under judgment, and

---

[112] Renz, *Zephaniah,* 489.

[113] BDB, 873; *hiphil* 3.

[114] *TDOT*, 12:540

[115] Roberts, *Zephaniah*, 178. Some see no specific referent underlying the invitees (Berlin, *Zephaniah*, 79). Since one expects guests to attend a communal sacrifice, the prophet fills out the metaphor by mentioning them (Motyer, "Zephaniah," 918). They are merely *dramatis personae*.

[116] John Hans de Jong, "Sanctified or Dedicated? הקדיש in Zephaniah 1:7," *VT* 68 (2018): 97. See also *NIDOTTE* (3:885), which states that the *hiphil* "has the sense of dedication, not with the implication of cultic qualification, but rather of transfer to the possession of God, to whom the person or thing dedicated now exclusively belongs."

the sacrificial meal is a part of the judgment that is unfolding in this chapter.[117]

In short, "The use of the Hiphil signifies that at this sacrificial meal the guests are not sanctified for cultic participation but have rather been dedicated irrevocably to Yahweh, which means they are the sacrifice."[118] Sweeney, commenting on the irony of this, observes, "Those invited to the sacrifice normally come to participate in the celebration and to consume a portion of the sacrificial meal." However, as the following verses indicate, in this context "those who are invited to the sacrifice are those who will be punished and destroyed if they are evil, thereby becoming the sacrifice themselves. This represents quite a play on the notion of purification or consecration for sacrifice."[119]

1.2.1.2 Punishment as "Sacrifice" (1:8–13)

1:8–9 The Lord will punish the corrupt royal court, including those who steal from others (1:8–9).

The Lord's day of sacrifice will be a day of judgment. The Lord announces (note the first-person verb forms) he will intervene to punish sinners.[120] It is uncertain if the introductory words, literally, "and it will be in the day of the sacrifice of the Lord," are spoken by the prophet or God. The third-person reference to the Lord suggests the prophet is the speaker since he refers to the Lord in the third person three times in verse 7. A shift in speaker would be abrupt in this case although rhetorically effective. The Lord interrupts the prophet and eagerly begins to elaborate on the point that the invitees (v. 7) are the sacrifice. On the other hand, the Lord refers to himself in the third person elsewhere in this chapter. In this case, the Lord's use of the divine name facilitates the transition from the prophet's words to his own[121]

[117] de Jong, "Sanctified or Dedicated?" 99–100.

[118] de Jong, "Sanctified or Dedicated?" 94. See also Patterson, *Zephaniah*, 311–12; Bailey, "Zephaniah," 428; David W. Baker, *Nahum, Habakkuk, Zephaniah,* TOTC (Downers Grove: Inter-Varsity, 1988), 94–95.

[119] Sweeney, *Zephaniah,* 81.

[120] In this case the first-person verb (note וּפָקַדְתִּי) is followed by the preposition עַל and then the object of judgment. The verb-preposition combination can be translated, "I will bring punishment upon," or, simply, "I will punish." This expression occurs as well in Zeph 1:9, 12; 3:7.

[121] Roberts (*Zephaniah,* 178) recognizes the transitional function of the references to the divine name. He is not certain if it was added by an editor or included by the prophet himself.

and highlights the fact that this sacrifice is orchestrated by the Lord, Judah's covenant God whose day of powerful intervention is near.[122]

In verse 8, the Lord singles out three objects of his judgment: "the officials, the king's sons, and all who are dressed in foreign clothing."[123] The "officials" (*śārîm*) comprised the royal administration and were responsible for dispensing justice among other things. Verse 8 gives no indication of why they would be punished, but the other passage where Zephaniah mentions them gives us a clue. We read in 3:3, "The princes (*śārîm*) within her are roaring lions; her judges are wolves of the night, which leave nothing for the morning." The comparison to ravenous wild beasts depicts them as violent. The immediate context, which mentions the "oppression" that characterizes the city (v. 1) in contrast to the Lord's commitment to justice (v. 5), suggests the officials act unjustly. In this regard, it is noteworthy that 1:9 speaks of "violence and deceit." Elsewhere in the prophets we read of Judah's officials (*śārîm*) perpetrating injustice against the vulnerable of society and corrupting the legal system by taking bribes (Isa 1:23; 3:14; Jer 34:8–11; Ezek 22:27; Mic 7:3).

The second object of the Lord's judgment is "the king's sons." This is the only occurrence of this phrase in the Latter Prophets.[124] The Lord provides no basis for the judgment.[125] If this prophecy comes from early in Josiah's reign before he reached adulthood, the referent might be sons of Manasseh who were still living and/or other sons of Amon besides Josiah. Since Josiah was a godly king, one might think his influence would positively impact his sons. However, his two sons who succeeded him, Jehoahaz and Jehoiakim, did not follow in their

---

[122] After noting that such abrupt shifts in person occur elsewhere in Zephaniah, Robertson (*Zephaniah*, 275) concludes that they "should be considered as a characteristic literary device for vivifying the Lord's own involvement."

[123] The Hebrew text reads lit., "And I will bring punishment *upon . . . and upon . . . and upon*." The repetition of the preposition עַל, "upon," and the addition of the conjunction "and" before the second and third occurrences indicate that three distinct objects are in view.

[124] There is some debate as to the referent of the phrase. Is it restricted in scope to literal sons of the king, or is it used of officials within the royal court (note the LXX, "house of the king")? See Renz, *Zephaniah*, 491; Berlin, *Zephaniah*, 79; Roberts, *Zephaniah*, 178; Ben Zvi, *Zephaniah*, 92; Sweeney, *Zephaniah*, 84–85.

[125] Renz (*Zephaniah*, 480) translates "the officials and the royal household, namely all those clothed in foreign clothing," understanding the conjunction on the third object as explicative (482). If correct, this would indicate that the king's sons (and perhaps the officials as well) had embraced foreign, pagan culture to some degree and would provide a basis for the Lord's judgment.

father's footsteps when they ascended to the throne (2 Kgs 23:31–32, 36–37; Jer 22:13–19).

The third object of judgment is "all who are dressed in foreign clothing" (lit., "the ones putting on a foreign robe"). This could include the officials and royal sons, but the use of "all" suggests a broader referent here. Dressing in foreign clothing may have been a symptom of a deeper problem: assimilation to foreign culture and religion (cf. Isa 2:6–9). As Renz observes, wearing foreign clothes possibly "portrays them here as being at home in an alien culture or at least as being unconcerned about preserving a distinct identity."[126] According to Hays, there is "iconographic evidence for Assyrian-style dress in the Levant during the period of Assyrian domination," which is likely alluded to in 1:8. Hays explains: "Elites were attempting to gain prestige by aligning themselves with Assyria even on the level of their clothing."[127]

In verse 9 the Lord identifies another object of judgment: "all who skip over the threshold, who fill their master's house with violence and deceit."[128] The meaning of "all who skip over the threshold" is unclear. The verb translated "skip" (*dālag*) occurs only four other times in the OT (2 Sam 22:20 = Ps 18:29 [30]; Song 2:8; Isa 35:6).[129] Twice the action is that of a deer (Song 2:8–9; Isa 35:6). The verb connotes speed and eagerness in all its uses. The noun translated "threshold" (*miptān*) is used elsewhere of the threshold of a temple (lit., "house," 1 Sam 5:4–5; Ezek 9:3; 10:4, 18; 47:1) or temple gate (Ezek 46:2).

Citing 1 Sam 5:4–5, most see this as a cultic action that provides further evidence of how pagan religion corrupted Judah's worship (see vv. 3–5).[130] The passage informs us the priests of Dagon in the Philistine town of Ashdod had a cultic practice of not stepping on the threshold of Dagon's temple, following the incident where Dagon's head and hands, separated from his torso, were found lying on the

---

[126] Renz, *Zephaniah*, 492.

[127] Hays, "Humility," 478.

[128] As in verse 8, the first-person verb (וּפָקַדְתִּי) is followed by the preposition עַל and then the object of judgment ("all who skip over the threshold"). The preposition does not appear before the participle הַמְמַלְאִים, lit., "the ones who fill," indicating that "the ones who fill" is appositional to "all who skip." For this reason, CSB translates with a relative pronoun, "who fill."

[129] The verb appears in the *qal* stem in Zeph 1:9. Elsewhere the *piel* is used. The preposition עַל, "over," appears with the verb here and in Song 2:8, where the woman's lover, compared to a gazelle or young deer, leaps over the mountains (that is, bounds over the mountainsides).

[130] Roberts, *Zephaniah*, 179; Patterson, *Zephaniah*, 312–13.

threshold of his temple. This would probably entail their skipping over the threshold, though the verb "skip" is not used there. Nevertheless, this understanding of Zeph 1:9 seems unlikely since 1 Sam 5:5 seemingly confines the practice to the Ashdod temple and gives no indication that it was widespread.[131]

It is more likely the focus is social oppression as suggested by the second half of verse 9, which mentions violence and deceit.[132] It makes sense to correlate this verse with 3:3, which depicts officials as ravenous lions and wolves. In this case, the first line of verse 9 depicts the culprits swiftly and violently breaking into houses, leaping over the thresholds in their haste to pilfer what is inside. Violence and deceit are used metonymically (cause for effect) for the things acquired by these means. If royal officials are in view (cf. v. 8), then the logical referent of "master" would be the king.[133] It is unlikely this refers to godly Josiah, but it could describe practices occurring early in Josiah's reign when he was still a boy.[134] Officials in the royal court may have been perpetuating the sins of Josiah's predecessors Manasseh (cf. 2 Kgs 21:16) and Amon (2 Kgs 21:20).

1:10–11 This next section of the speech begins in formulaic fashion. The temporal indicator *wəhāyâ bayyôm hah(h)ûʾ*, literally, "and it will be in that day," appears, followed by the prophetic speech formula *nəʾūm yhwh*, literally, "declaration of the LORD." The temporal statement occurs thirty-three times in the OT, exclusively in the Latter Prophets. This is the lone occurrence in Zephaniah.[135] In this context,

---

[131] Ben Zvi, *Zephaniah,* 98.

[132] Renz, *Zephaniah*, 494; S. D. Snyman, "Violence and Deceit in Zephaniah 1:9," *Old Testament Essays* 13 (2000): 89–102.

[133] The suffixed noun translated "their master" (אֲדֹנֵיהֶם) is morphologically plural and could be translated "their masters." The singular "house" can be collective when a house is common to the members of the group designated by a following plural genitive. See, for example, Exod 6:14; 8:3 [Hb. 7:28], 24 [Hb. v. 20]; 1 Sam 31:9; 2 Kgs 17:29. However, most prefer to take the suffixed noun as singular, understanding the plural as one of degree (or, more accurately, as a concretized abstract plural meaning "lordship"). The plural of אָדֹן, "lord," is often used of an individual master. For examples after the construct of "house," see Gen 39:2; 40:7; 44:8; 2 Sam 12:8; 2 Kgs 10:3; Isa 22:18.

[134] Ben Zvi, *Zephaniah*, 280–81.

[135] Elsewhere it appears thirteen times in Isaiah (7:18, 21, 23; 10:20, 27; 11:10–11; 17:4; 22:20; 23:15; 24:21; 27:12–13), twice in Jeremiah (4:9; 30:8), three times in Ezekiel (38:10, 18; 39:11), three times in Hosea (1:5; 2:16 [Hb. v. 18], 21 [Hb. v. 23]), once in Joel (3:18 [Hb. 4:18]), once in Amos (8:9), once in Micah (5:10 [Hb. 5:9]), and eight times in Zechariah (12:3, 9; 13:2, 4; 14:6–8, 13).

"that day" refers to the day of the Lord's sacrifice when he unleashes his punishment (vv. 8–9).

As noted earlier, the prophetic speech formula appears 239 times in the OT, all but nine of which occur in the Latter Prophets. It appears four times in Zephaniah (see also 1:2–3; 3:8). In 2:9 "declaration" (*nəʾūm*) appears before "LORD of Armies, the God of Israel." In each of the other instances in Zephaniah, the Lord speaks in the first person in conjunction with the formula. No first-person forms occur in verses 10–11, but the Lord speaks in the first person right before (vv. 8–9) and after this (vv. 12–13), so, as implied by the formula itself, it is reasonable to understand the Lord as the speaker in verses 10–11.

The Lord declares, "There will be an outcry from the Fish Gate, a wailing from the Second District, and a loud crashing from the hills." These are the sounds of destruction. The expression *qôl səʿāqāh*, literally, "sound of an outcry," occurs in three other passages (1 Sam 4:14; Jer 25:36; 48:3). In each case it is used of an anguished response to ruin and devastation. The same is the case with the noun translated "wailing" (*yəlālâ*) in its three other uses (Isa 15:8; Jer 25:36; Zech 11:3). The phrase translated "loud crashing" (*šeber gādôl*) occurs in six other texts, all in Jeremiah (4:6; 6:1; 14:17; 48:3; 50:22; 51:54), where it refers to the devastation of battle.

Three different locations are mentioned. The Fish Gate, mentioned elsewhere in conjunction with Manasseh's and Nehemiah's building projects (Neh 3:3; 12:39; 2 Chron 33:14), was located on the northern side of Jerusalem and provided entry to the fish market.[136] The Second District (lit., "the second," also mentioned in 2 Kgs 22:14 = 2 Chron 34:22), may refer to the newer quarter of the city.[137] Sweeney locates it west of the temple.[138] The "hills" are not identified, but the referent may be the "ridges west of the Tyropoeon Valley."[139] Renz suggests the hills are "those on either side of the Central Valley,"[140] while Sweeney understands the referent to be "the hills that surround Jerusalem in all directions, especially to the north and west."[141] By mentioning different sites (see "the Hollow" in v. 11) the Lord draws attention to the

[136] Berlin, *Zephaniah*, 86; Sweeney, *Zephaniah*, 89.
[137] *HALOT*, 650.
[138] Sweeney, *Zephaniah*, 89.
[139] Roberts, *Zephaniah*, 180.
[140] Renz, *Zephaniah*, 496.
[141] Sweeney, *Zephaniah*, 90.

thorough destruction that will encompass and overtake the entire city (v. 12).

Verse 11 transitions from straightforward predictive discourse (v. 10) to hortatory discourse, more specifically a call to mourn.[142] For rhetorical purposes, the Lord now speaks as if the coming judgment has arrived, urging the "residents of the Hollow" to "wail," an imperative form.[143] He speaks of the merchants having been silenced and cut off.

The verb forms in the second half of the verse are perfects, indicating completed action from the standpoint of the speaker: *nidmâ*, "has been silenced," and *nikrətû*, "have been cut off." CSB uses the English future tense ("will be silenced . . . will be cut off") to translate these perfects of certitude.[144] Both are in the passive stem (*niphal*), indicating that the subject (the merchants) is acted upon by an outside agent, the Lord (vv. 8–9, 12).

The meaning of the first verb (from *dāmâ*) is debated. BDB understands the primary meaning as "cease," used here in the sense of "be destroyed,"[145] but *HALOT* sees distinct roots, one meaning "be silent" (a by-form of *dāmam*), and the other "be destroyed,"[146] placing Zeph 1:11 under the second of these. CSB prefers the first option. The parallelism with "cut off" may favor "have ceased" or "have been destroyed" here.[147] Elsewhere when the *niphal* of *dāmâ* is used in the

---

[142] Floyd, *Minor Prophets,* 198.

[143] The verb is morphologically ambiguous. The *hiphil* form with an -*û* ending could be an imperative, second masculine plural, or a perfect, third common plural form. However, the presence of כִּי, "because," after the form strongly favors the imperatival understanding. See especially texts where "wail" is distinctly imperatival (masculine or feminine singular) or parallel to distinctly imperatival forms that are then followed by "because": Isa 14:31; Jer 4:8; 25:34; 48:20; 49:3; Ezek 21:17; Joel 1:5, 13; Zech 11:2. As in Zeph 1:11, a perfect verbal form appears in the causal clause in each of these texts. The ambiguous form with an -*û* ending is clearly functioning as a perfect in only two texts—Jer 48:39, where it is accompanied by another perfect, and Amos 8:3, where it is prefixed with *waw* and is used in predictive discourse. In neither case does "because" follow. Isolated/ambiguous examples (where the form could be perfect or imperatival) followed by "because" occur in Isa 13:6; 23:1, 14; Joel 1:11 (parallel to another ambiguous form). However, note that in Isa 23:6 the ambiguous form is imperatival (parallel to an imperative). The same is the case in Joel 1:5, 13. Finally, the ambiguous form occurs with an imperative (without a following "because") in Jer 51:8.

[144] See also the NIV, NET, and NASB. The ESV and KJV use the present tense.

[145] BDB, 198.

[146] *HALOT*, 225, lists three homonyms: דָּמָה (1) "be like, resemble," (2) "be silent," (3) "be destroyed."

[147] The verb כָּרַת, "cut off," in the *niphal* stem carries the nuance "cease, be destroyed" in prophetic judgment contexts. See Zeph 3:7, as well as the numerous texts listed in *HALOT,* 501,

prophets in a context of judgment, it usually means "be destroyed" (Isa 15:1; Hos 4:6; 10:7 [cf. v. 8], 15; Obad 5), although it can mean "be silenced" in Jer 47:5, where mourning rites are in view. Either "be destroyed" or "be silenced" fits in Isa 6:5.

"Hollow" translates the rare Hebrew word *maktēš*, which is used in only two other texts—Judg 15:19, where it is a geographical term for an area in which God opened a spring from the ground, and Prov 27:22, where it appears to refer to a mortar in which one crushes grain with a pestle. Since a mortar is bowl-like in shape, most understand the term in Zeph 1:11 as referring to a hollow or low-lying area where merchants operated.[148] However, Robertson, rather than understanding the word as referring to another district of the city (cf. v. 10), prefers to see the term as a metaphor for the entire city: "Encircled by higher hills, Jerusalem itself may be compared to a mortar, a pounding place. God in his judgment shall grind the whole of the city as though it were encased in a mortar."[149]

The first phrase used of the merchants reads literally, "the people of Canaan" (cf. NASB). This phrase occurs nowhere else in the OT, but "Canaan" refers to a merchant in Hos 12:7[8], while "land of Canaan" is used idiomatically of Babylon, viewed as a commercial nation in Ezek 16:29 and 17:4. The term "Canaanite" is used of a merchant in Prov 31:24 and possibly Zech 14:21 (see CSB margin). An alternative form of "Canaanite" refers to merchants in Isa 23:8, where it corresponds to "traders" in the parallel structure.[150] The terms "Canaan," "land of Canaan," originally referring to a geographical area populated by a distinct ethnic group, and "Canaanite," referring to inhabitants of that area, developed a derived meaning, "merchant," because Canaanites engaged in commercial activity with Israelites.[151] The synonymous parallelism in Zeph 1:11 favors this derived meaning. The corresponding phrase, literally, "all (those) weighing out [or perhaps, "weighed down by] silver,"[152] describes merchants.

---

under categories 2a and 2b. Zephaniah 1:11 is the only passage where דָּמָה and כָּרַת appear in parallelism.

[148] Note NIV, "market district." See Berlin, *Zephaniah*, 87; Roberts, *Zephaniah*, 180; Patterson, *Zephaniah*, 317–18; Sweeney, *Zephaniah*, 90.

[149] Robertson, *Zephaniah*, 279. Renz (*Zephaniah*, 497–98) agrees, explaining that all the city's residents should mourn "the end of trade."

[150] See Ben Zvi, *Zephaniah*, 106–7; Renz, *Zephaniah*, 483 (n. m).

[151] Robertson, *Zephaniah*, 279.

[152] Renz, *Zephaniah*, 483 (n.m.), 500.

1:12–13 This next section of the speech begins, like verse 10, with a temporal indicator, in this case *wəhāyâ bāʿēt hah(h)îʾ*, literally, "and it will be in that time." This is the only place in the OT where this introductory formula occurs.[153] Returning to predictive discourse,[154] the Lord announces he will "search Jerusalem with lamps and punish those who settle down comfortably." The verb translated "search" appears in the *piel* stem, drawing attention to the thorough nature of the search.[155] The verb is used in this stem elsewhere of Laban's search for his idols among Rachel's baggage (Gen 31:44), Joseph's servant's search for the silver cup in the sacks of Joseph's brothers (Gen 44:12), Saul's proposed search to track down David (1 Sam 23:23), Ben Hadad's demand he be allowed to search Ahab's palace (1 Kgs 20:6), Jehu's command to the servants of Baal that they search their temple to make sure only Baal's servants are present (2 Kgs 10:23), the psalmist's soul-searching during the night (Ps 77:6[7]), and the Lord's worldwide search for his enemies (Amos 9:3). By using this form in Zeph 1:12, the Lord emphasizes he will hunt down sinners within the city. The addition of "with lamps" lends further emphasis.[156] Sinners will not be able to hide from the Lord in dark places. This may even anticipate verse 15, where the day of the Lord is described as "a day of darkness and gloom."

For the third time in this speech the Lord says he will "punish" the object of his judgment (cf. vv. 8–9). He specifies the object as "those who settle down comfortably." CSB's translation is an interpretive paraphrase of the Hebrew, which reads literally, "who thicken on their dregs" (see CSB margin).

The metaphor comes from wine making. Clark explains: As the wine fermented, "sediment known as lees would gradually settle at the bottom" of the jar or wineskin. Typically, the wine would then

---

[153] The formula with וַיְהִי, "and it was" (rather than וְהָיָה, "and it will be"), when used with "in that time," introduces a new narrative unit three times (Gen 21:22; 38:1; 1 Kgs 11:29). The phrase "in that time," without "and it was," occurs often (see, for example, Zeph 3:19–20).

[154] Note the first-person singular imperfect form ("I will search"), followed by the *weqatal* form ("and I will punish").

[155] The *piel* probably has a reiterative function. The *qal* stem is used four times in the Old Testament (Ps 64:6 [Hb. v. 7]; Prov 2:4; 20:27; Lam 3:40), while the *piel* appears eight times (Gen 31:35; 44:12; 1 Sam 23:23; 1 Kgs 20:6; 2 Kgs 10:23; Ps 77:6 [Hb. v. 7]; Amos 9:3; Zeph 1:12). The distinction is not a thorough search (*piel*), as opposed to a superficial one (*qal*). Rather, the *qal* simply states the fact, while the *piel* is rhetorical, drawing attention to the thorough nature of the search.

[156] Roberts, *Zephaniah*, 180; Motyer, "Zephaniah," 921; Renz, *Zephaniah*, 501.

be separated and "poured into another jar or skin." However, "if this was not done, the wine would become too sweet and thick and spoil." According to Clark, this is the background for the metaphor in verse 12, where the men thickening on their lees (or dregs) "have become spoiled and deserve the displeasure of the Lord."[157] Not everyone is convinced spoiled wine is in view. Some prefer to see the metaphor as describing the process of fermenting wine. In this case, the main point is inactivity that leads to complacency, which appears to be the case in Jer 48:11.[158] Wine was sometimes allowed to age on its dregs and then strained before use (cf. Isa 25:6).[159]

The reality behind the metaphor follows. Those who thicken on their dregs are identified as those "who say to themselves [lit., "in their heart"]: The Lord will do nothing—good or bad."[160] They were practical atheists.[161] While they acknowledged the Lord's existence, they denied his just character and were convinced he would not intervene to bless or judge. They were content to enjoy their prosperity (cf. v. 13), which was achieved through dishonest means (v. 9). Roberts states,

> They had been secure so long in their wealth, despite their means of attaining it, that they no longer took seriously any thought that Yahweh might affect the outcome of business or politics. They were self-sufficient, self-made men, and God was no factor in their calculations (cf. James 4:13–17).[162]

The quotation of their words reads literally, "The Lord does not do good, and he does not do bad."[163] The two verb forms (*hiphil* of

---

[157] David J. Clark, "Wine on the Lees (Zeph 1.12 and Jer 48:11)," *The Bible Translator* 32, no. 2 (1981): 241. See also Berlin, *Zephaniah*, 87–88; James Nogalski, *The Book of the Twelve: Micah-Malachi*, SHBC (Macon, GA: Smyth & Helwys, 2011), 720.

[158] See Ben Zvi, *Zephaniah*, 111, and Roberts, *Zephaniah*, 180–81.

[159] The form שְׁמָרִים means "dregs of wine," which by metonymy refers to aged wine (*HALOT*, 1585). However, after a detailed analysis of the term, Barker concludes that it refers to excellent wine that is contrasted with dregs-filled wine. See William D. Barker, *Isaiah's Kingship Polemic: An Exegetical Study of Isaiah 24–27*, Forschungen zum Alten Testament II:70 (Tubingen: Mohr Siebeck, 2014), 79–84. The modifier מְזֻקָּקִים, from זָקַק, "to filter," describes the aged wine as "filtered clear . . . of sediments." See Roberts, *First Isaiah*, 322.

[160] The substantival participle "those who say" is appositional to "the men who thicken," equating the two.

[161] Motyer, "Zephaniah," 921; King, "The Day of the Lord in Zephaniah," 20.

[162] Roberts, *Zephaniah*, 180–81.

[163] The imperfect verbal forms can be translated as present or future. In either case, they refer to typical behavior. Both verbs are in the *hiphil* stem, which has an exhibitive function in

yāṭab, "be good," and of *rāʿaʿ*, "be bad") appear together in the *hiphil* stem in only six other texts. In three texts they are used of humans in a moral sense (Lev 5:4; Jer 4:22; 13:23). In two cases they are used of the pagan gods' inability to do good or bad (Isa 41:23; Jer 10:5). Only in Josh 24:20 is the combination used in reference to the Lord. There we read, "If you abandon the LORD and worship foreign gods, he will turn against you, harm [*hiphil* of *rāʿaʿ*, "be bad"] you, and completely destroy you, after he has been good [*hiphil* of *yāṭab*, "be good,"] to you." This verse makes clear the Lord is capable of both actions, causing harm and doing good. The *hiphil* stem of both verbs can have a moral sense in some contexts, but this need not be the case. The *hiphil* of *rāʿaʿ* can mean "do evil," but it can also have the nuance, "do harm, injure, hurt," which is the preferred meaning when God is subject, as in Zeph 1:12. The NET translation reflects the meaning nicely: "The LORD neither rewards nor punishes."

In verse 13 the Lord's announcement of judgment shifts from a declaration he will intervene to a description of the results of his intervention.[164] The group described in verse 12 will lose their wealth, which will become[165] plunder for others, while their houses become a desolate ruin. They will build houses but not live in them. They will plant vineyards but not enjoy the fruit of their labors. The judgment, which was realized when Nebuchadnezzar invaded the city (2 Kgs 25:9), would be appropriate because the preceding context (v. 9) indicates their wealth was accumulated through violence and deceit.

The second half of the verse presents a chronological and logical difficulty. If their wealth is plundered and their houses destroyed, as announced in the first half of the verse, then how will they build houses and plant vineyards? Perhaps the second half of the verse envisions a time of rebuilding after an initial judgment, followed by a second wave of judgment. However, this is not what happened when the Babylonians invaded (2 Kgs 25). The statements in verse 13b may reflect formulaic curses associated with the Mosaic covenant (cf. Deut

---

both cases: "The Lord does not act well, and he does not act badly." See Paul Joüon and T. Muraoka, *A Grammar of Biblical Hebrew* (Rome: Pontifical Biblical Institute, 2000), 163, par. 54d. They call this use of the stem "adverbial," referring to a "mode of action."

[164] Sweeney, *Zephaniah*, 95; Floyd, *Minor Prophets,* 196.

[165] Note the idiom הָיָה with the preposition -לְ, "to become."

28:30, 39; Amos 5:11; Mic 6:15), sometimes labeled "futility curses."[166] In reality, the house building and vineyard planting had in some cases already occurred or, in other cases, was underway or would soon commence prior to the judgment announced in verse 13a. The *weqatal* verb forms (lit., "they will build . . . And they will plant"), which are typical of predictive discourse, most likely refer to future activities that would occur prior to the announced judgment. The verbs may be viewed as future perfective and translated this way: "And they will have built houses but will not live (in them), and they will have planted vineyards but will not drink their wine." In this scenario, the verbs "they will not live . . . and will not drink" describe the aftermath of the judgment depicted in verse 13a.

1.2.2 A Day of Devastation for the World (1:14–18)

The approaching day of the Lord will bring devastation and ruin on a widespread scale against those who have sinned against him. Their wealth will not protect them from his fiery wrath.

This subunit begins with an announcement of the approaching day of the Lord (v. 14) that is accompanied by a detailed characterization of this day (vv. 15–16). A formal judgment speech follows, including an announcement by the Lord of his intervention, a description of the results of judgment, the formal basis (*kî*, "because") for judgment, and a detailed elaboration on the results of judgment (v. 17). The concluding verse highlights the inescapability of judgment "on the day of the LORD's wrath" (v. 18) and ends with a reference to the Lord's intervention (v. 18b).

The arrangement of the word "day" in verses 14–18 is noteworthy:

1:14a "the great **day** of the LORD"
1:14b "the **day** of the LORD"

1:15a "a **day** of wrath is that **day**"
1:15b "a **day** of trouble and distress"
1:15b "a **day** of destruction and desolation"

---

[166] See Ben Zvi, *Zephaniah*, 115–16; and Renz, *Zephaniah*, 504, who prefers to call the statements "proverbial motifs." For a study of the use of this curse in biblical texts, with a focus on the eighth-seventh centuries BC, see Jeremy D. Smoak, "Building Houses and Planting Vineyards: The Early Inner-Biblical Discourse on an Ancient Israelite Wartime Curse," *JBL* 127, 1 (2008): 19–35.

1:15b “a **day** of darkness and gloom”
1:15b “a **day** of clouds and total darkness”
1:16a “a **day** of ram’s horn and battle cry”

1:18a “the **day** of the wrath of the LORD”

“Day” appears twice with “the LORD” as a following genitive in verse 14. It then occurs seven times in verses 15–16 without “the LORD” after it. Renz observes that this “sevenfold use . . . suggests completeness, stressing the totality as well as the devastating impact of the destruction.”[167] The final appearance of “day” in verse 18 rounds off this unit of the speech in two ways. (1) By referring to the day as one of wrath (*ʿebrāh*), it forms a link with verse 15a. (2) By including “the LORD,” it forms a link with 1:14. In this way it signals closure for verses 14–18 as a unit.

1.2.2.1 DEVASTATION FOR THE PROUD (1:14–16)

The approaching day of the Lord will bring the bitterness of war. The Lord will direct his anger against human pride and the fortifications that symbolize it. Trouble, destruction, darkness, and the sounds of battle will characterize this day.

1:14–16. Zephaniah returns to the opening theme of this speech—the nearness of the day of the LORD (v. 7). In fact, he uses *qārôb*, “near,” twice to emphasize the point. The prophet characterizes the coming day as “great” and as “rapidly approaching,”[168] once more drawing attention to its imminence.[169]

The poetic structure and syntax of the second half of verse 14 require comment. CSB follows the traditional accentuation, which takes *mar*, “bitter,” with what follows: “Listen, the day of the LORD—then the warrior’s cry is bitter.” In this case, *qôl*, “sound,” is understood as an exclamation, in the sense of “listen,”[170] and “bitter” describes the warrior’s cry. Another option is to combine *mar* with what precedes: “The sound of the day of the LORD is bitter; the mighty man cries

---

[167] Renz, *Zephaniah*, 506.

[168] The form מַהֵר is best understood as a *piel* infinitive functioning, like קָרוֹב, “near,” as a predicate. The following מְאֹד is adverbial. Lit., verse 14a reads like this: “The great day of the LORD (is) near; (it is) near and (is a) quickly hurrying (day).”

[169] See Wendland (“The Drama of Zephaniah,” 34–35), who calls this “heightening.”

[170] See *HALOT,* 1085, category 8.b; Motyer, “Zephaniah,” 916; Patterson, *Zephaniah*, 326; Ben Zvi, *Zephaniah*, 118.

aloud there" (ESV, cf. NET, NIV11). In this case *mar* characterizes the day and describes its impact on those experiencing its judgment. Since the adverb *šām*, "there," refers to the day of the Lord, it is best translated in a temporal sense here: "then, at that time."[171] The verb *ṣōrēaḥ*, "cries out," is used only here and in Isa 42:13, where it describes the Lord's battle cry. He is compared to a mighty warrior who "roars aloud." In Zeph 1:14 a warrior's battle cry is probably in view if "bitter" goes with the preceding line.[172] If "bitter" modifies the cry adverbially, it could refer to a defeated warrior's bitter cry of lamentation.[173] However, if the Lord is the warrior (as in Zeph 3:17), then it is used of the negative impact of his battle cry on the objects of his judgment.[174]

The description of the day continues in verses 15–16. The initial statement in verse 15, "That day is [or perhaps, "will be"] a day of wrath," characterizes the day of the Lord (v. 14). The noun translated "wrath" (*ʿebrâ*) is used several times in the prophets of the Lord's anger revealed in judgment.[175] Verse 18, which speaks of "the day of the LORD's wrath" (*yôm ʿebrat yhwh*), gives a vivid description of this angry judgment (see discussion below). As K.-D. Schunck points out, "Yahweh's wrath . . . is always a reaction to false human behavior that runs counter to Yahweh's revealed will; as such, it is commensurate with Yahweh's holiness, majesty, and power."[176]

Following the initial statement of verse 15, the word "day" (*yôm*) occurs five more times in verses 15–16, in each case before a compound genitive consisting of two closely associated nouns that form a hendiadys:[177]

1. "a day of trouble and distress." The expression "day of trouble" (*yôm ṣārâ*) occurs fifteen times in the OT. It refers generally

---

[171] See NET; *HALOT,* 1546, category 2; Berlin, *Zephaniah*, 89; Ben Zvi, *Zephaniah*, 120; Motyer, "Zephaniah," 922; Renz, *Zephaniah*, 484 (note x).

[172] Ben Zvi, *Zephaniah*, 120–21, in contrast to Robertson, *Zephaniah*, 282, and Roberts, *Zephaniah*, 184.

[173] See the Akkadian cognate, cf. *HALOT,* 1055, as well as Patterson, *Zephaniah*, 322.

[174] Renz (*Zephaniah*, 505) takes מַר with the second line and understands it as referring to the Lord's fierce battle cry. See as well Motyer, "Zephaniah," 923.

[175] See *HALOT*, 782; *TDOT*, 10:428–30.

[176] *TDOT*, 10:430.

[177] See Rosmari Lillas, *Hendiadys in the Hebrew Bible* (Gothenburg: University of Gothenburg, 2012), 519–20. She lists four of the five pairs as examples of hendiadys.

to a time of trouble and danger that can be life-threatening.[178] Typically, the Lord is a refuge for his people in such times (Nah 1:7), but this will not be the case on the day of the Lord, when he brings trouble upon them. The accompanying synonym "distress" (*məṣûqâ*) occurs elsewhere with "trouble" (*ṣārâ*) only once (Ps 25:17).[179] Ironically, the Lord delivered his people from their "distress" throughout their history in response to their cry for help (Pss 107:6, 13, 19, 28), but on the day of the Lord, he will bring distress upon them. By pairing the synonyms, the prophet draws attention to the coming calamity and the intensity of the trouble/distress that will characterize it.

2. "A day of destruction and desolation": This phrase is unique to Zephaniah. Neither noun occurs with "day" elsewhere.[180] The words "destruction" (*šōʾâ*) and "desolation" (*məšôʾâ*) are joined in Job 30:3 and 38:27, where they describe a "desolate/ parched wasteland" that is uninhabited. The word *šōʾâ* is associated with a storm in some texts, as it is here (cf. Prov 1:27; Ezek 38:9). It is used of destruction in a more generic sense in several texts.[181] The pairing of these nouns, both of which are related to the verb *šāʾâ*, "be desolate," emphasizes the degree of destruction.
3. "A day of darkness and gloom": The expression (*yôm ḥōšek waʾăpēlâ*) also appears in Joel 2:2 in a description of the day of the Lord.[182] They appear in a construct relationship in Exod 10:22, describing the "thick darkness" that engulfed Egypt in conjunction with the ninth plague. They occur in poetic parallelism and are contrasted with light in Isa 58:10 and 59:9. Once more synonyms, in this case "darkness" (*ḥōšek*) and "gloom" (*ʾăpēlâ*), are paired for rhetorical effect, drawing attention to the extreme darkness.

---

[178] Gen 35:3; 2 Kgs 19:3; Pss 20:2; 50:15; 77:2 [Hb. v. 3]; 86:7; Prov 24:10; 25:19; Isa 37:3; Jer 16:19; Obad 12, 14; Nah 1:7; Hab 3:16; Zeph 1:15.

[179] The term is associated with צַר, "trouble," in Job 15:24; Pss 107:6, 13, 19, 28; 119:143.

[180] In Isa 10:3 שׁוֹאָה, translated "devastation" in CSB, occurs parallel to יוֹם פְּקֻדָּה, "day of punishment."

[181] Job 30:14; Pss 35:8; 63:9 [Hb. v. 10]; Prov 3:25; Isa 10:3; 47:11. The plural of מְשׁוֹאָה may refer to the ruins of a city in Ps 74:3, if the consonantal text is revocalized as מְשֹׁאוֹת (*HALOT*, 643).

[182] The phrase "day of darkness" occurs in Job 15:23.

4. “A day of clouds and total darkness”: This expression (*yôm ʿānān waʿărāpel*) also appears in Ezek 34:12 and Joel 2:2.[183] In addition to these three texts where they are joined after “day,” the words “clouds and total darkness” (*ʿānān waʿărāpel*) are also joined in Deut 4:11; 5:22 (both with the article in this case); and Ps 97:2. They occur in poetic parallelism in Job 38:9.
5. “A day of ram’s horn and battle cry”: This phrase is unique to Zephaniah.[184] The nouns translated “ram’s horn” (*šôpār*) and “battle cry” (*tərûʿâ*) are joined by *waw*, “and,” only here, but they are closely associated in several texts,[185] five times in a context of war.[186]

It is noteworthy four of the terms used in the last three of the five pairs appear in the accounts of the Sinai theophany (*ḥōšek*, “darkness,” *ʿānān*, “cloud,” *ʿărāpel*, “total darkness,” *šôpār*, “ram’s horn”), as well as “fire,” which is mentioned in Zeph 1:18.[187] All four terms appear in Deut 5:22–23. The awesome God who appeared in the dark clouds and fire at Sinai and commanded Israel to obey his commandments appears on the day of the Lord in the dark clouds and fire to judge those who had convinced themselves that he does not hold people accountable for their behavior (see Zeph 1:12).

Specifically, this judgment on the day of wrath (v. 15) is directed “against the fortified cities [*heʿārîm habbəṣūrôt*], and against the high corner towers [*happinnôt haggəbōhôt*]” (v. 16). “Fortified cities” are mentioned twenty times in the OT. The earliest references are to the

---

[183] The phrase יוֹם עָנָן, lit., “day of a cloud,” occurs in Ezek 30:3.

[184] The phrase יוֹם תְּרוּעָה, “day of trumpet blasts,” occurs in Num 29:1.

[185] Lev 25:9; Josh 6:5, 20; 2 Sam 6:15; 1 Chr 15:28; 2 Chr 15:14; Job 39:25; Ps 47:5 [Hb. v. 6]; Jer 4:19; Amos 2:2.

[186] Josh 6:5: “When there is a prolonged blast of the horn and you hear its sound (קוֹל שׁוֹפָר), have all the troops give a mighty shout (תְּרוּעָה).”
Josh 6:20: “So the troops shouted, and the rams’ horns sounded. When they heard the blast of the ram’s horn (קוֹל שׁוֹפָר), the troops gave a great shout (תְּרוּעָה), and the wall collapsed.”
Job 39:25: “When the ram’s horn (שׁוֹפָר) blasts, he snorts defiantly. He smells the battle from a distance; he hears the officers’ shouts and the battle cry (תְּרוּעָה).”
Jer 4:19: “My heart pounds; I cannot be silent. For you, my soul, have heard the sound of the ram’s horn (קוֹל שׁוֹפָר)—the shout (תְּרוּעָה < תְּרוּעַת) of battle.”
Amos 2:2: “Moab will die with a tumult, with shouting (תְּרוּעָה) and the sound of the ram’s horn (קוֹל שׁוֹפָר).”

[187] See Exod 19:9, 16, 18–19; 20:18, 21; Deut 4:11–12, 15, 33; 5:4–5, 22–26. On the connection to the Deuteronomic portrayal of the Sinai theophany, see King, “The Day of the Lord in Zephaniah,” 27.

Canaanite cities Israel was to conquer (Num 13:28; Deut 1:28; 3:5; 9:1; Josh 14:12).[188] Israel captured these cities (Neh 9:25) because the Lord is sovereign over all fortified cities (2 Kgs 19:25 [= Isa 37:26]; Isa 25:2). Judah built fortified cities (Hos 8:14), thinking they would provide security and protection; but on the day of the Lord destruction would overtake them, along with the high corner towers that symbolized the people's pride.[189] The word translated "high" (*gābōah*), used here of the physical height of the corner towers, refers in Isa 5:15 to proud people who are brought low by the Lord's judgment. In Isa 2:15 the words "high" (*gābōah*) and "fortified" (*bəṣûrâ*) are used of a tower and wall, respectively. As symbols of human pride (cf. 2:17) they will be brought low on the day of the Lord (2:12).

1.2.2.2 Devastation for Sinners (1:17–18)

The Lord will intervene in judgment against those who have sinned against him. The results will be devastating and inescapable.

1:17–18 The Lord speaks once more in verse 17. (Note the first-person verb in "I will bring distress," the first such form since v. 12.) The first half of the verse takes the form of a judgment speech. There is an announcement of judgment containing a first-person declaration of the Lord's intervention ("I will bring distress on mankind") and a description of its results ("and they will walk like the blind"). The basis for judgment follows: "because [*kî*] they have sinned against the Lord."

The verb translated "I will bring distress" (*wahăṣērōtî*), from the root *ṣārar*, conveys the literal idea of "cause to be cramped, restricted."[190] It is used of besieging a city in Deut 28:52; 1 Kgs 8:37; and 2 Chr 6:28. At other times it is used in an abstract sense of causing distress and suffering, as in verse 17 (2 Chr 28:20, 22; 33:12; Neh 9:27; Jer 10:18). The noun *ṣārâ*, "trouble" (translated "distress" in NIV11, ESV, and others), used of the day of the Lord in verse 15, is related to this verb.

---

[188] Sweeney (*Zephaniah*, 101) sees ironic reversal in Zeph 1:16: "Judah has taken the role played by Canaan in the time of Joshua."

[189] See Zeph 3:6 as well. Patterson (*Zephaniah*, 324, n. 68) aptly observes, "The synecdoche of citing towns and towers for the devastation of all cities and lands is an effective one. If the strongest defenses will collapse, everything will be laid waste."

[190] *HALOT*, 1058.

The recipient of this distress is identified as "mankind" (*ʾādām*).[191] Does the word refer to the people of Jerusalem or to the people of the world (humankind)? The sinners of Judah and Jerusalem have been the focus of verses 4–16, but in verses 17–18 the judgment broadens in scope to include the world. Nevertheless, this worldwide day of the Lord still includes Judah. The only other appearance of the word "mankind" (*ʾādām*) in Zephaniah is in 1:3, where it refers twice to humankind in the context of a cosmic, flood-like judgment that reverses creation. Judgment sweeps humankind from upon the face of the earth along with "animals . . . the birds of the sky and the fish of the sea." This broader referent is likely in view here in verse 17. Of course, the sinners of Judah and Jerusalem would be part of this group as the special target of divine judgment (see vv. 4–6). This is implied by the inclusion of the covenantal name (Yahweh) in the accompanying accusation.

The Lord's intervention in judgment will leave the objects of judgment helpless. To use the Lord's own metaphor, "they will walk like the blind [*ʿiwrîm*]," lost in a world of darkness as they stumble around, groping and feeling their way along until they fall (cf. Deut 28:29; Isa 59:10; Lam 4:14). There may be an allusion to or at least an echo of the curse in Deut 28:29, where the objects of the Lord's judgment grope "as a blind person [*ʿiwwēr*] gropes in the dark."[192] The word translated "dark" is the same term used in Zeph 1:15 (*ʾăpēlâ*, "gloom").

The basis for the Lord's judgment is stated in a straightforward manner: "because they have sinned against the Lord." The expression "sinned against the Lord" (*ḥāṭāʾ lyhwh*) is used several times in the OT,[193] but it is rare for the Lord's name to precede the verb as in verse 17 (cf. 1 Sam 2:25; Jer 3:25; 50:14). The word order highlights the one who has been offended rather than the offensive act.[194]

This is the third time in this chapter the Lord refers to himself in the third person for rhetorical reasons (vv. 5–6, 8). As noted above, in verses 5–6 the technique makes the Lord's accusation more objective

---

[191] The recipient is introduced by the preposition -לְ, "to." This is also the case in the other instances where the *hiphil* of צָרַר occurs (Deut 28:52; 1 Kgs 8:37; 2 Chr 6:28; 28:20, 22; 33:12; Neh 9:27; Jer 10:18), except for the substantival participle in Jer 48:41 and 49:22.

[192] King, "The Day of the Lord in Zephaniah," 28.

[193] Exod 10:16; Num 32:23; Deut 1:41; Josh 7:20; 1 Sam 7:6; 12:23; 14:34; 2 Sam 12:13; 2 Kgs 17:7; Jer 8:14; 16:10; 40:3; 44:23; 50:7.

[194] In this regard, see Renz, *Zephaniah*, 509.

and formal in tone. Using the first person would focus on personal offense and injury; but by using the third person, the Lord speaks more as prosecutor than defendant and assumes the point of view of those hearing his case and his verdict against the guilty party. In verse 8 using the third person highlights this sacrifice as orchestrated by *the Lord*, Judah's covenant God whose day of powerful intervention is near. In verse 17 the third person functions similarly. The Lord is coming in judgment because people have had the audacity to sin against *the Lord*. As noted above, this suggests the people of Jerusalem and Judah are still in view and included within the larger *ʾādām*, "mankind."

Verse 17b expands on the results of the Lord's intervention in vivid terms: The sinners' "blood will be poured out like dust and their flesh like dung." It is not clear if the Lord is still speaking or the prophet is responding to the Lord's announcement. In the Hebrew text *waw*, "and," is prefixed to the clause *wəšuppak dāmām keʿāpār*, "[and] their blood will be poured out like dust," suggesting this clause is a continuation of the Lord's words in verse 17a.

The image of blood (*dām*) being poured out (*šāpak*) is common in the Old Testament. "Dust" (*ʿāpār*, better as "dirt") is used with "pour out" once (Lev 14:41), so it is surprising to see dust in the simile. Nevertheless, the usage in Lev 14:41 is instructive, where Israelites are commanded to scrape the "plaster" (*ʿāpār*) off a contaminated wall and to dump it outside the city. One envisions a container being filled with the debris from the wall. If blood is disposed of in this way, it indicates a significant volume of bloodshed. There may also be an implication the blood in this case lacks value.[195]

The word translated "flesh" (*ləḥûm*) is used only here and in Job 20:23, where it refers to the flesh of the body.[196] The proposed meaning makes sense in Zeph 1:17, given the parallelism with "blood" and the existence of an Arabic cognate.[197] In this case the comparison is to "dung" (*gəlālîm*). Since the verb "poured out" is understood by ellipsis in this poetic line, one envisions a large quantity of dung being swept

---

[195] In this regard see Roberts (*Zephaniah*, 185), who speaks of their blood being "as worthless as dust." Likewise, Patterson (*Zephaniah*, 324) states, "Human life (flesh and blood) is thus reduced to a thing of no value, with even corpses being treated as despicable refuse."

[196] However, some emend the form to read, "while he is eating" (see CSB), which makes sense in this context (cf. "when he fills his stomach" at the beginning of the verse).

[197] *HALOT*, 525.

up and loaded in a container and dumped out in an appropriate location, probably to be burned. This explains why "dung" is used in the plural here, indicating a large quantity. The word appears in only one other passage, 1 Kgs 14:10, which speaks of burning (from the verb *bāʿar*; CSB reads "sweep away") dung [*gālāl*, singular] until it is gone. This may suggest burning up a pile of dung (hence the singular form of the noun) after it has been collected and disposed of. Regardless, the comparison to dung indicates that flesh in this case is expendable.

As noted above, it is unclear if the Lord or the prophet is speaking in verse 17b. Nevertheless, it is apparent the prophet is the speaker in verse 18. The third-person reference to the Lord (note "the day of the LORD's wrath") by itself does not rule out the possibility the Lord is still speaking (see vv. 5–6, 8, 17, where the Lord uses his own name when speaking). However, two more third-person references follow. Furthermore, the clauses containing these third-person references are linked:

> "Their silver and their gold will be unable to rescue them on the day of the LORD's wrath,
>
> [**and: note *waw***] the whole earth will be consumed by the fire of *his* jealousy,
>
> **for** *he* will make a complete, yes, a horrifying end of all the inhabitants of the earth."

The prophet reiterates the devastation described in verse 17b will be inescapable (v. 18a).[198] Even the wealth of sinners in the form of silver and gold will be unable to rescue them[199] on the day of the Lord's wrath.[200] While "silver and gold" refers to the riches of the wealthy (cf. v. 13), Ball suggests the statement could reflect "the hope that silver and gold paid in tribute could save them from their enemies" (cf. Isa 13:17).[201] If so, the prophet makes clear that the Lord cannot be bought off.[202]

---

[198] See Sweeney, *Zephaniah,* 104.

[199] The juxtaposition of גַּם . . . גַּם followed by the negative particle is best translated "neither . . . nor" (*HALOT*, 196; GKC, 500, par. 162b).

[200] An almost identical statement appears in Ezek 7:19. For a discussion of the meaning of עֶבְרָה, "wrath," see verse 15 above.

[201] Ball, *Zephaniah,* 91.

[202] Robertson, *Zephaniah,* 286.

The Lord's fiery judgment will devour all the earth. Fire, one of the most destructive forces known to humankind, was especially formidable in ancient times before modern firefighting techniques were developed. Fire is particularly untamable when it emanates from the Lord. The initial fulfillment of the prophecy came when the Babylonians destroyed Jerusalem with fire.[203]

The Hebrew word *qinʾâ*, translated "jealousy" here, requires comment. On several occasions the OT affirms the Lord God of Israel is a jealous God. In Exod 34:14 he says this of himself: "The Lord is jealous for his reputation. . . . He is a jealous God" (lit., "The Lord, whose name is Jealous, is a jealous God" (cf. Exod 20:5; Deut 4:24; 5:9; 6:15). In what sense is God "jealous"?

A survey of the semantic field of the Hebrew root (*qnʾ*) in its nominal (*qinʾāh*), verbal (*qinnēʾ*), and adjectival (*qannāʾ*, and *qannôʾ*) forms, especially as applied to God, reveals the following shades of meaning.

1. In the Pentateuch God's "jealousy" is primarily his passionate desire and demand for his people's allegiance that arises from the covenantal relationship binding him to Israel. The adjectival forms clearly have this sense in Exod 20:5 (= Deut 5:9); 34:14; Deut 4:24; 6:15; and Josh 24:19, where they appear in motivating statements attached to prohibitions against worshipping other gods.

2. When this demand is violated, God becomes angry and acts against those who are unfaithful. In Deut 29:20 the noun refers metonymically to the response (jealous anger) that God's violated demand for loyalty produces. The word is used in a similar sense in Ezek 8:3, 5, which refer to the "offensive statue," the "idol of jealousy," which when worshipped by God's unfaithful people, rouses his jealous anger and results in judgment. The word carries this same force in Ezek 16:38, 42, where Jerusalem is compared to an adulteress whose unfaithfulness has roused her husband's jealous anger and desire for vengeance. (Note that the noun is used of a husband's jealousy for his wife in Num 5:14, 30 and Prov 6:34.) See also Ps 79:5; Ezek 5:13; 23:25.

3. In several prophetic texts the noun and in one case an adjective refers to God's anger against proud and hostile nations that moves him to judge and destroy. In some cases, this anger is motivated by a desire for vengeance (see Isa 59:17–18; Nah 1:2). In most instances

[203] Lam 1:13; 2:3–4; 4:11; see Robertson, *Zephaniah,* 286–87.

God is depicted as a warrior eager for battle (see Isa 42:13; 59:17; Ezek 36:5–6; 38:19; Nah 1:2).

4. In some prophetic texts God's "jealousy" is his intense love for and commitment to his people, which move him to show compassion (Joel 2:18; cf. Isa 63:15), to seek reconciliation (Zech 8:2), to restore (Isa 9:7; 37:32), and to protect/vindicate (Isa 26:11; Zech 1:14). This same semantic sense of intense love and commitment appears in Ezek 39:25, which speaks of God's "jealousy" for his own name. The noun has a similar sense in Song 8:6, where it is used of human love.

God's "jealousy" is better understood as "zeal." This divine character quality reflects his great love for his people and his desire to have a lasting and intimate relationship with them. God cares enough about his relationship with his people to act decisively when it is threatened and to seek reconciliation when the decisive punishment has had its intended effect. His zeal also moves him to vindicate and avenge his people when they have suffered at the hands of cruel oppressors, and it guarantees that hostile nations will not overrun God's world and turn it into chaos.

The noun *qinʾāh* occurs twice in Zephaniah. The use of the term in Zeph 3:8, where God's judgment upon the nations is in view, fits best under the third category above. In 1:18 the immediate context does not as clearly indicate that worldwide judgment is in view. A decision depends in part on how one understands the referent of "the whole earth" (*kol hāʾāreṣ*).

The noun *ʾereṣ*, "earth, land," occurs eight times in Zephaniah:

1:18 "The whole **earth** will be consumed by the fire of his jealousy, for he will make a complete, yes, a horrifying end of all the inhabitants of the **earth**."

2:3 "Seek the Lord, all you humble of the **earth**, who carry out what he commands."

2:5 "The word of the Lord is against you, Canaan, **land** of the Philistines."

2:11 "When he starves all the gods of the **earth.**"

3:8 "For the whole **earth** will be consumed by the fire of my jealousy."

3:19 "I will make those who were disgraced throughout the **earth** receive praise and fame."

3:20 "I will give you fame and praise among all the peoples of the **earth.**"

The referent of "humble" of the earth/land in 2:3 is ambiguous. The prophet addresses "an undesirable nation" (Judah) in 2:1 yet refers to various nations in 2:4–15. The word has a local sense ("land") in 2:5, where it refers specifically to the "land of the Philistines." The referent is worldwide ("earth") in (1), 2:11, where "all the gods of the earth" are mentioned in connection with "the distant coasts and islands of the nations;" (2) 3:8 where the Lord judges "nations" and "kingdoms;" and (3) 3:19–20 where Israel's exiles throughout the earth are in view and the "peoples of the earth" are mentioned.

As for 1:18, the judgment of the day of the Lord encompasses all of Judah, so one could translate "all the land" and "all the inhabitants of the land" (note "all the residents of Jerusalem" in v. 4).[204] Nevertheless when one correlates 1:14–18 with 1:2–3, which describe a flood-like judgment that reverses creation and sweeps away everything (note *kōl* in v. 2; cf. v. 18), including humankind (*ʾādām*; v. 3; cf. v. 17), one can understand the phrases as broader in scope ("the whole earth" and "all the inhabitants of the earth").[205] It becomes apparent in 2:4–15 that the coming judgment will destroy nations in the four directions of the compass. This judgment culminates with the scene depicted in 3:8, where *qinʾâ* also appears and, as in 1:18, is associated with fiery judgment. The term *ʾereṣ* is best understood as "world" in 1:18, but this does not mean it refers to the nations in contrast to Judah. The worldwide day of the Lord includes Judah, for ironically the Lord's covenant nation is depicted as proud, hostile, and rebellious.[206]

Consequently, the use of *qinʾâ* in 1:18 as in 3:8 fits well under the third semantic category listed above. Nevertheless, since Judah's idolatry is in view in this chapter (vv. 4–6) and the next chapter denounces "all the gods of the earth" and anticipates a time when "all the distant coasts and islands of the nations will bow down and worship" the Lord (2:11), "jealous anger" also works well for 1:18. The Lord expects his covenantal people and the nations to recognize him as the one true God, and their failure to do so ignites the fire of his jealous anger.

The syntactical structure and meaning of verse 18b require attention: "For he will make a complete, yes, a horrifying end of all the inhabitants of the earth." The opening word *kî*, "for" [or "because"]

---

[204] See Renz, *Zephaniah,* 481, 511.

[205] Robertson, *Zephaniah,* 287.

[206] Ben Zvi (*Zephaniah,* 136) proposes that the ambiguity in 1:18 is intentional and that this is "a sophisticated literary double entendre."

draws a logical connection with the preceding statement ("The whole earth will be consumed by the fire of his jealousy"). The whole earth will be consumed by the fire of the Lord's zeal because he will make the fire so thorough in its impact that it encompasses all the inhabitants of the earth. The noun *kālâ*, "complete destruction,"[207] is an adverbial accusative of product in relation to the verb *yaʿăśeh*, "he will make," which takes a double accusative here.[208] The particle *ʾak* has an emphasizing function that in combination with the following *niphal* participle *nibhālâ*, intensifies *kālâ*.[209] CSB understands the participle to mean "horrifying" (cf. NET/NASB1995, "terrifying,"), relating it to the usual meaning of the verb *bāhal* in the *niphal* stem. However, when used with this meaning, the *niphal* is passive, a nuance that does not fit in Zeph 1:18. It is more likely that the *niphal* has the nuance "sudden," here, like the *niphal* of *bāhal* in Prov 28:22 ("A greedy one is in a hurry for wealth") and Eccl 8:3 ("Do not be in a hurry").[210] The term *kol*, "all," is the direct object of *yaʿăśeh*, "he will make." It takes the accusative sign (*ʾēt*) because of the presence of the article on the last word in the construct chain: *kol yōšebê hāʾāreṣ*, literally: "all of [the] inhabitants of the earth." One may translate verse 18b literally: "For complete destruction, even sudden (destruction), he will make all the inhabitants of the earth."

---

[207] *HALOT*, 477. The noun is related to the verb כָּלָה, "stop, come to an end."

[208] See BDB, 794, II. 1. g. See on the grammatical point GKC, 371, par. 117ii. For other examples of עָשָׂה with a direct object and כָּלָה as the adverbial accusative, see Neh 9:31; Jer 30:11; 46:28; Ezek 11:13; 20:17; Nah 1:8.

[209] *HALOT*, 45.

[210] See the LXX (*spoudēn*, translated by NET as "swift"), NIV/ESV ("sudden"), KJV ("speedy"). For a discussion of the meaning of נִבְהָלָה, see Ben Zvi, *Zephaniah*, 133–34.

SECTION OUTLINE

2 The Lord's Angry Judgment: Devastation Mixed with Glimpses of Hope (2:1–15)
- 2.1 Imminent Devastation Demands Preparation (2:1–3)
- 2.2 Widespread Devastation Has a Surprising Aftermath (2:4–15)
  - 2.2.1 Devastation of the Philistines to the West (2:4–7)
  - 2.2.2 Devastation of Moab and Ammon to the East (2:8–11)
  - 2.2.3 Devastation of Cush to the South (2:12)
  - 2.2.4 Devastation of Assyria to the North (2:13–15)

2 THE LORD'S ANGRY JUDGMENT: DEVASTATION MIXED WITH GLIMPSES OF HOPE (2:1–15)

1 *Gather yourselves together;*
gather together, undesirable nation,
2 *before the decree takes effect*
and the day passes like chaff,
before the burning of the LORD*'s anger overtakes you,*
before the day of the LORD*'s anger overtakes you.*
3 *Seek the* LORD*, all you humble of the earth,*
who carry out what he commands.
Seek righteousness, seek humility;
perhaps you will be concealed
on the day of the LORD*'s anger.*

4 *For Gaza will be abandoned,*
and Ashkelon will become a ruin.
Ashdod will be driven out at noon,
and Ekron will be uprooted.
5 *Woe, inhabitants of the seacoast,*
nation of the Cherethites!
The word of the LORD *is against you,*
Canaan, land of the Philistines:
I will destroy you until there is no one left.
6 *The seacoast will become pasturelands*
with caves for shepherds and pens for sheep.
7 *The coastland will belong*
to the remnant of the house of Judah;

they will find pasture there.
They will lie down in the evening
among the houses of Ashkelon,
for the Lord *their God will return to them*
and restore their fortunes.

8 *I have heard the taunting of Moab*
and the insults of the Ammonites,
who have taunted my people
and threatened their territory.
9 *Therefore, as I live*
—this is the declaration of the Lord *of Armies,*
the God of Israel—Moab will be like Sodom
and the Ammonites like Gomorrah:
a place overgrown with weeds,
a salt pit, and a perpetual wasteland.
The remnant of my people will plunder them;
the remainder of my nation will dispossess them.
10 *This is what they get for their pride,*
because they have taunted and acted arrogantly
against the people of the Lord *of Armies.*
11 *The* Lord *will be terrifying to them*
when he starves all the gods of the earth.
Then all the distant coasts and islands of the nations
will bow in worship to him,
each in its own place.

12 *You Cushites will also be slain by my sword.*

13 *He will also stretch out his hand against the north*
and destroy Assyria;
he will make Nineveh a desolate ruin,
dry as the desert.
14 *Herds will lie down in the middle of it,*
every kind of wild animal.
Both eagle owls and herons
will roost in the capitals of its pillars.
Their calls will sound from the window,
but devastation will be on the threshold,

for he will expose the cedar work.
15 *This is the jubilant city*
that lives in security,
that says to herself:
I exist, and there is no one else.
What a desolation she has become,
a place for wild animals to lie down!
Everyone who passes by her
scoffs and shakes his fist.

The prophet urges the sinful nation to prepare for the day of the Lord's angry judgment. He then tells the obedient humble to maintain their quest for righteousness and humility, for there is a possibility they will be hidden from judgment. It is vital to heed this warning because the coming judgment will devastate nations far and wide, from west to east and south to north.

Chapter two contains two main literary units (2:1–3, 4–15). The first is a two-part exhortation directed first to the "undesirable nation" (Judah) (vv. 1–2) and then to the "humble of the earth, who carry out what [the Lord] commands" (v. 3). The exhortation is supported by (note *kî*, "for" at the beginning of v. 4) a series of judgment announcements against nations to the west (vv. 4–7, Philistia), east (vv. 8–11, Moab and Ammon), south (v. 12, Cush), and north (vv. 13–15, Assyria).

The two-part exhortation is transitional in the structure of the book.[1] The two references to the day of the Lord (vv. 2–3) link the exhortation to the announcement of the impending day of the Lord in 1:7–18. The exhortation forms a suitable conclusion to the judgment announcements of chapter 1. At the same time, it introduces the following oracles of judgment against the nations, as indicated by *kî*, "for" at the beginning of verse 4.[2] In this case the link is not simply a formal grammatical link between verses 3 and 4 but a signal of a conceptual link between the two literary units.[3] In other words, the exhortations demand a response, for the day of the Lord is indeed coming

[1] Nicholas R. Werse, "Reconsidering the Problematic Tripartite Structure of Zephaniah," *ZAW* 130 (4) (2018): 575–76.

[2] Wendland, "The Drama of Zephaniah," 41–42, 60–61.

[3] BDB (474) observes that sometimes כִּי "relates not to the v[erse] which immed[iately] precedes or follows, but to several."

on "the whole earth" and all its inhabitants (1:18), as represented by the nations mentioned in verses 4–15.[4]

Roberts calls the causal link "bogus."[5] He states that "the superficiality of this link is immediately obvious" because verses 4–15 make "no mention of the day of Yahweh" and contain "no judgment against Judah." Furthermore, "there is no integral connection to the preceding composition in 1:2–2:3 at all."[6]

But why should one assume there needs to be a direct reference to the day of the Lord? After all, 1:18 speaks of the "whole earth" (*kol-hāʾāreṣ*) being consumed and "all the inhabitants of the earth" (*kol-yōšebê hāʾāreṣ*) being destroyed. Verses 4–15 (if we accept the link as appropriate for the sake of argument) unpack this with "specificity,"[7] as we read that the Lord will leave the land (*ʾereṣ*) of the Philistines without inhabitants (*mēʾên yôšēb*) (2:5).

Other substantive thematic links with 1:1–2:3 appear in 2:4–15, making clear that the judgment of the nations is the outworking of the day of the Lord. The prophet prays for the Lord to stretch out his hand against the north (that is, Assyria) (2:13), just as he will do against Judah (1:4). The ruin (*šəmāmâ*) caused by the judgment upon Jerusalem (1:13) is replicated in Ashkelon (2:4), Moab and Ammon (2:9), and Nineveh (2:13), as *šəmāmâ* becomes a key word to describe the aftermath of judgment. The arrogance of the residents of Jerusalem is a fundamental reason for their demise (1:12). They say in their heart (note *hāʾōmərîm bilbābām*), "The Lord will do nothing—good or bad." This arrogance is replicated in the proud city of Nineveh, who says in her heart (note *hāʾōmerâ zerāh bilbābâ*), "I exist, and there is no one else" (2:15). The statement epitomizes her pride and is a fundamental reason for her demise.

As for the absence of judgment upon Judah, it is important to see and appreciate the prophet's rhetorical strategy as he moves from judgment to restoration. After describing the devastating judgment the day of the Lord will bring upon Judah and the whole earth, he offers

---

[4] Arguing for a causal link, Sweeney ("Form Criticism of Zephaniah," 397) explains how 2:4–7 supports 2:1–3: "Certainly 2:4 provides a clear example of impending disaster and as such, provides a basis for the exhortation to seek Yhwh in 2:1–3. In other words, the disaster which will overtake the Philistine cities in 2:4 is the motivation for the audience to seek Yhwh, justice, and poverty in v 3 and perhaps to be saved. If they do not, the same fate can befall them."

[5] Roberts, *Zephaniah,* 196.

[6] Roberts, *Zephaniah,* 195.

[7] Floyd, *Minor Prophets,* 216.

a flicker of hope that some may be spared (2:3). As he expands on the devastating worldwide results of judgment, he also begins to develop a secondary theme in 2:7, 9, where he envisions a future for the "remnant" of God's people. He concludes the prophecy with a vision of their restoration; the secondary theme swallows up and replaces the theme of judgment. Even the nations will be reclaimed by the one true God. The prophet introduces this theme in 2:11 and develops it more fully in 3:9–10.[8]

2.1 Imminent Devastation Demands Preparation (2:1–3)

The prophet urges (1) the "undesirable nation" to prepare itself as kindling for the day of the Lord's angry judgment and (2) "the humble of the earth, who carry out what [the Lord] commands" to seek the Lord by seeking righteousness and humility. For the obedient humble there is a possibility they will be hidden from judgment.

The first exhortation consists of two imperatives and a vocative with an embedded accusation (v. 1). It is linked to a series of three temporal clauses introduced by "before" that describe the day for which they must prepare (v. 2). The second exhortation consists of three imperatives urging the obedient humble to seek the Lord, righteousness, and humility. It is followed by a motivating statement that holds out the possibility of escaping the judgment for those who heed the imperatives (v. 3).

In verses 1–2 the prophet addresses the "undesirable nation" (*haggôy lōʾ niksāp*). Though not specifically identified, Judah, the only nation named earlier (1:4), is the referent.[9] The modifying phrase (*lōʾ niksāp*) means "not desired," if the *niphal* verb form is understood as passive.[10] This would reflect the Lord's attitude toward them. However, the verb *kāsap* occurs in four other passages, twice in the *qal* stem and twice in the *niphal* stem. There is no apparent semantic difference between the stems; in each case, the verb means "long for, desire": Gen 31:30 ("because you *long* [*niphal*] for your father's family"); Job 14:15

[8] For more on this subject, see King, "The Remnant in Zephaniah," 414–27.

[9] Wendland and Clark propose that Philistia is the nation in view. Ernst R. Wendland and David J. Clark, "Zephaniah: Anatomy and Physiology of a Dramatic Prophetic Text," *Journal of Translation and Textlinguistics* 16 (2003): 8–9. For a critique of the proposal on syntactical grounds, see Jason S. DeRouchie, "The Addressees in Zephaniah 2:1, 3: Who Should Seek YHWH Together?" *BBR* 30, 2 (2020): 185.

[10] In addition to CSB, see NET ("undesirable nation"), KJV ("nation not desired").

(“you would *long* [*qal*] for the work of your hands”); Ps 17:12 (“they are like a lion *eager* [*qal*] to tear”); Ps 84:2[3](“I *long* [*niphal*] and yearn for the courts of the LORD”).[11] In all four cases the verb is used with the preposition *lə-* introducing the object for which the subject longs. Consistent with usage, one could translate in 2:1, “the nation that does not desire” and assume the object (the Lord/righteousness?) is implied.[12] Nevertheless, the absence of an object could indicate the verb is passive in this case. Because of these difficulties, some prefer to understand the verb as meaning “be ashamed” (as in Aramaic),[13] referring to their lack of shame over their sin.[14]

Addressing the people of the nation (note the plural verbs), the prophet tells them, “Gather yourselves together, gather together.” Both verb forms derive from *qāšaš*,[15] which in turn is derived from the noun *qaš*, “straw, stubble.”[16] The first form (*hitqôšəšû*) is a *hithpoel* imperative, while the second (*qôššû*) is a *qal* imperative.[17] Neither stem is attested for this verb elsewhere. The verb appears six times in the *poel* stem, where it is used of gathering stubble for brickmaking (Exod 5:7, 12) or wood for kindling (Num 15:32–33; 1 Kgs 17:10, 12). The *hithpoel*, understood as reflexive in relation to the *poel*, could mean “gather yourselves together as stubble/kindling.” The nuance of the otherwise unattested *qal* form is uncertain. Possibly it is functionally equivalent to an emphatic infinitive absolute.[18] The *qal* may indicate the purpose or consequence of the previous action:[19] “gather yourselves (as kindling)

---

[11] See *HALOT*, 490; BDB, 493–94.

[12] DeRouchie, “The Addressees in Zephaniah 2:1, 3,” 185–86.

[13] Marcus Jastrow, *A Dictionary of the Targumim, the Talmud Babli and Yerushalmi, and the Midrashic Literature* 2 vols. (Brooklyn: P. Shalom, 1967), 655.

[14] See NIV (“shameful nation”), ESV/NLT (“shameless nation”), NASB (“nation without shame”). For further discussion of the problem, see Ben Zvi, *Zephaniah*, 139–43; Roberts, *Zephaniah*, 187; Renz, *Zephaniah*, 518, n.c.; Ball, *Zephaniah*, 97–98; Sweeney, *Zephaniah*, 115.

[15] For the second verb, some have proposed to remove the *dagesh* from the *shin* and read קוֹשׁוּ from קוֹשׁ, understood to mean “set traps,” or “stoop, bend.” For a summary and critique of these proposals, see Roberts, *Zephaniah*, 186–87.

[16] *HALOT*, 1154.

[17] Ben Zvi (*Zephaniah*, 137) and Sweeney (*Zephaniah*, 114) prefer to understand the second form as a *poel.*

[18] See DHS, 122, par. 88, Rem. 4. Davidson states, “A force akin to that of the inf. abs. is sometimes obtained by repeating the verb in another form. In addition to Zeph 1:18, he cites Ps 118:11 (two *qal* forms of סָבַב); Isa 29:9 (*hithpael* [if emended] and *qal* of תָּמַהּ [if the first form is emended], and *hithpalpel* and *qal* of שָׁעַע); Hab 1:5 (*hithpael* and *qal* of תָּמַהּ).

[19] On this use of the imperative when following another imperative, see GKC, 324–25, par. 110f.

in order to be kindling/so that you will be kindling."[20] In any case, the repetition of the root is rhetorical; the sound-play focuses one's attention and prompts one to think of stubble/kindling. This is significant in relation to the reference to the fire of judgment in the preceding verse. For sinners the command is ominous; it seems they are being told to prepare for their own destruction (cf. 2:2). They are the kindling for the Lord's fiery judgment. This image of fire devouring kindling also fits well with the earlier image of the Lord's sacrifice, where the sinners are the sacrifice. Here they are the kindling for the sacrificial fire.[21] The militant irony of 1:7–8 continues here.

Verse 2 contains three temporal clauses (each introduced by *bəṭerem*, "before") that modify the imperatives of verse 1. In other words, the people should gather themselves as kindling before the events described in verse 2 take place:

1. "Before the decree takes effect and the day passes like chaff."

As it stands, the Hebrew text reads literally, "Before the birthing of a decree, like chaff it passes a day." The form *ledet* is an infinitive construct of the verb *yālad*, "give birth," with *ḥōq*, "decree" following as a genitive.[22] Giving birth is metaphorical here, referring to the time when the "decree" will be implemented and take effect.[23] In this context *ḥōq*, which can refer to a statute, law, or regulation, is the formal pronouncement of judgment associated with the day of the Lord (see 2:2b–3 and 1:7–18).

The comparative statement describes how suddenly the decree, once figuratively given birth, will be realized: "Before the birthing of (the) decree, (which) like chaff will have passed by[24] [that is, be blown

[20] This seems to be the case in Isa 29:9 and Hab 1:5, where the imperative of a reflexive stem is followed by the imperative of the *qal* stem of the same verb. For this understanding of the two examples in Isa 29:9, see Smith, *Isaiah 1–39*, 499.

[21] See Sweeney (*Zephaniah*, 114–15), who, after observing that the people are the "sacrificial victims" in chapter 1 (see v. 8), writes regarding 2:1: "The gathering of sticks or wood is an essential element of the preparation of the sacrificial altar, and the prophet's use of these verbs in the command to gather builds on this metaphorical and ironic strategy by portraying the gathering of the people as the gathering of the very sticks that are to be burned up as part of the sacrifice on the Day of YHWH."

[22] The infinitive לֶדֶת, without a prefixed preposition, also takes a common noun as genitive in Job 39:1.

[23] See Patterson, *Zephaniah*, 332.

[24] The perfect (*qatal*) verb form can be translated as a future perfect ("will have passed by") or perfect of certitude ("will pass by"). In either case the rhetorical perspective is that of the

away] (in) a day." The verb *ʿābar*, "pass by," is used with *mōṣ*, "chaff," in Isa 29:5 to describe chaff that is blown away quickly. Here in 2:2, "day" refers to how relatively suddenly the chaff will disappear (cf. 1:18b).[25] Rather than using one of the terms that appears in Isa 29:5 (*ləpetaʿ pitʾōm*, "suddenly, in an instant"), Zephaniah chooses "day" to maintain the link with the day of the Lord mentioned before and after this (1:18; 2:2). While "day" may not suggest as quick a disappearance as Isa 29:5 envisions, it does indicate suddenness if one assumes there will be a large pile of chaff to eliminate as suggested by the extent of the coming judgment in chapter 1.[26]

2. "Before the burning of the LORD's anger overtakes you."

In this line and the next *bəṭerem*, "before," is followed by the negative particle *lōʾ*, a combination that occurs only here in the OT and seems to convey a meaning that is the opposite of what one expects.[27] The grammars propose the double negative has an emphatic function.[28]

The coming judgment has been described in terrifying detail prior to this and even called a day of "wrath" (*ʿebrâ*, 1:15, 18), but now the prophet states this more emphatically, using the word *ʾap*, "anger," three times in verses 2–3. To reflect the intensity of the Lord's anger, he combines this first use of *ʾap* with *ḥārôn*, "burning," a combination

---

future day of judgment.

[25] See the helpful observations of Motyer, "Zephaniah," 926–27.

[26] Jeffrey Niehaus prefers to see a homonym here (and in Gen 3:8), meaning "storm," cognate to Akkadian *ūmu*. See also *HALOT*, 401. Niehaus proposes a translation: "(that) storm sweeps on like chaff." He paraphrases in a footnote: "The storm of coming judgement advances quickly, driving all before it like chaff driven by the wind." Acknowledging that "day" appears in the immediate context, he suggests that the traditional understanding could be retained with an allusion to the homonymic "storm." See his article, "In the Wind of the Storm: Another Look at Genesis III 8," *VT* 44, 2 (1994): 263–67. For a critique of this proposal, see Christopher L. K. Grundke, "A Tempest in a Teapot? Genesis III 8 Again," *VT* 51, 4 (2001): 548–51.

[27] One is tempted to simply omit the particle as a scribal error, but in this case one is hard pressed to explain how such an addition was made in this graphic environment not once but twice!

[28] GKC 483, §152y. See also Joüon and Muraoka, *A Grammar of Biblical Hebrew*, 608–9, par. 160p, and *HALOT*, 379. In this regard, טֶרֶם without the preposition is a negative, often translated "not yet" (see GKC, 481, par. 152r; *HALOT*, 379; BDB, 382). When the preposition -בְּ is prefixed to the form, it is typically translated "before" as if the negation had disappeared. But this is simply a problem of conveying the underlying negation of Hebrew into English. For example, one can paraphrase Zeph 2:2a: "Gather . . . (in the time during which) the birthing of the decree (is not yet occurring)." We can paraphrase Zeph 2:2b: "Gather . . . (in the time during which) the burning of the LORD's anger is (not yet—yea, not [for emphasis]) overtaking you."

used thirty-three times in the Old Testament—always of God's burning anger.

3. "Before the day of the LORD's anger overtakes you."

The prophet makes clear the coming time of judgment is the day of the Lord. For the third time he characterizes the day by placing a genitive between "day" and the Lord's name: "day of the sacrifice of the LORD" (1:8), "day of the wrath of the LORD" (1:18), and now "day of the anger of the LORD."

The logical relationship between the imperatives of verse 1 and the temporal clauses of verse 2 is difficult to discern. The command to gather as kindling for the coming fire of judgment (cf. 1:18) does not readily allow for a positive interpretation. However, in this context, where the temporal clauses describe coming judgment and the imperative of verse 3 calls for positive behavior, one expects the imperatives of verse 1 to contain, at least implicitly, a warning to heed before disaster comes.[29] This is the case in Jer 13:16, the only other example of this syntactical sequence: "Give [imperative] glory to the LORD your God before (*bəṭerem*) he brings darkness [and] before (*bəṭerem*) your feet stumble." It is no surprise many interpreters understand the imperatives in a positive sense, as summoning the people to assemble for repentance[30] or as warning them to change their behavior.[31]

Nevertheless, at least at the locutionary level it is better to understand the imperatives for what they appear to be—a highly rhetorical sarcastic call to sinners to "be kindling" for the fiery judgment of cosmic proportions described in chapter 1. The militant irony continues in verse 2, where this preparation of kindling needs to occur before the fire of judgment arrives. Through these ironic imperatives the prophet transforms what might be expected—a call to repent before judgment falls—in such a way as to drive home one of the key themes of the

---

[29] See Renz (*Zephaniah*, 524), who writes, "But the haunting and insistent repetition of *before* in the next verse [v. 2] makes the call sound more like an earnest plea that the addressees use what little time is left than a sarcastic taunt that gleefully points out that there is nothing more that can be done."

[30] Ben Zvi, *Zephaniah*, 138, 296; Patterson, *Zephaniah*, 328; Motyer, "Zephaniah," 926; Sweeney, *Zephaniah*, 116; Floyd, *Minor Prophets*, 215–16.

[31] Roberts, *Zephaniah*, 189; Renz, *Zephaniah*, 524. This sometimes entails emendation of the first clause in verse 2 to make clear that a warning is in view. See Roberts, *Zephaniah*, 187–88. Sweeney (*Zephaniah*, 116) gives a list of the various proposals that have been made.

previous chapter—the inescapability and thorough extent of the coming judgment.[32] In this case, the prophet may be indicating the Lord has given these sinners over to destruction, a theme that often appears in the Bible. There may still be hope for the humble obedient (cf. v. 3) to become a righteous remnant (3:12–13), but there is no indication the Lord is offering the sinners denounced in chapter 1 an opportunity for repentance on a mass scale.[33]

At first glance, verse 3 seems to call this interpretation into question, for it includes a call to obedient behavior and holds out the possibility of escaping judgment. This matter of the relationship between the imperatives of verse 1 and those in verse 3 requires closer attention.

The exhortations in verse 3 are addressed to "all you humble of the earth [or perhaps "land"], who carry out what he commands." Daniel Ryou observes some interpreters understand the addressees to be the same audience as in verses 1–2, while others see a different audience in verse 3.[34] More specifically, DeRouchie explains there are three main views concerning the addressees in 2:1, 3: (1) Both verses "address Judah collectively as a rebellious nation." (2) Verse 1 "addresses Judah collectively as a rebellious nation, but verse 3 addresses the rebellious foreign nations." (3) Verse 1 "addresses Judah collectively as a rebellious nation," while verse 3 "addresses Judah's faithful remnant."[35] After surveying the views and interacting with their major proponents, he argues for a fourth view that is a modified version of the third position. This proposal, with which I agree, sees Judah's remnant as the "primary" addressee in verse 3, but, in the larger context of the book, makes room for "other rebellious nations and their remnants" as well.[36]

As in 1:18, the scope of *hāʾāreṣ*, "the earth," is not immediately clear. Since the exhortation of 2:1 is addressed to the "undesirable

---

[32] In this regard, see the remarks of A. Vanlier Hunter, *Seek the Lord: A Study of the Meaning and Function of the Exhortations in Amos, Isaiah, Micah, and Zephaniah* (Baltimore: St. Mary's Seminary and University, 1982), 267–70.

[33] For a study that reaches this conclusion, see Tyler Kelly, "'After Such Knowledge, What Forgiveness?': The Polemic against the Wealthy and Zephaniah's Day of Yhwh," *VT* 72, 4/5 (2022): 594–608.

[34] Ryou, *Zephaniah's Oracles against the Nations*, 326–28.

[35] DeRouchie, "The Addressees in Zephaniah 2:1, 3," 188–99.

[36] DeRouchie, "The Addressees in Zephaniah 2:1, 3," 200–206. His proposal follows the lead of Floyd, *Minor Prophets,* 216, and Daniel C. Timmer, *The Non-Israelite Nations in the Book of the Twelve: Thematic Coherence and the Diachronic-Synchronic Relationship in the Minor Prophets,* Biblical Interpretation 135 (Leiden: Brill, 2015), 151–68, especially 166–67.

nation" of Judah, one is inclined to understand the "humble" as a subgroup within the nation. If so, then *hāʾāreṣ* refers to "the land" of Judah.[37] On the other hand, the scope of the day of the Lord is broader than Judah, making it possible the humble of "the earth" are in view as well (see 1:18). In this regard it is noteworthy that 2:4, which is connected to verse 3 by *kî*, "for," begins a description of the Lord's judgment on the nations.

It seems odd this call to righteousness and humility is addressed to "all you humble of the earth, who carry out what he commands," in other words, to people who are already humble and demonstrating obedience.[38] Elsewhere in the Prophets, "humble" (the plural of *ʿānāw* is used here) is a sociological term, referring to those who are poor and/or oppressed, vulnerable, and in need of protection and/or deliverance.[39] This is clearly the case in the three other texts where the word is modified by the genitive "earth" (see Ps 76:9 [10]; Isa 11:4; Amos 8:4 [*kethib*]).[40] The sociological sense is usually present in Psalms and Proverbs as well.[41] On a few occasions it refers to humility in contrast to pride and is used of a humble, contrite attitude before the Lord.[42] In Zeph 2:3 it could refer to the oppressed (cf. 1:9; 3:3), but the focus here is on obedience, for these humble people "carry out what he commands." The relative clause need not imply all the humble carry out the commands. As Renz points out, it could be "restrictive," referring to the obedient as a "subgroup" of the humble.[43] After all, being socially oppressed does not automatically make one obedient. The closely related word *ʿānî*, "meek" appears in 3:12 (with *dal*), where

[37] NET, NIV, ESV, NASB margin.

[38] Sweeney, *Zephaniah,* 118. There is an easy "solution" to the problem, discussed by Ben Zvi, *Zephaniah,* 146; Ryou, *Zephaniah's Oracles against the Nations,* 328, and Renz, *Zephaniah,* 519, note h. One could add a *kaph* to the front of כָּל־עַנְוֵי, read "like all the humble," and argue that MT is due to haplography. In this case, the "undesirable nation" is addressed in verse 3 and told to seek the Lord *like* the humble of the earth do. If they seek the Lord through obedience and fear, they have a chance to be spared. However, there is no textual support for this emendation. The proposal cuts, rather than unties, the interpretive knot. So does the proposal to eliminate these words as a later gloss. See Hadjiev, "Survival, Conversion and Restoration," 571. If they create incoherence, why would a redactor add them? If there is a good answer to this question, then we do not need to propose a redactor.

[39] Isa 11:4; 29:19; 32:7; 61:1; Amos 2:7; 8:4.

[40] In these three texts the article does not appear with אֶרֶץ.

[41] Pss 9:12 [Hb. v. 13], 18 [Hb. v. 19]; 10:12, 17; 22:26 [Hb. v. 27]; 34:2 [Hb. v. 3]; 37:11; 69:32 [Hb. v. 33]; 76:9 [Hb. v. 10]; 147:6; 149:4; Prov 14:21; 16:19.

[42] Ps 25:9; Prov 3:34. See also Num 12:23, where it is used of Moses.

[43] Renz, *Zephaniah,* 525.

the "meek and humble" are contrasted with the proud (see v. 11) and "take refuge in the name of the LORD" (v. 12). King concludes these texts . . .

> are not simply sociological descriptions nor do they merely supply information about the financial status of the remnant. They also tell of the contrite spirit and meek attitude of these people. They are a people whose confidence is not in their own possessions or abilities. Rather, they place their trust in Yahweh alone.[44]

Perhaps it is best to view them as righteous people, committed to following the Lord's commands, who, because of that commitment are powerless and vulnerable if not poor and destitute economically. This need not imply all who are powerless, vulnerable, poor, and/or destitute are righteous.

The verb translated "carry out" is *pāʿal*; "do" understood in the sense of "practice, perform." The perfect verb form is probably present perfective in function ("have done"), indicating completed action with continuing results. This may explain how obedient humble people can be commanded to do what they have already done. The prophet urges them to sustain their obedient spirit before the Lord. If this is correct, we are reminded obedience is an ongoing responsibility. One can never rest complacently on past performance. There is always the need to "seek" the Lord by obeying and fearing him.

The object of the verb is *mišpāṭô*, the precise meaning of which is not immediately clear, given the broad semantic range of *mišpāṭ*. This is the only passage where *pāʿal* is used with *mišpāṭ*. However, the synonymous verb *ʿāśāh*, "do" (note the parallelism of *pāʿal* and *ʿāśāh* in Prov 21:15, where *mišpāṭ* is the object of *ʿāśāh*) is frequently used with *mišpāṭ* in the sense of "doing justice" (that is, acting justly and promoting justice).[45] In Zeph 2:3 the third-person suffix on *mišpāṭô* refers to the Lord, who establishes the principles of justice. The prophet describes the obedient humble as those who live by the Lord's principles of justice.[46]

---

[44] King, "The Remnant in Zephaniah," 419. See more recently DeRouchie, "The Addressees in Zephaniah 2:1, 3," 187–88.

[45] Ben Zvi, *Zephaniah,* 148. See, among others, Gen 18:19, 25; Deut 10:18; 2 Sam 8:15; Jer 5:1; 7:5; 22:3, 15; 23:5; 33:15; Ezek 18:5, 21, 27; 33:14, 19; Mic 6:8.

[46] Though פָּעַל, "do," does not occur with מִשְׁפָּט, "justice," elsewhere, it is used in Ps 15:2 with צֶדֶק, "righteousness," which is often paired with מִשְׁפָּט. See Ben Zvi, *Zephaniah,* 148.

Three times the prophet exhorts the obedient humble to "seek," first the Lord, then righteousness, and then humility. The command to seek the Lord runs counter to the behavior described in 1:6, where the Lord announced that he would judge those in Judah and Jerusalem who turned their backs away from following him and were not seeking him.[47] As noted in my comments on that passage, seeking the Lord can refer to seeking him in repentance and/or obedience (Deut 4:29; 2 Chr 15:4; Jer 29:13; 50:4; Hos 3:5; 7:6 [the verb is negated as in Zeph 1:6]) or through sacrifice (Hos 5:6). On several occasions seeking the Lord means seeking his favor (2 Chr 11:16; 15:15; 20:4; Zech 8:22–23) or enablement (1 Chr 16:10–11; Ps 105:3–4). In at least one case the expression may refer to seeking a reliable message from the Lord, though this is uncertain (Isa 45:19). In 2:3 obedience is in view, as the second and third exhortations make clear. One seeks the Lord by seeking righteousness (*ṣedeq*; cf. Isa 51:1) and humility (*ʿănāwâ*).[48] In this case "seek" can be paraphrased: "make every effort to put into practice."[49]

In this context "righteousness" is ethical in nature and focuses on just actions,[50] in contrast to the behavior described in 1:9 and 3:3. The term *ʿănāwâ*, "humility," appears with certainty in only three other texts,[51] all in Proverbs: (1) 15:33: "The fear of the Lord is what wisdom teaches, and humility comes before honor," (2) 18:12: "Before his downfall a person's heart is proud, but humility comes before honor,"

---

[47] See Sweeney, *Zephaniah,* 119.

[48] See Renz, *Zephaniah,* f 527. The terms "righteousness" and "humility" occur only here in Zephaniah. The expressions "seek righteousness" and "seek humility" occur only here in the Old Testament.

[49] Note NET, "strive," both here and in Ps 34:14 [Hb. v. 15]: "Strive for peace and promote it" (lit., as in CSB, "seek peace and pursue it"). Note also that BDB lists both Zeph 2:3 and Ps 34:15 under the gloss "aim at, practice" (p. 134, *piel,* category 2. b).

[50] *HALOT,* 1005, category 2; BDB, 841, category 5. See also Bailey, "Zephaniah," 447–49.

[51] The word appears in Ps 18:35 [Hb. v. 36), where the psalmist says to God, "Your humility exalts me." This probably refers to God's willingness to condescend to help the psalmist. However, the parallel in 2 Sam 22:36 has a different reading: "Your help [lit., "your answer"] exalts me." (4QSam[a] reads *ʿzrtk,* "your help," which is interpretive.) "Your answer" refers to God's response to the psalmist's prayer that gave him the strength needed to defeat the enemy. More specifically, it probably alludes to an oracle of salvation or victory that preceded the battle and guaranteed the enablement needed to defeat the enemy. If so, the statement correlates with 22:31b, which speaks of the reliability of God's word of promise. It also provides a nice contrast to 22:42, where the psalmist's enemies received no answer from the Lord. Some also see עֲנָוָה in Ps 45:4 [Hb. v. 5], where the otherwise unattested עַנְוָה appears with צֶדֶק. God's chosen king's commitment to justice is in view here.

and (3) 22:4: "Humility, the fear of the LORD, results in wealth, honor, and life."[52] Usage, though limited, is instructive. Humility is contrasted with pride and closely associated with, if not equated with, the fear of the Lord,[53] which entails humbly submitting to his sovereign authority and turning from evil behavior. The description of the idolatrous people of Judah and Jerusalem in 1:4–15 and 3:2–4 shows they were sorely lacking when it came to humility and the fear of the Lord.[54] This is perhaps most evident in their blatant denial of the Lord's just character: "The LORD will do nothing—good or bad" (1:12).

The final clause of verse 3 is puzzling because it does not guarantee safety for the obedient humble. The prophet says, "*Perhaps* you will be concealed (that is, "hidden, protected")[55] on the day of the LORD's anger." The word *ʾûlay*, "perhaps," often has a hopeful tone,[56] but, even so, it reflects a degree of uncertainty about the destiny of the obedient humble. After all, the judgment will be so severe the humble obedient may be engulfed in its fire and be collateral damage. If the prophet is talking in such contingent terms, one wonders what will decide their destiny in the end. Perhaps the best course of action is that of the king of Nineveh, who, when he heard Jonah's seemingly unconditional announcement of judgment, recognized God's sovereignty, committed himself to doing what was right, and said, "Who knows? God may turn and relent; he may turn from his burning anger so that we will not perish" (Jonah 3:9). At this point in Zephaniah's unfolding message, King's observation is noteworthy. He proposes that *ʾûlay*, "perhaps,"

> preserves the absolute sovereignty and freedom of Yahweh. In other words, it depends entirely on Yahweh whether he wants to show mercy. Yahweh is not indebted to respond by saving a

---

[52] On the thematic connection between Zeph 2:3 and Prov 22:4, see Ben Zvi, *Zephaniah,* 148. For a survey of the usage of עֲנָוָה in the Old Testament, see Stephen B. Dawes, "עֲנָוָה in Translation and Tradition," *VT* 41, 1 (1991): 38–48.

[53] Renz, *Zephaniah,* 527.

[54] Dawes ("עֲנָוָה in Translation and Tradition," 42) lists 1:5–6; 2:8, 10, 15; 3:1–2, 11 as passages in Zephaniah where the theme of pride is present, and 3:12 where the theme of humility appears.

[55] Emphasis added. Understanding the *niphal* as passive is preferable here to taking it as reflexive, as Ball (*Zephaniah,* 120) does.

[56] BDB, 19. See, among others, Gen 16:2; 18:24, 28–32; 1 Sam 6:5; 9:6; 14:6; 2 Sam 14:15; 16:12; Isa 37:4; Jer 21:2; 26:3; 36:3, 7; 51:8; Ezek 12:3; Amos 5:15; Jonah 1:6; Lam 3:29.

remnant. On the contrary, He reacts in His sovereignty and freedom, and salvation springs out of His grace and love.[57]

As noted earlier, it is also important to recognize the exhortation in 2:3 reflects the prophet's perspective as he identifies with his audience. It is his response to the preceding announcement of judgment (1:2–18) and complements the sarcastic exhortation that immediately precedes it (2:1–2). The use of *ʾûlay*, "perhaps," coming on the heels of the description of the devastation that will accompany the day of the Lord, emphasizes the degree of destruction judgment will bring. As the prophet stands in the shoes of those who have heard the announcement of 1:2–18, his words reflect what some might be thinking: Given the coming reversal of creation and unleashing of divine fury, does anyone have a chance to escape?

We now need to return to the matter of the implication of verse 3 for understanding the imperatives in verse 1. Does verse 3 support a positive or a negative understanding of verses 1–2? Although verse 3 contains a call to righteous living characterized by the fear of the Lord consistent with our interpretation of verses 1–2, there is an element of irony present since the threefold imperative "seek" is directed only to the "humble" who have already carried out "what he commands." This is not an extension of the exhortation in verses 1–2, which addresses more broadly the "undesirable nation." The irony persists when the prophet tells the humble, "*Perhaps* you will be concealed on the day of the LORD's anger." Verse 3 may qualify verses 1–2 slightly, but, even so, one is inclined to say with the apostle Peter, "If a righteous person is saved with difficulty, what will become of the ungodly and the sinner?" (1 Pet 4:18).

The highly ironic tone of verses 1–3 reinforces the point that the coming judgment of the day of the Lord will be thorough and inescapable. The sovereign Lord alone determines the destiny of everyone. Nevertheless, the hint that some may escape peeks through the dark clouds of judgment and gives cause for hope that a remnant may be saved.

I have made a case for a straightforward reading of the imperatives in verses 1–3, at least at the surface, or locutionary, level. Nevertheless it is worth considering another option, given (1) the prophet's

[57] King, "The Remnant in Zephaniah," 421.

rhetorical stance, where he assumes the perspective of the recipients of the announcement of judgment given in chapter 1 (see above), and (2) the message of the book when considered as a literary unit that ends on a positive note.

An interpreter should view any given passage in a book in the light of the message of the larger context of the entire book, especially its conclusion.[58] The judgment announcement of chapter 1 and the prophet's apparent sarcastic response to it in 2:1–2 depict destruction as inescapable. His address to the righteous in verse 3, given from the same rhetorical perspective as verses 1–2, offers only the possibility of escape and, at best, just a hint of protection for some. However, the rest of the book makes clear that Judah does have a future. There will be a remnant (2:7, 9), and it will become the "Israel" that populates restored Zion (see 3:12–15).

Wendland explains that a "key thematic question" raised in the prophecy is this: "On the day of the LORD, will there be any hope?" The book's three major sections (for him, "dialogues") give different answers, namely, "Not at all!" (chap. 1), "Maybe?" (chap. 2), and "Yes, indeed!" (chap. 3). He observes "a perceptive audience," having heard 1:2–18, "would conclude there is absolutely no hope." But then part 2 (2:1–15) "presents a glimmer of hope," while part 3 (3:1–20, especially 3:14–17) celebrates hope "that is not only possible, but also one that has been fully realized as a result of the purifying and protective actions of YHWH."[59]

This shift from inescapable judgment for sinners and possible escape for the righteous to ultimate salvation for the Lord's covenant community (3:12–20) suggests we should reconsider verses 1–3 in the light of speech act theory. While judgment appears to be inescapable, the book, viewed as a whole, especially its conclusion, qualifies this. This suggests that the perlocution (intended response) of the prophetic rhetoric of verses 1–3 is more positive than the locutionary, or even illocutionary, levels appear to indicate. The sarcasm of verses 1–2 and the uncertainty expressed in verse 3 emphasize the gravity of the

[58] I have addressed this vital hermeneutical principle with respect to the interpretation of Ecclesiastes and Job in Robert B. Chisholm Jr., "The Fear of the Lord/God: A Thematic Key to the Unity of the Wisdom Books," in *The Law, the Prophets, and the Writings*, ed. A. M. King, W. R. Osborne, and J. M. Philpott (Nashville: B & H Academic, 2021), 271–90, especially 273, 283–84, 289–90. The principle also applies to prophetic books, including Zephaniah.

[59] Wendland, "The Drama of Zephaniah," 59.

situation described in chapter 1. From the perspective of those hearing the message, the future looks hopeless or at best uncertain. Yet once we read on, we discover that there is hope because the Lord has a plan for the restoration of the covenant community and even the nations. As we read the book a second time, we detect the real intent of the hortatory discourse in verses 1–3. As they gather as kindling in preparation for the judgment that will come in the immediate future, sinners must come to their senses before the fiery judgment arrives. They need to join the group of the humble obedient, for whom there is some hope (v. 3; cf. Ezek 18:21–23). As for the obedient humble, they need to persist in righteousness, placing their destiny in the hands of a sovereign God who has revealed himself as merciful and faithful (Exod 34:6–7; Jonah 4:2). House puts it this way: "2.1–2 attempts to shock and insult Judahites into joining the remnant. Such as it is, this biting invitation is the book's first offer of redemption."[60]

Using the categories of speech act theory, we can paraphrase the meaning and intent of 2:1–3:

2:1–2

Locution (what is stated at the surface level): Sinners must gather in anticipation of the fiery judgment to come, for they will be the kindling for the fire!

Illocution (deeper meaning of what is stated): Sinners will not be able to escape the destruction that is imminent.

Perlocution (intended response to what is stated, understood within the totality of Zephaniah's message): Given the inevitability of destruction for sinners, those persisting in sin must respond with a sense of urgency and through repentance join the ranks of the obedient (cf. v. 3), for whom there is some hope of escape.

2:3

Locution (what is stated at the surface level): The humble obedient must persist in seeking the Lord, for there is at least some hope that the sovereign God will protect them in the day of judgment.

---

[60] Paul R. House, *Zephaniah: A Prophetic Drama,* JSOTSup 69 (Sheffield: Sheffield Academic, 1989), 64. DeRouchie ("The Addressees in Zephaniah 2:1, 3," 196–97) cites House with approval. See also Ryou, *Zephaniah's Oracles against the Nations*, 333, and Sweeney, "Form Criticism of Zephaniah," 398.

Illocution (deeper meaning of what is stated): The future is in the hands of the sovereign Lord, who alone determines the destiny of people. One can escape the severity of the coming judgment only through his decision to be merciful.

Perlocution (intended response to what is stated, understood within the totality of Zephaniah's message): The Lord's decision to preserve a remnant (cf. 2:7, 9; 3:12–20) shows he will extend mercy amid and beyond judgment. Those who seek the Lord through humble obedience will survive the coming destruction (cf. Hab 2:4; 3:16–19; Ezek 9:4–6) and become the remnant. It is imperative that all take heed to the commands given in verse 3.

When viewed in the larger context of the book, the exhortations of 2:1–3 are not simply warnings of impending divine judgment but, rather, an invitation to escape that judgment and experience the Lord's mercy.

In addition to the internal evidence of Zephaniah's prophecy, when read as a literary unit, historical factors support this interpretation of Zeph 2:1–3. Zephaniah prophesied during the reign of Josiah (641–609 BC). He was a contemporary of Jeremiah, whose prophetic ministry began in Josiah's reign and continued until the fall of Jerusalem to the Babylonians in 587 BC (Jer 1:1–3). Since both prophets were spokesmen for the Lord, one expects consistency in their messages regarding judgment as imminent or contingent upon the people's response. Jeremiah 26, which dates to the beginning of the reign of Josiah's son, Jehoiakim, is instructive in this regard. Jehoiakim ruled from 609 to 598 BC after the career of Zephaniah.

As the Lord commissioned Jeremiah to proclaim his word, he told the prophet,

> "This is what the LORD says: Stand in the courtyard of the LORD's temple and speak all the words I have commanded you to speak to all Judah's cities that are coming to worship there. Do not hold back a word. **Perhaps they will listen and turn—each from his evil way of life—so that I might relent concerning the disaster that I plan to do to them because of the evil of their deeds.** You are to say to them, 'This is what the LORD says: **If you do not listen to me by living according to my instruction that I set before you and by listening to the words of my servants the prophets—whom I have been sending to you time and time again, though you did not listen—I will make this temple like Shiloh.** I will make this city an

example for cursing for all the nations of the earth'" (Jer 26:2–6, emphasis added).

At this point in time, judgment is clearly contingent on the people's response to Jeremiah,[61] as the bolded portions of the passage indicate. The following narrative, in which some in the royal court compare Jeremiah's message to the contingent message of judgment delivered by Micah in 701 BC, supports this (26:7–19).[62] In the course of time, the Lord did decree inescapable judgment upon Judah (4:28; 15:1–6), but this development postdated Zephaniah's message. Like Jeremiah's message from the earlier part of his career, Zephaniah's announcements of judgment upon Judah and Jerusalem should be seen as implicitly contingent. While judgment was inevitable for sinners, there was hope for those who sought the Lord. Nevertheless the situation was dire and demanded urgency. Jeremiah's message, when compared to Zeph 2:1–3, indicates that even the fiery judgment of the day of the Lord could have been averted or at least postponed if the nation responded properly to the message of the prophets.

2.2 Widespread Devastation Has a Surprising Aftermath (2:4–15)

The judgment of the day of the Lord will be widespread, devastating nations far and wide. In the aftermath of this judgment, the Lord will reverse the situation of Judah's survivors (vv. 7, 9) and even make distant nations his genuine worshippers (v. 11).

The oracles against the nations are linked to the exhortation of verses 1–3 by *kî*, "for."[63] Verses 4–15 in their entirety provide the reason the addressees should heed the exhortations: the day of the Lord will bring worldwide ruin.[64] The oracles include judgment announcements against nations to the west (vv. 4–7, Philistia), east (vv. 8–11,

---

[61] In verse 5 the Lord refers to "my servants the prophets," which would include Jeremiah and others, such as Zephaniah, who had been warning the people of impending judgment and calling them to repent.

[62] For a fuller discussion of this passage, see Robert B. Chisholm Jr., "Does God 'Change His Mind?'" *BSac* 152 (1995): 396–97.

[63] Some prefer to translate כִּי "indeed, certainly." See NET; Ben Zvi, *Zephaniah,* 150. NIV and NLT leave it untranslated.

[64] See the helpful discussion in Motyer, "Zephaniah," 931.

Moab and Ammon), south (v. 12, the Cushites), and north (vv. 13–15, Assyria).[65]

2:4–7 The first oracle announces judgment against the Philistines to the west of Judah. It begins with a description of the results of judgment (v. 4). A woe (*hôy*) oracle follows, accompanied by a formal announcement of the Lord's intervention (v. 5) and an additional description of the results of judgment (v. 6). The oracle ends on a positive note for the "remnant of the house of Judah," who will occupy Philistine territory as "the LORD their God" reverses their situation (v. 7).

The prophet mentions four of the five major Philistine cities (Gath is omitted; cf. Josh 13:3; 1 Sam 6:17), listed from south to north (and then east).[66]

1. Gaza "will be abandoned." The sound-play in Hebrew between Gaza (*ʿazzâ*) and "abandoned" (*ʿăzûbâ*, *qal* passive participle) grabs the listeners' attention. When used of a city, the passive of the verb *ʿāzab*, "to abandon," pictures the city as deserted (*qal passive:* Isa 17:2, 9; 60:15; Jer 4:29; *niphal*: Isa 27:10; 62:12 [negated]; Ezek 36:4; *pual*: Isa 32:14; Jer 49:25 [negated]).

2. Ashkelon "will become a ruin."[67] Its destiny is the same as the houses of Jerusalem (1:13, where the noun *šemāmâ*, "ruin," also appears; 2:9). Often the word describes a land as deserted. When used of a city, it pictures an uninhabitable heap of ruins.[68]

---

[65] Dietrich comments on the significance of Assyria's placement at the end of the list: "Assyria and Nineveh effectively form the target and the end point in a series of words of God, which are directed against the enemies in the west, east, south, and north. This goal means God even puts a stop to this greatest and most dangerous hostile power of all." See Walter Dietrich, "Three Minor Prophets and the Major Empires: Synchronic and Diachronic Perspectives on Nahum, Habakkuk, and Zephaniah," in Rainer Albertz, James D. Nogalski, and Jakob Wöhrle, eds., *Perspectives on the Formation of the Book of the Twelve: Methodological Foundations—Redactional Processes—Historical Insights*, BZAW 433 (Berlin: De Gruyter, 2012), 149.

[66] Starting from Gaza in the south, he moves north to Ashkelon, then north to Ashdod and finally east to Ekron. The same four cities mentioned by Zephaniah appear in a different order in Jer 25:20; Amos 1:7–8; and Zech 9:5–6. On the omission of Gath, see Kahn, "Zephaniah's Oracles," 440.

[67] The verb "will be" (תִּהְיֶה) from the first line is understood by ellipsis in this line. It combines with the preposition -לְ to indicate entry into a state and is translated "become."

[68] For a discussion of the historical fulfillment of this prophecy in 604 BC, see above, under "Prophecy and Fulfillment: Historical Fulfillment of Zephaniah's Prophecies." Cp. Josh 8:28; Isa 17:9; 62:4 [Note that עֲזוּבָה, CSB, "deserted" and שְׁמָמָה, CSB, "desolate," are parallel, as in Zeph 2:4a.]; 64:10 [Hb. v. 9]; Jer 6:8; 10:22; 34:22; 44:6; 49:2, 33; 50:13; 51:26, 62; Mic 1:7; Zeph 2:13.

3. Ashdod "will be driven out at noon." The text reads literally, "Ashdod, at noon they will drive her out."[69] Three texts in Jeremiah speak of noon as the time when an army attacks:[70] (a) 6:4: "Set them apart for war against her; rise up, let's attack at noon," (b) 15:8: "I brought a destroyer at noon against the mother of young men," and (c) 20:16: "Let him hear an outcry in the morning and war cry at noontime." First Kings 20:16 describes an Israelite army marching out to fight the Arameans at noon.[71] On the Moabite Stone King Mesha describes his victory over the town of Nebo this way: "And Kemosh said to me: 'Go, take Nebo from Israel!' And I went in the night, and I fought against it from the break of dawn until noon, and I took it, and I killed [its] whole population" (*COS*, 2:138 [lines 14–16a]).[72] Stuart relates this to the "sovereign's day of conquest," which he proposes is the background of the day of the Lord.[73] As such, it is an idiom emphasizing the swift and decisive nature of his victory over his enemies on any given occasion. If this is correct, then Zephaniah depicts the defeat of Ashdod as particularly swift.

The prophet describes an invader driving out the residents of Ashdod. What exactly does "driven out" entail? The verb (*piel* of *gāraš*) has the primary meaning "expel, remove, drive away," as is evident in nonmilitaristic texts.[74] However, in militaristic contexts, the verb may refer to driving people out to occupy their territory, or removing

---

[69] The third masculine plural verb has no stated subject or antecedent for the subject. Zephaniah envisions enemies, functioning as God's instruments (note "I will destroy" in v. 5), driving out the people of Ashdod. Since warriors are typical participants in such a scene, the prophet can refer to them without directly mentioning them. The feminine singular suffix with the verb refers to the town of Ashdod. This use of the feminine for towns is typical in Hebrew (GKC, 391, par. 122h). Ashdod stands by metonymy (container for contents) for its residents.

[70] *NIDOTTE*, 1:717.

[71] According to H. Niehr (*TDOT*, 12:265), "Midday is unfavorable for military operations because of the sun's high position in the sky, making it all the more surprising when the enemy does indeed attack at this time" (1 Kgs 20:16; Jer 6:4). Niehr proposes that בַּצָּהֳרַיִם, "in the noon," in Zeph 2:4 means, "already by noon," indicating "a battle lasting merely half a day."

[72] "Noon" translates Moabite *hṣhrm*, lit., "the noon," which is cognate with Hebrew צָהֳרַיִם. In Zeph 2:4 the noun has a prefixed preposition vocalized to indicate the presence of the article, בַּצָּהֳרַיִם, lit., "at the noon." The presence of the article is typical with this noun in biblical Hebrew, though there are a few exceptions (see *HALOT*, 1008).

[73] Stuart, "The Sovereign's Day of Conquest," 163.

[74] See, among others, Gen 3:24; 4:14; 21:10; Exod 2:17; 6:1; 10:11; 11:1; 12:39; Lev 21:7, 14; 22:13; Num 30:9 [v. 10]; Judg 9:41; 11:2, 7; 1 Sam 26:19; 1 Kgs 2:27; Job 30:5; Ps 34:1 [Hebrew = heading in English]; Prov 22:10; Ezek 31:11; 44:22; Hos 9:15; Jonah 2:4; Mic 2:9.

people by killing them; yet most texts are ambiguous, giving no indication "drive out" means "to kill."[75] In Exod 23:28–31, the idea of "expel" is perhaps favored by verse 27 (cf. CSB, "I will make all your enemies turn their backs to you in retreat"), if it refers to retreating enemies. The text reads literally, "I will give all your enemies to you, neck." However, verse 23 speaks of wiping out (*hiphil* of *kāḥad*) the inhabitants of the land. Josh 24:12 (and, by extension v. 18) appears to coincide with Exod 23:28–31. Note the reference to the Lord sending "hornets," or, perhaps better, "terror, panic," in both passages.[76] The one text which favors equating "drive out" with "kill" is Deut 33:27: "[God] drives out the enemy before you and commands: 'Destroy!'" Furthermore, in the accounts of Israel's conquest of Canaan, language for "driving out," including synonyms of *gāraš*, and for "killing" is used.[77] On the other hand, "drive out" language sometimes appears independently (Deut 4:38; 11:23; 18:12).

Most likely, the variety of language reflects the reality of war. Attackers may intend to kill their enemies and succeed to varying degrees. Concomitantly, defeated enemy warriors will retreat and noncombatants will flee and become refugees. The "kill" language of these passages may reflect the attackers' mission and goal, while the "drive out" language reflects the practical reality. The language need not be collapsed into one ("drive out by killing"). As William Webb and Gordon Oeste conclude, the variety of language expresses a "shared-goal equivalency," kill and/or drive out. In any case, the enemy must be removed from the area to be occupied.[78]

We need to return to the question regarding the description of Ashdod in Zeph 2:4. When the enemy warriors attack, many will die, while others will try to retreat. The use of "drive out" need not mean all will die. The focus is on the result: Ashdod will be deserted and uninhabited.

---

[75] Exod 33:2; 34:11; Num 22:6, 11 [king of Moab speaking in both verses]; Judg 2:3; 6:9; 1 Chr 17:21; 2 Chr 20:11; Pss 78:55; 80:8 [Hb. v. 9].

[76] Josh 24:12 is problematic because of the reference to "the two Amorite kings," Sihon and Og, whom the Israelites destroyed. Note Josh 2:10, which uses the *hiphil* of חָרַם. See also 24:8, which tells how Israel destroyed the Amorites east of the Jordan. However, Josh 24:11–13 is clearly referring to the conquest west of the Jordan River. The LXX reads "twelve" for "two."

[77] In addition to Exod 23:23, 28–31, and Deut 33:27, see Deut 7:1–2, 16–17, 22–24; 9:3–4; 12:29–30; 19:1–2; 31:3–5; Josh 23:4–5. See Webb and Oeste, *Bloody Brutal and Barbaric?*, 232–34.

[78] See Webb and Oeste's chapter "Drive Out: An Equivalent Alternative," in *Bloody Brutal and Barbaric?*, 231–62.

Ekron "will be uprooted." The sound-play in Hebrew between Ekron (*ʿeqrôn*) and "uprooted" (*tēʿāqēr*) grabs the listeners' attention. The Hebrew verb appears seven times in the Old Testament.[79] Five times it is used in the *piel* stem of crippling an ox or horse.[80] In Eccl 3:2 it appears in the *qal* stem (lit., "a time to plant and a time to *uproot* what is planted"). In this context where contrasting actions are paired, the verb refers to uprooting a plant. The *niphal* in Zeph 2:4 is passive: "be uprooted." Ekron is pictured as a plant pulled up by its roots and, in a context of judgment, probably connotes death.

Welch proposes the image of uprooting reflects Ekron's status in the seventh century BC as the leading producer of olive oil in its region. He estimates that Ekron's olive oil industry produced roughly 245,000 liters (= 64,722 US gallons) each year. This required roughly 3,500 dunams (= 865 acres) of cultivated olive trees.[81] One can see behind the verb "uprooted" the metaphor of olive trees being torn up, an apt image for the judgment that would come upon Ekron, the region's leading producer of olive oil.

The first three lines of verse 4 picture the Philistine cities as uninhabited. This is consistent with the Lord's statement in verse 5b: "I will destroy you until there is no one left." Gaza is abandoned, Ashkelon is an uninhabitable heap of ruins, and an enemy has made Ashdod a deserted place. In all three there is an absence of life, and each city is no longer functioning as a city. At the surface level, the image of an uprooted plant is not as readily associated with the description of the first three cities. Nevertheless, there is thematic continuity. An uprooted plant (probably an olive tree) is deprived of life and no longer functions in accordance with its design. Such was the destiny of Ekron as a city.

Lawrence Zalcman detects the metaphor of a destitute woman in verse 4.[82] The proposal, perhaps more creative than convincing, is viable since these cities are viewed as feminine. Note the feminine passive participle "abandoned" in line one, the feminine pronominal suffix

[79] It appears once in biblical Aramaic, in Dan 7:8 where it refers to uprooting animal horns (*HALOT*, 1952).

[80] *HALOT*, 874. BDB (785) sees homonyms here, listing this verb separately from the other two uses (*qal* and *niphal*), which it places under a different root.

[81] Eric Lee Welch, "The Roots of Anger: An Economic Perspective on Zephaniah's Oracle Against the Philistines," *VT* 63 (2013): 479.

[82] Lawrence Zalcman, "Ambiguity and Assonance at Zephaniah II 4," *VT* 36, 3 (1986): 365–71.

on "drive out" in line three, and the feminine verb "uprooted" in line four. Ashkelon has no modifier in line 2, but a feminine noun "ruin" describes the city's destiny. Zalcman sees Gaza as an abandoned wife (cf. Isa 54:6; 62:4), Ashkelon as a woman deserted by her fiancé (cf. Isa 54:1; 62:4), Ashdod as a divorced woman (cf. Lev 21:7, 14; 22:13; Num 30:10; Ezek 44:22), and Ekron as a barren woman (note the wordplay with *ʿāqār*, "infertile, barren"). Robert Gordis modifies Zalcman's analysis to reflect a "rising tide" of misery: Gaza is "deserted (like a betrothed woman)," Ashkelon is "desolate (like a deserted wife)," Ashdod is "driven out . . . (like a divorced woman)," and Ekron is "uprooted (like a barren woman)."[83] Marvin Sweeney proposes the metaphor of a woman is chosen to contrast the plight of the Philistine cities with the portrait of Daughter Zion in 3:14–20, "whose husband, YHWH, has come home."[84]

Verse 5 begins with a woe (*hôy*) oracle, which is unsurprising and harmonizes with the theme of the absence of life in verse 4 (see above). The interjection *hôy*, "woe," was used in funeral laments (see 1 Kgs 13:30; Jer 22:18–19; 34:5; Amos 5:16). When used in prophetic judgment speeches, it carries the connotation of death and would alert the audience as it conveys urgency.

A woe oracle is a subcategory of the judgment speech. It is formally introduced with a pronouncement of woe (*hôy*), typically accompanied by an accusation (sometimes implicit in the description of the addressee).[85] However, this is not the case in Zeph 2:5. The inhabitants of the seacoast,[86] the nation of the Cherethites,[87] are addressed. There is no formal accusation accompanying the woe pronouncement, nor is there an embedded accusation in the vocative that merely identifies the addressee.[88]

---

[83] Robert Gordis, "A Rising Tide of Misery; A Note on a Note on Zephaniah II 4," *VT* 37, 4 (1987): 389.

[84] Sweeney, *Zephaniah*, 123.

[85] See, for example, the woe oracle in Zeph 3:1–5. For a convenient list of woe oracles with their introductions, see Ryou, *Zephaniah's Oracles against the Nations*, 334–36.

[86] "Seacoast" reads lit., "rope of the sea" (חֶבֶל הַיָּם), which might picture the coast as "a long, narrow [that is, ropelike] strip of land" (*HALOT*, 286). For a more likely explanation, see Motyer, "Zephaniah," 932, who understands "rope" as alluding to measurement of land. See also Renz, *Zephaniah*, 554–55.

[87] The Cherethites were an ethnic group (called here a גּוֹי "nation") that originated in Crete and was identified with the Philistines, who lived along the Mediterranean coast (cf. Ezek 25:16).

[88] Roberts (*Zephaniah*, 197) suggests the mentioning of Canaan might have a negative connotation and provide a reason it must be destroyed.

The prophet formally introduces the announcement of judgment in verse 5: "The word of the LORD is against you, Canaan, land of the Philistines."[89] The "word of the LORD" appears in the following quotation in which the Lord speaks in the first person: "[and] I will destroy you[90] until there is no one left." The presence of the *waw* on the following verb makes it unlikely "Canaan, land of the Philistines," is part of the quotation of the Lord's words. Rather, the prophet here addresses the recipients of the Lord's word. For the quotation to begin with *waw* is not problematic. The introductory *weqatal* pattern signals predictive discourse. There are two other examples of *wəhaʾăbadtî*, "and I will destroy" (*hiphil* perfect first singular with prefixed *waw*) with a prefixed conjunction directly after an introductory speech formula (Ezek 30:13; Obadiah 8).

Nine other times in the OT the Lord says, *wəhaʾăbadtî*, "I will destroy." Eight of these are in the Prophets (Lev 23:30 being the exception), most often in the context of judgment against foreign nations.[91] The destruction will be devastating, leaving the land without inhabitants (*mēʾên yôšēb*, lit., "from there is not an inhabitant"). In this idiomatic expression, the preposition *min*, "from," indicates a negative consequence, "so that not."[92] The negative *ʾên* adds emphasis.[93] One can paraphrase here: "So that there will not be, certainly not, an inhabitant" (cf. Zeph 3:6). As Ehud Ben Zvi points out, in several cases the idiom appears with terms for "ruin" (*šammâ*, *šəmāmâ*) so one expects to see it in verse 5 after the appearance of *šəmāmâ* in verse 4 to describe Ashkelon's demise.[94]

---

[89] Canaan is larger than just the Philistine territory (Gen 10:15–19; cf. Num 13:29; Josh 13:2–3). The synecdoche involves whole for part. See Berlin, *Zephaniah,* 105.

[90] The antecedent of the second feminine singular suffix on the verb is the *land* of the Philistines.

[91] See Jer 49:38 (against Elam); Ezek 25:7 (Ammon), 16 (Philistines/Cherethites); 30:13 (idols of Egypt); 32:13 (cattle of Egypt); Obadiah 8 (wise men of Edom). In Jer 25:10 Judah and the immediately surrounding nations are the objects of destruction, while in Mic 5:10 [b. v. 9] the Lord destroys Judah's chariots.

[92] See BDB, 583, category 7b. In other cases where the *hiphil* of אָבַד occurs with an object and the preposition מִן, "from," the verb is pregnant, meaning "destroy (and remove) from." See, for example, Num 24:19 (lit., "he will destroy [and remove] survivors from a city"); Deut 7:24 ("I will destroy [and remove] their name from under the heavens"); 8:20 ("nations whom the Lord is about to destroy [and remove] from before you"). See also Jer 25:10; 49:38; Ezek 25:7; 32:13; Obad 8.

[93] BDB, 35, category 6d. For other examples of the idiom מֵאֵין יוֹשֵׁב, lit., "there is not an inhabitant," see Isa 5:9; 6:11; Jer 4:7; 26:9; 33:10; 34:22; 44:22; 46:19; 48:9; 51:29; Zeph 3:6.

[94] Ben Zvi, *Zephaniah,* 156.

Verse 6 describes the aftermath of the Lord's destructive intervention. The verse begins with a *weqatal* verb form. It may continue the Lord's statement, "I will destroy you," in which case the Lord is the speaker in verse 6.[95] Another option suggests it continues the prophet's statement, "the word of the LORD is against you," in which case the prophet is the speaker in verse 6, as he seems to be in verse 7.[96]

The judgment upon the seacoast will reduce it to pastureland and sheepfolds.[97] The noun *nəwōt* is the plural of *nāwâ*, "grazing place," elsewhere spelled with an *aleph* (*nəʾôt*).[98] The meaning of the next word, *kərōt,* is unclear. In this context it would appear to be a plural of *kar*, "pasture," but elsewhere this noun appears as *kārîm*.[99] Perhaps the feminine ending *-ōt* is used here for the sake of assonance with *kərētîm*, "Cherethites," in verse 5.[100] In this case, one could translate literally, "grazing places of pastures of shepherds."[101] CSB (see also

95 Sweeney, *Zephaniah,* 128.

96 However, some suggest the Lord continues to speak in verse 7, referring to himself in the third person. See Roberts, *Zephaniah,* 199. Berlin, *Zephaniah,* 108, is open to the idea.

97 The appearance of a third feminine singular verb (הָיְתָה) at the beginning of verse 6 is problematic because the apparent subject, the following חֶבֶל, "rope," is masculine elsewhere (BDB, 286). One is tempted to emend the form to third masculine singular (הָיָה, cf. v. 7), but there is no way to explain the corruption of the form (added *taw*) in this graphic environment. Some propose an original defectively written second feminine singular וְהָיִת (for the usual וְהָיִית, attested in eight places in the Old Testament), "and you will be" (note the second feminine singular suffix on "I will destroy you" in verse 5, the antecedent of which is אֶרֶץ, "land"). One would have to explain the final *he* as due to virtual dittography of the *heth* at the beginning of the following חֶבֶל. However, in this case, "seacoast" would have to be understood as vocative, and we are back to the original problem. Why would the masculine חֶבֶל be addressed as feminine? (The antecedent of the second feminine suffix on "I will destroy you" is אֶרֶץ, "land.") Perhaps it is best to regard חֶבֶל הַיָּם, "rope/region of the sea," as a proper name understood conceptually as feminine due to its close association with the "land of the Philistines" (v. 5). See Ben Zvi, *Zephaniah,* 156, note 456, and Sweeney, *Zephaniah,* 128. Motyer ("Zephaniah," 932) understands אֶרֶץ, "land," as the subject of the feminine verb, with "seacoast" being "in amplificatory apposition" to the implied subject.

98 *HALOT*, 678.

99 *HALOT*, 496.

100 See Motyer ("Zephaniah," 933), who states that there is no "reason to refuse Zephaniah the right to coin an assonantal word for his own purposes. It subtly recapitulates the reference to the Philistines as Cherethites." See also Sweeney, *Zephaniah,* 128, and Ben-Zvi, *Zephaniah,* 157, who lists other nouns that are attested with both masculine and feminine plural endings, especially in the construct form.

101 Another option is to take נְוֹת as an interpretive gloss for the rhetorically modified כְּרֹת (see Ben Zvi, *Zephaniah,* 158) or vice versa due to the unusual spelling of נְוֹת without the aleph. However, Renz (*Zephaniah,* 539, n. j) observes one would expect the normal spelling in the former case. Sweeney (*Zephaniah,* 128) suggests the omission of the *aleph* is "deliberate" to make the form "morphologically similar" to כְּרֹת.

NASB95) reads "caves" here, while NIV11 opts for "wells." In either case the form is derived from *kārâ*, "to dig."[102] The noun *gidrôt* (plural of *gədērâ*, "stone wall"), when modified by "sheep" as it is here, refers to sheepfolds.[103] The sheepfolds may sarcastically mimic the cities ("enclosures" for people) they have replaced.[104]

Verse 7 provides a sudden "turning point" in Zephaniah's message.[105] Up to this point, devastating judgment has been the theme of the prophecy. A flicker of hope was offered to the obedient humble within Judah, but it was prefaced with the word "perhaps" (v. 3). Now we hear of "the remnant of the house of Judah"[106] occupying Philistine territory as the Lord their God returns to them and reverses their situation.[107] The day of the Lord's anger recedes, albeit briefly (see 2:8–11), as the Lord comes to restore his people.

This stunning reversal is mirrored in the use of the verb *pāqad*, "visit" (KJV), which has a positive nuance here (CSB, "return to," NIV/NASB "care for," NET "intervene for," ESV, "be mindful of"). The verb *pāqad* has the primary meaning "pay attention to, observe with care, interest." Here it refers by metonymy to the consequence of the Lord's attention and has the connotation "visit graciously" (see Gen 21:1; 50:24–25; Exod 13:19; Ruth 1:6; 1 Sam 2:21; Ps 65:9 [Hb. v. 10]). This contrasts sharply with the negative use of this same verb for judgment ("I will punish") in 1:8–9, 12.[108]

---

[102] See BDB, 500; Patterson, *Zephaniah,* 342.

[103] BDB, 155.

[104] Ben Zvi, *Zephaniah,*158.

[105] King, "The Remnant in Zephaniah," 421.

[106] "House of Judah" occurs thirty-nine times, twenty-seven of which are in the Latter Prophets. The phrase refers to the tribe of Judah, that is, the family descended from Judah. Zephaniah 2:7 is the only occurrence of the expression "remnant [שְׁאֵרִית] of the house of Judah." "Remnant of/to Judah" occurs eight times in Jeremiah without the intervening "house." A similar construct chain ("the remnant of the house of Israel") appears in Isa 46:3. The synonym פְּלֵיטָה, "remnant," occurs before "house of Judah" in 2 Kgs 19:30 = Isa 37:31.

[107] Sweeney ("The Form Criticism of Zephaniah," 404) does not see the remnant as future. He states, "The announcements concerning a remnant do not indicate the survivors of impending disaster, that is, they do not represent the doom of the people. Instead, they are survivors of past punishment who represent the divine pledge of national restoration." Even if one were to accept this view, the reference to a remnant here in a prophecy of judgment upon Philistia (and Moab/Ammon, v. 9) indicates that total judgment (as threatened in 2:1–3) will be averted.

[108] This is a case of polysemantic wordplay, where the same word is used with two different shades of meaning. In 1:8–9, 12 the verb (וּפָקַדְתִּי) is followed by the preposition עַל and then the object of judgment. The verb-preposition combination can be translated, "I will bring punishment upon," or, "I will punish." In 2:7 the verb simply takes an object suffixed to the verb (יִפְקְדֵם). Likewise, in other positive uses of the verb, the object appears without the

The first two Hb. words of verse 7 (*wəhāyâ ḥebel*, CSB*:* "the coastland will") pose a challenge. The term *ḥebel*, "rope, region," does not have the accompanying *hayyām*, "the sea," as in verse 6, and a third *masculine* singular verb appears before it, rather than the *feminine* form, as in verse 6. The LXX adds "the sea" after *ḥebel*, but it is difficult to see how if it were originally in the MT, the phrase was omitted in this graphic environment. It is far more likely it was added to harmonize the text with verse 6. Noting the gender of the verb is important here. If *ḥebel*, a masculine noun, is the original reading (minus "the sea"), then the verb form is expected. We can translate literally: "and a region [that is, an area allotted by measurement with a rope] will be for [that is, belong to][109] the remnant of the house of Judah."[110] One quickly discovers this region is Philistine territory.

The words *ʿălêhem yirʿûn*, literally, "upon them they will graze" (CSB*:* "They will find pasture there") pose a syntactical problem. There is no antecedent for the masculine plural pronoun suffix on the preposition.[111] Some suggest an emendation of *ʿălêhem* to *ʿal hayyām*, "at/by the sea."[112] If the latter is original, one can trace the corruption in the consonantal, unvocalized text as follows: *ʿl.hym* > *ʿl.yhm* (transposition of *he* and *yod*) > *ʿlyhm* (fusion of separate forms). In this case, the two

---

preposition: Gen 21:1; 50:24–25; Exod 3:16; 4:31; 13:19; Ruth 1:6; 1 Sam 2:21; Pss 65:9 [Hb. v. 10]; 80:14 [Hb. v. 15]; 106:4; Jer 15:15; 27:22; 29:10; 32:5. In Zech 10:3 both negative and positive nuances appear: "I will punish the leaders" [וְעַל־הָעַתּוּדִים אֶפְקוֹד, lit., "upon the leaders I will bring punishment" and "For the LORD of Armies has tended his flock" [כִּי־פָקַד יְהוָה צְבָאוֹת אֶת־עֶדְרוֹ] Note that the negative use "I will bring punishment" is combined with the preposition עַל, "upon," introducing the recipient of punishment, while the positive use ("has tended") simply has the recipient as the direct object (introduced by the accusative sign אֶת in this case).

[109] The combination of הָיָה and the preposition -לְ can sometimes indicate possession. For examples, see BDB, 226, II. 2h and 553, 5b. For a syntactical parallel to Zeph 2:7a, with חֶבֶל combined with possessive -לְ, see 1 Kgs 4:13, which reads lit., "to him [Ben-geber] (belong) the villages of Jair which are in Gilead, to him (belongs) the region (lit. "measuring rope") of Argob which is in Bashan."

[110] Those supporting this basic approach include Roberts, *Zephaniah,* 192, n. 3; Renz, *Zephaniah,* 537. One could add an article to חֶבֶל, and read "the [aforementioned, cf. v. 6] region will . . ." The prefixed *he* could have dropped out by haplography (note the *he* on the end of the preceding verb and the *heth* that begins חֶבֶל).

[111] Some see the pastures and enclosures of verse 6 as the antecedent and are content to understand this as an example of lack of gender agreement. See Berlin, *Zephaniah,* 107; Motyer, "Zephaniah," 933. Sweeney (*Zephaniah,* 130–31) sees the suffix as anticipating the houses mentioned in the next line. In support of his proposal, one could cite Isa 27:10, where a calf both grazes and lies down in an abandoned city.

[112] Roberts, *Zephaniah,* 192, n. 4; Renz, *Zephaniah,* 540, n. m.

elements in the composite expression *ḥebel hayyām*, "rope/region of the sea," in verse 6 are divided and used in parallel lines in verse 7.[113]

The grazing remnant is likened to sheep (cf. 3:13), implying the Lord is the shepherd (cf. 3:19; Ezek 34:15). In the evening the sheep will lie down in the houses of Ashkelon, presumably within their ruins (cf. v. 4), from which sheepfolds can be built.[114] Of course, this portrait of sheep grazing in ruins operates strictly at the locutionary (surface) level. At the illocutionary (deeper) level, the reality is the remnant of Judah will occupy former Philistine territory and reside in Ashkelon.[115] In this regard, Motyer sees an allusion to the conquest of Canaan, mentioned in verse 5 in conjunction with the land of the Philistines. He sees verse 7 as depicting a fulfillment of an unrealized promise.[116] However, in the period of the judges, Judah conquered Ashkelon, along with Gaza and Ekron (Judg 1:18), so it is more precise to say that verse 7 pictures a reactualization of that earlier event, perhaps with the hope of greater and lasting success (cf. Judg 1:19).

The Lord will be the one who brings all this about: "For the Lord their God will return to them and restore their fortunes" (cp. Zeph 3:20). The reference to "the Lord their God" invites correlation with other texts (thirty-three in number apart from Zeph 2:7) that use the expression. In Exod 29:46 the Lord says Israel "will know that [he is] the Lord their God" who delivered them from Egyptian bondage. He then repeats the assertion: "I am the Lord their God." Even when Israel experiences the covenant curses, the Lord says he will not abandon them, "For [he is] the Lord their God" (Lev 26:44). Unfortunately, the Former Prophets tell the story of how Israel/Judah rejected "the Lord their God."[117] The Latter Prophets also speak of this,[118] but

---

[113] See Renz, *Zephaniah,* 540, n. m, 558, n. 337. For examples of this poetic technique ("'breakup' of a composite phrase"), see Wilfred G. E. Watson, *Classical Hebrew Poetry: A Guide to Its Techniques*, JSOTSup 26 (Sheffield: JSOT, 1984), 328–32.

[114] For other texts using the verbs רָעָה, "graze, shepherd," and רָבַץ, "lie down," in proximity, see Song 1:7; Isa 11:7; 13:20; 14:30; 27:10 (where a calf grazes and lies down in an abandoned city); Jer 33:12; Ezek 34:14–15; Zeph 3:13.

[115] It is peculiar that only Ashkelon is mentioned and not the other towns listed in verse 4. It is likely the prophet is using a part for whole technique, with Ashkelon representative of the others. Kahn ("Zephaniah's Oracles," 441, n. 13) prefers a redactional explanation, suggesting that verse 7 may have been "edited after the conquest of Ashqelon, but before the destruction of the other Philistine cities, since only Ashqelon is mentioned twice."

[116] Motyer, "Zephaniah," 932.

[117] Judg 3:7; 8:34; 1 Sam 12:9; 1 Kgs 9:9; 2 Kgs 17:7, 9, 14, 16; 2 Kgs 18:12.

[118] Jer 3:21; 22:9; Hos 7:10.

they envision a time when the people will experience the blessings of "the LORD their God" as they return to him.[119]

The expression translated "restore their fortunes" (*šāb šəbût* [*kethib*]/*šəbît* [*qere*])[120] was once thought by many to mean "turn the captivity" or "do away with a sentence of imprisonment," with *šəbût*/*šəbît* understood as a derivative from *šābâ*, "be captive."[121] However, *šəbût*/*šəbît* may be a cognate accusative of *šûb*, "return."[122] In any case, usage, not etymology, must be determinative for the meaning of the expression. Bracke surveys its usage and concludes the term identifies "a model of restoration." Usually it "is associated with promises which indicate Yahweh's reversal of judgment, and the restoration of a condition of well-being." It often "includes Yahweh's correction of that which led to his judgment." Granted, sometimes restoration includes a return from captivity, but at times this is just one element of the restoration.[123] Furthermore, there are texts where captivity is not in view (cf. Job 42:10; Ezek 16:53; Lam 2:14).

When the Prophets use the expression to speak of the Lord's restoration of Israel/Judah,[124] literary allusion is at work. In Deut 30:1–10 Moses set the pattern for how restoration from exile would unfold.[125] When in exile (v. 1), the Lord's people will turn to him and obey him (v. 2). Then the Lord will *restore the fortunes* of the exiles and extend his compassion to them (v. 3). He will bring them back to the land (vv. 4–5), transform their hearts (v. 6), defeat their enemies (v. 7), and restore his blessings in response to their renewed commitment (vv. 8–10). Twice in his prophecy (2:7; 3:20) Zephaniah speaks of this time of restoration.

---

119 Jer 30:9; 50:4; Ezek 28:26; 34:30; 39:22, 28; Hos 1:7; 3:5; Zech 9:16; 10:6.

120 The form שְׁבוּת occurs seventeen times without a *qere* and seven times with שְׁבִית as a *qere*. Conversely, שְׁבִית occurs two times without a *qere* and four times with שְׁבוּת as a *qere*. See Bracke, "*šûb šəbût*, 235.

121 See BDB, 985–86, and Bracke's summary of the views of Preuschen and Baumann in "*šûb šəbût*," 233–35.

122 Another option is that שְׁבִית is a scribal attempt to suggest "captivity" as the meaning. See Sweeney's discussion, *Zephaniah*, 131–32.

123 Bracke, "*šûb šəbût*," 243.

124 Jer 29:14; 30:3, 18; 31:23; 32:44; 33:7, 11, 26; Ezek 39:25; Hos 6:11; Joel 3:1 [Hb. 4:1]; Amos 9:14.

125 Robertson, *Zephaniah*, 301.

2.2.2 *Devastation of Moab and Ammon to the East (2:8–11)*

The second oracle announces judgment upon Moab and Ammon to the east of Judah. It begins with the Lord speaking, stating his accusation against Moab and Ammon (v. 8). Using an oath, he then announces the coming judgment, focusing on its results without including a formal statement about his intervention (v. 9a). As in the preceding oracle (cf. v. 7), there is a statement about the remnant of Judah, called here "my people," occupying the territory of the objects of judgment (v. 9b). The two references to the Lord in verses 10–11 suggest the prophet is reflecting on the judgment.[126] In verse 10 he correlates the description of the judgment (cf. v. 9a) with the accusation (v. 8). After affirming the Lord's awesome position (v. $11a^1$), he puts the judgment of Moab and Ammon in broader, worldwide perspective (vv. $11a^2$–11b). The Lord will weaken (CSB, "starve") the "gods of the earth," prompting the distant nations to worship him.

2:8–11 The Lord heard the "taunting of Moab" and "insults of the Ammonites" against his people (v. 8). Both the noun *ḥerpâ*, "taunting," and the related verb (*piel* of *ḥārap*, "taunted") occur here. There are several texts where these terms refer to a crime, sometimes of a verbal nature, that deserves and/or receives retribution (cf. 1 Sam 25:39; Ps 79:12; Isa 65:7; Jer 15:15). As Kutsch notes, the verb carries the meaning "abuse (verbally), blaspheme, scoff." He adds, "The one who scoffs at another seeks to denigrate the latter in significance, worth, and ability; he makes clear that he scorns and despises the other."[127]

These verbal insults and threats which reveal an underlying hostility are the basis for the Lord's judgment. Significantly, the Lord speaks of "my people" (*ʿammî*), identifying with his covenant nation. In verse 9 he identifies himself as the God of Israel and refers to "the remnant of my people" (*šəʾērît ʿammî*) and "the remainder of my nation" (*yeter gôyî* [*qere*]), which sharply contrasts with "undesirable nation" in 2:1.

---

[126] See Ryou, *Zephaniah's Oracles against the Nations*, 301, though he sees it as a later addition. Floyd, *Minor Prophets,* 224, calls verses 10–11 a "summary-appraisal." See also Sweeney, *Zephaniah,* 141. Roberts, *Zephaniah,* 201, suggests that the Lord may still be speaking in verse 10.

[127] *TDOT*, 5:211. The synonymous noun גִּדּוּף, "reviling," appears in its masculine form only here and in Isa 43:28. The related feminine noun גִּדּוּפָה occurs with חֶרְפָּה in Isa 51:7, where the terms refer to verbal abuse. Another feminine noun גְּדוּפָה is used with חֶרְפָּה in Ezek 5:15. The related verbs (*piel* of גָּדַף and *piel* of חָרַף) are joined in 2 Kgs 19:22 (= Isa 37:23) and Ps 44:16 [Hb. v. 17] and refer to verbal abuse. See Ben Zvi, *Zephaniah,* 164.

In verse 10 the prophet calls the recipients of the taunts "the people of the LORD of Armies." When Moab and Ammon verbally assaulted the Lord's people, they were assaulting him,[128] which explains the severity of the punishment.

In this regard David's confrontation with Goliath is instructive. When David heard the Philistine's challenge (1 Sam 17:23), he expressed his indignation that the Philistine would disgrace Israel and, worse yet, defy "the armies of the living God" (v. 26). David's word choice is significant.[129] Goliath boasted of defying the battle lines of Israel (v. 10), and the soldiers spoke of the Philistine defying Israel (v. 25). But David viewed the Philistine's challenge from a theological perspective.[130] He had not simply defied Israel or Israel's army; he had defied the "armies of the living God" (cf. v. 36) and "the LORD of Armies, the God of the ranks of Israel" (v. 45). The Lord was closely linked with Israel and its armies. This puts the Philistine's challenge in proper perspective. He had defied Israel's God as if the Lord was not present with his people or incapable of defending them. The Philistine had no right to heap verbal abuse on the army of Israel and, by extension, the living God. David, as the Lord's instrument of justice, would kill the Philistine, demonstrating the Lord's greatness and punishing the Philistine for his blasphemous defiance (cf. vv. 45–47). David's treatment of Goliath was an act of justice whereby he vindicated the Lord's honor by silencing the Philistine blasphemer, whose crime had to be punished. David stepped forward as the instrument of justice. In a similar way Moab and Ammon, by taunting the Lord's people, taunted the Lord himself and must pay a heavy price for doing so.

The final line of verse 8 poses some challenges. It reads literally, "And they magnified (themselves) against/regarding their border/territory" (CSB: "and threatened their territory"). The *hiphil* of the verb *gādal*, "be great," has no stated object here, so it is best understood as having an exhibitive function. They exhibited "greatness" ("strength"), but in a negative sense through their boasting.[131] Other examples of this expression "boasting against/regarding (*ʿal*)" someone include Ps

---

[128] Roberts, *Zephaniah*, 200; House, *Zephaniah,* 65.

[129] See T. A. Boogaart, "History and Drama in the Story of David and Goliath," *Reformed Review* 38 (1985): 208–9.

[130] David G. Firth, *1 & 2 Samuel, AOTC* (Nottingham: Apollos, 2009), 198. See also Mark K. George, "Yhwh's Own Heart," *CBQ* 64 (2002): 456.

[131] BDB, 152, *hiphil*, category 3b.

55:12 [13] and Ezek 35:13, and perhaps also Pss 35:26; 38:16 [17]; and Lam 1:9. The relationship of the prepositional phrase ("against/regarding their border") to the verb is unclear. One could understand the pronominal suffix as referring to Moab/Ammon, the implied subject of the verb. In this case they boasted about their territory being superior to that of the Lord's people. The other option is that the suffix refers to "my people," the object of the parallel verb "taunted" in the preceding line. In this case the self-magnification in the form of boasting was directed against the territory of the Lord's people. Since "territory" refers to land, it is possible that the boasting included threats to take their land.[132]

The announcement of judgment (v. 9) is introduced with "therefore," establishing the logical cause-effect relationship between what precedes and what follows. Preceding the announcement proper, the Lord prefaces and seals it with an oath, the content of which is concise, *ḥay-ʾānî*, literally, "alive (am) I," that is, "(as surely as) I live."[133] Of the twenty-two times this precise formula appears, the following message is a negative one twenty times, the exceptions being Isa 49:18 and Ezek 33:11.[134] This is not a mere affirmation of existence but an assertion he is alive and active in the world. The affirmation should be understood in the light of the designation the "living God" (*ʾĕlōhîm ḥay/ḥayyîm* or *ʾēl ḥay*), which emphasizes God's active presence and powerful intervention. David used the title *ʾĕlōhîm ḥayyîm* when getting ready to face Goliath (1 Sam 17:26, 36). This title occurs only once in the OT prior to this. In Deut 5:26 Moses recalled that Israel heard the voice of the "living God" speaking from the fire at Sinai and lived to tell about it. The title *ʾĕlōhîm ḥay* appears later in 2 Kgs 19:4, 16 (= Isa 37:4, 17), where Hezekiah said that Sennacherib had ridiculed the living God, the same verb (*piel* of *ḥārap*) used to describe the Philistine's defiance of Israel (1 Sam 17:10). Jeremiah used the title *ʾĕlōhîm ḥayyîm* when affirming the Lord's sovereignty over the nations and his incomparability to the pagan gods (Jer 10:10–11). The Lord told Jeremiah to warn the people not to misrepresent the words of the "living God," who rules over all (Jer 23:36). The form *ʾēl ḥay* occurs

132 Sweeney, *Zephaniah*, 136.

133 The Lord uses this formula twenty-three times: Num 14:21, 28; Deut 32:40 [with אָנֹכִי]; Isa 49:18; Jer 22:24; 46:18; Ezek 5:11; 14:16, 18, 20; 16:48; 17:16, 19; 18:3; 20:3, 31, 33; 33:11, 27; 34:8; 35:6, 11; Zeph 2:9. The word נְאֻם, "declaration," follows in nineteen cases.

134 Robertson, *Zephaniah*, 304.

in Josh 3:10, where Joshua told the people they would know the "living God" was among them when he drove out their enemies before them. (This form of the title also appears in Pss 42:2, 8 [3, 9]; 84:2 [3]; and Hos 1:10 [2:1].) This title is not simply affirming God is alive as opposed to dead or that he merely exists. The contexts in which it appears associate the title with God's sovereignty, powerful presence, and ongoing intervention in the experiences of his people. He is the living God in the sense he actively intervenes for his people. We see this in David's case, where God delivered (1 Sam 17:37, 47) his servant and gave him the victory over the enemy.

Following the affirmation, "(as surely as) I live," the prophetic speech formula, "this is the LORD's declaration" (*nəʾum yhwh*) appears (cf. 1:2–3, 10; 3:8), as is typical.[135] In this case the divine name *yhwh* is modified by *ṣəbāʾôt*, "Armies" (cf. v. 10 as well), and then the additional title "God of Israel."[136] Mettinger argues that the title *yhwh səbāʾôt* fundamentally refers to the Lord's royal position at the head of the heavenly assembly, not to a military role *per se*:

> First, the Sabaoth name belongs to the temple milieu and refers to God as the heavenly King on his cherubim throne. Second, 'Sabaoth' is linguistically related to the word *sabaʾ* which itself designates the heavenly host, God's divine council. It is important to recognize that these two lines actually converge. *The Sabaoth name designates God as the heavenly King, and the element sebaʾot directs our attention to the heavenly hosts around the throne of God.* These heavenly hosts have multiple functions: they sing the eternal praise of God in the heavenly sanctuary; they serve as members of God's heavenly government; and they carry out God's assignments on earth.[137]

The numerous instances where the title depicts the Lord as sovereign King without any direct military connotation support this. However, at times the title is associated with God's royal function of warrior-judge. When the context so dictates, it is legitimate to see the title as having

---

[135] Ben Zvi, *Zephaniah*, 167.

[136] The expression נְאֻם יְהוָה צְבָאוֹת occurs twenty-five times, but only here does "God of Israel" follow. The combination יְהוָה צְבָאוֹת אֱלֹהֵי יִשְׂרָאֵל occurs (apart from נְאֻם) thirty-seven times, thirty-two of which are in Jeremiah. See Ben Zvi, *Zephaniah*, 167.

[137] Mettinger, *In Search of God*, 134–35 (emphasis in original).

a strong military connotation.[138] Zephaniah 2:9, which describes judgment in connection with the day of the Lord, is such a case.

The additional title, "God of Israel," fits nicely here. As pointed out above, the Lord identifies with his people in this oracle: "my people" (vv. 8, 9), "my nation" (v. 9), "the people of the LORD of Armies" (v. 10). It may seem peculiar that "Israel" is mentioned here rather than Judah, but the form of the traditional title is rooted deeply in Israel's past and had become standardized by Zephaniah's time.[139] The title "God of Judah" never appears in the Old Testament.

The content of the announcement per se begins with *kî*, which is typically causal, "for." Nevertheless, in this context there seems to be no causal connection with what precedes. For this reason, one might understand *kî* as emphasizing: "surely" (KJV, NIV, NASB95), "assuredly" (NASB), "be certain that" (NET). Ryou prefers to subordinate *kî* to what follows and translates "when."[140] The main clause in this case is "the remnant of my people will plunder them."

In any case, Moab and Ammon will be like Sodom and Gomorrah, respectively, upon which the Lord rained burning sulfur, leaving the entire region like a smoking furnace (Gen 19:24, 28). In the aftermath of the judgment, the region was left "a burning waste of sulfur and salt, unsown, producing nothing, with no plant growing on it" (Deut 29:23). Likewise, Moab and Ammon will be left "overgrown with weeds, a salt pit, and a perpetual wasteland" (Zeph 2:9). It makes sense the Lord would use Sodom and Gomorrah as illustrations of the desolation of Moab and Ammon, since both these peoples originated in an incestuous relationship between Lot and his daughters after they fled the judgment on the twin cities (Gen 19:30–38).[141] Perhaps there is a hint here that judgment finally caught up with Lot.

The precise meaning of the phrase *mimšaq ḥārûl*, "overgrown with weeds," is uncertain, since *mimšaq* occurs only here and its root (*mšq*) is unattested as a verb. The term *ḥārûl* occurs in two other texts. In Prov 24:31 the plural form is used of weeds that have overgrown

[138] Note especially the use of the title in 1 Sam 17:45; Pss 24:10; 46:7, 11 [Hb. vv. 8, 12]; 48:8 [Hb. v. 9]; 59:5 [Hb. v. 6]; 89:8 [Hb. v. 9]; Isa 1:9; 2:12; 5:9, 16; 9:19; 10:16, 23, 26, 33; 13:4, 13; 14:22–27; 28:22; 31:4; Jer 5:14–17; 6:6, 9; 9:7–11; 35:17; 38:17–18; Amos 3:13; 4:13; 5:14–16, 27; 6:8, 14; 9:5; Nah 2:13; 3:5; Mal 4:1–3.

[139] The title occurs 198 times in the OT, including 6 times in the Torah and 42 times in Joshua/Judges/1–2 Samuel.

[140] Ryou, *Zephaniah's Oracles against the Nations*, 108–9, 146.

[141] In this regard, see Sweeney, *Zephaniah*, 139, and *The Book of the Twelve*, 733.

the sluggard's field/vineyard. It is parallel to *qimməšōnîm*, another rare word for weeds (Isa 34:13; Hos 9:6). In Job 30:7 it refers in the singular to a large shrub in a desolate wasteland under which homeless, banished exiles huddle together for shelter. It is parallel to *śîḥîm*, "shrubs." The second phrase, *melaḥ*, "salt," is well attested. The preceding word, *mikrēh*, if related to the verbal root *kārâ*, "dig, hollow out," can refer to a salt pit or mine, but Akkadian and Aramaic cognates support a meaning "heap."[142] The third phrase begins with *šəmāmâ*, "wasteland," which also appears in 1:13; 2:4, 13. The noun is modified by *ʿad-ʿôlām*, "to perpetuity, perpetual" (cf. Jer 49:33).[143]

As in verse 7, a remnant of the Lord's people will occupy Moabite and Ammonite territory in the aftermath of the judgment. In verse 9 the language is more militaristic. The remnant will "plunder" and "dispossess" Moab and the sons of Ammon. "Plunder" (*bāzaz*) appears in the accounts of Israel's conquest of the land,[144] as does "dispossess" (*nāḥal*).[145] Moab and Ammon were exempt from conquest when Israel took the land (Deut 2:9, 19), but that will change.

One is tempted to ask, however, if the conquered territory is to be a perpetual wasteland, what would be the point of taking possession of it?[146] Robertson suggests the prophet "has simply mixed his imagery."[147] Likewise, Roberts warns against applying "hairsplitting logic to poetry that works with graphic and shifting imagery."[148] Indeed, the Lord mixes two sets of stereotypical judgment language here, annihilation on the one hand and dispossession on the other without being overly concerned with harmonizing them at the locutionary (surface) level.[149] At a deeper illocutionary level, the images agree: Moab and

---

[142] *HALOT*, 582. For discussion of the lexical problems in verse 9a, see Ben Zvi, *Zephaniah*, 168–69, n. 497; Sweeney, *Zephaniah*, 139–40; Ryou, *Zephaniah's Oracles against the Nations*, 38–39; Renz, *Zephaniah*, 541–42, n. y.

[143] The plural form of the noun appears with עוֹלָם without the preposition in Jer 25:12; 51:26, 62; Ezek 35:9.

[144] Deut 2:35; 3:7; Josh 8:2, 27; 11:14.

[145] Exod 23:30; 32:13; Deut 1:38; 3:28; 12:10; 31:7; Josh 1:6; 14:1.

[146] Ben Zvi, *Zephaniah*, 170.

[147] Robertson, *Zephaniah*, 305.

[148] Roberts, *Zephaniah*, 201.

[149] For a discussion of the prophets' hyperbolic use of stereotypical "destruction" language, see Heater, "Do the Prophets Teach that Babylonia Will Be Rebuilt in the *Eschaton*?," 23–43. Aside from Zephaniah 2, biblical examples include Isa 34:11–15; Jer 50:39–40 [used of Babylon]; 51:36–37 [used of Babylon]. For ancient Near Eastern examples, see the Sefire treaty [*COS*, 2:214] and Ashurbanipal's description of the destruction of Elam [*ARAB*, 2:310–11]).

Ammon will experience severe judgment through the instrumentality of the remnant of the Lord's people, while this remnant will be elevated to prominence over their defeated enemies. Roberts puts it this way:

> The main thought . . . is that Israel will drive Moab and Ammon out of their territories and take everything of value that belonged to them. There is no contradiction between this imagery and the portrayal of these conquered territories, following such a conquest, as wasteland.[150]

The prophet's summary begins by correlating the judgment (v. 9) with its root cause, pride (v. 10).[151] The desolation of Moab and Ammon is retribution for their arrogance, which took tangible form in their taunting and self-magnifying boasting directed against the Lord's people (cf. v. 8). More specifically, their taunts were "against the people of the LORD *of Armies*." As noted above, in these verses the Lord identifies with his people, so the taunts are ultimately against him. For the one hurling taunts, that is devastating when the one taunted is "the LORD of Armies," as Goliath could attest (see v. 9).

The Hebrew word translated "pride" (*gāʾôn*) is occasionally used in a positive sense of the Lord's majesty.[152] Nevertheless, when used of human pride it has a negative connotation. It is often associated with human strength[153] and characterizes the evil people of the earth,[154] including various nations and cities.[155] The Lord abhors human pride (Prov 8:13; Amos 6:8), which prompts his judgment (Isa 13:11; 23:9). This is why pride goes before destruction (Prov 16:18).

Verse 11 begins with an affirmation of the Lord's sovereignty. The *niphal* participle *nôrāʾ* describes him as worthy of fear, awe-inspiring or awesome. In this context, following a judgment speech against Moab and Ammon, this term refers to a future development in the aftermath of the judgment (cf. CSB/NASB, "will be terrifying," NET, "will

---

[150] Roberts, *Zephaniah*, 201.

[151] The Hebrew text reads lit., "this (is) for them in place of their pride." In this case, Hebrew תַּחַת carries the sense of "in place of, instead of" (BDB, 1065–66, category II. 2. b), with a connotation of "recompense" (*HALOT*, 1723, category 3).

[152] Exod 15:7; Isa 2:10, 19, 21; 24:14; Mic 5:3 [Hb. v. 4].

[153] Lev 26:19; Ezek 7:24; 24:21; 30:6, 18; 33:28.

[154] Isa 13:11; 23:9.

[155] Isa 14:11; 16:6; Jer 13:9; 48:29; Ezek 16:56; 32:12; Hos 5:5; 7:10; Zech 9:6; 10:11

terrify," ESV, "will be awesome"). In a context of judgment, one might reasonably understand the preposition *ʿal* as adversative, "against," especially with the pronominal suffix likely referring to Moab and Ammon (cf. ESV). However, with *nôrāʾ* it is more likely the preposition is used in the sense of "above, over," with the connotation "superior to."[156] See Pss 89:7 [Hb. v. 8], "more awe-inspiring than all who surround him," 96:4, "feared above all gods" (cf. 1 Chr 16:25).[157] So the prophet affirms that the Lord will, through his judgment upon Moab and Ammon, prove himself to be more worthy of fear than these two defeated nations, despite all their threatening, insulting taunts against his people and, as his people's God, against him. Furthermore, since the Lord identifies with his people (cf. vv. 8–10), standing behind Moab and Ammon are their gods, Chemosh and Milcom, respectively. So, by implication, the assertion of the Lord's superiority to Moab and Ammon is also an assertion of his preeminence over their gods.

The following clause takes us in this direction (CSB*:* "when he starves all the gods of the earth"), while also broadening the scope from Moab/Ammon to all nations. The opening *kî* may be understood as causal ("for") or temporal ("when"). The following perfect verbal form (*rāzâ*), if retained, has a future perfect function (lit., "he will have weakened").[158] The verb appears to mean "weaken."[159] It appears in only one other text, Isa 17:4, where a *niphal* form describes Jacob as emaciated. In the preceding parallel line, the corresponding verb (*yiddal*, from *dālal*, "be tiny") describes the fading of Jacob's splendor. The verb appears to refer to a weakening or diminishing of one's strength or vigor. Related words support this idea, including an adjective *rāzeh*, "thin, gaunt" (Num 13:20 [used of land]; Ezek 34:20 [used of a sheep]) and a noun *rāzôn*, "emaciation, leanness, consumption,"

---

[156] BDB, 755, category II. 3; *HALOT*, 826, category 1. f.

[157] In the few texts where the *niphal* participle נוֹרָא combines with the preposition עַל, the combination three times means "worthy of fear above," in a comparative sense ("more worthy of fear than") (1 Chron 16:25; Pss 89:7 [Hb. v. 8]; 96:4). In Ps 66:5 נוֹרָא, used of God's work (note the parallel line, "wonders of God"), combines with עַל־בְּנֵי אָדָם, perhaps meaning "toward the sons of man." However, the comparative nuance is possible, "more worthy of fear than (the work of) the sons of man." Renz, *Zephaniah*, 542, n. hh, prefers the comparative view.

[158] Since the event in view is future, it is tempting to emend the verb to an imperfect, understanding the MT form to be the product of haplography. Note the *yod* at the end of the preceding כִּי. Proponents of an emendation usually opt for a *piel* form, יְרַזֶּה, though the *piel* is not attested and the *qal* is transitive here.

[159] Since the *qal* is otherwise unattested, the presence of an object in Zeph 2:11 favors a transitive meaning.

used of a wasting or emaciating disease (Ps 106:15; Isa 10:16) and a short measure (Mic 6:10). The meaning of *rāzî* in Isa 24:16 is uncertain. Interpreters offer various options, but most likely it is a related noun referring to wasting away.[160]

The logical connection between this clause and the preceding one may be paraphrased this way: Through his judgment on Moab and Ammon (v. 10), the Lord will prove himself more worthy of fear than these boastful nations, for the Lord's judgment upon Moab and Ammon, as part of the day of the Lord, will encompass all nations and in defeating them he will weaken their gods.[161]

Verse 11b takes another surprising turn, moving from judgment of the nations' gods to worship of the Lord among the nations. The introductory verb (a *weyiqtol* form, imperfect with nonconsecutive *waw*) can be coordinated with (1) the preceding causal/temporal clause or (2) the first clause of the verse:[162]

1. The Lord will prove to be more worthy of fear than them,
   for he will have weakened all the gods of the earth,
   and all the coasts of the nations will worship him, each from its place.[163]
2. The LORD will prove to be more worthy of fear than them,
   for he will have weakened all the gods of the earth,
   so all the coasts of the nations will worship him, each from its place.

[160] *HALOT*, 1210. Rudman, appealing to Babylonian and Egyptian evidence, suggests that the Lord weakens the gods of the earth by depriving them of their daily offerings, viewed as food by their worshippers. He attributes this to the conversion of the nations, mentioned in the second half of the verse. Dominic Rudman, "A Note on Zephaniah," *Biblica* 81, 1 (1999): 109–12. However, it is just as likely that this alludes to the defeat of the nations, which would prevent worshippers from feeding their gods. This notion of deprivation of food for the gods may lie behind the CSB translation: "starves."

[161] This is the only passage in the OT where כָּל־אֱלֹהֵי הָאָרֶץ, "all the gods of the earth," appears.

[162] For a summary and critique of the various ways the syntax of verses 10–11 has been understood, see Ryou, *Zephaniah's Oracles against the Nations*, 146–50.

[163] It is rare to find a *weyiqtol* verb form following a כִּי-clause containing a *qatal*/perfect verb form. In relation to the כִּי-clause, the *weyiqtol* form can indicate purpose (Jer 23:18; Lam 1:19), consequence (Ps 91:14; Hos 4:6), or simple sequence (Job 3:13; Ezek 47:9; Hos 6:1). All three of these would work in this proposed syntactical structure. However, none of these examples is strictly parallel to Zeph 2:11 because in each case the subject is the same for both verbs.

In the case of (1), the final line gives an additional reason the Lord will prove worthy of fear. In the case of (2), the final line states a consequence of the Lord being worthy of fear.

The future worshippers of the Lord are designated "all the distant coasts and islands of the nations" (*kol ʾîyê haggôyim*).[164] The phrase *ʾîyê haggôyim* occurs in only one other passage, Gen 10:5, which explains: "From these descendants [that is, the offspring of Noah's son Japheth through his sons Gomer and Javan, v. 4], the peoples of the coasts and islands [*ʾîyê haggôyim*, lit., "the coasts of the nations"] spread out into their lands according to their clans in their nations, each with its own language." The noun *ʾî* occurs thirty-five times. It is often associated with the sea and/or geographical names associated with the sea.[165] Sometimes it is equated with far-off regions.[166] The coastlands probably stand by synecdoche for all nations (cf. 3:9–10). If even these distant nations recognize the Lord as King, the implication is that all will.

The distant nations will worship the Lord, "each in its own place" (*mimməqômô*). The verb translated "bow in worship" (*hishtaphel* of *ḥāwāh*) is used with the preposition *min*, "from," in only one other passage, Exod 24:1, where the preposition is locative: "bow in worship at [lit., from] a distance." In other words, the worship will take place at a distance. This parallel suggests that the object of the preposition indicates where the worship will take place.[167] The point seems to be they will not travel to Israel but will worship the Lord in their own countries. Similar scenes appear in Isa 19:19–25 and Mal 1:11.[168] This does not preclude the nations journeying to Zion for special occasions, including the resolution of disputes and the celebration of the Festival of Shelters (Isa 2:2–4; Mic 4:1–4; Zech 14:16).[169] The emphasis

[164] This expression occurs only here in the OT.

[165] Esth 10:1; Ps 72:10; Isa 23:2, 6; 24:15; 42:10; 60:9; 66:19; Jer 2:10; 25:22; 47:4; Ezek 26:15, 18; 27:3, 6–7, 15.

[166] Isa 41:5; 42:10; 49:1; Jer 31:10. See the discussion of the word's usage in Renz, *Zephaniah*, 567.

[167] Another option would be to take the preposition as pregnant: "And they will worship, each (having come) from his own place."

[168] Robertson, *Zephaniah*, 308.

[169] For a discussion of the phrase "from its place," and a defense of the position I have taken, see J du Preez, "An Interpretation of Zephaniah 2:11 with Special Reference to the Phrase *ʾîš mimqômô* [*sic*]," *Scriptura* 19 (1986): 18–24. See also Ryou, *Zephaniah's Oracles against the Nations*, 237.

in Zeph 2:11 appears to be the vast, worldwide extent of the Lord's eschatological reign. All regions of the earth come under his rule.

2.2.3 Devastation of Cush to the South (2:12)

2:12 The third oracle announces judgment upon the Cushites in the distant south: "You Cushites will also be slain by my sword." The text reads literally, "Also you, Cushites, slain of my sword (are) they." The verse poses several interpretive challenges. The most basic interpretive issue is the identity of the Cushites (*kûšîm*). Berlin discusses five options, the order of which I have rearranged, placing my preference last.[170]

1. Egypt:[171] If Egypt were intended, why is it not mentioned specifically? As Berlin points out, Cush and Egypt are often mentioned together, but they are not equated.[172]

2. Midian: Numbers 12:1 speaks of Moses having a Cushite wife. Moses's wife Zipporah was the daughter of Jethro, a Midianite priest (Exod 2:16, 21); but should we assume this Cushite wife is the same person? Habakkuk 3:7 mentions Cushan and Midian together, but Cushan is not Cush, as the spelling of the words indicates. Second Chronicles 21:16 mentions Arabians living beside Cushites, but this could refer to Cushite migrants who had settled near the Arabians.

3. Tribes of the Arabian Peninsula: Genesis 10:7 (= 1 Chr 1:9) mentions some Arabian peoples as descendants of Cush, but Seba, associated elsewhere with Egypt, is also listed. According to the Table, descendants of Cush ended up in various places, but this need not mean they were known collectively as Cushites in Zephaniah's time.

4. Mesopotamia, more specifically, Assyria: According to Gen 10:8–12, Nimrod, who settled in Assyria and built Nineveh, both of which are mentioned in Zeph 2:13, was a descendant of Cush. The literary proximity of the Cushites with Assyria in verses 12–15 is striking, but it hardly means the Cushites should be equated with the Assyrians

---

[170] Berlin, *Zephaniah,* 111–13. For an additional view that the Cushites lived on the southern border of Judah, perhaps having migrated from Ethiopia, see Robert D. Haak, "'Cush' in Zephaniah," in Steven W. Holloway and Lowell K. Handy, eds., *The Pitcher Is Broken: Memorial Essays for Gösta W. Ahlström*, JSOTSup 190 (Sheffield: Sheffield Academic, 1995), 238–51.

[171] See Patterson, *Zephaniah*, 349–50.

[172] Gen 10:6; 1 Chr 1:8; 2 Chr 12:3; Ps 68:31 [Hb. v. 32]; Isa 11:11; 20:3–5; 43:5, 14; Ezek 30:4, 9; Nah 3:9; Dan 11:43. See also Ben Zvi, *Zephaniah*, 176–77, who points out that in many cases Cush and Egypt cannot be equated.

here, as Berlin prefers.[173] In fact, in choosing a southern nation, Zephaniah may have decided to mention the Cushites, rather than Egypt, because of the ancient connection between Cush and Nimrod.[174]

5. Ethiopia or Nubia: If Cush/Cushites refers to Ethiopia/Nubia and its residents, its proximity to Egypt would readily explain the numerous texts where Cush/Cushites and Egypt are mentioned together. This view is overwhelmingly supported by usage and fits the context of Zeph 2:4–15 well, providing the southern point in the prophet's arrangement of nations in accordance with the four directions of the compass.[175] Referring to such a distant people also makes sense coming on the heels of the reference to the coastlands in verse 11. Michael Floyd observes that mention of "far-flung nations and their gods" at the end of verse 11 "leads naturally to the mention of particular kingdoms that lie outside the surrounding areas of Judah's immediate neighbors." He adds, "Ethiopia and Assyria represent this larger sphere of influence as nations representing the ancient Near Eastern centers of power in North Africa and Mesopotamia."[176]

The syntax of verse 12 also requires comment. Since the verse describes judgment (note "slain by my sword"), the initial *gam*, "also," if indicating correspondence, is to be understood in relation to the judgment portion of the preceding Moab-Ammon oracle.[177] Another option is to understand the word as an emphasizer, "even," in relation to the following word.[178] "Cushites" (*kûšîm*) is appositional to "you" (*ʾattem*). "Slain" (*ḥallê*) is a predicate nominative, modified by a genitive of instrument ("of [that is, by] the sword").[179] The final "they"

---

173 Berlin, *Zephaniah,* 113.

174 Nogalski detects in Zeph 2:12 an allusion to Genesis 10, which parallels Genesis 1, to which Zeph 1:2–3 alludes. He sees an undoing of creation in Zeph 1:2–3 and an undoing of the lines of Japheth and Ham (founded in Genesis 10) in Zeph 2:4–15. See his "Zephaniah's Use of Genesis 1–11," 356–60. Similarly, he sees a reversal of the Babel punishment in Zeph 3:9–10 (360–63).

175 E. Wendland, "The Drama of Zephaniah," 45.

176 Floyd, *Minor Prophets,* 226. For a survey of the history of the Cushites, see J. Daniel Hays, "The Cushites: A Black Nation in Ancient History," *BSac* 153 (1996): 270–80. For a recent study of the Cushites, see Kevin Burrell, *Cushites in the Hebrew Bible: Negotiating Ethnic Identity in the Past and Present,* Biblical Interpretation Series 181 (Leiden: Brill, 2020).

177 See Roberts, *Zephaniah*, 202.

178 Ryou, *Zephaniah's Oracles against the Nations*, 239. Renz, *Zephaniah*, 543, n. oo, mentions both options.

179 Renz, *Zephaniah*, 543, n. rr.

(*hēmmâ*) is appositional to "you" and serves as the subject of "slain."[180] Robertson detects a rhetorical purpose for the change in person: "The swift sword of the executioner has found its victim immediately upon the Lord's uttering the name of the Cushites."[181]

The major syntactical issue is the question of tense, which is related to identification of the discourse type. Since there is no verb, the sentence could be understood as past, present, or future. The verse follows two judgment oracles and precedes another, so the discourse appears to be anticipatory/predictive, favoring a future translation.

Some prefer to understand the time frame as present or past.[182] If, for the sake of argument, we grant the nominal sentence is best translated with the present (descriptive or expository discourse) or past tense (historical discourse) at the surface level of syntax, the usage could be rhetorical in this environment of anticipatory/predictive discourse, referring to the future in a more graphic manner as already unfolding or realized.

Renz objects to a future tense translation based on the historical background of the passage and its syntax. I have just addressed the syntactical point, but the appeal to historical background needs a reply. Renz states correctly that "it is implausible that *Cushites* stands for 'Egypt' here." He adds that "the relative obscurity of the *Cushites* from the mid-seventh century onward would make them a surprising target of a future attack. Cush is still mentioned in later oracles, but only alongside other peoples, mostly in oracles against Egypt (e.g. Jer 46:9; Ezek 30:4–5)."[183] However, I have proposed above there is good reason rhetorically for including Cush here, rather than Egypt, namely the literary proximity of references to Assyria (v. 13) and to distant nations (v. 11). Furthermore, the references to Cush in some of the later judgment speeches should not be so quickly dismissed. The focal point of Jeremiah 46 is Egypt, with Cushite involvement (v. 9) mentioned in passing. Cush is associated with Egypt in Ezekiel 30, but not as a mere subordinate. Devastating judgment will fall on Egypt, Cush,

---

[180] For discussion with numerous examples of this so-called *casus pendens* construction, see S. R. Driver, *The Use of the Tenses in Hebrew* 3rd ed. (Oxford: Clarendon, 1892), 268, par 198, Obs. 2. After the vocative there is a change to third person. See also Ryou, *Zephaniah's Oracles against the Nations*, 43–44, 238–39 (though he does not cite Driver).

[181] Robertson, *Zephaniah*, 309.

[182] See Ben Zvi, *Zephaniah*, 179; Renz, *Zephaniah*, 569.

[183] Renz, *Zephaniah*, 569.

Put [Libya], and Lud [Lydia] (Ezek 30:4–5). The judgment of Cush is distinct from that of Egypt (30:9). In Ezek 38:5 Cush appears as part of a coalition of nations headed up by Gog that includes nations from the north (vv. 3, 6: Magog, Meschech, Tubal, Gomer, Beth-togarmah), east (Persia), and south (Cush, Put [Libya]). As appears to be the case in Zeph 2:4–15, Cush, along with Put, is used to represent nations from the distant south. When one understands the rhetorical function of Cush, here and in the Ezekiel passages, appeals to historical background are largely immaterial.

2.2.4 Devastation of Assyria to the North (2:13–15)

2:13–15 The fourth oracle pronounces judgment upon Assyria to the distant north. The prophet begins in highly rhetorical fashion by calling a curse down upon Assyria and the city of Nineveh. Verse 13 contains three *weyiqtol* verb forms (prefixed forms with nonconsecutive *waw*). Most English translations treat them as imperfects and use the future tense (cf. CSB: "He will also stretch out . . . and destroy . . . he will make"). However, the first and third verb forms are distinctly jussive (*wəyēṭ . . . wəyāśēm*), while the second is ambiguous (*wîʾabbēd*) and should be understood as jussive in this context. So one should translate, "*May he* [the Lord] *stretch out* his hand against the north and *destroy* Assyria; *may he make* Nineveh a desolate ruin, dry as a desert." While some might think imperfects would be needed in this context, which contains predictive discourse, Driver long ago correctly observed, "There is no reason why the verbs should not be understood strictly as jussives" in this context.[184] Indeed, calling a justifiable curse down upon someone is a more forceful way of sealing his doom than simply predicting it. When one pronounces a curse, one appeals to the righteous Judge to activate judgment and to do so immediately, which is what the prophet does here. Furthermore, the use of the jussive with its sense of immediacy fits well in Zephaniah's historical context, for the downfall of Assyria was unfolding during Josiah's reign.

After the curse, which appeals for divine intervention, the prophet, confident his prayer will be answered, describes in verse 14 the results of judgment with the standard verb forms that characterize predictive discourse: a *weqatal* (perfect with *waw* consecutive) form and two

---

[184] Driver, *The Use of the Tenses in Hebrew*, 213, par. 172. See Motyer, "Zephaniah," 936; Robertson, *Zephaniah*, 312; and Berlin, *Zephaniah*, 114, who recognizes the jussives as rhetorical.

imperfects. In verse 15a he provides the accusation, or basis for judgment: Nineveh's arrogance. Verse 15b is a further description of the results of judgment, with the prophet using a perfect of certitude to indicate the situation described is already accomplished, followed by two imperfects.[185] Another option proposes after Assyria fell (612 BC) Zephaniah appended this description of the aftermath of judgment to the original curse and prophecy.

Zephaniah begins his appeal by calling upon the Lord to "stretch out his hand against the north" (v. 13). The next line indicates Assyria is in view. Though Assyria was located northeast of Israel, it is spoken of as being in the north because Assyrian armies would invade from that direction.[186] As noted earlier (cf. 1:4), "stretch out the hand against" is a divine judgment idiom in the Prophets.[187] This action sets in motion destructive judgment, for which the prophet prays. He then gets more specific as he asks the Lord to make Nineveh into a desolate ruin (*šəmāmâ*), a term he has already used to describe the destruction of Judah's houses (1:13), Ashkelon (2:4), and Moab/Ammon (2:9). For emphasis, he adds a simile, describing the ruins as being "dry as a desert," where there is no water to sustain life.[188]

The ruins of the once great city Nineveh[189] will be inhabited by flocks/herds (v. 14).[190] As the subject changes to the flocks/herds, the prophet switches from hortatory discourse (curses in this case) to predictive discourse (note the *weqatal* verb *wərābəṣû*, "will lie down") as he begins his description of the results of judgment. The inclusion of "in the middle of it" indicates that the destruction will be thorough, reaching to the interior of the city.[191]

---

[185] Whether Nineveh's fall is described as good as done (perfect of certitude) or as already accomplished (present perfect), the imperfects are best understood as present progressive in function within the framework of the prophet's depiction of Nineveh's ruination and the response of onlookers.

[186] Roberts, *Zephaniah*, 203; Motyer, "Zephaniah," 936–37.

[187] Isa 5:25; 14:26; Jer 6:12; 15:6; 51:25; Ezek 6:14; 14:9, 13; 16:27; 25:7, 13, 16; 35:3; Zeph 1:4.

[188] See Ps 107:35; Isa 35:2; 41:18; Jer 2:6; 50:12; Ezek 19:13; Hos 2:3 [Hb. v. 5].

[189] Werse ("Realigning the Cosmos," 118) proposes that verse 14 depicts the destruction of a temple. For support he points to the architectural features and the reference to singing.

[190] *HALOT*, 794; BDB 727.

[191] See Jer 51:47; Ezek 13:14; 22:21–22; 28:23. For a discussion of the prophets' hyperbolic use of stereotypical "destruction" language, including here in Zeph 2:13–15, see Heater, "Do the Prophets Teach that Babylonia Will Be Rebuilt in the *Eschaton*?," 23–43.

In addition to the domesticated flocks/herds that lie in the city's ruins, the usual assumption is that wild creatures are also present (cf. CSB, "every kind of wild animal"),[192] with two such animals then being specified. Nevertheless, the word *ḥayyâ* can be used of domesticated animals (cf. Num 35:3; Isa 46:1) and could refer here to a diversity of livestock/domesticated animals. The syntax allows for this: There is no conjunction before "every" and the following *gam*, "also" (used before both animals mentioned) could refer to additional animals (probably birds), rather than specifying *ḥayyāh*. The wording may point in this direction, since the word *gôy*, "nation," appears as the modifier after "animal," rather than "earth," "field," or "forest." Furthermore, in verse 15 the phrase *marbēṣ laḥayyāh*, "resting place for an animal," need not refer to the "lair" for a wild animal (cf. CSB, NIV). In fact, the only other time *marbēṣ* occurs, it refers to a sheepfold (Ezek 25:5). Likewise, the related verb *rābaṣ*, "lie down," can be used of domesticated flocks and herds (see v. 14a) and the related noun *rēbeṣ* in its two occurrences refers to the resting place of domesticated animals (Isa 65:10; Jer 50:6).[193] The scene depicted here may be comparable to what is described in 2:7, where the remnant of Judah, pictured as sheep, makes the ruins of Ashkelon their abode.

Interpreters have debated the precise identity of the specific animals mentioned.[194] The first word (*qāʾat*) refers to an unclean bird (Lev 11:18; Deut 14:17) that dwells in a desert (Ps 102:6 [7]) or in ruins (Isa 34:11).[195] The second word (*qippōd*) occurs in Isa 14:23; 34:11 and refers to an animal that inhabits ruins. Some opt for a bird, others

---

[192] The Hebrew text is difficult; it reads lit., "every animal of a nation." The alternative construct form (with *-ô* ending) of חַיָּה, "animal," appears elsewhere with "earth" (Gen 1:24 [note the normal form in v. 25]; Ps 79:2), "forest" (Pss 50:10; 104:20; note Isa 56:9, where "in the forest" follows), or "field" (Ps 104:11; Isa 56:9) as modifying genitive. See GKC, 254, par. 90o. The appearance of גּוֹי, "nation," as a genitive here is surprising. In this graphic environment it is difficult to see how any of the attested genitives could have been corrupted to גּוֹי. (The LXX has *gēs*, "earth.") If retained, one can only guess at a meaning. Perhaps the idea is that the ruins will be the abode of all the typical animals one finds in a typical nation.

[193] *HALOT*, 1181.

[194] See David J. Clark, "Of Birds and Beasts: Zephaniah 2:14," *The Bible Translator* 34 (1982): 243–46.

[195] CSB: "eagle owls" (margin: "pelicans"); NASB: "pelican" (margin: "owl," "jackdaw"); NIV: "desert owl;" ESV: "owl."

for a hedgehog.[196] The animals lodge (the root is *lîn*, "to lodge")[197] in the "capitals of its pillars," presumably lying broken on the ground.[198]

The sound of one or both of these animals will be heard in/through a window (cf. CSB: "Their calls will sound from the window"). The Hebrew text reads literally, "A voice will sing in/through the window."[199] Renz, in a lengthy discussion of the verb *šîr*, "sing," points out this Hebrew verb is always used of human singing, never of birds singing.[200] Yet in this context the human inhabitants are gone. It would appear that irony is at work.[201] In Nineveh's ruins, the only sounds approximating singing are those of the birds/animals inhabiting the ruins. The prophet continues describing the sights and sounds of the city's ruins. As the animals' "singing" is heard from the window, "devastation" (*ḥōreb*; cf. CSB, ESV) is visible on the threshold. If "devastation" is the correct reading, it probably refers by metonymy to the visible signs of devastation, such as rubble and debris (cf. NET, NIV: "rubble").[202] This will be, at least in part, the result of (note *kî*, "for") woodwork being exposed and presumably scattered about.[203]

In verse 15 "this" refers to the description of ruined Nineveh in verse 14. One may paraphrase: "This (the desolate city Nineveh just described) is the destiny of the jubilant city, that lives in security, that says to herself: I exist and there is no one else" (cf. CSB, NASB). In this case the two substantival participles are translated as present. This

---

[196] CSB: "herons" (margin: "hedgehogs"); NASB: "hedgehog;" NIV: "screech owl;" ESV: "hedgehog."

[197] CSB has "roost" because they see both animals as birds.

[198] If both animals are birds, then the pillars could be standing. See Renz, *Zephaniah*, 572.

[199] The Hebrew verb form is a *polel* imperfect from שִׁיר, "to sing." The *polel* form draws attention to the "continuation . . . of the action" as "recurring" (*HALOT*, 1480). If an owl is the bird making the sound, then "hooting" (NIV11) or "hoot" (ESV) is a suitable translation.

[200] Renz, *Zephaniah*, 572–76.

[201] Sweeney, *Zephaniah*, 153.

[202] Since animals (including at least one bird) have just been mentioned and "devastation" seems a bit abstract for this description, some prefer to emend חֹרֶב, "devastation," to עֹרֵב, "raven." The term עֹרֵב, "raven," appears in Isa 34:11 with קָאַת and קִפֹּד, the two animals mentioned in Zeph 2:14. This reading has the support of the Septuagint and the Vulgate. See CSB margin, "ravens."

[203] See the discussions in Patterson, *Zephaniah*, 356, and Sweeney, *Zephaniah*, 154. The Hebrew text reads lit., "For cedar work he/one will have exposed." The noun אַרְזָה occurs only here in the Old Testament. It appears to be the feminine form of אֶרֶז, "cedar." Renz, *Zephaniah*, 545, n. hhh, suggests a collective use. The verb עֵרָה is a *piel* perfect meaning "to expose, uncover." The *qatal*/perfect has a future perfect function, describing an action that will occur before the preceding situation. The subject may be the Lord, or it could be simply indefinite ("someone").

approach fits well with verse 14, which views the judgment as future. Another option is to translate the participles as past and understand the rhetorical perspective as future: "This (the desolate city Nineveh just described) is what is left of the once jubilant city, that lived in security, that said to herself: I exist and there is no one else" (cf. NET, NIV, ESV). This fits well with the statement that follows in verse 15: "What a desolation she has become" [note the *qatal*/perfect verb form].

In either case the prophet provides the basis for judgment, namely, Nineveh's hubris.[204] The first word he uses to describe the city is *ʿallîzâ* (the feminine form of *ʿallîz*), which refers to joyful celebration. It can have a positive (Isa 13:3) or a negative (Isa 22:2; 23:7; 24:8; 32:13; Zeph 3:11) connotation, depending on the context.[205] In Zeph 2:15 it is negative, referring to boastful arrogance.

Nineveh also lived in security. The expression used here (the verb *yāšab*, "live," combined with the prepositional phrase *lābeṭaḥ*, "according to [that is, in a state of] security)[206] refers to physical security without the threat of harm or, in the case of a city or nation, invasion (see Deut 12:10; 1 Sam 12:11; Ezek 34:28).[207] Living in such security can make one confident (Ps 4:8), unsuspecting (Jud 18:7; Prov 3:29; Ezek 38:11), and in some cases arrogant and overconfident, like Nineveh (cf. Isa 47:8, used of Babylon). Nineveh's arrogance was evident in her words, spoken "to herself" (lit., "in her heart"): "I exist, and there is no one else" (lit., "I, and there is none besides").[208] The statement's grammatical structure makes it a declaration of incomparability and an affirmation of uniqueness and superiority. Nineveh is in a class all by herself. One may paraphrase: "I am unique! No one can compare to me" (NET).

After a declaration of such hubris, Zephaniah's sudden exclamation marks a striking contrast: "What a desolation she has become"

---

[204] Ryou, *Zephaniah's Oracles against the Nations*, 251.

[205] The same can be said for the related verb עָלַז, which can be positive (Pss 28:7; 60:6 [Hb. v. 8]; 68:4 [Hb. v. 5]; 96:12; 108:7 [Hb. v. 8]; 149:5; Prov 13:16; Hab 3:18; Zeph 3:14) or negative (2 Sam 1:20; Ps 94:3; Isa 23:12; Jer 11:15; 15:17; 50:11; 51:39).

[206] On the use of the preposition, see BDB, 516, category 5. j.

[207] Apart from Zeph 2:15, the expression occurs in twenty-one other texts: Lev 25:18–19; 26:5; Deut 12:10; Judg 18:7; 1 Sam 12:11; 1 Kgs 4:25 [Hb. 5:5]; Ps 4:8 [Hb. v. 9]; Prov 3:29; Isa 47:8; Jer 32:37; 49:31; Ezek 28:26; 34:25, 28; 38:11, 14; 39:6, 26; Zech 14:11.

[208] The *yod* ending on אַפְסִי may be paragogic or a suffix (if the latter, "except me"). See GKC, 253, par. 90l; *HALOT*, 79; BDB, 67; Ryou, *Zephaniah's Oracles against the Nations*, 119. The same construction appears in Isa 47:8, 10, where Babylon is the speaker.

(v. 15).[209] In the other uses of this exclamation, one sees a similar contrast. In Ps 73:19 the psalmist's exclamation about the demise of the arrogant wicked ("How suddenly they become a desolation!") contrasts with the earlier description of their pride and ease (vv. 3–12). In Jer 50:23 the Lord's exclamation about Babylon's demise ("What a horror [lit. "desolation"] Babylon has become among the nations!") contrasts with her former exalted status as "the hammer of the whole earth." Similarly, in Jer 51:41 the Lord's exclamation about Babylon's fall ("What a horror [lit., desolation] Babylon has become among the nations!") stands in contrast to her former honor as "the praise of the whole earth."

By using the *qatal*/perfect form *hāyətâ*, "she has become," the prophet takes a rhetorical stance in the not too distant future beyond Nineveh's fall. As noted above, it is possible that once Nineveh fell (612 BC) Zephaniah appended this description of the aftermath of judgment to the original curse and prophecy. At any rate, he now elaborates on Nineveh's ruined condition. The city has become a place for animals to lie down.[210] Whoever passes by the abandoned ruins "scoffs and shakes his fist." The verb translated "scoffs" literally means "whistle, hiss." Apparently, such whistling and shaking the fist (lit., hand) were taunting, derisive gestures.

---

[209] This same exclamation (אֵיךְ+ the perfect of לְשַׁמָּה + הָיָה), lit., "How she has become a desolation," occurs in Ps 73:19 (third common plural form of the perfect) and in Jer 50:23; 51:41 (third feminine singular form of the perfect in both cases).

[210] See the above discussion of *marbēṣ laḥayyāh* in the comments on verse 14, where I make the point that the phrase need not refer to the "lair" of a "wild animal." In this regard, Michael B. Dick's reading of Zeph 2:13–15 against the backdrop of Assyrian royal lion hunts lacks substantive textual support. See his "The Neo-Assyrian Royal Lion Hunt and Yahweh's Answer to Job," *JBL* 125, 2 (2006): 261.

SECTION OUTLINE

3 Glimpses Become Reality: Judgment Gives Way to Salvation (3:1–20)
- 3.1 The Necessity of Judgment and Patience (3:1–10)
  - 3.1.1 The Necessity of Judgment upon Jerusalem (3:1–5)
  - 3.1.2 The Necessity of Judgment upon the Nations (3:6–7)
  - 3.1.3 The Necessity of Waiting upon the Lord (3:8–10)
- 3.2 The Transformation of the Lord's People (3:11–20)
  - 3.2.1 Jerusalem's Joy (3:11–15)
  - 3.2.2 The Lord's Joy (3:16–19)
  - 3.2.3 The Lord's Restoration of the Exiles (3:20)

3 GLIMPSES BECOME REALITY: JUDGMENT GIVES WAY TO SALVATION (3:1–20)

1 *Woe to the city that is rebellious and defiled,*
the oppressive city!
2 *She has not obeyed;*
she has not accepted discipline.
She has not trusted in the LORD;
she has not drawn near to her God.
3 *The princes within her are roaring lions;*
her judges are wolves of the night,
which leave nothing for the morning.
4 *Her prophets are reckless—treacherous men.*
Her priests profane the sanctuary;
they do violence to instruction.
5 *The righteous* LORD *is in her;*
he does no wrong.
He applies his justice morning by morning;
he does not fail at dawn,
yet the one who does wrong knows no shame.
6 *I have cut off nations;*
their corner towers are destroyed.
I have laid waste their streets,
with no one to pass through.
Their cities lie devastated,
without a person, without an inhabitant.
7 *I said: You will certainly fear me*

and accept correction.
Then her dwelling place
would not be cut off
based on all that I had allocated to her.
However, they became more corrupt
in all their actions.
8 *Therefore, wait for me—this is the LORD's declaration—until*
the day I rise up for plunder.
For my decision is to gather nations,
to assemble kingdoms,
in order to pour out my indignation on them,
all my burning anger;
for the whole earth will be consumed
by the fire of my jealousy.

9 *For I will then restore*
pure speech to the peoples
so that all of them may call
on the name of the LORD
and serve him with a single purpose.
10 *From beyond the rivers of Cush*
my supplicants, my dispersed people,
will bring an offering to me.
11 *On that day you will not be put to shame*
because of everything you have done
in rebelling against me.
For then I will remove
from among you your jubilant, arrogant people,
and you will never again be haughty
on my holy mountain.
12 *I will leave*
a meek and humble people among you,
and they will take refuge in the name of the LORD.
13 *The remnant of Israel will no longer*
do wrong or tell lies;
a deceitful tongue will not be found
in their mouths.
They will pasture and lie down,
with nothing to make them afraid.

[14] *Sing for joy, Daughter Zion;*
shout loudly, Israel!
Be glad and celebrate with all your heart,
Daughter Jerusalem!
[15] *The* L*ORD* *has removed your punishment;*
he has turned back your enemy.
The King of Israel, the L*ORD*, *is among you;*
you need no longer fear harm.
[16] *On that day it will be said to Jerusalem:*
"Do not fear;
Zion, do not let your hands grow weak.
[17] *The* L*ORD* *your God is among you,*
a warrior who saves.
He will rejoice over you with gladness.
He will be quiet in his love.
He will delight in you with singing."

[18] *I will gather those who have been driven*
from the appointed festivals;
they will be a tribute from you
and a reproach on her.
[19] *Yes, at that time*
I will deal with all who oppress you.
I will save the lame and gather the outcasts;
I will make those who were disgraced
throughout the earth
receive praise and fame.
[20] *At that time I will bring you back,*
yes, at the time I will gather you.
I will give you fame and praise
among all the peoples of the earth,
when I restore your fortunes before your eyes.
The L*ORD* *has spoken.*

Chapter 3 continues the judgment theme that has predominated to this point. The prophet denounces Jerusalem's sins (vv. 1–5). The Lord expected the city to repent when the people saw the devastating judgment he brought upon the nations, but they persisted in their sinful ways (vv. 6–7). Consequently, those hoping for restoration of blessing must wait for judgment to run its course (v. 8). The Lord will bring another round of judgment upon the whole earth, culminating in the spiritual transformation of the nations (vv. 9–10) and of Jerusalem, which will be populated by a faithful remnant. Jerusalem and her people will celebrate the Lord's powerful presence and the security he provides (vv. 11–20).[1]

The section consists of two major literary units (3:1–10, 11–20). Judgment is the focus in the first unit (vv. 1–8). However, a salvation announcement suddenly swallows up judgment (vv. 9–10) as the Lord expands the theme of 2:11, which foresees a time when the distant nations will worship the Lord. The second unit, introduced by the formula "in that day" (v. 11), expands the salvation announcement to include Jerusalem and her people. It develops in greater detail the salvation hint and notices of 2:7, 9.

3.1 The Necessity of Judgment and Patience (3:1–10)

The first unit begins with a woe oracle in which the prophet denounces the city for its sins committed despite the Lord's presence within it (vv. 1–5). The Lord suddenly speaks, addressing the city (vv. 6–7; note "I have cut off" at the beginning of v. 6).[2] He explains the city and her people have not repented despite his expectations. He then addresses a group, probably the remnant mentioned in verse 12, urging them to wait patiently for judgment to run its course (v. 8). The message takes a positive turn as the Lord describes the transformation of the nations to genuine worshippers (vv. 9–10). "Therefore" at the beginning of verse 8 formally links the exhortation with what precedes, but the switch from a feminine singular addressee in verse 7 to a masculine plural addressee in verse 8 marks the transition to a new subunit. Three causal/explanatory clauses introduced by "for" (*kî*) follow (two in v. 8b and one at the beginning of v. 9). They may provide motivation for obeying the exhortation to "wait" (see discussion below).

---

[1] In addressing the macrostructure of the book, Sweeney prefers to view 2:1–3:20 as one literary unit, which he labels a "Prophetic Exhortation Proper." He sees the entire book as having a hortatory purpose and calls it a "Prophetic Exhortation to Seek Yahweh." See his "Form Criticism of Zephaniah," 403–4.

[2] Sweeney (*Zephaniah*, 169–70, 172) takes verse 5 with verses 6–13.

3.1.1 The Necessity of Judgment upon Jerusalem (3:1–5)

The Lord will judge the rebellious city, Jerusalem, who has rejected him (vv. 1–2). Her civil and religious leaders are corrupt (vv. 3–4), in contrast to the just Lord who dwells within the city (v. 5).

3:1–5 This woe oracle is strictly accusatory, with no formal announcement of judgment, though the "woe" connotes impending doom. The address contains accusatory elements as the prophet calls the city rebellious, defiled, and oppressive (v. 1).

A first-time reader might think this oracle is directed to Nineveh (cf. 2:13–15).[3] James Nogalski sees a rhetorical dimension comparable to what Amos does in his oracles in chapters 1–2.[4] The audience, thinking Nineveh and the Assyrians are still in view, is in for a surprise as the prophet turns the threat of judgment toward Jerusalem, a fact that becomes clear in verse 2. Jerusalem will not escape the judgment about to come upon the nations.

This rhetorical move has an additional function. It serves to associate Nineveh and Jerusalem morally. Nathan Hays says, "The rapid and unmarked transition from the oracle against Assyria/Nineveh . . . to the condemnation of Jerusalem . . . rhetorically underscores the deep and troubling continuity between Jerusalem and Assyria/Nineveh."[5] The Lord has already denounced Jerusalem for embracing foreign astral worship and dress (1:5, 8). According to Hays, astral worship "was especially prominent in Assyria and material evidence for astral worship in the Levant increases considerably with greater contact with Assyria." Furthermore, there is "iconographic evidence for Assyrian-style dress in the Levant during the period of Assyrian domination," which is likely alluded to in 1:8. Hays explains: "Elites were attempting to gain prestige by aligning themselves with Assyria even on the level of their clothing."[6]

Hays points out that pride is a developing theme in chapter 2 (see v. 10), culminating in the oracle against Assyria (vv. 13–15). Nineveh is a "jubilant [*ʿallîzâ*] city that lives in security [*lābeṭaḥ*], that says to herself: I exist, and there is no one else" (v. 15).[7] Hays shows how the

---

[3] Wendland, "The Drama of Zephaniah," 47–48.

[4] Nogalski, *The Book of the Twelve*, 736.

[5] Hays, "Humility," 472.

[6] Hays, "Humility," 477–78.

[7] Hays, "Humility," 479–81.

theme escalates in 3:1–7. Jerusalem is "rebellious" (v. 1); she rejects the Lord's will and refuses to trust (*bāṭāḥâ*) him (v. 2). Rather than fearing the Lord and accepting discipline, she becomes increasingly corrupt (v. 7). In the next part of the speech (v. 11) where the Lord announces the transformation of the city, he describes her condition as rebellious. However, he will remove her "jubilant, arrogant people" (*ʿallîzê gaʾăwātēk*) who are "haughty." By developing this theme of pride, the Lord attempts to motivate the sinful people to join the ranks of the humble (cf. 2:3; 3:12).[8]

As the prophet continues his indictment of the personified city, he accuses her of failure in four areas, using four negated *qatal*/perfect verb forms (v. 2). He next exposes the sins of four groups within the city: princes, judges, prophets, and priests (vv. 3–4). One expects a formal announcement of judgment to appear, but instead the prophet describes the Lord, focusing on his just character and actions (v. 5a-b[1]). The pattern of four (see vv. 2–4) continues as he makes four assertions about the Lord.[9] This description has a twofold function. (1) Like the introductory woe in verse 1, it hints that judgment is impending because the just Lord who dwells within the city will not tolerate what he sees happening within it (see especially v. 3). (2) The description creates a sharp contrast between the just Lord, on the one hand, and the sinful city and its sinful residents, on the other hand. As such it heightens their guilt and supports the formal accusation that precedes. To reinforce the contrast, the prophet follows the description with the statement, "Yet the one who does wrong knows no shame" (v. 5b[2]).

After the introductory woe, the prophet addresses "the city that is rebellious and defiled, the oppressive city." The text reads literally, "Woe, rebellious and defiled one, the oppressive city." As noted earlier (see 2:5), the interjection *hôy*, "woe," was used in funeral laments (see 1 Kgs 13:30; Jer 22:18–19; 34:5; Amos 5:16). Consequently, when the prophets used it in conjunction with a pronouncement of impending judgment, it would evoke the listeners' attention for it connotes death and conveys a sense of urgency.

The meaning of the first word (*mōrəʾâ*) after "woe" is uncertain. The simplest explanation is to understand the form as related to the verbal root *mārâ*, "rebel," with the third *he* verb following a third

[8] Hays, "Humility," 481–83.

[9] Ball (*Zephaniah*, 201–2, 223) also observes the use of four in this speech.

aleph pattern. In this case, the form is a *qal* active participle, feminine singular, "rebellious one."[10] This understanding of the form fits well with the description of the city in verse 2, characterized as disobedient and failing to accept discipline. However, some relate the form to a noun, attested in postbiblical Hebrew, meaning "excrement"[11] (see KJV, NET: "filthy"). This interpretation fits well with the verb that immediately follows: "defiled."[12]

This next word (*nigʾālâ*) is a *niphal* participle from *gāʾal*, meaning "be defiled." It appears in this stem (*niphal*) in two other texts. In Isa 59:3 the Lord confronts his people with their sinful deeds (cf. v. 2). He accuses them of having "hands defiled with blood" because they have committed unjust acts of violence against others (cf. vv. 4–8). In Lam 4:14 the author laments over the judgment that has come upon Jerusalem because of the sins of her prophets and priests "who shed the blood of the righteous" (cf. v. 13) and thereby defiled themselves. In both texts the defilement by blood is the result of violent crimes against others. This is the background for Zeph 3:1 as well (see v. 3; cf. 1:9).

In the second half of the verse, the prophet more specifically identifies the one who is "rebellious and defiled" as "the oppressive city." The *qal* participle *yônâ*, "oppressive," used here as an attributive adjective modifying "the city," appears in three other texts, all in Jeremiah: (1) 25:38: The Lord announces judgment upon the shepherds (a metaphor for the leaders of the nations), which will come through a violent oppressor. (2) 46:16: The prophet announces that an "oppressor's sword" will devour Egypt. (3) 50:16: The Lord will judge Babylon through an "oppressor's sword." There is another *qal* form of the verb in Ps 74:8, where the conquerors of God's people say, "Let's oppress them relentlessly" before burning down every place throughout the land where God met with his people. In each of these passages, militaristic violence is in view, which is not the case in Zeph 3:1. Nevertheless, the motif of violence is common to all the texts in which the *qal* form of the verb appears, Zeph 3:1 included (cf. v. 3). This

[10] See GKC, 216–17, par. 75rr, as well as CSB, NASB, NIV, ESV, and Ben Zvi, *Zephaniah*, 184–85.

[11] In this case, it could be a *hophal* denominative. See *HALOT*, 630. On the noun רֵאִי II, see Jastrow, *Dictionary,* 1436. This word may occur in Nah 3:6 (cf. רֹאִי), where "filth" (שִׁקֻּץ) appears earlier in the verse, but the word more likely means "spectacle." Others relate it to מֻרְאָה, which refers to a bird's craw in Lev 1:16 (cf. *HALOT,* 630).

[12] For discussions of other proposals, see Roberts, *Zephaniah*, 206.

verb occurs more commonly (fourteen times) in the *hiphil* stem, where unjust, oppressive actions against those living in one's own country (often resident aliens) occur in thirteen of the texts as in Zeph 3:1.[13]

In verse 2 the prophet accuses the personified city of failing to do four things. First, "she has not obeyed,"[14] literally, "she has not listened to a voice."[15] When used with a human subject, the idiom connotes disobedience or failure to hear and act accordingly. Elsewhere in this commonly used expression, "voice" is invariably modified by a pronominal suffix or a genitive, often the Lord. Only here does "voice" appear without a modifier. In this context, the Lord's voice is the implied object of the verb. However, by omitting the modifier, the prophet draws attention to her established character as unresponsive and disobedient.[16]

Second, "she has not accepted discipline." The expression "accept discipline" (the verb *lāqaḥ*, "accept," with *mûsār*, "discipline" as object) occurs eleven times.[17] In Prov 24:32 it refers to a favorable response to an object lesson. The author says he "received instruction" from observing the negative consequences of laziness. In other words, he learned an important lesson about diligence in work that impacted his behavior. In some cases, the expression refers to changing (or failing to change) one's behavior after experiencing the negative consequences of disobedience. Jeremiah 2:30 and 5:3 describe how the Lord severely punished his people but they failed to accept it as discipline and refused to change their sinful behavior. The expression carries this sense in Zeph 3:2. The Lord's attempts to change the behavior of the sinful city have proven futile because of her unwillingness to respond favorably to disciplinary punishment.

Third, "she has not trusted in the LORD." In the Hebrew text, "in the LORD" precedes the verb for emphasis.[18] If there were any doubt about which city the prophet is addressing, the words "in the

---

[13] Exod 22:21 [Hb. v. 20]; Lev 19:33; 25:14, 17; Deut 23:16; Jer 22:3; Ezek 18:7, 12, 16; 22:7, 29; 45:8; 46:18. The lone exception is Isa 49:26, where foreign oppressors are in view.

[14] As reflected in the CSB translation, the perfect/*qatal* verb forms are best understood here as perfective.

[15] The Hebrew text reads, לֹא שָׁמְעָה בְּקוֹל. On the use of the preposition -בְּ with the verb "to hear," see GKC, 380, par. 119k; BDB, 90, IV. d.

[16] In this regard, see Bailey, "Zephaniah," 475; and Sweeney, *Zephaniah*, 161.

[17] In addition to its two appearances in Zeph (3:2, 7), it occurs three times in Proverbs (1:3; 8:10; 24:32) and six times in Jeremiah (2:30; 5:3; 7:28; 17:23; 32:33; 35:13).

[18] In this regard, see Bailey, "Zephaniah," 476–77.

LORD" and "her God" in the next line make clear that Jerusalem is the addressee.[19] The expression "trust in the LORD" is associated with Hezekiah's obedience to the Lord's commands (2 Kgs 18:5; cf. vv. 4, 6). The psalmist declares his "trust in the LORD" in a context where he affirms his unwavering devotion to the Lord and his obedience (Ps 26:1). Trusting in the Lord entails doing what is right (Ps 37:3). According to Prov 3:5, the one who trusts in the Lord does "not rely on" his "own understanding." He recognizes the Lord's authority, fears the Lord, and turns away from evil (vv. 6–7). Indeed, putting one's confidence in human beings, rather than the Lord, is deadly and deprives one of the Lord's blessing (Jer 17:5, 7), while the one who trusts in the Lord experiences deliverance (Pss 21:7 [Hb. v. 8]; 28:7; 40:3 [Hb. v. 4]; 84:12 [Hb. v. 13]; 115:9–11; Prov 29:25; Jer 39:18) and the Lord's blessing (Ps 32:10; 125:1; Prov 16:20). Trusting in the Lord means to obey him and rely on him for security. The people of Jerusalem in Zephaniah's day had not done this and would forfeit the benefits of their covenantal relationship with the Lord.[20] They were trusting in their wealth, military strength, foreign alliances, and false gods.[21]

Fourth, "she has not drawn near to her God." In the Hebrew text, "to her God" precedes the verb for emphasis. This expression "draw near to God" (*qal* of *qārab*, "draw near," with the preposition *ʾel* followed by *ʾĕlōhîm*, "God") occurs elsewhere only once. In 1 Sam 14:36 the priest accompanying Saul and the Israelite army advises the king: "Let's approach God here." Saul then seeks an oracle from God (v. 37). In Isa 48:16 the Lord summons Israel to draw near to him to hear his word. The sample size of usage is small, but one could conclude that Zeph 3:2 speaks of Jerusalem's failure to consult God's will. The inclusion of the pronoun, "*her* God," highlights this relational failure.

In verses 3–4 the prophet denounces four groups within the city: princes, judges, prophets, and priests. He begins with the civil leaders, namely princes and judges (v. 3). The princes (*śārîm*) appear earlier in 1:8 (cf. CSB "officials"), where they are associated with the king's sons and with those who wear foreign clothes. They worked within the royal administration and were responsible for justice, among other things. The earlier reference gives no indication of why they would be

---

[19] Sweeney, *Zephaniah*, 161.

[20] In this regard, see Ben Zvi, *Zephaniah*, 188.

[21] Roberts, *Zephaniah*, 212.

punished. Nevertheless, here in 3:3 we get a clue: "The princes within her are roaring lions." The metaphor (they *are* lions) is more rhetorically powerful than a mere simile would be (they are *like* lions). Identifying them as ferocious lions depicts them as powerful and violent. Ezekiel's description of a roaring lion is terrifying in the extreme. He compares the false prophets[22] of Jerusalem to a "roaring lion tearing its prey: they devour people, seize wealth and valuables, and multiply the widows within her" (22:25).

The immediate context of Zeph 3:3 suggests a similar scenario. In contrast to the Lord's commitment to justice (v. 5), oppression characterizes the city (v. 1), suggesting injustice is in view. In fact, 1:9 speaks of "violence and deceit." Elsewhere in the Prophets we read of Judah's officials (*śārîm*) perpetrating injustice against the vulnerable of society and corrupting the legal system by taking bribes (Isa 1:23; 3:14; Jer 34:8–11; Ezek 22:27; Mic 3:1–9; 7:3).

The city's judges were also corrupt (v. 3b). The word translated "judges" (*šōpəṭîm*) can refer to civil leaders in a general sense, as in the book of Judges, but often refers more specifically to those who carry out a judicial function.[23] In this context, where justice is a theme, this appears to be the case. These judges are identified as "wolves of the night," a phrase used only here and in Hab 1:8.[24] Ezekiel compares Jerusalem's officials to "wolves tearing their prey, shedding blood, and destroying lives in order to make profit dishonestly" (22:27). Genesis 49:27 describes the tribe of Benjamin as a wolf that "tears his prey. In the morning he devours the prey, and in the evening he divides the plunder." The description depicts the wolf hunting in the evening and finishing his meal in the morning. As with the image of the roaring lion, injustice, accompanied by violence, is the background of the imagery.

The meaning of the final clause is uncertain. It reads literally, "they have not gnawed at morning." The verb (*gāram*) is related to the noun *gerem*, "bone." The verb, which is in the *qal* stem in verse 3, occurs in two other passages in the *piel* stem (probably indicating reiterative action) of breaking or gnawing on bones (Num 24:8) or on the pieces

---

22 The Hebrew text has "prophets," while the Septuagint has "leaders" (cf. NET).

23 See, for example, Deut 1:16; 16:18; 17:9, 12; 19:17–18; 21:2; 25:1–2; 1 Sam 7:15–17; 8:1–2 (cf. v. 3); 2 Sam 15:4; 1 Kgs 3:9, 18; Mic 7:3.

24 Some emend עֶרֶב, "evening," to עֲרָבָה, "desert" (cf. NET), but "evening" forms a nice parallel with "morning" in the next line (cf. Gen 49:27). For discussion see Ryou, *Zephaniah's Oracles against the Nations*, 55; Ben Zvi, *Zephaniah*, 192; Roberts, *Zephaniah*, 207, n. 6; Berlin, *Zephaniah*, 128; Sweeney, *Zephaniah*, 164.

of a broken cup (Ezek 23:34). The point here in verse 3 may be that the "wolves" (unjust judges) of Jerusalem are so eager to devour that they leave nothing for morning (cf. CSB, "which leave nothing for the morning," cf. NASB95; NIV; NET).[25]

The city's religious leaders were also corrupt. Zephaniah characterizes the prophets as "reckless" and "treacherous" (v. 4).[26] The verb (participle) translated "reckless" (*pāḥaz*) appears in the OT only here and in Judg 9:4, where it is combined with the word "empty" to describe the morally bankrupt thugs Abimelech hired to help him murder his half brothers and carry out his coup. Related terms occur in Gen 49:4 to describe "turbulent" (*paḥaz*) water and in Jer 23:32, which denounces prophets who mislead the people with "reckless [*paḥăzût*] lies." The word translated "treacherous" (*bōgədôt*) is related to the well-attested verb *bāgad*, which refers to using deceit to exploit and betray others.[27]

The priests also come under fire, for they profaned what is holy (v. 4b).[28] The verb translated "profaned" (*piel* of *ḥālal*) appears with "what is holy" (*qōdeš*) as its object in six passages. In three texts ritually holy offerings are in view (Lev 19:8; 22:15; Num 18:32), while in three others the object (holy thing[s]) is mentioned without specificity (Ezek 22:8, 26 [Sabbaths are included]; Mal 2:11). In several passages the verb is used with the Lord's name, characterized as "holy," as the object,[29] while the holy Sabbath is the object in Exod 31:14. The reference in Zeph 3:4 lacks specificity, but since the priests are the subjects of "profane[d]," cultic objects (cf. Ezek 22:26) or the worship center itself could be in view.[30]

The priests also did violence to the law. The verb *ḥāmas*, "treat violently," which is related to the well-attested noun *ḥāmās*, "violence,"

---

[25] For a helpful discussion of the hunting and eating habits of wolves, see Renz, *Zephaniah*, 589–90. Appealing to cognate evidence, BDB (175) understands a homonymic verb here, meaning "lay aside, leave, save," which fits the context. For discussion, see Ryou, *Zephaniah's Oracles against the Nations*, 55–57.

[26] The text reads lit., "Her prophets are reckless ones, men of treachery." "Men of" is in apposition to "reckless ones." The modifying attributive genitive after the construct tells what type of men they are.

[27] See, among several others, Isa 24:16; Jer 3:20; 12:6; Hos 5:7.

[28] The *qatal*/perfect verb forms are perfective (see NET).

[29] Lev 20:3; 22:2, 32; Ezek 20:39; 36:20–22; Amos 2:7.

[30] CSB has "the sanctuary" (cf. KJV, NASB, NIV), while NET and ESV have "what is holy." One would expect to see מִקְדָּשׁ, "sanctuary," as the object if the worship center was in view (cf. Lev 21:12, 23; Ezek 23:39; 24:21; 28:18; 44:7; Dan 11:31), but קֹדֶשׁ could conceivably stand by metonymy for the place of worship.

occurs at least seven times.[31] It takes as its object the resident alien, the fatherless, the widow (Jer 22:3), grapes (Job 15:33), an individual (Job 21:27; Prov 8:36), and a shelter (Lam 2:6). In Ezek 22:26, as in Zeph 3:4, *tôrāh* is the object. However, in that passage, where the priests are also the perpetrators of the violence, the text specifies the *tôrāh* as the Lord's (note "my instruction"), which is likely the case in Zeph 3:4 as well. The word *tôrāh* refers generally to "instruction(s)." In this context, where priests are profaning what is holy, it probably refers to the covenant stipulations regulating ritual holiness and cultic purity. For the verb *ḥāmas* to be used of their actions, their violations must have been blatant and excessive.

With the guilt of the city and its leaders established beyond a shadow of a doubt, one expects a formal announcement of judgment at this point. Instead, as noted above, the prophet suddenly makes four assertions about the Lord, who will judge the guilty before wrapping up his accusation (v. 5). The rhetorical technique is reminiscent of Amos 5:7–10, where the prophet's accusation (vv. 7, 10) is interrupted by a hymnic description of the Judge himself (vv. 8–9):

AMOS 5:7–10	ZEPHANIAH 3:4–5
7 Those who turn justice into wormwood also throw righteousness to the ground.	4 Her prophets are reckless— treacherous men. Her priests profane the sanctuary; they do violence to instruction.
8 **The one who made the Pleiades and Orion, who turns darkness into dawn and darkens day into night, who summons the water of the sea and pours it out over the surface of the earth— the Lord is his name.**	5 **The righteous Lord is in her; he does no wrong. He applies his justice morning by morning; he does not fail at dawn,**
9 **He brings destruction on the strong, and it falls on the fortress.**	
10 They hate the one who convicts the guilty at the city gate, and they despise the one who speaks with integrity.	yet the one who does wrong knows no shame.

Some question or deny the originality of Amos 5:8–9, but, as I have pointed out elsewhere, this "begs the real question for . . . someone

[31] The *niphal* form of verb in Jer 13:22 could derive from חָמַס, "treat violently" (see BDB, 329), but *HALOT* (329) lists it as a homonym meaning "devise."

. . . felt this hymnic description of God was appropriate here." Indeed, "the very awkwardness of these verses draws attention to them and highlights their content." Furthermore, verses 8–9 occupy "the central and pivotal position in a chiastic" structure within verses 1–17 that many have observed:

A Israel's demise deserves a *lament* (vv. 1–3).
  B The people must *repent* for judgment is imminent (vv. 4–6),
    C and they are guilty of *injustice* (v. 7).
      D They will encounter the divine Judge (vv. 8–9).
    C[1] The people are guilty of *injustice* and judgment is imminent (vv. 10–13),
  B[1] so the people must *repent* (vv. 14–15).
A[1] Divine judgment will bring widespread *lamentation* (vv. 16–17).[32]

Likewise, Zeph 3:5a-b[1] seemingly interrupts the accusation of 3:4, 5b,[2] but its awkwardness draws attention. As explained above, the description has an important twofold rhetorical function.

Zephaniah begins by affirming, "The righteous LORD is in her."[33] In this context, where the Lord's justice is the focus, the adjective "righteous" (*ṣaddîq*) is best translated "just."[34] The addition of "in her" (*bəqirbâ*) is significant in the light of verse 3, where Jerusalem's princes "within her" (*bəqirbâ*) are described as roaring lions, a metaphor that depicts them as violent oppressors. The repetition of the prepositional phrase in verse 5 serves to juxtapose and contrast the Lord who dwells within the city with the unjust leaders who also dwell there. As noted above, it supports the introductory woe, which implies impending judgment, for the just Lord will not tolerate what is going on within his city. This theme of what is transpiring within the city is developed further in 3:11–12.

Second, the prophet states the Lord "does no wrong."[35] The statement complements the preceding one, affirming through a negated

---

[32] Chisholm, *Handbook on the Prophets*, 391–92.

[33] Rather than taking "righteous" as an attributive adjective, some prefer to take it as predicative: "The LORD is righteous within her" (NASB, cf. NIV, ESV).

[34] *HALOT,* 1003, category 6. b; BDB, 843, category 1.d.

[35] Outside of Zephaniah 3 (cf. vv. 5, 13), the verb עָשָׂה, "do," is combined with עַוְלָה, "wrong," only in Ps 37:1, where עֹשֵׂי עַוְלָה refers to "those who do wrong."

sentence the reality of the Lord's just character. The *yiqtol*/imperfect verb form (*yaʿăśeh*, from *ʿāśâ*, "do") has a generalizing function, characterizing the Lord. The noun *ʿawlâ*, "wrong," in this context probably refers primarily to acts of injustice. This well-attested word often refers to evil in a general, unspecified way; but it is sometimes associated with specific forms of wrongdoing, including violence (Ps 58:2 [Hb. v. 3]), murder and lies (Isa 59:3), robbery (Isa 61:8), bloodshed (Mic 3:10; Hab 2:12), and bribery (2 Chr 19:7).[36]

Third, Zephaniah says the Lord "applies his justice morning by morning."[37] In this context the verb *yittēn* (from *nātan*, "give") has the nuance "to grant, bestow" in the sense of "execute." The *yiqtol*/imperfect verb form has a generalizing function, characterizing the Lord's behavior. Given the context, justice in the social and legal arena is primarily in view. The execution of legal justice is also associated with morning in Jer 21:12: "Administer justice every morning, and rescue the victim of robbery."

Fourth, the prophet states the Lord "does not fail at dawn."[38] This statement complements the preceding one, affirming through a negated sentence the reality of the Lord's commitment to justice each day. In the parallelism of the doublet the prepositional phrase *lāʾôr*, "at the light," refers to sunrise each morning.[39] The verb *neʿdār* (a *niphal* participle) means "to be missing"[40] and when negated as here, "is not missing" (CSB, "does not fail").

The revelation of the Lord and his justice at the morning light (cf. "morning by morning," "at dawn" [lit., "light"]) stands in stark contrast to the ravenous activity of the "wolves of the night" (v. 3), who

---

[36] The corresponding masculine nominal form, עָוֶל, can refer to legal injustice (Lev 19:15; Ps 82:2) and cheating for profit (Lev 19:35; Deut 25:16 [cf. vv. 13–15]; Ezek 18:8; 33:15).

[37] The text reads lit., "In the morning, in the morning his justice he gives." The repetition of the prepositional phrase conveys the idea of "every morning." See GKC, 395, par. 123c, and Ben Zvi, *Zephaniah*, 209.

[38] It is possible to take מִשְׁפָּטוֹ, "his justice," as the subject. For discussion see Ryou, *Zephaniah's Oracles against the Nations*, 61, 124–25.

[39] See *HALOT*, 24, category 3. We understand לָאוֹר, "at the light," as going with what follows. For discussion see Ryou, *Zephaniah's Oracles against the Nations*, 60, 124–25, 258–59, and Ben Zvi, *Zephaniah*, 210–11. While acknowledging the strengths of the temporal view of the prepositional phrase, DeRouchie understands it differently, as going with what precedes as an adverbial modifier of "gives." He then interprets it as "a metaphor for 'that which guides to the right way.'" See Jason S. DeRouchie, "YHWH's Judgment Is New Every Morning: Zephaniah 3:5 and the Light of the World," *Trinity Journal* 43NS (2022): 131–46 (on the syntax, see esp. 133–35).

[40] See the use of the *niphal* in 1 Sam 30:19; 2 Sam 17:22; Isa 34:16; 40:26; 59:15.

perpetrate their injustice in the darkness.[41] The contrastive imagery facilitates the transition to the final statement of verse 5, where the prophet, having described the Lord's just character, resumes his accusation against the city's leaders: "Yet the one who does wrong knows no shame." In contrast to the Lord, who "does no wrong," the leaders were guilty of wrongdoing.[42] The noun *ʿawwāl*, "sinner," is related to *ʿawlâ*, "wrong," used earlier in the verse (and in v. 13). It occurs elsewhere only in Job 18:21; 27:7; 29:17; and 31:3, where it consistently refers to evildoers.

The expression "know shame" (the verb *yādaʿ*, "know," combined with the noun *bōšet*, "shame") occurs elsewhere in just one passage, Ps 69:19 [Hb. v. 20], where the psalmist says this: "You know the insults I endure—my shame and disgrace," using the verb "know" with the nuance, "be aware of." The verb has a different shade of meaning in Zeph 3:5, where the point seems to be that the wicked do not express (metonymy, know and feel/express) a sense of shame, remorse, or embarrassment over their wicked deeds to the point where they repent and change their ways.[43] The noun *bōšet*, "shame," appears to have such a nuance in at least two other texts:

Jer 3:25: "Let us lie down in our shame. . . . We have sinned against the Lord our God."
Dan 9:7–8: "Public shame belongs to us . . . because we have sinned against you."

The related verb *bôš*, "be ashamed," is used in this sense in several texts, including . . .

> Ezra 9:6: "I am too ashamed and disgraced, my God, to lift up my face to you, because our sins are higher than our heads and our guilt has reached to the heavens."

---

[41] Wendland, "The Drama of Zephaniah," 48–49.

[42] See Ball, *Zephaniah*, 278.

[43] In this case, the metonymic use of "know" with "shame" in the sense of "know and feel/express shame" is functionally equivalent to the verb בּוֹשׁ, "be/feel ashamed." Berlin (*Zephaniah*, 130–31) understands the statement differently. She takes "does not know" in the sense of "ignore," and "shame" as referring to the condemnation that sinful behavior will bring. In other words, they ignore the consequences of their wrongdoing.

Jer 6:15: "Were they ashamed when they acted so detestably? They weren't at all ashamed. They can no longer feel humiliation." (See also 8:12.)

Jer 31:19: "After I strayed, I repented; after I came to understand, I beat my breast. I was ashamed and humiliated."

Ezek 16:63: "When I make atonement for you for all you have done, you will remember and be ashamed."

Ezek 36:32: "Be ashamed and disgraced for your conduct, people of Israel!"

3.1.2 The Necessity of Judgment upon the Nations (3:6–7)

The Lord's people did not learn the intended lesson from his judgment upon the nations (v. 6) but instead persisted in their sinful ways (vv. 6–7).

3:6–7 After the description of the just Lord and the accusatory statement in verse 5, a formal announcement of judgment would certainly be in order, but that does not happen. The Lord breaks in and speaks, but he does not announce judgment. Instead, he elaborates on the accusation by giving a detailed account of his attempt to bring his people to repentance. Despite his efforts, they persisted in their sin and did so with enthusiasm.

The Lord brought devastating judgment upon nations and cities (v. 6).[44] He "cut off nations," an expression that refers to terminating them (Josh 23:4; Isa 10:7; cf. Jer 48:2). The description of judgment then focuses on the devastation of their cities. Their "corner towers," a reference to walled cities (synecdoche of part for whole), depicts their strongest defenses being destroyed (see 1:16). The Lord "laid waste" their streets so no one could pass through.[45] This detail makes clear that the destroyer breached the defenses and went through the city

---

[44] Motyer ("Zephaniah," 947) goes in a different direction than most, understanding the *qatal*/perfect verb forms as indicating certainty and looking to future developments.

[45] The expression מִבְּלִי־עוֹבֵר, "with no one to pass through," also occurs in Jer 9:12 [Hb. v. 11] and Ezek 14:15. As with מֵאֵין in 2:5 and later in this verse, the preposition מִן, "from," indicates a negative consequence, "so that not." See BDB, 583, category 7b. The negative בְּלִי adds emphasis. See BDB, 115; Ryou, *Zephaniah's Oracles against the Nations*, 64.

leaving it in ruins (cf. Ezek 19:7). Their cities were devastated[46] and left uninhabited.[47]

Verse 6 displays a symmetrical paneled structure that is modified for rhetorical purposes:[48]

A Lord's intervention (first person *hiphil* perfect): "I have cut off nations"

  B Results of intervention (third person *niphal* perfect): "their corner towers are destroyed"

A[1] Lord's intervention (first person *hiphil* perfect): "I have laid waste their streets"
Depopulation (prepositional phrase with *min: mibbəlî*): "with no one to pass through"

  B[1] Results of intervention (third person *niphal* perfect): "Their cities lie devastated"
  Depopulation (prepositional phrase with *min: mibbəlî*): "without a person"
  Depopulation (prepositional phrase with *min: mēʾên*): "without an inhabitant"

There is an intensification in the description as it progresses, mirroring the intensity of the judgment. A1 mirrors A (intervention), but with an additional phrase highlighting the depopulation resulting from the intervention. B[1] mirrors B (results of intervention), but also A[1] in that there are now two additional phrases describing depopulation. The first mirrors the one attached to A[1] (note *mibbəlî*) while the second switches to *mēʾên*, signaling closure through terminal deviation. There are seven syntactical units in all, indicating completeness. They are distinguished in the Hebrew text by the accentual system, with each unit containing two elements.

Verse 6 refers to the Lord's judgment upon nations and cities, so we can only speculate what specific historical events are in view. One thinks of the Assyrian conquests in the eighth century BC, which were

---

[46] The verb נִצְדּוּ is a *niphal* perfect from the verbal root צָדָה, which occurs only here in the Old Testament. It is attested in postbiblical Hebrew and Aramaic (Jastrow, *Dictionary,* 1262).

[47] The expression מִבְּלִי־אִישׁ, "without a person," also occurs in Jer 9:10 [Hb. v. 9] with עוֹבֵר, "passing through," following it. The expression מֵאֵין יוֹשֵׁב, "without an inhabitant," is more common, occurring elsewhere in Zeph 2:5, as well as Isa 5:9; 6:11; Jer 4:7; 26:9; 33:10; 34:22; 44:22; 46:19; 48:9; 51:29, 37. See earlier comments on 2:5.

[48] Ball (*Zephaniah*, 225–26) has also noticed the structural features of this verse but schematizes them differently.

orchestrated by the Lord (Isa 10:5–15), their conquest of the northern kingdom (cf. Amos 7:9; Mic 1:6–7), and their conquest of Thebes in 663 BC (Nah 3:8). If this oracle dates to the final years of Josiah, the fall of Nineveh in 612 BC anticipated in 2:13–15 could provide the historical referent.

Verse 7a reveals the Lord's purpose for judging the nations in relation to Jerusalem. He had expected the destruction of these nations to serve as a wake-up call for his people. Speaking to Jerusalem (note the second feminine singular verb forms), he said, "You will certainly fear me and accept correction." The emphasizer *ʾak*, "certainly" (cf. 1:18), highlights the Lord's expectation. To "fear" the Lord is to submit to his sovereign authority and turn from evil. To "accept correction" is to change one's behavior after experiencing or observing the negative consequences of flawed behavior (see 3:2). The Lord anticipated that observing his judgment on others would prompt the city and its residents to respond positively to the object lesson, but, as verse 2 states, "She has not obeyed; she has not accepted discipline."

Following the statement of the Lord's expectation, he indicates what the positive consequences of fearing him and accepting correction would be. We can paraphrase: "I said: You will certainly fear and accept correction and then/consequently her place will not be cut off by/after all [the punishment] that I will have brought upon her." The shift from the second to third person is a bit awkward, but the negated third-person *yiqtol*/imperfect with *waw* (*wəlōʾ-yikkārēt*, "will not be cut off") after the second-person imperfects indicates purpose or in this case result (consequence).[49] The term *kōl*, "all," is best taken as an adverbial accusative indicating manner (by) or time (after). What follows explains how or when the cutting off would occur. The *qatal*/ perfect verb form *pāqadtî* has a future perfect function ("I will have brought punishment upon") in relation to "will be cut off." In other words, the implementation of punishment would occur before or concomitantly with the cutting off.

As noted above, the transition of person is awkward. One would expect to read, "*Your* place will not be cut off. . . . I will have brought upon *you*." However, the line should be viewed within the larger

---

[49] For other examples, see Num 5:3 ("Send them outside the camp, so that they will not defile the camps"); Deut 24:15 ("You are to pay him his wages. . . . Otherwise he will cry out" [or, so that he will not cry out); Ruth 2:22 ("It is good for you to work with his female servants, so that nothing will happen to you in another field").

rhetorical framework of this speech. After the opening woe address (v. 1), the Lord speaks of the personified city in the third person in verses 2–5 (four third feminine singular verb forms and seven third feminine singular pronouns). After the historical review of verse 6, he addresses the city with two second feminine singular verbs in verse 7a, but then reverts to the third feminine singular in verse 7a[1]. Ironically, the Lord, though dwelling in the city (v. 5), has distanced himself from her due to her sin. He can speak *about* her, but only briefly does he speak *to* her and, only then by recalling what he said at an earlier time. Though it violates proper grammar, he reverts to the more impersonal third person.[50] Nevertheless, this will change radically in the next speech (vv. 11–20), where direct address to the restored city is predominant.

The Lord's intention was thwarted by the people's insistence on sinning (v. 7b). As already indicated in verse 2, "they became more corrupt in all their actions." The text reads literally, "However, they arose early and corrupted all their actions." The introductory *ʾākēn* is contrastive in this context.[51] The *hiphil* of the verb *šākam*, "to do (something) early," is often combined with another verb to indicate that an action was done early, or more figuratively, with eagerness, which is the case here where the next verb means to "make corrupt."[52]

The Lord shifts from feminine singular forms in addressing and describing the city (v. 7a) to third plural forms in referring to her residents' commitment to sinning (v. 7b). This same pattern was visible in verses 1–5, where the city's actions were the initial focus (note the four third feminine singular verbs in v. 2). While the city was still present in verses 3–5 (note six third feminine singular pronouns), the actions of her sinful leaders took center stage (note three third plural *qatal*/perfect verbs in vv. 3–4 and three nominal sentences describing them). We see the same shift in focus from city to residents here in verse 7. This same movement will appear in the next speech (vv. 11–20): city (vv. 11–12a)—people (vv. 12b–13)—city (vv. 14–19a)—people (vv. 19b–20; with direct address in v. 20).

---

[50] Renz (*Zephaniah,* 598) rightly observes that rhetoric is at work here and speaks of "distancing."

[51] *HALOT*, 47; BDB, 38.

[52] *HALOT,* 1493. The *qatal*/perfect verb forms are best understood as perfective here. Robertson (*Zephaniah,* 324) hears an echo of Deut 31:29 here.

3.1.3 The Necessity of Waiting upon the Lord (3:8–10)

The Lord urges his obedient followers to wait for his judgment to run its course and for the transformation of the nations into genuine worshippers.

3:8–10 With the appearance of *lākēn*, "therefore," at the beginning of verse 8, one expects to see the formal announcement of judgment. Instead, an exhortation follows, instructing an unidentified group (note the second masculine plural verb)[53] to wait patiently for judgment to run its course. The judgment will be worldwide in scope (note "nations" and "kingdoms"). The Lord's use of seven first-person singular pronouns comes close to making this a formal announcement of judgment, though one expects to see at least one first-person singular verb. Furthermore, while Judah will be included among these nations, she is not singled out to bring closure to verses 1–7. Suddenly the message takes a positive turn, as the Lord describes the transformation of the nations to genuine worshippers (vv. 9–10). This paves the way for a salvation announcement addressed to Zion (see v. 11).

The presence of *lākēn*, "therefore" (v. 8), indicates a logical connection to what precedes, but the change of addressee from the city (note the second feminine singular verbs in v. 7) to a group signals this is a new subunit. Since the residents of Jerusalem did not respond to the Lord's attempt to prompt repentance, the group addressed must wait for the Lord to bring about the restoration predicted earlier (cf. 2:7, 9) that will come about through judgment. It is likely the Lord speaks here to his obedient followers, whom he addressed with the second masculine plural in an earlier exhortation in 2:3: "Seek the Lord, all you humble of the earth, who carry out what he commands." This group is also described in 3:12 as "meek and humble people" who "take refuge in the name of the Lord." The exhortation to "wait for" [me, that is, the Lord] has a positive connotation which carries the nuance "wait in faith."[54] Such hopeful expectation will sustain God's people through the difficult time to come when he pours out his anger on the nations. The exhortation is supported by the prophetic speech

---

[53] The LXX has a singular imperative verb here, perhaps due to *yod-waw* confusion. In verse 7, the LXX has plural imperatives where the Hebrew has feminine singular forms.

[54] One finds this same positive connotation with this verb (חָכָה) in Ps 33:20; Isa 8:17; 30:18; 64:4 [Hb. v. 3]; Hab 2:3. See Sweeney, *Zephaniah,* 180.

formula, "this is the Lord's declaration" (*nəʾūm yhwh*), which appears for the fifth and final time within the prophecy (cf. 1:2–3, 10; 2:9).

The prepositional phrase "until [lit., "for"] the day I rise up for plunder" is appositional to "for me" and expands on its meaning. The question that arises from the exhortation (wait for me to do what?) is answered here. The Lord will arise for the purpose of taking plunder (or prey).[55] The combination "rise up" (*qûm*) and "plunder" (*ʿad*) occurs only here, but this appears to be a reference to rising up for war (cf. Jer 49:14), with plunder being a metonymy (effect for cause).[56]

The next clause is introduced by *kî*, the first of three such clauses in verses 8b–9. Each is best understood as causal in relation to "wait," providing a threefold explanation for why waiting is necessary.[57] As such, they provide motivation for responding positively to the imperative. In this case, waiting for the Lord to arise as a warrior is necessary because (1) he has decided to gather nations for judgment, (2) his zeal will devour all the earth, and (3) then he will turn the nations into genuine worshippers. It will be worth waiting for the Lord's judgment to run its course because judgment will culminate in restoration. Understood this way, the three clauses reflect a chronological progression as suggested by *ʾāz*, "then," following the third *kî*. The Lord gathers the nations for judgment, pours his anger out on them, and then transforms them.[58]

---

[55] Sweeney, *Zephaniah,* 181.

[56] The Septuagint understands the word as עֵד, "witness," here: "for the day of my arising as a witness" (NET). See NIV: "For the day I will stand up to testify." Other texts do speak of a witness (עֵד) arising (קום) to give testimony in a legal setting. See Deut 19:15–16; Job 16:8; Pss 27:12; 35:11. The presence of מִשְׁפָּט, used in the sense of a formal (legal) "decision" in the next clause, might support this (cf. Mal 3:5), though in this case the legal metaphor would be mixed (witness and judge). However, see Renz, *Zephaniah,* 599, who cites other examples of such a mixture and suggests a double entendre here. See also Ben Zvi, *Zephaniah,* 222–23, who proposes a triple entendre. For a study of the problem, see Adrian Schenker, "Israelite or Universal Horizon?: Zephaniah 3.8–10 in the Hebrew and Greek Bibles," *The Bible Translator* 64, 2 (2013): 151–58. Schenker argues that verses 8 and 10 (which are shorter in the Septuagint) must be considered together with the older (in his opinion) Greek reading reflecting a "universal perspective," in contrast to the Hebrew reading's "Israelite perspective" (see p. 157). Schenker assumes that the reference to "dispersed people" in verse 10 refers to Israelite exiles. However, see the commentary on 3:8–10 below.

[57] See Sweeney, *Zephaniah,* 171, 181, 183.

[58] For other examples where כִּי־אָז means "for then," see Josh 1:8; 2 Sam 5:24; Job 11:15; 22:26; Jer 22:22; Zeph 3:11. Another option is to understand each כִּי initiated clause in relation to what immediately precedes. The first could be understood as causal in relation to "for the day I rise up for plunder." It explains that the Lord's intervention as a warrior is the outworking of his decision to gather the nations for the purpose of pouring out his anger upon them. The second

Waiting is necessary because the Lord has made an important "decision" to "gather nations" and "assemble kingdoms" (v. 8b).[59] The word *mišpāṭ* refers here to a formal decision made by the Lord in his role of Judge.[60] The term occurs four times in Zephaniah. It refers to the Lord's standards of justice that he expects people to observe (2:3; see commentary above), the Lord's just actions (3:5), and the Lord's acts of judgment upon Jerusalem (3:15). Here in 3:8 it refers to his just decision to bring judgment upon nations.[61]

The synonyms "gather" (*ʾāsap*) and "assemble" (*qābaṣ*) occur in proximity in ten other texts. The connotation is often positive, referring to the Lord gathering his people from exile (Isa 11:12; Ezek 11:17; Mic 2:12; 4:6). In other texts the nations are gathered for a legal confrontation with the Lord (Isa 43:9), the Lord's people gather to repent (Joel 2:16), Babylon gathers the nations to dominate them (Hab 2:5), and birds gather to devour the flesh of Gog's armies (Ezek 39:17).[62] Here in Zeph 3:8 the connotation is negative as the following infinitive, "to pour out my indignation [*zaʿmî*] on them," makes clear. This

כִּי initiated clause could be understood as temporal, "when," in relation to what immediately precedes. The Lord will pour out his fury when the whole earth is devoured by his fiery zeal. The third *kî* initiated clause does not seem to be related logically to what precedes, so the כִּי here would need to be understood as an emphasizer, "surely." For other examples where כִּי־אָז means "surely then," see Deut 29:20 [Hb. v. 19]; 2 Sam 2:27; 19:6 [Hb. v. 7].

59 The suffixed infinitival form קָבְצִי is best translated "assemble to me," with the suffix having a dative function. See *HALOT*, 1063, and Ryou, *Zephaniah's Oracles against the Nations*, 68.

60 Sweeney, *Zephaniah,* 181. For other examples of this shade of meaning for מִשְׁפָּט, see BDB, 1048, categories 1.a ("act of deciding a case") and 1.e ("sentence, decision of judgment"). However, BDB puts Zeph 3:8 under category 1.f, "execution of judgment."

61 The antecedent of the third plural pronominal suffix on עֲלֵיהֶם is most naturally understood as the "nations" (with its parallel term "kingdoms") mentioned just before this. However, some prefer to understand the referent as the Lord's sinful people described at the end of verse 7. In this case the assembled nations are the Lord's instrument of judgment that he uses to pour out his anger on his sinful people. See, for example, Roberts, *Zephaniah,* 216–17. This necessitates understanding כָּל־הָאָרֶץ at the end of the verse as "the whole land." For a survey of views (Jerusalem and its "elite," the nations, Jerusalem and the nations), see Judith Gärtner, "Jerusalem—the City of God for Israel and for the Nations in Zeph 3:8, 9–10, 11–13," in Rainer Albertz, James D. Nogalski, and Jakob Wöhrle, eds., *Perspectives on the Formation of the Book of the Twelve: Methodological Foundations—Redactional Processes—Historical Insights*, BZAW 433 (Berlin: De Gruyter, 2012), 271–72. She opts for a redaction critical explanation involving three updates, but she does state that "from a synchronic point of view" the third update ("*Fortschreibung*") "specifies the perspective of the first and second" (p. 278).

62 The two remaining uses are in Isa 62:9 (gathering grain and grapes) and Ezek 29:5 (Pharaoh and his army will not be gathered for burial).

indignation is identified as "all my burning anger" (*kōl ḥărôn ʾappî*).[63] In Zeph 2:2 the Lord's burning anger is associated with "the day of the LORD's anger," suggesting the judgment described in 3:8 coincides with the judgment of the day of the Lord in 1:2–2:3.

The verb "pour out" (*šāpak*) is used with the noun "indignation" (*zaʿam*) in three other texts (Ps 69:24 [Hb. v. 25]; Ezek 21:31 [36]; 22:31). As in Zeph 3:8 "fire" (*ʾēš*) accompanies this outpouring in Ezek 21:31 and 22:31, and "burning anger" (*ḥărôn ʾap*) accompanies it in Ps 69:24. The verb "pour out" is used with "burning anger" in Lam 4:11, where it is associated with "fire." The terms for anger (*zaʿam* and *ḥărôn ʾap*) occur together in Pss 69:24; 78:49; and Nah 1:6. As Nahum points out, no one can "withstand [God's] indignation" or "endure his burning anger." Waiting is also necessary because (note *kî*, "for") "the whole earth will be consumed by the fire of" the Lord's "jealousy" (v. 8b[1]). This statement also appears in 1:18 with one minor difference. A third-person suffix appears with *qinʾâ* there ("*his* jealousy"), while a first-person suffix occurs here ("*my* jealousy") with the Lord as the speaker. This is another indication the judgment described in 3:8 is the judgment of the day of the Lord depicted in 1:2–2:3. For discussion of "the whole earth" and "jealousy," see the commentary on 1:18 above.

The third reason for waiting is remarkable. The Lord will "restore pure speech to the peoples so that all of them may call on the name of the LORD and serve him with a single purpose" (v. 9). With the first-person singular verb "I will restore" (*ʾehpōk*), we finally see the expected formal statement of the Lord's active intervention. However, he does not announce his intervention in judgment but rather for restoration. Waiting will allow judgment to run its course and to culminate in its final goal: restoration. Though the Lord will pour out his anger and consume the whole earth (v. 8), judgment is not the end. Beyond judgment the Lord intends to restore the nations (vv. 9–10) and his covenant people (vv. 11–20).

The verb translated "restore" (*hāpak*) has the primary meaning of "turn." It is often used of overturning or overthrowing an object in judgment. Nevertheless, it can also refer to changing or altering in a

[63] The phrase "all my burning anger" (כֹּל חֲרוֹן אַפִּי) is in apposition to "my indignation" (זַעְמִי).

positive sense as it does here.[64] Used with the preposition "to" (*ʾel*), it has the nuance "restore."

The beneficiaries of the Lord's restorative intervention are "peoples" (*ʿammîm*), referring to the nations. However, there is a shift in language here in verse 9 from the terms used in verse 8, where the nations are referred to as *gôyim*, "nations," and *mamlākôt*, "kingdoms." The words are synonymous, but the shift may be significant nevertheless. The word "kingdoms" appears only here in Zephaniah but *gôy*, "nation," occurs seven times:

1. 2:1: "undesirable nation" (referring to sinful Judah)
2. 2:5: "nation of the Cherethites" (referring to the Philistines)
3. 2:9: "remainder of my nation" (referring to the remnant of Judah)
4. 2:11: "islands of the nations" (referring to distant nations that will worship the Lord)
5. 2:14: "every kind [*gôy*] of wild animal" (referring to types of animals)
6. 3:6: "I have cut off nations" (referring to nations that have been judged by the Lord)
7. 3:8: "my decision is to gather nations" (referring to nations that will be judged)

The plural form is used negatively twice (3:6, 8) of nations under judgment but positively once (2:11) of "islands of the nations" as future worshippers.

The term *ʿam*, "people," also appears seven times:

1. 1:11: "all the merchants" [*ʿam kənaʿan*, lit., "people of Canaan," an idiom for merchants)
2. 2:8: "my people" (referring to Israel, cf. v. 9)
3. 2:9: "remnant of my people" (referring to the future remnant of Israel)
4. 2:10: "the people of the LORD of Armies" (referring to Israel)
5. 3:9: "the peoples" (referring to the restored nations of the future)

---

[64] See, for example, (1) Deut 23:5 [Hb. v. 6]: "He turned the curse into a blessing for you," (2) Jer 31:13: "I will turn their mourning into joy," (3) Ps 30:11 [Hb. v. 12]: "You turned my lament into dancing," and (4) Ps 66:6: "He turned the sea into dry land." On the irony in Zeph 3:9, see Wendland, "The Drama of Zephaniah," 52–53.

6. 3:12: "a meek and humble people" (referring to the future remnant of Israel, cf. v. 13)
7. 3:20: "all the peoples of the earth" (referring to the restored nations of the future, cf. v. 9)

The plural form is used twice of the nations of the future who worship the Lord and live in harmony with the remnant of Israel (of whom the singular "people" is used three times). The shift from *gôyim* (2:11; 3:8) to *ʿammîm* in 3:9 mirrors the change that will come to the nations (*gôyim*) in the aftermath of judgment. They have a new name, one that is used in the singular of the Lord's covenant people (except for the idiomatic expression in 1:11).

The Lord will restore to the peoples "pure speech." The text literally reads, "a purified lip" (*śāpâ bərûrâ*). "Lip" is used here by metonymy for words, specifically a language.[65] The passive participle (or, perhaps, adjective) *bərûra*, "purified," is derived from the verb *bārar*, "purify, select."[66]

Developing a theme already introduced in 2:11b, the Lord anticipates a time when he will restore purified speech to the peoples, enabling them to praise the Lord in unison as they serve him (vv. 9b–10). The people of the earth will again speak one language. This is a reversal of the Babel event, when God confused the unified language of the people and caused them to scatter across the earth.[67] At that time "the whole earth had the same language (lit., "one lip") and vocabulary (lit., "the same words")" (Gen 11:1, cf. v. 6). But the Lord "confused the language (lit., "lip") of the whole earth" (Gen 11:9). Nevertheless, in the day of salvation depicted in Zeph 3:9, the Lord will give the peoples a purified lip. They will once more speak one common language.[68] The appearance of the Hebrew word "lip" echoes the Babel episode, and the term *bərûrâ*, "purified," plays on the sound of the verb *bālal*, "confused," employed in Genesis 11.[69]

Some prefer to understand "purified lip" as having an ethical connotation. "Lip" (= speech) is followed on occasion by a modifier indicating deception (see Ps 12:2 [3]; Prov 17:4, 7). In Job 33:3 Elihu says,

---

[65] Gen 11:1, 6–7, 9; Isa 19:16.

[66] BDB, 140–41.

[67] Nogalski, *The Book of the Twelve,* 744; Floyd, *Minor Prophets,* 235.

[68] See Sweeney, *Zephaniah,* 184.

[69] Both words contain duplicated liquid phonemes (the letter *r* in בָּרַר and the letter *l* in בָּלַל).

"My lips speak with sincerity [*bārûr*] what they know." According to Zeph 3:13, "the remnant of Israel will no longer do wrong or tell lies; a deceitful tongue will no longer be found in their mouths." Consequently, Ben Zvi, who does not see an intertextual connection with Genesis 11, understands "purified lip" to refer to ethically "pure, sincere speech."[70] There are problems with this proposal, however. Verse 13 describes the remnant of Israel, while verse 9 speaks of the nations. Furthermore, verse 9 associates a purified lip with invoking the name of the Lord in the context of service, not speaking in an honest or sincere manner.

Despite these objections, Ben Zvi's proposal could be on the right track. Perhaps there is a deeper meaning behind the expression "purified lip." In addition to referring to the purification of human language through the restoration of a common tongue, the expression could hint at an ethical purification of human speech. First, the judgment on the nations described in verse 8 includes judgment on the Lord's covenant people, as in 1:18; consequently, verse 9 can be connected with verses 12–13. Second, in Prov 17:4 the phrase *śəpat-ʾāwen*, "lip of evil" (cf. CSB, "malicious talk") appears. The noun *ʾāwen* refers to evil in a generic sense. In Gen 11:3–4 the whole earth (cf. v. 1), speaking one language ("one lip"), articulated a plan designed to "make a name for" themselves to prevent their being "scattered throughout the earth." In this way they attempted to counter God's mandate to fill the earth and to rule it as his vice-regents. Their words can be classified as evil rebellion against their King. In the day when the Lord restores a common language, "a purified lip," as it were, the nations will invoke the name of the Lord, looking to him as their King. The movement from "make a **name** *for ourselves*" (Gen 11:4) to invoking "the **name** *of the* LORD" (Zeph 3:9) points to an ethical purification of human language.[71]

The Lord expressed a dual purpose for purifying the speech of the peoples (note the two infinitives construct with prefixed *lə-*). First, they will all call on the name of the Lord. This expression (*qārāʾ* combined with *bəšēm* followed by the Lord's name or a pronominal suffix referring to the Lord) is used of invoking the Lord's name in prayer.[72]

---

[70] Ben Zvi, *Zephaniah,* 225. See also Renz, *Zephaniah,* 608.

[71] In this regard, see Ball, *Zephaniah,* 236–38.

[72] See Gen 4:26; 12:8; 13:4; 21:33; 26:25; 1 Kgs 18:24; 1 Chr 16:8; Ps 105:1; Isa 12:4; 41:25; 64:7 [Hb. v. 6]; Joel 2:32 [Hb. 3:5]; Zech 13:9.

Particularly illustrative are (1) 1 Kgs 18:24–26, where Elijah and the prophets of Baal invoke their respective deities. When they call upon their deity, they expect a response (v. 24), and the prophets of Baal specifically ask Baal to answer them (v. 26). (2) 2 Kgs 11:5, where Naaman anticipates Elisha will invoke the Lord's name as part of a healing ritual. (3) Zech 13:9, where the Lord answers the one who calls in his name.

This is another example of the Lord referring to himself in the third person (cf. 1:5–6, 8, 17). In this case, he uses the idiom "call in the name of the LORD" (*qal* of *qārāʾ* followed by *bəšēm yhwh*) which is used eleven times (see above) and is more common than "call in my name" (*qal* of *qārāʾ* followed by *bišmî*), which appears only two times (Isa 41:25; Zech 13:9).

Second, they will serve the Lord "with a single purpose," literally, "(with) one shoulder."[73] To serve the Lord entails obeying and worshipping him, including through offerings and sacrifices. The expression "one shoulder" refers to serving in unison/one accord. The shoulder is sometimes associated with carrying a load, an image that is consistent with the use of "serve."[74] Nevertheless, there is no negative connotation here of service being oppressive.

Verse 10 elaborates on this description of worldwide recognition of the Lord's kingship: "From beyond the rivers of Cush my suppliants, my dispersed people, will bring an offering to me." The reference to the Lord's supplicants/dispersed people from beyond the rivers of Cush (cf. Isa 18:1) highlights the extent of his kingdom. In 2:12 the Lord announced the Cushites, representing the people of the distant south, will experience his judgment, symbolized by his sword. But now those beyond the rivers of Cush in even more remote regions of the south will bring an offering or tribute to the Lord as their King. The point seems clear: where there was widespread judgment there will be even more widespread worship as the prophet has already depicted in 2:11.

The terms used to describe these worshippers are significant. The form *ʿătāray*, "my supplicants," is typically understood as a suffixed plural form of an otherwise unattested noun *ʿātār*.[75] However, it is

---

[73] "Shoulder" is an adverbial accusative of manner.

[74] *HALOT*, 1494. Cp. Gen 21:14; 24:15; 49:15; Ps 81:6 [7]; Isa 10:27; 14:25. See Roberts, *Zephaniah*, 217.

[75] *HALOT*, 905; BDB, 801.

preferable to vocalize the form as a suffixed *qal* active participle *ʿōtəray* from the verb *ʿātar*, "plead, supplicate." This verb is used in the *qal* stem in five texts, referring in each case to petitionary prayer: (1) Gen 25:21: "Isaac prayed to the LORD on behalf of his wife because she was childless"; (2) Exod 8:30 [Hebrew v. 26]: "Moses . . . appealed to the LORD"; (3) Exod 10:18: "Moses . . . appealed to the LORD"; (4) Judg 13:8: "Manoah prayed to the LORD"; and (5) Job 33:26: "He will pray to God, and God will delight in him." The nations will bring their needs and requests to the Lord, recognizing him as their King.

The next expression, "my dispersed people," reads literally *bat-pûṣay*, "daughter of my dispersed ones." If retained, *pûṣay* is probably a suffixed *qal* passive participle from *pûṣ*, "disperse." The use of *bat*, "daughter," is peculiar here but most likely is a personification of the dispersed people as is often the case when the word appears before the name of a city, land, or people (cf. Zeph 3:14) with the name being appositional.[76] Perhaps the closest parallel is the phrase *bat ʿammî*, "daughter of my people," picturing "my people" as a daughter. As such, it is a term of endearment. If this explanation is correct, then the Lord here views his "dispersed ones" as his daughter just as he does Zion in verse 14.

But who are these dispersed ones? One's first inclination may be to identify them as the exiles of Israel.[77] They may be included in the larger group since Moses foresaw Israel being dispersed among the peoples in distant places (cf. Deut 4:27; 28:64). But one would expect the exiles to return to the land of Israel to live (Isa 11:12), not simply bring an offering/tribute. It is more likely the tribute bearing suppliants/dispersed ones of verse 10 belong to the peoples mentioned in verse 9 (cf. 2:11).

The reference to the peoples being "dispersed" (v. 10) is an additional allusion to the Babel event described in Genesis 11, where the verb used here (*pûṣ*) appears three times to describe how the Lord "dispersed" the people of the earth (vv. 4, 8–9).[78] At Babel the rebellious people joined forces to build a tower as a monument to their greatness to avoid filling the earth, as Adam and Noah had been commanded

---

[76] See BDB, 123, category 3.

[77] See, among many other passages, Deut 4:27; 28:64; Isa 11:12; Jer 9:16 [Hb. v. 15]; Ezek 28:25. For a defense of this view, see Daniel Timmer, "Political Models and the End of the World in Zephaniah," *Biblical Interpretation* 24 (2016): 316–18.

[78] See Sweeney, *Zephaniah*, 183.

to do. They were punished by having their language confused and by being forced to disperse. In the future age they will serve the Lord in the lands where they were dispersed (cf. 2:11), invoke the Lord's name, serve him, pray to him, and bring him tribute. The creation mandate will be realized.

Ehud Ben Zvi objects to this line of interpretation.[79] Relegating his response to a footnote, he rejects any substantive link with Genesis 11. He contends Gen 11:1–9 and Zeph 3:9–10 "share no common language." He then backpedals by observing that "only two significant words occur in both" (namely, "lip" and "name") but then points out that "lip" "occurs elsewhere many times" and "name" appears "hundreds of times." He seems to be suggesting the occurrence of both in these texts is merely coincidental.

Nevertheless, when assessing whether intertextuality is present, one should not simply look at words in isolation but for clusters or combinations of words. Especially noteworthy are those that appear together only in the two passages being considered as intertextually linked by authorial design. Such is the case with Gen 11:1–9 and Zeph 3:9–10. Singular "lip" and singular "name" occur in proximity only in Gen 11:1–9 and Zeph 3:9. The verb "confuse" (*bālal*) occurs with "lip" only in Gen 11:7, 9. The verb *bārar*, "purify," from which *bərûrâ* is derived, occurs with "lip" only in Zeph 3:9. When one recognizes the sound play involved (see above), this becomes further evidence of intertextual linking. Ben Zvi also asserts "name" does not correlate in meaning between Zeph 3:9 and Gen 11:4. A superficial glance might lead to this conclusion, but a closer examination reveals subtle thematic intertextuality of a contrastive nature that points to the radical change the Lord will bring to pass. In Gen 11:4 the rebels want to make a name for themselves to avoid being dispersed, while in Zeph 3:9 the nations invoke the name of the Lord. Their focus completely changes as they are transformed from rebels to worshippers. Finally, the references to the dispersing of the people in Gen 11:4, 8, 9, when compared with Zeph 3:10, add another substantive term to the cluster of key words linking Zeph 3:9–10 with Gen 11:1–9.

The following list of verses highlights the clustering and intertextual links:

---

[79] Ben Zvi, *Zephaniah,* 225, n. 736.

Gen 11:1: "The whole earth had the same language [one **lip,** *śāpāh*] and vocabulary."

Gen 11:4: "Let's make a **name** [*šēm*] for ourselves; otherwise, we will be **scattered** [*pûṣ*] throughout the earth."

Gen 11:6: "one people all having the same language" [one **lip,** *śāpāh*]

Gen 11:7: "Let's go down and **confuse** [*bālal*] their language [**lip,** *śāpāh*] so that they will not understand one another's speech" [**lip,** *śāpāh*].

Gen 11:8: "The LORD **scattered** [*pûṣ*] them throughout the earth."

Gen 11:9: "Therefore it [its **name,** *šēm*] is **called** [*qārā'*] Babylon, for there the LORD **confused** [*bālal*] the language [**lip,** *śāpāh*] of the whole earth, and from there the LORD **scattered** [*pûṣ*] them throughout the earth."

Zeph 3:9: "For I will then restore **pure** [*bərûrāh*] speech [**lip,** *śāpāh*] to the peoples so that all of them may **call** [*qārā'*] on the **name** [*šēm*] of the LORD and serve him with a single purpose."

Zeph 3:10: "From beyond the rivers of Cush my supplicants, my **dispersed** [*pûṣ*] people, will bring an offering to me."

If the supplicants/dispersed ones who "bring an offering" (*minḥâ*) in verse 10 belong to the peoples of verse 9, then what is the precise content of this offering? It could simply be a literal offering, perhaps given as tribute (cf. Hos 10:6), a meaning well-attested for *minḥâ*.[80] In light of the reference to invoking the Lord's name in verse 9, Sweeney proposes, "It is to be presented at the temple in order to acknowledge

[80] See *HALOT*, 601, category A. 5, though *HALOT* places Zeph 3:10 under category B. 1, "offering."

YHWH and Jerusalem as the center of creation."[81] However, it is possible to identify the offering as exiles in the light of Isa 66:20: "They will bring all your brothers from all the nations as a gift [*minḥâ*] to the LORD . . . just as the Israelites bring an offering [*minḥâ*] in a clean vessel to the house of the LORD" (cf. Isa 49:22).

3.2 The Transformation of the Lord's People (3:11–20)

The transformation of the nations will be accompanied by a transformation of the Lord's covenant community. Jerusalem and her people will celebrate the Lord's powerful presence and the security he provides.

This second unit of the speech begins with the formula "in that day" (v. 11), followed by a salvation announcement addressed to Jerusalem (vv. 11–19) and her people (v. 20) that describes her spiritual transformation and the restoration of blessing. The Lord speaks first (vv. 11–13), followed by an exhortation from the prophet (vv. 14–15).[82] Another "in that day" formula marks the beginning of a new subunit in which the prophet speaks first (vv. 16–17), followed by the Lord (vv. 18–19).[83] The final subunit begins with the formula "at that time" (v. 20) and contains a message from the Lord to the remnant (note the five second masculine plural pronouns).

In verses 11–19 there is a chiastic arrangement of key words and themes:

A The Lord will remove **shame** (11a) (cf. *lōʾ tēbôšî*, "you will not be put to shame.")

  B The Lord will restore a remnant (11b-13) (**shepherd** motif)

---

[81] Sweeney, *Zephaniah*, 186.

[82] The first-person verbs in verses 11–12 indicate the Lord is speaking, despite the fact he is mentioned in the third person at the end of verse 12 (see discussion below). Since verse 13 seems to be linked to verse 12 through the remnant motif and appears to elaborate on the character of the meek and humble mentioned in verse 12, it is best assigned to the Lord as well. The twofold reference to the Lord in the third person in verse 15, in the absence of any first-person statements by the Lord, suggests the prophet is speaking at this point. Since verse 15 appears to give the motivation accompanying the preceding exhortation, verse 14 is best assigned to the prophet.

[83] In the absence of any first-person statements by the Lord in verses 16–17, the third person references to the Lord in these verses are best assigned to the prophet. However, the first-person verbs in verses 18–19 indicate the Lord is speaking at this point.

C Jerusalem/Zion should **rejoice** (14) (cf. *ronnî*, "sing for joy," and *śimḥî*, "be glad")

D The Lord turned back the enemy (15a) (**warrior** motif)

E Jerusalem/Zion **need not fear because the Lord is present** (15b) (cf. *lōʾ tîrəʾî*, lit., "you will not fear," and *yhwh bəqirbēk*, "the LORD is among you")

E' Jerusalem/Zion **need not fear because the Lord is present** (16–17a[1]) (cf. *ʾal-tîrəʾî*, "Do not fear," and *yhwh . . . bəqirbēk*, "The LORD . . . is among you")

D' The Lord is "a warrior who saves" (17a[2]) (**warrior** motif)

C' The Lord will **rejoice** over Jerusalem/Zion (17b) (cf. *śimḥâ*, "gladness," and *rinnâ*, "singing")[84]

B' The Lord will restore a remnant (18–19a) (**shepherd** motif [cf. Mic 4:6–8])

A' The Lord will remove **shame** (19b) (cf. *boštām*, lit., "their shame")

These verses also have a framework around them that depicts Jerusalem's restoration within a worldwide setting. Verses 9–10 depict the peoples (*ʿammîm*) worshipping the Lord, while verse 20 describes the Lord giving his people "fame and praise among all the peoples of the earth" (*ʿammê hāʾāreṣ*).

3.2.1 *Jerusalem's Joy (3:11–15)*

The Lord will purge Jerusalem, replacing the proud with a righteous remnant that is humble and meek (vv. 11–13). It will be a time of celebration for Jerusalem and all Israel (v. 14), for their King will turn away his judgment, dwell among them, and protect them (v. 15).

---

[84] Wendland ("The Drama of Zephaniah," 54–55) gives a slightly different, more detailed explanation of the corresponding elements in the chiasmus: A Zion/Israel/Jerusalem sings/rejoices (14), B Reason: YHWH's forgiveness and protection (15a), C King Yahweh is within the city (15b), D You will never again fear (15c), E Focus on "that day" (16a), D' Do not fear (16b-c), C' Warrior Yahweh is within the city (17a), B' Reason: His salvation and love (17b-c), A' Yahweh sings/rejoices for Zion (17d). See also Baker, *Zephaniah*, 87, whose even more detailed concentric outline has a pivotal "G" element corresponding to Wendland's pivotal "E."

The introductory formula ("on that day") and the transition to a feminine singular addressee signal a shift in focus back to the oppressive city (cf. v. 1) described and addressed in verses 1–7. This is confirmed at the end of verse 11, where the Lord mentions his "holy mountain."

Verses 11–13 comprise a salvation announcement. It begins with a description of the city's future security (v. 11a) as a result (note *kî*, "for") of the Lord's intervention in salvation (vv. 11–12; note "*I will remove* from among you" and "*I will leave* a meek and humble people among you") with positive consequences for the "remnant of Israel" (v. 13). The statement "I will remove from among you your jubilant, arrogant people," when viewed in isolation, sounds like the long-awaited first-person announcement of intervention in judgment; however, in this context it is simply the first stage in the city's moral transformation.

Verses 11–13 are predictive discourse, as is evident in the verb forms:

11a "In that day you will feel no shame" (negated second feminine singular *yiqtol*/imperfect)
 11b[1] "for then I will remove " (*kî ʾāz* + first singular *yiqtol*/imperfect)
 11b[2] "and you will never again be haughty" (*waw* + negated second feminine singular *yiqtol*/imperfect)
 12a "but I will leave " (first singular *weqatal*/perfect consecutive)
 12b "and they will take refuge " (third plural *weqatal*/perfect consecutive)
13a "The remnant of Israel will do no wrong" (negated third masculine plural *yiqtol*/imperfect)
13a[1] "and tell no lies" (*waw* + negated third masculine plural *yiqtol*/imperfect)
13a[2] "Nor will a deceitful tongue be found" (*waw* + negated third masculine singular *yiqtol*/imperfect)
 13b "for they will feed" (kî + subject + third masculine plural yiqtol/imperfect)
 13b[1] "and lie down " (third plural *weqatal*/perfect consecutive)

There are two panels, with the division clearly marked by the asyndetic subject + verb sequence at the beginning of verse 13. Each panel consists of a main sequence, followed by a subordinate clause introduced by *kî*, "for." The main sequence contains negated *yiqtol*/imperfect forms, one in the first panel, three in the second. The subordinate causal sequences begin with a *yiqtol*/imperfect form after *kî*. In panel one (vv. 11–12) the causal sequence is then carried along by a negated *yiqtol*/imperfect and two *weqatal*/perfect consecutive forms. In panel two (v. 13) it is carried along by a *weqatal*/perfect consecutive form.

An exhortation in the form of a call to celebrate appears in verse 14, addressed to Daughter Zion, Israel, and Daughter Jerusalem (note the four imperatives).[85] This call and celebration take place in the future, once restoration has occurred (cf. *bayyôm hahûʾ*, "in/on that day" in vv. 11 and 16). Though not formally introduced with a *kî*, the reasons for celebration follow (v. 15).

3:11–13 As this portion of the speech begins, the Lord assures the city she will not experience shame because of her past rebellious actions (v. 11a). This statement plays off the last clause of verse 5: "yet the one who does wrong knows no shame." Verse 5 says that the wicked do not express a sense of shame over their wicked deeds to the point where they repent and change their ways. They should have felt shame over their sinful deeds because their actions were evidence of their rebellion against the Lord. The verb *pāšaʿ* ("be haughty") refers to rebelling against a higher authority. For this reason, judgment will fall upon them. Beyond the judgment there will no longer be a need for shame because the Lord will have removed proud sinners from the city (v. 11b), leaving a righteous remnant (vv. 12–13). In other words, judgment will be purifying and redemptive. As Motyer puts it, lack of shame in verse 5 "speaks of deadness of conscience; now, however, there is a clear conscience."[86]

The statement "I will remove *from among you*" (*miqqirbek*) in verse 11 highlights the reversal that will take place. In verse 3 the city's "princes *within her*" (*bəqirbâ*) are compared to roaring lions and ravenous wolves, depicting their violent oppression of the vulnerable right in the heart of the city within which (*bəqirbâ*) the righteous Lord dwells (v. 5). The Lord will remove the oppressors from the midst of

---

[85] The feminine singular is used in addressing Daughter Zion and Daughter Jerusalem, while the masculine plural is used in addressing Israel.

[86] Motyer, "Zephaniah," 953.

the city and replace them with those who humbly seek the Lord (v. 12, note "among you" [*bəqirbek*]).

The sinners are called "jubilant, arrogant people" (lit., "jubilant ones of your pride," that is, "your proud jubilant ones"). As noted above (see 2:15), *ʿallîz* refers to joyful celebration. It can have a positive (Isa 13:3) or a negative connotation (Isa 22:2; 23:7; 24:8; 32:13; Zeph 2:15) depending on the context.[87] In Zeph 3:11, as in 2:15, it is negative, referring to boastful arrogance. The words *ʿallîz*, "jubilant," and *gaʾăwâ*, "arrogance," are combined elsewhere only in Isa 13:3 where they describe warriors raised up by the Lord as his instruments of judgment (cf. NET, "my boasting, arrogant ones"). While the word *gaʾăwâ*, "arrogance," can have a positive connotation when used of the Lord (Deut 33:26, 29; Ps 68:34 [Hb. v. 35]), more often it refers to human "arrogance," something the Lord opposes and destroys.[88]

The Lord will eliminate such people from the city. Consequently, the personified city "will never again be haughty" on the Lord's "holy mountain." The verb *yāsap* (in the *hiphil* stem), used to indicate repetition or continuation of the following condition, is joined with the infinitive construct (*ləgobhâ*) of the verb *gābah*, "to be high, exalted, haughty." The adverb *ʿôd*, "still, again," appears as well, emphasizing that the city's haughty condition will end once and for all.

The concluding prepositional phrase "on [lit., in] my holy mountain" reminds the audience of Jerusalem's ideal character and the people's corruption of it with their arrogance (cf. v. 4). The city will once more be the Lord's holy hill. Elsewhere *har qodšî* (lit., "mountain of my holiness" = "my holy mountain") refers to the Lord's dwelling place (Joel 3:17 [Hb. 4:17]), which ideally is a place of submission to the Lord (Isa 11:9), of pure worship (Isa 56:6; Ezek 20:40), and of peace (Isa 65:25), where the Lord's chosen vice-regent rules (Ps 2:6).

When the Lord intervenes in judgment, he will not only "remove" the "jubilant, arrogant people" but will also "leave a meek and humble people" within the city (v. 12). The verb translated "leave" literally means "cause to remain" (*wəhišʾartî*, from the verbal root *šāʾar*). The noun "remnant" (*šəʾērît*), which appears at the beginning of verse 13, is related to this verb. As noted above, "among you" (*bəqirbēk*, lit., "in

---

[87] The same can be said for the related verb עָלַז, which can be positive (Pss 28:7; 60:6 [Hb. v. 8]; 68:4 [Hb. v. 5]; 96:12; 108:7 [Hb. v. 8]; 149:5; Prov 13:16; Hab 3:18; Zeph 3:14) or negative (2 Sam 1:20; Ps 94:3; Isa 23:12; Jer 11:15; 15:17; 50:11; 51:39).

[88] Pss 10:2; 31:18, 21; 73:6; Prov 29:23; Isa 9:9 [Hb. v. 8]; 13:11; 16:6; 25:11; Jer 48:29.

your midst") plays off "from among you" (*miqqirbēk*) in verse 11. It will be a case of out with the old (the arrogant) and in with the new (the humble).

The words "meek and humble" (*ʿānî* and *dāl* [pausal form of *dal*]) occur in proximity in five other texts (Job 34:28; Ps 82:3; Prov 22:22; Isa 10:2; 26:6). In each case the word pair refers to those who are poor and oppressed economically. In Isa 26:6 they are also viewed as "righteous" (see v. 7). It may be that the future "meek and humble" remnant will consist of those who were once socially oppressed; however, it is more likely the text refers to the humble obedient (*ʿanwê hāʾāreṣ*, "humble of the earth") first addressed in 2:3. As discussed in our comments on that verse, the term translated "humble" is used elsewhere primarily as a sociological term, referring to those who are poor and/or oppressed, vulnerable, and in need of protection and/or deliverance. On a few occasions it refers to humility in contrast to pride and is used of a humble, contrite attitude before the Lord. In 2:3 the term refers to the oppressed (cf. 1:9; 3:3), but the focus is on obedience, for these humble people "carry out what [God] commands." The same may be the case in 3:12, where the closely related word *ʿānî*, "meek," appears (with *dal*). In verse 12 the "meek and humble" are contrasted with the proud (see v. 11),[89] and they "take refuge in the name of the LORD" (v. 12). The focus is on their attitude toward the Lord rather than their economic status. King concludes these texts . . .

> are not simply sociological descriptions nor do they merely supply information about the financial status of the remnant. They also tell of the contrite spirit and meek attitude of these people. They are a people whose confidence is not placed in their own possessions or abilities. Rather, they place their trust in Yahweh alone.[90]

As stated earlier, perhaps it is best to view them as righteous people, committed to following the Lord's commands, who, because of that commitment, are powerless and vulnerable if not poor and destitute

[89] See also 2 Sam 18:27 (= Ps 18:27 [Hb. v. 28]), where the group designated עַם עָנִי, "oppressed people," translated "meek . . . people" in Zeph 3:12, is contrasted with the proud and associated with the righteous (vv. 20–25).

[90] King, "The Remnant in Zephaniah," 419. See also Patterson, *Zephaniah,* 375–76; Robertson, *Zephaniah,*331.

economically. This need not mean, however, that all who are powerless, vulnerable, poor, and/or destitute are righteous.

The expression "take refuge in the *name* of the LORD" occurs only here in the OT. The name of the Lord sometimes represents by metonymy the Lord himself.[91] When the "name of the LORD" is specifically mentioned, the Lord is revealing in a special way the character trait suggested by his personal name. The name Yahweh (translated "LORD") means "he is [with]," or, perhaps better, "he will be [with]" (cf. Exod 3:12–15). The name focuses on his protective presence with his people.

The verb *ḥāsâ,* when used of taking "refuge" in the Lord, refers to seeking his protection. This act presupposes and demonstrates the subject's loyalty. The one who takes refuge in the Lord is often contrasted with rebels. For example, in Psalm 2 the rebellious rulers of the earth (vv. 2–3, 10–12a) are admonished to submit to the Lord's chosen king (cf. vv. 7–9, 12). Their attitude stands in stark contrast to those who take refuge in the Lord and receive a blessing (v. 12). In Psalm 5 David asks that wicked rebels (vv. 9–10 [10–11]) be held guilty in order that all who take refuge in the Lord might rejoice (v. 11 [12]).This same contrast with the wicked appears in Pss 31:17–19 [18–20] and 34:22 [23]; Isa 57:13; and Zeph 3:11–13. Those who take refuge in the Lord are identified with those who love his name (Ps 5:11 [12]), fear him (Ps 31:19 [20]), and are his servants (Ps 34:22 [23]).

The act of taking refuge in the Lord is also closely related to a verbal affirmation of loyalty on occasion. In Psalm 16 David, after indicating that he has sought the Lord's protection (v. 1), asserts he has worshiped the Lord alone (vv. 2–4). In Psalm 31 he takes refuge in the Lord (v. 1 [2]) and then disavows any relationship to foreign gods (v. 6 [7]). A similar pattern can be observed in Psalms 71 (vv. 1 and 5–6), 91 (vv. 4 and 14–16), and 141 (vv. 8 and 1–7).

Taking refuge in the Lord also serves as the basis for a request for protection. In Ps 16:1 David asks God to guard him. The motivation, introduced by *kî*, "for," is the fact he has sought refuge (v. 7). Similarly, in Ps 25:20 he asks for protection and deliverance because he has taken shelter in the Lord (cf. also Pss 37:40 and 57:1 [2]). The use of "take refuge" in the motivation clause suggests it is the *significance*

---

[91] See, among many others, Pss 5:11 [Hb. v. 12]; 7:17 [Hb. v. 18]; 9:10 [Hb. v. 11]; 18:49 [Hb. v. 50]; Isa 18:7; 24:15; 26:8; 30:27; 48:1; 50:10; 56:6; 59:19. For a full list of examples, see BDB, 1028, category 3.

of the act as an expression of loyalty and not the act itself that is primary. The fact that taking refuge in the Lord frequently warrants divine *ḥesed*, "faithful love," supports this interpretation (cf. Pss 17:7; 36:7 [8]; 57:1, 4 [2, 5]).

Verse 13 characterizes this future remnant,[92] which is specifically identified as the "remnant of Israel."[93] Prior to this, "Israel" has been mentioned just once in Zephaniah (in 2:9 in the traditional title "God of Israel"), but now this righteous remnant of the future is viewed as what remains of the covenant community. In verses 14–15 they are called "Israel" and comprise the covenant community. In this regard, Floyd observes,

> The whole notion of the remnant is extended by referring to it as 'Israel' (v. 13), indicating that the new existence of Yahweh's people will not be any mere reconstruction of the state of Judah but rather a re-creation in some new form of the ancient entity that predated the separation of the northern from the southern kingdom.[94]

The remnant will not act or speak deceptively. The noun *ʿawlâ*, "wrong," in this context refers primarily to acts of injustice. This well-attested word often refers to evil in an unspecified way although in some instances the term is associated with specific forms of wrongdoing, including violence (Ps 58:2 [3]), murder and lies (Isa 59:3), robbery (Isa 61:8), bloodshed (Mic 3:10; Hab 2:12), and bribery (2 Chron 19:7).[95] The repetition of this phrase is significant. According to verse 5, the Lord "does no wrong" within the city. According to verse 13, he will produce a remnant that will mirror his character[96]

---

[92] Sweeney, *Zephaniah*, 188.

[93] The phrase "remnant of Israel" (שְׁאֵרִית יִשְׂרָאֵל) occurs in seven other texts. In three passages it refers to Jerusalem and its residents as those who remained from the nation Israel in the time of Jeremiah and Ezekiel (Jer 6:9; Ezek 9:8; 11:13). It refers to the northern tribes at the time of David (1 Chr 12:39), those remaining from the northern tribes in the time of Josiah (2 Chr 34:9), and the exiles from the northern tribes in Jeremiah's day (Jer 31:7). In Mic 2:12 it is used of the exiles in general—if that passage is taken as describing deliverance.

[94] Floyd, *Minor Prophets*, 235.

[95] The corresponding masculine nominal form, אָוֶל, can refer to legal injustice (Lev 19:15; Ps 82:2) and cheating for profit (Lev 19:35; Deut 25:16 [cf. vv. 13–15]; Ezek 18:8; 33:15).

[96] In this regard see Robertson, *Zephaniah*, 331; Ben Zvi, *Zephaniah*, 235.

and do no wrong. The remnant will not speak lies,[97] nor will deceit be on their tongues.[98]

Why does the Lord focus on the avoidance of deceptive speech as the distinguishing trait of the restored remnant? Ben Zvi asks why the prophet would single out this particular characteristic rather than more weighty sins like "killing, stealing, adultery, idolatry, indifference to the poor and needy"?[99] The answer is readily apparent if one observes human nature and takes a closer look at a couple of key texts. Deceptive speech is a diagnostic symptom of a morally corrupt nature that, given the "right" circumstances, expresses itself in more heinous ways. In Psalm 5 "speakers of lies" (v. 6) are associated with "boastful . . . evildoers" (v. 5) who are "violent and deceitful" (v. 6). They use deceptive speech to destroy others and to advance their own interests (v. 9). In Psalm 58 "those who tell lies" (v. 3) are associated with the "wicked" who "practice injustice" and "weigh out violence" (v. 2). They are as dangerous as a venomous snake (vv. 4–5) or a young, subadult lion (v. 6; cf. Judg 14:5). The entrance liturgies in Psalms 15 and 24 also make proper speech a requirement for worship.[100] It is no surprise that Paul in his description of sinful human nature, whether Jew or Gentile, begins with sins of speech (Rom 3:13–14) before moving to sins of violence (vv. 15–18). The former is the prelude to the latter.

Jesus spoke of this as well, exposing the Pharisees' flawed moral character:

> A tree is known by its fruit. Brood of vipers! How can you speak good things when you are evil? For the mouth speaks from the overflow of the heart. A good person produces good things from his storeroom of good, and an evil person produces evil things from his storeroom of evil. I tell you that on the day of judgment people will have to account for every careless word they speak.

---

[97] The expression "speak [*piel* of דָּבַר] a lie" occurs in four other texts: Judg 16:10, 13 (Delilah complains that Samson has spoken lies to her); Hos 7:13 (rebellious Israel speaks lies against the Lord); Dan 11:27 (the kings of the north and south will lie to each other). The expression "speakers [*qal* of דָּבַר] of lies" appears in Pss 5:6 [Hb. v. 7] and 58:3 [Hb. v. 4].

[98] The noun תַּרְמִית, "deceit," occurs in four other passages. In Ps 119:118 and Jer 8:5 it refers to straying from the Lord's commandments and turning away from him, while in Jer 14:14 [*qere*] and 23:26 it refers more specifically to false prophecies that do not come from the Lord.

[99] Ben Zvi (*Zephaniah*, 235) does well to raise the issue. His explanation, which is sociopolitical, is inadequate (235–36).

[100] See Sweeney, *Zephaniah*, 192.

For by your words you will be acquitted, and by your words you will be condemned (Matt 12:33b–37).

James chimes in, too:

The tongue is a fire. The tongue, a world of unrighteousness, is placed among our members. It stains the whole body, sets the course of life on fire, and is itself set on fire by hell. Every kind of animal, bird, reptile, and fish is tamed and has been tamed by humankind, but no one can tame the tongue. It is a restless evil, full of deadly poison (3:6–8).

The second half of verse 13 shifts the focus from the remnant's moral character to their security. They will be like flocks lying in their pasture with no reason to fear harm (cf. 2:7). Picturing the community as a flock paves the way for portraying the Lord as King (v. 15, see comments below).[101] Freedom from fear[102] portrays the fulfillment of the Lord's promise in Lev 26:6: "I will give peace to the land, and you will lie down with nothing to frighten you."[103]

The structure of verse 13 appears to mirror verse 12, where a similar pattern is visible:

12a But I will leave a meek and humble people among you [character],
12b and they will take refuge in the name of the LORD [security].
13a The remnant of Israel will no longer do wrong or tell lies;
13a¹ a deceitful tongue will not be found in their mouths [character].
13b They will pasture and lie down, with nothing to make them afraid [security].

The presence of *kî*, "for" (see KJV, NASB, ESV), at the beginning of verse 13b suggests a logical connection with the first half of the verse. Nevertheless, some translations (like CSB, cf. NIV) leave the term untranslated or understand it as an emphasizer (cf. NET, "indeed").[104] At first glance a logical connection between verse 13a and verse 13b is not readily apparent. How does the remnant's lying down securely

---

[101] See Robertson, *Zephaniah*, 332.

[102] Note the presence of the expression אֵין מַחֲרִיד, lit., "no one/nothing causing fear," in both Zeph 3:13 and Lev 26:6. See also Jer 30:10; 46:27; Ezek 34:28; 39:26; Mic 4:4.

[103] See Robertson, *Zephaniah*, 332.

[104] See Berlin, *Zephaniah*, 137; Patterson, *Zephaniah*, 376.

provide the reason for ethical purity? Perhaps the security that comes from obedience and seeking refuge in the Lord motivates the remnant to avoid the type of behavior that would jeopardize that security and relationship as illustrated by the purifying judgment that eliminated those who rebelled against the Lord. Actually, it makes perfect sense. Why take the risk of forfeiting the Lord's protective presence by rejecting his authority? When sinners rebel against their Protector, their disobedience is a form of moral insanity that is self-destructive.

3:14–15—The announcement of the transformation of the covenant community through the "remnant of Israel" is cause for celebration. In verse 14 the prophet calls for celebration: "Sing for joy, Daughter Zion; shout loudly, Israel! Be glad and celebrate with all your heart, Daughter Jerusalem!"[105] There is an escalation of emotion in the parallelism as the longer third exhortation contains two verbs ("be glad and celebrate") and adds the prepositional phrase, literally, "with a whole heart," suggesting sincerity and intense devotion.[106]

It is noteworthy the "remnant of Israel" (v. 13) is now addressed as "Israel" and closely associated with Daughter Zion/Daughter Jerusalem.[107] As stated above, the remnant, centered in Zion/Jerusalem, is now the covenant community and heir to the Lord's promises.

Some of the language used in the call to celebrate highlights the reversal that will take place when the Lord establishes the remnant in Zion/Jerusalem. The verb translated "shout loudly" (*hārîʿû*, from *rûaʿ*) in verse 14 is the verbal root from which the noun *tərûʿâ*, "battle cry," used in 1:16 is derived. Battle once came upon fortified cities, including

---

[105] Wendland ("The Drama of Zephaniah," 54) observes, "YHWH's oracle of salvation (vv. 8–13) is so awesome, so earth-shaking in its implications, that the prophet cannot, as it were, contain himself."

[106] Usually "heart" has a suffixed pronoun; but in a few cases, as in Zeph 3:14, the phrase is simply "with a whole heart." See 2 Kgs 23:3; Pss 111:1; 119:2, 34, 58, 69, 145.

[107] For a defense of the view that "Zion" is an appositional genitive in relation to "daughter" (thus yielding the translation "Daughter Zion"), see J. Andrew Dearman, "Daughter Zion and Her Place in God's Household," *Horizons in Biblical Theology* 31 (2009): 144–59, especially 149–50 (regarding Zeph 3:14–20). For a list of places where "daughter" is followed by a proper name functioning as an appositional genitive, see Sweeney, *Zephaniah*, 198. For the alternative view, that the phrase should be understood as "Daughter of Zion," see Michael H. Floyd, "Welcome Back, Daughter of Zion," *CBQ* 70 (2008): 484–504, and then Floyd's "The Daughter of Zion Goes Fishing in Heaven," in *Daughter Zion: Her Portrait, Her Response*, ed. M. J. Boda, C. J. Dempsey, and L. S. Flesher (Atlanta: Society of Biblical Literature, 2012), 177–200. In Floyd's view Jerusalem/Zion is the oppressing city of 3:1, while her daughter (= the next generation) experiences the restoration of the Lord's blessing (see Floyd, *Minor Prophets,* 238). For a survey of the debate, see Udoekpo, *Re-thinking the Day of YHWH,* 167–70.

Jerusalem, but there will be genuine joy in Zion over the Lord's royal presence. The verb translated "celebrate" (*ʿolzî*) in 3:14 is the verbal root from which *ʿallîzâ*, "jubilant" (2:15) and *ʿallîzê*, "jubilant" (3:11) are derived. Nineveh was once jubilant (2:15), but she will be judged, while Jerusalem will experience joy. Jerusalem was once inhabited by jubilant, arrogant people (3:11), but they too will be judged and replaced by a joyful righteous remnant.[108]

Verse 15 gives the reasons for celebration. The four clauses reflect the time perspective of the future celebration. The first two describe what the Lord has done (note the two *qatal*/perfect verbs: "has removed," "has turned back"), the third (a verbless clause) speaks of the present ("The King of Israel, the LORD is among you"), and the fourth looks to the future (note the *yiqtol*/imperfect verb: "you need no longer fear harm," cf. NIV: "never again will you fear any harm," ESV: "you shall never again fear evil").[109]

The first cause for celebration will be the cessation of judgment with its consequences. The first clause of verse 15 literally reads, "The LORD has removed your judgments [plural]." The noun *mišpāṭ* has several shades of meaning. The word appears three times before this in Zephaniah. It refers to the Lord's standards of justice he expects people to observe (2:3), the Lord's just actions (3:5), and the Lord's just decision to bring judgment upon nations (3:8). Here in verse 15 the plural form refers to the acts of judgment against Jerusalem[110] the Lord had executed.[111] The term is used by metonymy (cause for effect) for the destructive consequences of judgment.

There is a play on the verb "remove" (*hiphil* of *sûr*) that highlights the reversal that will occur when the Lord restores the city. Earlier the Lord announced he would "remove" the arrogant residents of the city through judgment (3:11). Once the Lord does that and replaces them

---

[108] On the contrast see King, "The Remnant in Zephaniah," 416.

[109] Ben Zvi, *Zephaniah*, 238, speaks of the "finite actions of YHWH" (= the perfects), "the continuous situation of YHWH's presence" (= the verbless clause), and "the new circumstances for Jerusalem" (= the imperfect).

[110] The antecedent of the second feminine singular suffix on the plural noun form is Daughter Zion/Jerusalem, mentioned in the previous verse. Since the noun has an underlying verbal idea (acts of judgment), the suffix can be understood as objective (the acts of judgment directed toward/against you).

[111] See BDB, 1048, category 1.f, "*execution* of judgment." Other instances of the plural noun used of acts of judgment occur in Pss 48:11 [Hb. v. 12] (cf. vv. 4–7 [Hb. vv. 5–8]); 97:8 (cf. vv. 3–7); 105:5, 7; Isa 26:8–9; Jer 1:16; Ezek 5:8.

with the humble and meek followers of the Lord (v. 12), he will also remove the effects of past judgments and restore the city.

The second cause for celebration will be the elimination of the city's enemy: "He has turned back your enemy." The verb translated "turned back" is *pinnâ* (the *piel* form of *pānâ*, "turn"). Elsewhere the *piel* form refers to clearing away or eliminating obstacles.[112] The "enemy" is not identified.[113] One might think of Assyria, whose judgment was impending (cf. 2:13–15) and materialized before the end of Josiah's reign in 609 BC.[114] However, the Babylonians quickly became the new enemy and sacked Jerusalem in 587 BC. Trying to explain these verses strictly against the historical background of Zephaniah's time is inadequate. The prophet envisions events that are broader and eschatological in scope. The enemy is the final enemy of that culminating time.

The third cause for celebration will be the Lord's presence within the city. Of course, the Lord resided in the city during Josiah's time, setting the standard for justice he expected his people to follow (3:5). Nevertheless, only a few observed those standards (2:3), necessitating the outpouring of the Lord's anger and the destruction of the city. But now, with the effects of judgment being removed along with the enemy, the Lord's presence would be a cause for celebration and a guarantee of a future free from harm.

The reference to the Lord being within the city plays off the earlier uses of *bəqereb*, "within, among," in the chapter. In verse 3 Jerusalem's princes "within her" (*bəqirbâ*) are described as "roaring lions," a metaphor that depicts them as violent oppressors. The repetition of the phrase (*bəqirbâ*) in verse 5 ("in her") contrasts the Lord who dwells within the city with the unjust leaders who also dwell there. As noted above, it supports the introductory woe, which implies impending judgment, for the just Lord will not tolerate disobedience within his city. This theme of what transpires within the city is developed further in 3:11–12. The statement "I will remove *from among you*" (*miqqirbēk*) in verse 11 highlights the reversal that will take place.

[112] It is used of cleaning up a house (Gen 24:31; Lev 14:36), clearing the terrain as a first stage in building a road (Isa 40:3; 57:14; 62:10; Mal 3:1), and preparing the ground before planting a vine (Ps 80:9 [Hb. v. 10]).

[113] Ben Zvi (*Zephaniah*, 241–42) takes the singular as collective and understands the city's jubilant, arrogant people as the referent. Berlin (*Zephaniah*, 143) gives this as an option but also mentions the nations, the instruments of judgment, as a possibility.

[114] See Sweeney, *Zephaniah*, 199.

The just Lord (v. 5) will remove the oppressors (v. 3) from the midst of the city and replace them with those who humbly seek him (v. 12, note "among you" [*bəqirbēk*]). In contrast to verse 5, where the Lord's presence highlighted their guilt, his presence in the time of restoration will make the city secure (v. 15, see also v. 17).[115]

The Lord is called "the King of Israel." The phrase appears 132 times in the OT, but only twice (here and Isa 44:6) is it used of the Lord. Nevertheless, the Lord's kingship over Israel is mentioned in several passages.[116] The title is appropriate in this context where the remnant is portrayed as sheep (vv. 13, 19). Throughout the ancient Near Eastern world kings were viewed as divinely appointed shepherds of their people.[117] For example, a Sumerian text tells how the god Enlil chose Shulgi (2094–2047 BC) to be a shepherd-king: "Enlil chose Shulgi in (his) pure heart, he entrusted the people to him. The lead-rope and the staff he hung on his arm—he is (henceforth) the shepherd of all the lands."[118] According to a Babylonian text, the god Ea enabled King Ammiditana (1683–1647 BC) to shepherd his people. The king led them to "fine pastures and watering places" and made "them lie down in (safe) pastures."[119] The royal metaphor of a shepherd was an apt one, because a king, like a shepherd, was responsible for the safety and security of those entrusted to him. The kingship motif also fits well in a context where the Lord is depicted as a warrior (*gibbôr*) who delivers his people (v. 17) and turns back their enemy. One of the chief responsibilities for an ancient Near Eastern king was to lead his armies against the enemies of his people.

The fourth cause for celebration will be the cessation of any need to fear: "You need no longer fear harm."[120] The verb is modified here

---

[115] Roberts (*Zephaniah*, 222) puts it well: "One should note the contrast with v. 5, where Yahweh was also said to be in Jerusalem, but his earlier presence in the city brought destruction because the corruption of the city's officials made Yahweh hostile to it. A holy God will not live comfortably in a moral slum. In the future, however, Yahweh's presence in Jerusalem will be salvific, not destructive, for then the remnant inhabiting Zion will be righteous, fit to enjoy God's company." See also Ball, *Zephaniah*, 277.

[116] Deut 33:5; 1 Sam 12:12; Pss 5:2 [Hb. v. 3]; 10:16; 29:10; 44:4 [Hb. v. 5]; 48:2 [Hb. v. 3]; 68:24 [Hb. v. 25]; 74:12; 84:3 [Hb. v. 4]; 145:1; 149:2; Isa 41:21; 43:15; 44:6.

[117] For numerous examples from Egypt and Mesopotamia, see Niehaus, *Ancient Near Eastern Themes in Biblical Theology*, 34–50.

[118] *COS*, 1:553.

[119] Niehaus, *Ancient Near Eastern Themes*, 46.

[120] The negative particle לֹא appears with the second feminine singular *yiqtol*/imperfect of יָרֵא, only here and in Isa 54:14 and 57:11. Other second-person *yiqtol*/imperfect forms of יָרֵא

by the adverb *ʿôd*, "still, again." This is one of only three texts where *yārēʾ*, "to fear," is combined with *ʿôd.*[121] In Jer 23:4 the combination is used with a pastoral metaphor where sheep (the Lord's people) will no longer fear when the Lord replaces their evil shepherds (leaders) with morally competent shepherds.

The noun translated "harm" (*raʿ*) often refers to moral evil, but in several contexts as here it refers to something that is harmful. In Ps 23:4, the only other text where the verb "to fear" (*yārēʾ*) takes *raʿ* as its object, the noun refers to "harm." At the locutionary level of the shepherd-sheep metaphor of verses 1–4, dangerous predators are likely in view. They, in turn, represent David's enemies (v. 5). In Zeph 3:15 the focus is on the calamities that overcame the city through the Lord's judgment—invasion, destruction, and death. As in Jer 23:4 and Ps 23:4, a shepherd-sheep motif is present. The remnant will not need to fear because the Lord, the Shepherd-King of Israel, will care for his sheep (cf. vv. 13, 19). This cessation of fear contrasts with the city's earlier refusal to fear the Lord (cf. 3:7).[122]

3.2.2 The Lord's Joy (3:16–19)

Another "on that day" formula marks the beginning of this new subunit in which the prophet speaks first (vv. 16–17), followed by the Lord (vv. 18–19). In the concentric structure of verses 11–19 (see above), the themes of verses 11–15 are reiterated. In the day of restoration, there will be no need for fear because the Lord, the mighty warrior, will be present in the city (vv. 16–17a, cf. v. 15). Just as Zion rejoices over the Lord (v. 14), so the Lord will rejoice over his people (v. 17b). He will restore a remnant and remove his people's shame (vv. 18–19, cf. vv. 11–13).

In that day Jerusalem/Zion, representing her people, will be told not to fear (v. 16). Within the framework of predictive discourse ("On that day it will be said to Jerusalem"), the message is clearly hortatory, as the presence of the negative particle *ʾal* before the two prefixed verb forms (jussives) indicates: "Do not fear; . . . do not let your hands grow

occur with לֹא fifteen times. Of the eighteen total occurrences eleven are in hortatory discourse, two in expository-interrogative discourse (Isa 57:11; Jer 5:22), and five in predictive-promissory discourse (Job 5:21; 11:15; Ps 91:5; Isa 54:14; Zeph 3:15).

[121] (1) 1 Sam 18:29: "[Saul] became even more afraid of David" (the *yiqtol*/imperfect has a past progressive nuance in this context); (2) Jer 23:4: "They will no longer be afraid."

[122] See Ball, *Zephaniah*, 278.

weak." The exhortation "do not fear" marks this as a salvation oracle, in which the words of reassurance are followed by the substantiating announcement of salvation (cf. v. 17).

The parallel exhortation, "Do not let your hands grow weak," is metonymic, describing an effect of fear. The idiom refers literally to the hands dropping due to a cessation of activity. When the verb (*rāphâ*) occurs in the *qal* verbal stem and is used of hands, it invariably describes a fearful response to a threat.[123]

Verse 17 gives two basic reasons there will be no need for fear—the Lord's presence among his people and his delight in them. As in verse 15 the prepositional phrase *bəqirbēk*, "among you," is used of the Lord's presence. In verse 15 he is called "the King of Israel, the LORD." Here in verse 17 "your God" is added to the divine name, emphasizing his relationship to Zion,[124] and the King's role as warrior (*gibbôr*) is highlighted. More specifically, he is "a warrior who saves."[125] Since these words are spoken in the day of restoration (cf. v. 16) as the reason Zion should not fear, the *yiqtol*/imperfect verb form is best taken as generalizing or habitual here (see CSB, NIV "who saves").[126]

Three consecutive clauses declare the Lord's delight in Zion. Most translations, including CSB, translate all three with the future tense; but if these words are spoken to Zion in the day of restoration (vv. 16–17a), then the present tense is better. See NET: (1) "he takes great delight in you," (2) "he renews you by his love," (3) "he shouts for joy over you."[127]

The first declaration of delight reads literally, "He takes delight over you with joy." The verb (*yāśîś*, from *śûś/śîś*) is combined with the noun *śimḥâ*, "joy," from the synonymous verb *śāmaḥ*, "to rejoice" for emphasis.[128] The preposition *ʿal*, "over," is best understood as hav-

---

[123] See 2 Sam 4:1; Neh 6:9; 2 Chr 15:7; Isa 13:7; Jer 6:24; 50:43; Ezek 7:17; 21:7 [Hb. v. 12].

[124] The expression "the LORD your God" occurs in four other passages with a second feminine singular suffix. In each case the addressee is either Zion (Isa 60:9 [see v. 14]; Mic 7:10 [see v. 11]) or Israel (Jer 2:17, 19; 3:13).

[125] "Warrior" is in apposition to "the LORD your God" and the relative pronoun is omitted after "warrior." On the syntax, see DHS, 191, par. 143. Floyd (*Minor Prophets,* 243) speaks of the "divine warrior" reconfirming "his kingship with a new victory."

[126] NET ("can deliver") gives the verb a modal nuance, indicating potential: the Lord is capable of delivering.

[127] The future is preferable *if* the quotation from the future day ends with verse 17a and the prophet, speaking from his stance in history prior to that day, is predicting what will transpire.

[128] The expression occurs elsewhere only once: Ps 68:3 [Hebrew v. 4].

ing a causal function: "He takes delight because of you."[129] The gloss "delight" is appropriate, for the verb describes an emotional response. This is evident in Isa 62:5, which uses the imagery of a groom delighting in his bride to describe the Lord's delight in Zion/Jerusalem.

The second statement in the Hebrew text reads, "He is silent in his love."[130] However, the verb (*hiphil* of *ḥāraš*, "be silent") does not fit well in this context, where the preceding and following statements describe an outburst of joy.[131] The Septuagint reads, "He will renew you with his love," apparently understanding the verb as *yəḥaddēš*. Confusion of the letters *dalet* and *resh* accounts for the variation in readings. If we treat the Greek reading as original, the lack of a direct object ("you" is expected in the light of the parallel lines) is problematic. The direct object "you" should be understood either through ellipsis or by possible virtual haplography, with the suffixed *kaph* having been dropped before the similar looking *bēt* at the beginning of the next word. The concept of renewal or restoration fits well in this context. The noun "love" (*ʾahăbâ*) refers here to the Lord's covenantal love that prompts his work of renewal on behalf of the city.[132]

The third statement mirrors the first as the main verb (*yāgîl*, from *gîl*, "delight, rejoice") is combined with a noun, in this case *rinnâ*, "cry of joy," related to the synonymous verb *rānan*, "to shout for joy," for emphasis. The contrast with the language used earlier of the day of the Lord is striking. In 1:15, 18; 2:2–3 the Lord's anger against sinners, including his people, is highlighted as he comes as a warrior to judge. Now, however, joy is the focus. In those earlier texts, four different words or phrases are used for the Lord's anger (*ʿebrâ*, *ʾēš qinʾātô*, *ḥărôn ʾap yhwh*, *ʾap yhwh*). In 3:17 four different words are used for the Lord's joy (*śûś*, *śimḥâ*, *gîl*, *rinnâ*) as he reveals himself as the warrior who saves.

---

[129] The verb שׂוּשׂ/שִׂישׂ is used with עַל elsewhere in Deut 28:63; 30:9; Ps 119:162; Isa 62:5; Jer 32:41.

[130] For a critique of alternative ways to understand the verb חָרַשׁ, see Ben Zvi, *Zephaniah*, 250–51. Sweeney (*Zephaniah*, 202–3) opts for the reading "plow," understanding it as having romantic connotations within the metaphorical framework of husband-wife.

[131] For a summary of attempts to explain חָרַשׁ in a way that fits the context, see Ben Zvi, *Zephaniah*, 251–52. See also Patterson, *Zephaniah*, 383. Ben Zvi proposes that the verb here refers to the Lord's refraining from judgment since the people have confessed their sins. See also Ball, *Zephaniah*, 184–86. For a critique of this proposal, see Renz, *Zephaniah*, 631.

[132] The word is used of the Lord's covenantal love for his people in Deut 7:8; Isa 63:9; Jer 31:3.

The Lord speaks in verse 18. This verse has puzzled and challenged interpreters.[133] It reads literally, "The grieved, from an assembly, I have gathered, from you, they were; tribute, upon her, a reproach." A sampling of translations does little to offer clarification:[134]

CSB I will gather those who have been driven from the appointed festivals; they will be a tribute from you and a reproach on her. [A marginal note says the Hb. is "obscure."]

ESV I will gather those of you who mourn for the festival, so that you will no longer suffer reproach. [A marginal note says, "The meaning of the Hebrew is uncertain."]

KJV I will gather *them that are* sorrowful for the solemn assembly, *who* are of thee, *to whom* the reproach of it *was* a burden. [Emphasis added.]

NASB I will gather those who are worried about the appointed feasts—They came from you, *Zion*; *The* disgrace *of exile* is a burden on them.

NET As for those who grieve because they cannot attend the festivals—I took them away from you; they became tribute and were a source of shame to you.

NIV The sorrows for the appointed feasts I will remove from you; they are a burden and a reproach to you.

NIV11 I will remove from you all who mourn over the loss of your appointed festivals, which is a burden and reproach for you.

A word-for-word analysis of the Hebrew text is in order, followed by a tentative interpretation:

---

[133] For a helpful summary of the interpretive challenges and scholarly attempts to make sense of the text, see Tchavdar S. Hadjiev, "The Translation Problems of Zephaniah 3, 18: A Diachronic Solution," *ZAW* 124 (2012): 416–20. Unfortunately, his complicated redaction critical proposal is more of a testimony to his creativity than a compelling solution.

[134] On the ancient versions (Septuagint, Vulgate, Targum, Syriac Peshitta), see Ball, *Zephaniah*, 187–88. As for modern translations, Ball (188) states, "Among modern translators and commentators, of over thirty translations checked, no two were exactly the same."

nûgê The form appears to be a *niphal* participle, masculine plural construct, from a hypothetical *qal* verb *yāgâ*, "suffer."[135] A construct form can occur, as here, before a prepositional phrase beginning with *min*, "from."[136] The *niphal* participle occurs in Lam 1:4, where the feminine plural form (*nûgôt*) refers to grieving young women.[137] It is parallel to Zion's personified mourning roads and groaning priests. So the term appears to refer to those who are suffering emotionally or grieving.[138]

mimmôʿēd The prepositional phrase means "from an assembly." The preposition is probably causal, while *môʿēd* may refer to a festival. In Lam 1:4 Zion's personified roads grieve for lack of having travelers to a festival. Similarly, Zeph 3:18 may be describing those who are grieving "because of a festival," in the sense that festivals no longer took place during the time of Zion's judgment.

ʾāsaptî The *qatal*/perfect verb form goes with what precedes (see the disjunctive accent). It could be past or perfective, "I gathered"/"I have gathered," if it refers to judgment (cf. 1:2–3; 3:8).[139] However, in verses 19–20 the discourse is predictive, so, if this gathering is positive, the perfect would indicate certitude and can be translated as future.

---

[135] BDB, 387; GKC, 191, par. 69t. (On the contraction of *aw* to the vowel *ô* and the subsequent change to *û*, see GKC, 90, par. 27n.) This verb does not occur in the *qal* verbal stem, but does appear in the *niphal, piel,* and *hiphil.*

[136] GKC, 421, par. 130a.

[137] The *hiphil* of יָגָה occurs in Lam 1:5, 12 with the meaning "cause to suffer," that is, "afflict."

[138] Patterson (*Zephaniah*, 385) proposes taking נוּגֵי from a root *nwg*, "depart," attested in Ugaritic. He translates "those who have been driven" (from your appointed feasts). This meaning would also fit in Lam 1:4, referring to virgins who have departed. Gordon lists the Ugaritic root tentatively as *nwg.* Cyrus H. Gordon, *Ugaritic Textbook,* Analecta Orientalia 38 (Rome: Pontifical Biblical Institute, 1965), 442, no. 1624. Gibson lists it as *ngy*. J. C. L. Gibson, *Canaanite Myths and Legends* 2nd ed. (Edinburgh, T & T Clark, 1978), 152. The verb appears in Kirtu in the following clause: *wng.mlk.lbty*, which Gibson translates: "And flee away, king, from my house." The verb is parallel to *rhq*, "keep far" (Gibson, 86, Keret 14:131–32). See also Simon B. Parker, ed., *Ugaritic Narrative Poetry,* SBL Writings from the Ancient World 9 (Atlanta: Society of Biblical Literature, 1997), 17, where Greenstein translates: "But fly, O king, from my palace" (Kirta, *CAT* 1.14 III:27–28). In *COS*, 1:335, Pardee translates: "Leave, king, my house" (Kirta,*CAT* 14 iii:131–32).

[139] See Renz, *Zephaniah*, 635, n.e; Floyd, *Minor Prophets,* 247.l

mimmēk	The prepositional phrase goes with the following verb. The second-person feminine singular suffix refers to personified Zion.
hāyû	The subject of the third-person plural verb could be the grieving ones or the festivals, if *môʿēd* is collective. The verb may have the nuance here, "came."[140]

Though any interpretation must be tentative, the first half of the verse could be paraphrased this way: Those suffering grief because of lost festivals I will gather. They [the grieving ones] came from you [Zion]. The implication is that they have gone into exile, from where the Lord will gather them.

maśʾēt	This noun refers to an offering or tribute. The corresponding masculine form *maśśāʾ* sometimes refers to a burden or load, a meaning that BDB proposes for *maśʾet* in Zeph 3:18.[141]
ʿāleyhā	This prepositional phrase means, "upon her." The likely antecedent of the third feminine singular suffix is Zion, though this entails a shift from direct address in the preceding clause and then back to direct address in the next verse.[142]
ḥerpâ	This noun refers to a "reproach." It could be appositional to *maśʾēt* or function as an adverbial accusative.

A tentative paraphrase of the second half of the verse might be, Tribute [offered to Assyria] (was) upon her [Zion] [that is, weighed her down] (as) a reproach.

If the verse is understood as suggested here, it provides a backdrop for the restoration described in verses 19–20. The Lord will gather from exile those who grieved the loss of their festivals when they left Zion. Prior to that tragic event, Zion had been forced to pay tribute to Assyria. This was a humiliating reproach. In verses 19–20 the Lord

---

140 For examples of this use of הָיָה, see BDB, 225–26, category II. 1.

141 BDB, 673, category 3.

142 Sweeney (205) suggests that verse 18b "could be the prophet's own third person aside, which aids in explaining the significance of the preceding statement by YHWH."

promises to gather the exiles, remove Zion's humiliation, and restore his people's honor.

In rhetorical fashion the Lord announces he will execute justice against Zion's oppressors (v. 19a). The first clause reads literally: "Look, I am dealing with your oppressors."[143] By using suffixed *hinnēh* with the participle, he draws attention to himself as the One who is about to act decisively. The phrase "at that time" places the action in the future, as does the predictive discourse structure in verse 19b. Note the verb forms: (1) a *weqatal* (*wəhôšaʿtî*, "and I will save"), (2) a *yiqtol*/imperfect (*ʾăqabbēṣ*, "[I will] gather"), and (3) another *weqatal* (*wəśamtî*, "[and] I will make"). The oppressors are not specifically identified, but one thinks of the taunting Moabites and Ammonites (2:8, 10), as well as the Assyrians (2:13–15).

This is the fourth time the verb *ʿāśâ* appears in Zephaniah. In each case the Lord's justice is the focus. The Lord will make "a complete, yes, a horrifying end of all the inhabitants of the earth" (1:18). This judgment will be just because the Lord "does no wrong" and executes justice "morning by morning" (3:5). He will preserve a "remnant of Israel" that mirrors his just character. They will "no longer do wrong" (3:13). As the just Judge he will "deal with" the oppressors of Zion, which represents his people. He will vindicate his people and restore them to a position of honor (3:19).

In connection with executing judgment, the Lord "will save the lame and gather the outcasts" (v. 19). His power as a warrior enables him to save (cf. v. 17). As indicated in the chiastic poetic parallelism of verse 19b, salvation takes the form of gathering. The text reads literally: "And I will save (b) **the lame** // (b') **and the outcast(s)** (a') I will gather."[144] There is a contrast with verse 8, where the Lord gathers the nations for fiery judgment. This judgment is alluded to in verse 19a, but in verse 19b the act of gathering is salvific.

The ones saved and gathered are identified as the "lame" and the "outcasts." The form translated "lame" is a feminine singular *qal* participle (*ṣōlēʿāʿ*)[145] from the verb *ṣālaʿ*, which refers to Jacob limp-

143 The verb עָשָׂה, in combination with the preposition אֵת, can be understood as "deal with." See BDB, 86, 1. d, and 794, I. 2. For other examples, see Ps 109:21; Ezek 20:44; 22:14.

144 Regarding the chiastic structure, Renz (*Zephaniah*, 641) observes that the verb-object-object-verb pattern "surrounds those in need of care with YHWH's action."

145 The feminine singular participle indicates a collective here. See DHS, 16–17, par. 14. 2; cf. also GKC, 394, par. 122s.

ing in Gen 32:31 [Hb. v. 32].[146] In Mic 4:6 the Lord says he "will assemble (*ʾāsap*) the lame (the feminine singular *qal* participle *ṣōlēʿāʿ*, as in Zeph 3:19) and gather (*qābaṣ*) the scattered."[147] According to verse 7, he "will make the lame (feminine singular participle again) into a remnant." The reference to the "watchtower for the flock" in verse 8 suggests the lame and scattered sheep are in view at the surface (locutionary) level of the metaphor. The reality behind the metaphor is the exiled people. This is probably the case in Zeph 3:19 as well. The form translated "outcasts" is a feminine singular *niphal* participle (*niddāḥâ*) from *nādaḥ*, "be scattered." The *niphal* is used elsewhere of scattered sheep,[148] as well as the exiles of Israel.[149] The use of the verb here to describe the gathering of the scattered ones is an ironic reversal of Moses's words in Deut 30:1, where he speaks of the exiled people being "in all the nations where the Lord . . . God has driven [them]."[150]

The image of the shepherd gathering his sheep is consistent with the kingship motif (see v. 15).[151] The promise to "gather" them, here and in verse 20, echoes the promise of Moses in Deut 30:3–4: "Then he will restore your fortunes, have compassion on you, and gather you again from all the peoples where the Lord your God has scattered you. Even if your exiles are at the farthest horizon, he will gather you and bring you back from there."

Having gathered his sheep, the Lord will replace their shame with honor (v. 19b[1]). The text reads literally: "And I will make them into praise and into a name in all the earth, their shame."[152] "Praise" (*təhillâ*) is a metonymy here for an object of praise,[153] while "name" is a

---

[146] A related noun צֶלַע refers to stumbling and falling in Job 18:12; Pss 35:15; 38:17 [Hb. v. 18]; Jer 20:10.

[147] On intertextual links between Mic 4:6–8 and Zeph 3:11–19, see Mark J. Boda, *Exploring Zechariah, Part 1: The Development of Zechariah and Its Role within the Twelve*, Ancient Near Eastern Monographs 16 (Atlanta: SBL, 2017), 240.

[148] See Deut 22:1; Ezek 34:4, 16.

[149] See Deut 30:4; Neh 1:9; Ps 147:2; Isa 11:12; 27:13; 56:8. See Ben Zvi, *Zephaniah*, 257.

[150] In Deut 30:4 he calls them "your exiles" (lit., "your scattered ones," *niphal* participle [*niddaḥ*] from *nādaḥ*).

[151] See Roberts, *Zephaniah*, 223.

[152] The verb שִׂים, when combined with the preposition -לְ, can refer to making something into something else, with the preposition introducing the product. For examples, see *HALOT*, 1325, category 18, d. iii; BDB, 964, category 5. a.

[153] See BDB, 240, category 5. c.

metonymy for "fame, glory,"[154] referring to the sheep/exiles as those to whom fame is ascribed, that is, those who possess fame. There is an echo here of Deut 26:19 (cf. Jer 13:11), where Moses describes the covenantal ideal in terms of the Lord elevating his people "to praise, fame, and glory above all the nations he has made." The Lord announces in Zeph 3:19–20 the realization of this ideal.[155]

With attention grabbing abruptness, "their shame" is tacked on to the end of the sentence. It is best understood as appositional to "them," the object of the verb "make." It specifies that their shame (that is, the shame that defines them as exiles) will be transformed into honor and praise. This stands in contrast to the present, where the unjust inhabiting the city "know no shame" (v. 5), despite their sinful actions, and must pay the consequences. However, here in verse 19 the Lord announces that the consequences experienced by the city because of judgment upon her sinful inhabitants will be eliminated. Their judgment will result in the elimination of any need for shame (v. 11).

3.2.3 The Lord's Restoration of the Exiles (3:20)

In this final verse the Lord speaks to his people (note the second-person plural pronouns), assuring them that he will restore them and give them honor among the nations.

The Lord begins by promising, "At that time I will bring [*hiphil* of *bôʾ*] you." In this context, this refers to gathering the exiles as the next line indicates (cp. v. 19). For this reason, CSB translates the line this way: "I will bring you back." There is an intertextual link here with Deut 30:5, where Moses promised, "The Lord your God will bring [*hiphil* of *bôʾ*] you into the land your ancestors possessed, and you will take possession of it."

The syntax of the next line is difficult. It reads literally, "And in the time, my gathering you." The verb form is a *piel* infinitive with a first-person singular pronominal suffix. This could be a substitute for a finite verbal form, namely, a first-person imperfect "I will gather" (cf. v. 19).[156] The traditional accentuation, which places this line with what precedes, favors this. Nevertheless, it is odd for the preposition *bēt* in

---

[154] See BDB, 1028, category 2. b.

[155] In this regard, see the comments of Ball, *Zephaniah*, 274.

[156] See DHS, 129, par. 96, Rem. 3.

ûbāʿēt to be vocalized with *qamets*, indicating definiteness.[157] If the vocalization is retained, then it is best to understand the prefixed *waw* as explicative, "namely,"[158] and assume a suppressed relative clause after *ʿēt*: "namely, in the time (in which) I gather you."[159]

In conclusion the Lord reiterates the transformation he will bring about (cf. v. 19).[160] He will make those whom he gathers famous and an object of praise among all the peoples of the earth.[161] This will occur when he restores their fortunes[162] before their very eyes (see 2:7). As noted earlier, there is an intertextual link with Deut 30:3: "Then he will restore your fortunes." The prophecy ends with a statement: "The LORD has spoken," which forms a thematic connection with the first words of the prophecy: "The word of the LORD" (1:1). However, the terrifying start to the book, where the Lord says, "I will completely sweep away everything," has been radically transformed as restoration replaces destruction.

---

157 In other instances where the preposition is prefixed to עֵת followed by an infinitive construct, the *beth* invariably has a *shewa* beneath it. See Gen 31:10; 38:27; 1 Sam 18:19; 2 Chron 28:22; Jer 11:14. Roberts (*Zephaniah*, 221, n. 12) emends the text accordingly.

158 On this use of the conjunction, see GKC, 484, par. 154, n. 1 (b), and DHS, 185, par. 136, Rem. 1 (c). Patterson (*Zephaniah*, 387) prefers this explanation. See also Motyer, "Zephaniah," 961.

159 One could understand the line with what follows and read: "And in the time (in which) I gather you, surely I will make." See Berlin, *Zephaniah*, 141–42; Sweeney, *Zephaniah*, 193, 208. In this case כִּי would have an emphasizing function rather than being causal. However, this violates the placement of the *athnaq*, which indicates this line goes with what precedes, and disturbs the poetic parallelism.

160 Ball (*Zephaniah*, 273) states that the repetition "creates a mighty climax of salvation in a chapter in which repetition plays an important role."

161 The verb נָתַן, when combined with the preposition -לְ, can refer to making something into something else, with the preposition introducing the product. For examples, see *HALOT*, 734, category 13; BDB, 681, category 3. B; Renz, *Zephaniah*, 636, n. p. On לְשֵׁם, "for a name," and לִתְהִלָּה, "for praise," see the comments above on verse 19.

162 On the form שְׁבוּתֵיכֶם, see GKC, 258, par. 91l.

BIBLIOGRAPHY

Abernethy, Andrew T. and Gregory Goswell. *God's Messiah in the Old Testament: Expectations of a Coming King*. Grand Rapids: Baker Academic, 2020.

Anderson, Roger W., Jr., "Zephaniah Ben Cushi and Cush of Benjamin: Traces of Cushite Presence in Syria-Palestine." In *The Pitcher Is Broken: Memorial Essays for Gösta W. Ahlström*, JSOTSup 190, 45–70. Edited by Steven W. Holloway and Lowell K. Handy. Sheffield: Sheffield Academic, 1995.

Aster, Shawn Zelig. "The Image of Assyria in Isaiah 2:5–22: The Campaign Motif Reversed." *JAOS* 127 (2007): 249–78.

Bailey, Waylon. "Nahum, Habakkuk, Zephaniah." In Kenneth L. Barker and Waylon Bailey, *Micah, Nahum, Habakkuk, Zephaniah*. NAC 20. Nashville: Broadman & Holman, 1998.

Baker, David W. *Nahum, Habakkuk, Zephaniah*. TOTC. Downers Grove: Inter-Varsity, 1988.

Ball, Ivan J. *A Rhetorical Study of Zephaniah*. Berkely, CA: BIBAL Press, 1988.

Barker, William D. *Isaiah's Kingship Polemic: An Exegetical Study of Isaiah 24–27*, Forschungen zum Alten Testament II:70. Tubingen: Mohr Siebeck, 2014.

Beaulieu, Jean-Alain. "Judah in the Shadow of Babylon." *Hebrew Bible and Ancient Israel* 9 (2020): 4–19.

Ben Zvi, Ehud. *A Historical-Critical Study of the Book of Zephaniah*, BZAW 198. Berlin: Walter de Gruyter, 1991.

Berlin, Adele. *Zephaniah*. AB. New York: Doubleday, 1994.

Betlyon, John W. "Neo-Babylonian Military Operations Other Than War in Judah and Jerusalem." In *Judah and the Judeans*, 263–83. Edited by Oded Lipschits and Joseph Blenkinsopp. Winona Lake, IN: Eisenbrauns, 2003.

Blaising, Craig A. "The Day of the Lord: Theme and Pattern in Biblical Theology." *BSac* 169 (2012): 3–19.

Boda, Mark J. *Exploring Zechariah, Part 1: The Development of Zechariah and Its Role within the Twelve*, Ancient Near Eastern Monographs 16. Atlanta: SBL, 2017.

Boogart, T. A. "History and Drama in the Story of David and Goliath." *Reformed Review* 38 (1985): 204–14.

Borowski, Oded. "Hezekiah's Reforms and the Revolt against Assyria," *BA* 58 (1995): 148–55.

Bracke, John M. "*šûb šəbût:* A Reappraisal," *ZAW* 97, 2 (1985): 233–44.

Bruce, F. F. *1 & 2 Thessalonians*. WBC. Waco, TX: Word Books, 1982.

Burnett, Joel S. *A Reassessment of Biblical Elohim*, SBLDS 183. Atlanta: Society of Biblical Literature, 2001.

Burrell, Kevin. *Cushites in the Hebrew Bible: Negotiating Ethnic Identity in the Past and Present*, Biblical Interpretation Series 181. Leiden: Brill, 2020.

Charlesworth, James, ed. *The Old Testament Pseudepigrapha*. 2 vols. Garden City, NY: Doubleday, 1983, 1985.

Childs, Brevard S. *Introduction to the Old Testament as Scripture*. Philadelphia: Fortress, 1979.

_______. *Isaiah*. OTL. Louisville: Westminster John Knox, 2001.

Chisholm, Robert B., Jr., "Does God 'Change His Mind?'" *BSac* 152 (1995): 387–99.

_______. "The 'Everlasting Covenant' and the 'City of Chaos': Intentional Ambiguity and Irony in Isaiah 24." *Criswell Theological Review* 6 (1993): 237–53.

_______. "Evidence from Genesis." In *A Case for Premillennialism*, 35–54. Edited by D. Campbell and J. Townsend. Chicago: Moody, 1992.

_______. "The Fear of the Lord/God: A Thematic Key to the Unity of the Wisdom Books." In *The Law, the Prophets, and the Writings*, 271–90. Edited by A. M. King, W. R. Osborne, and J. M. Philpott. Nashville: B & H Academic, 2021.

_______. "God's Covenantal Suffering in Hosea 11." In *Divine Suffering: Theology, History, and Church Mission*, 100–18. Edited by Andrew J. Schmutzer. Eugene, OR: Pickwick/Wipf and Stock, 2023.

_______. *Handbook on the Prophets*. Grand Rapids: Baker Academic, 2002.

_______. "History or Story? The Literary Dimension in Narrative Texts." In *Giving the Sense*, 54–73. Edited by D. Howard and M. Grisanti. Grand Rapids: Kregel, 2003.

_______. "Israel according to the Prophets." In *The People, the Land, and the Future of Israel: Israel and the Jewish People in the Plan of God*, 53–69. Edited by D. Bock and M. Glaser. Grand Rapids: Kregel, 2014.

_______. "The Servant of the Lord: Covenant Mediator and Light to the Nations." In *The Future Restoration of Israel: A Response to Supersessionism*, McMaster Biblical Studies Series 10, 19–36. Edited by S. E. Porter and A. E. Kurschner. Eugene, OR: McMaster Divinity College Press and Pickwick/Wipf and Stock, 2023.

_______. "Suppressing Myth: Yahweh and the Sea in the Praise Psalms." In *The Psalms: Language for All Seasons of the Soul*, 75–84. Edited by A. J. Schmutzer and D. M. Howard. Chicago: Moody, 2013.

_______. "A Theology of the Minor Prophets." In *A Biblical Theology of the Old Testament*, 397–433. Edited by R. Zuck. Chicago: Moody, 1991.

_______. "When Prophecy Appears to Fail, Check Your Hermeneutic," *JETS* 53/3 (September 2010): 561–77.

Christensen, Duane L. "Zephaniah 2:4–15: A Theological Basis for Josiah's Program of Political Expansion." *CBQ* 46 (1984): 669–82.

Clark, David J. "Of Birds and Beasts: Zephaniah 2:14." *The Bible Translator* 34 (1982): 243–46.

_______. "Wine on the Lees (Zeph 1.12 and Jer 48:11)." *The Bible Translator* 32, no. 2 (1981): 241–43.

Clendenen, E. Ray. "Textlinguistics and Prophecy in the Book of the Twelve." *JETS* 46 (2003): 385–99.

Cogan, Mordechai and Hayim Tadmor. *II Kings*. AB. New York: Doubleday, 1988.

Cross, Frank M. *Canaanite Myth and Hebrew Epic*. Cambridge: Harvard University, 1973.

Davies, Graham I. *Hosea*. NCB. Grand Rapids: Eerdmans, 1992.

Dawes, Stephen B. "עֲנָוָה in Translation and Tradition." *VT* 41, 1 (1991): 38–48.

Day, John. *Yahweh and the Gods and Goddesses of Canaan,* JSOTSup 265. Sheffield: Sheffield Academic, 2000.

Dearman, J. Andrew. "Daughter Zion and Her Place in God's Household." *Horizons in Biblical Theology* 31 (2009): 144–59.

de Jong, John Hans. "Sanctified or Dedicated? הקדיש in Zephaniah 1:7." *VT* 68 (2018): 94–101.

DeRoche, Michael. "Contra Creation, Covenant and Conquest (Jer. viii 13)." *VT* 30 (1980): 280– 90.

_______. "The Reversal of Creation in Hosea." *VT* 31 (1981): 400–409.

_______. "Zephaniah i 2–3: The 'Sweeping' of Creation." *VT* 30 (1980): 104–9.

DeRouchie, Jason S. "The Addressees in Zephaniah 2:1, 3: Who Should Seek YHWH Together?" *BBR* 30, 2 (2020): 183–207.

_______. "YHWH's Future Ingathering in Zephaniah 1:2: Interpreting אָסֹף אָסֵף." *Hebrew Studies* 59 (2018): 173–91.

_______. "YHWH's Judgment Is New Every Morning: Zephaniah 3:5 and the Light of the World." *Trinity Journal* 43NS (2022): 131–46.

Dewrell, Heath D. "'Swearing to Yahweh, but Swearing by *Mōlek*-Sacrifices': Zephaniah 1:5b." *VT* 69 (2019): 737–41.

Dick, Michael B. "The Neo-Assyrian Royal Lion Hunt and Yahweh's Answer to Job." *JBL* 125, 2 (2006): 243–70.

Dietrich, Walter. "Three Minor Prophets and the Major Empires: Synchronic and Diachronic Perspectives on Nahum, Habakkuk, and Zephaniah." In *Perspectives on the Formation of the Book of the Twelve: Methodological Foundations—Redactional Processes—Historical Insights*, BZAW 433, 147–56. Edited by R. Albertz, J. D. Nogalski, and J. Wöhrle. Berlin: De Gruyter, 2012.

Driver, S. R. *The Use of the Tenses in Hebrew.* 3rd ed. Oxford: Clarendon, 1892.

Duguid, Iain M. and Matthew P. Harmon. "Zephaniah: Hope through the Darkness," in *Zephaniah, Haggai, Malachi*, Reformed Expository Commentary. Phillipsburg: P & R Publishing, 2018.

du Preez, J. "An Interpretation of Zephaniah 2:11 with Special Reference to the Phrase *ʾîš mimqômô* [*sic*]." *Scriptura* 19 (1986): 18–24.

Everson, A. Joseph. "The Days of Yahweh." *JBL* 93 (1974): 329–37.

Fenik, Juraj and Robert Lapko. "Annunciations to Mary in Luke 1–2." *Biblica* 96.4 (2015): 498–524.

Firth, David G. *1 & 2 Samuel.* AOTC. Nottingham: Apollos, 2009.

Fitzmyer, Joseph A. *The Aramaic Inscriptions of Sefîre*, Biblica et Orientalia 19. Rome: Pontifical Biblical Institute, 1967.

Floyd, Michael H. "The Daughter of Zion Goes Fishing in Heaven." In *Daughter Zion: Her Portrait, Her Response*, 177–200. Edited by M. J. Boda, C. J. Dempsey, and L. S. Flesher. Atlanta: Society of Biblical Literature, 2012.

_______. *Minor Prophets, Part 2*. FOTL. Grand Rapids: William B. Eerdmans, 2000.

_______. "Welcome Back, Daughter of Zion." *CBQ* 70 (2008): 484–504.

Gane, Roy. "The Role of Assyria in the Ancient Near East during the Reign of Manasseh." *AUSS* 35 (1997): 21–32.

Gärtner, Judith. "Jerusalem—the City of God for Israel and for the Nations in Zeph 3:8, 9–10, 11–13." In *Perspectives on the Formation of the Book of the Twelve: Methodological Foundations—Redactional Processes—Historical Insights*,

BZAW 433, 269–83. Edited by R. Albertz, J. D. Nogalski, and J. Wöhrle. Berlin: De Gruyter, 2012.

George, Mark K. "Yhwh's Own Heart." *CBQ* 64 (2002): 442–59.

Gibson, J. C. L. *Canaanite Myths and Legends.* 2nd ed. Edinburgh: T & T Clark, 1978.

Glassner, Jean-Jacques. *Mesopotamian Chronicles*, SBL Writings from the Ancient World 19. Atlanta: SBL, 2004.

Gordis, Robert. "A Rising Tide of Misery; A Note on a Note on Zephaniah II 4." *VT* 37, 4 (1987): 487–90.

Gordon, Cyrus H. *Ugaritic Textbook,* Analecta Orientalia 38. Rome: Pontifical Biblical Institute, 1965.

Greenspahn, Frederick E. "Syncretism and Idolatry in the Bible." *VT* 54, 4 (2004): 480–94.

Grundke, Christopher L. K. "A Tempest in a Teapot? Genesis III 8 Again." *VT* 51, 4 (2001): 548–51.

Haak, Robert D. "'Cush' in Zephaniah." In *The Pitcher Is Broken: Memorial Essays for Gösta W. Ahlström*, JSOTSup 190, 238–51. Edited by S. W. Holloway and L. K. Handy. Sheffield: Sheffield Academic, 1995.

Hadjiev, Tchavdar S. "Survival, Conversion and Restoration: Reflections on the Redaction History of the Book of Zephaniah." *VT* 61 (2011): 570–81.

________. "The Theological Transformations of Zephaniah's Proclamation of Doom." *ZAW* 126 (4) (2014): 506–20.

________. "The Translation Problems of Zephaniah 3,18: A Diachronic Solution." *ZAW* 124 (2012): 416–20.

Hagedorn, Anselm C. "When Did Zephaniah Become a Supporter of Josiah's Reform?" *The Journal of Theological Studies*, NS 62, 2 (October 2011): 453–75.

Hayes, John H. and Stuart A. Irvine. *Isaiah the Eighth Century Prophet: His Times and His Preaching.* Nashville: Abingdon, 1987.

Hays, J. Daniel. "The Cushites: A Black Nation in Ancient History." *BSac* 153 (1996): 270–80.

Hays, Nathan. "Humility and Instruction in Zephaniah 3.1–7." *JSOT* 44, 3 (2020): 472–89.

Heater, Homer, Jr. "Do the Prophets Teach that Babylonia Will Be Rebuilt in the *Eschaton*?" *JETS* 41 (1998): 23–43.

Hess, Richard S. *Israelite Religions: An Archaeological and Biblical Survey.* Grand Rapids: Baker Academic, 2007.

Hoffman Yair. "The Day of the Lord as a Concept and a Term in the Prophetic Literature." *ZAW* 93 (1981): 37–50.

House, Paul R. *Zephaniah: A Prophetic Drama,* JSOTSup 69. Sheffield: Sheffield Academic, 1989.

Hunter, A. Vanlier. *Seek the Lord: A Study of the Meaning and Function of the Exhortations in Amos, Isaiah, Micah, and Zephaniah.* Baltimore: St. Mary's Seminary and University, 1982.

Jastrow, Marcus. *A Dictionary of the Targumim, the Talmud Babli and Yerushalmi, and the Midrashic Literature.* Rep.; 2 vols. Brooklyn: P. Shalom, 1967.

Johnson, S. Louis, Jr. "Evidence from Romans 9–11." In *A Case for Premillennialism*, 199–223. Edited by D. Campbell and J. Townsend. Chicago: Moody, 1992.

Joüon, Paul and T. Muraoka. *A Grammar of Biblical Hebrew.* Rome: Pontifical Biblical Institute, 2000.

Kahn, Dan'el. "The Historical Setting of Zephaniah's Oracles against the Nations (Zeph 2:4–15)." In *Homeland and Exile,* VTSup 130, 439–53. Edited by G. Galil, M. Keller, and A. Millard. Leiden: Brill, 2009.

_______. "Judean Auxiliaries in Egypt's Wars Against Kush." *JAOS* 127 (2008): 507–16.

_______. "Nebuchadnezzar and Egypt: An Update on the Egyptian Monuments." *Hebrew Bible and Ancient Israel* 7 (2018): 65–78.

Kakkanattu, Joy Philip. *God's Enduring Love in the Book of Hosea: A Synchronic and Diachronic Analysis of Hosea 11:1–11*. Tübingen: Mohr Siebeck, 2006.

Kaminski, Carol M. *From Noah to Israel: Realization of the Primaeval Blessing after the Flood*, JSOTSup 413. London: T & T Clark International, 2004.

Keel, Othmar. *The Symbolism of the Biblical World: Ancient Near Eastern Iconography and the Book of Psalms*. Winona Lake, IN: Eisenbrauns, 1997.

Kelly, Tyler. "'After Such Knowledge, What Forgiveness?': The Polemic against the Wealthy and Zephaniah's Day of Yhwh." *VT* 72, 4/5 (2022): 594–608.

King, Greg A. "The Day of the Lord in Zephaniah." *BSac* 152 (1995): 16–32.

_______. "The Message of Zephaniah: An Urgent Echo." *AUSS* 32, 2 (1996): 211–22.

_______. "The Remnant in Zephaniah." *BSac* 151 (1994): 414–27.

Koole, J. L. *Isaiah. Part 3 Vol. 2: Isaiah 49–55*. Historical Commentary on the Old Testament. Translated by A. P. Runia. Leuven: Peeters, 1998.

Laato, Antti. "Assyrian Propaganda and the Falsification of History in the Royal Inscriptions of Sennacherib." *VT* 45 (1995): 198–226.

Labahn, Antje. "The Delay of Salvation within Deutero-Isaiah." *JSOT* 85 (1999): 71–84.

Levenson, Jon D. *Creation and the Persistence of Evil*. San Francisco: Harper & Row, 1988.

Levin, Christoph. "Zephaniah: How This Book Became Prophecy." In *Constructs of Prophecy in the Former & Latter Prophets & Other Texts,* Ancient Near East Monographs 4, 117–39. Edited by L. L. Grabbe and M. Nissinen. Atlanta, SBL, 2011.

Lichtheim, Miriam. *Ancient Egyptian Literature*. 3 vols. Berkeley: University of California, 1975–80.

Lillas, Rosmari. *Hendiadys in the Hebrew Bible*. Gothenburg: University of Gothenburg, 2012.

Lipschits, Oded. *The Fall and Rise of Jerusalem: Judah under Babylonian Rule*. Winona Lake, IN: Eisenbrauns, 2005.

Macky, Peter W. *The Centrality of Metaphors to Biblical Thought: A Method for Interpreting the Bible*. Lewiston, NY: Edwin Mellen, 1990.

Mason, Steven D. "Another Flood? Genesis 9 and Isaiah's Broken Eternal Covenant." *JSOT* 32 (2007): 177–98.

Master, Daniel M. "Nebuchadnezzar at Ashkelon." *Hebrew Bible and Ancient Israel* 7 (2018): 79–92.

Mettinger, Tryggve N. D. *In Search of God: The Meaning and Message of the Everlasting Names*. Translated by Frederick H. Cryer. Philadelphia: Fortress, 1988.

Moore, Michael S. "Yahweh's Day." *Restoration Quarterly* 29 (1987): 193–208.

Motyer, J. Alec. *The Prophecy of Isaiah: An Introduction & Commentary*. Downers Grove, IL: InterVarsity, 1993.

_______. "Zephaniah." In J. Alec Motyer, Thomas E. McComiskey, and Douglas Stuart. *Zephaniah, Haggai, Zechariah, Malachi*. In *The Minor Prophets: An Exegetical and Expository Commentary, Vol. III*. Edited by Thomas E. McComiskey. Grand Rapids: Baker Books, 1998.

Na'aman, Nadav. "Sennacherib's Campaign to Judah and the Date of the *lmlk* Stamps." *VT* 29 (1979): 61–86.

Niccacci, Alviero. "Isaiah XVIII-XX from an Egyptological Perspective." *VT* 48 (1998): 217–24.

Niehaus, Jeffrey J. *Ancient Near Eastern Themes in Biblical Theology*. Grand Rapids: Kregel, 2008.

________. "In the Wind of the Storm: Another Look at Genesis III 8." *VT* 44, 2 (1994): 263–67.

Nogalski, James. *The Book of the Twelve: Micah-Malachi*. SHBC. Macon, GA: Smyth & Helwys, 2011.

________. "Zephaniah's Use of Genesis 1–11." *Hebrew Bible and Ancient Israel* 2 (2013): 351–72.

North, Christopher R. *The Second Isaiah*. Oxford: Clarendon, 1964.

Oswalt, John N. *The Book of Isaiah, Chapters 40–66*. NICOT. Grand Rapids: William B. Eerdmans, 1998.

Parker, Simon B., ed. *Ugaritic Narrative Poetry.* SBL Writings from the Ancient World 9. Atlanta: Society of Biblical Literature, 1997.

Parunak, H. van Dyke. "Some Axioms for Literary Architecture." *Semitics* 8 (1982): 1–16.

Patterson, Richard D. *Nahum, Habakkuk, Zephaniah*. Wycliffe Exegetical Commentary. Chicago: Moody, 1991.

Penchansky, David. *What Rough Beast? Images of God in the Hebrew Bible*. Louisville: John Knox, 1991.

Pope, Marvin H. and Jeffrey H. Tigay. "A Description of Baal." *Ugarit-Forschungen* 3 (1971): 117–30.

Raabe, Paul R. "The Particularizing of Universal Judgment in Prophetic Discourse." *CBQ* 64 (2002): 652–74.

Radine, Jason. "The 'Idolatrous Priests' in the Book of Zephaniah." In *Priests and Cults in the Book of the Twelve*. Ancient Near Eastern Monographs 14, 131–48. Edited by Lena-Sofia Tiemeyer. Atlanta: SBL, 2016.

Renz, Thomas. *The Books of Nahum, Habakkuk, and Zephaniah*. NICOT (Grand Rapids: William B. Eerdmans, 2021.

Rice, Gene. "The African Roots of the Prophet Zephaniah." *The Journal of Religious Thought* 36, 1 (Spring-Summer, 1979): 21–31.

________. "Two Black Contemporaries of Jeremiah." *The Journal of Religious Thought* 32, 1 (Spring-Summer 1975): 95–109.

Roberts, J. J. M. *First Isaiah: A Commentary*. Hermeneia. Minneapolis: Fortress, 2015.

________. *Nahum, Habakkuk, and Zephaniah: A Commentary.* OTL. Louisville: Westminster/John Knox, 1991.

Robertson, O. Palmer. *The Books of Nahum, Habakkuk, and Zephaniah*. NICOT. Grand Rapids, William B. Eerdmans, 1990.

Rudman, Dominic. "A Note on Zephaniah." *Biblica* 81, 1 (1999): 109–12.

Ryou, Daniel Hojoon. *Zephaniah's Oracles against the Nations: A Synchronic and Diachronic Study of Zephaniah 2:1–3:8*, Biblical Interpretation 13. Leiden: Brill, 1995.

Sabottka, L. *Zephanja*. Rome: Pontifical Biblical Institute, 1972.

Schenker, Adrian. "Israelite or Universal Horizon: Zephaniah 3.8–10 in the Hebrew and Greek Bibles." *The Bible Translator* 64, 2 (2013): 151–58.

Seely, Paul H. "The Geographical Meaning of 'Earth' and 'Seas' in Genesis 1:10." *WTJ* 59 (1997): 231–55.

Seibert, Eric A. *Disturbing Divine Behavior: Troubling Old Testament Images of God.* Minneapolis: Fortress, 2009.

Smith, David. "What Hope after Babel? Diversity and Community in Gen 11:1–9; Exod 1:1–14; Zeph 3:1–13; and Acts 2:1–3." *Horizons in Biblical Theology* 18, 2 (1996): 169–91.

Smith, Gary V. *Isaiah 1–39*. NAC 15A. Nashville: B & H Publishing, 2007.

Smoak, Jeremy D. "Building Houses and Planting Vineyards: The Early Inner-Biblical Discourse on an Ancient Israelite Wartime Curse." *JBL* 127, 1 (2008): 19–35.

Snyman, S. D. "Violence and Deceit in Zephaniah 1:9." *Old Testament Essays* 13 (2000): 89–102.

Stadelmann, Luis I. J. *The Hebrew Conception of the World*. Analecta Biblica 39. Rome: Biblical Institute, 1970.

Stager, Lawrence E. "Ashkelon and the Archaeology of Destruction: Kislev 604 B.C.E." *Eretz-Israel* 25 (1996): 61*–74*.

Stuart, Douglas. *Hosea-Jonah*. WBC. Waco, TX: Word, 1987.

________. "The Sovereign's Day of Conquest." *BASOR* 220/221 (1975–76): 159–64.

Sweeney, Marvin A. "A Form-Critical Reassessment of the Book of Zephaniah." *CBQ* 53 (1991): 388–408.

________. *Zephaniah: A Commentary*. Hermeneia. Minneapolis: Fortress, 2003.

Taylor, J. Glen. "A Response to Steve A. Wiggins, 'Yahweh: The God of Sun?'" *JSOT* 71 (1996): 107–19.

________. *Yahweh and the Sun: Biblical and Archaeological Evidence for Sun Worship in Ancient Israel*, JSOTSup 111. Sheffield: Sheffield Academic, 1993.

Thomas, Heath A., Jeremy Evans, and Paul Copan, eds. *Holy War in the Bible: Christian Morality and an Old Testament Problem*. Downers Grove, IL: IVP Academic, 2013.

Timmer, Daniel. "Political Models and the End of the World in Zephaniah." *Biblical Interpretation* 24 (2016): 310–31.

Timmer, Daniel C. *The Non-Israelite Nations in the Book of the Twelve: Thematic Coherence and the Diachronic-Synchronic Relationship in the Minor Prophets*. Biblical Interpretation 135. Leiden: Brill, 2015.

Udoekpo, Michael Ufok. *Re-thinking the Day of YHWH and Restoration of Fortunes in the Prophet Zephaniah: An Exegetical and Theological Study of 1:14–18; 3:14–20*. Bern: Peter Lang, 2010.

Ussishkin, David. "The Destruction of Lachish by Sennacherib and the Dating of the Royal Judean Storage Jars." *Tel Aviv* 4 (1977), 28–60.

Vanderhooft, David. "Babylonian Strategies for Imperial Control in the West: Royal Practice and Rhetoric." In *Judah and the Judeans*, 235–62. Edited by Oded Lipschits and Joseph Blenkinsopp. Winona Lake, IN: Eisenbrauns, 2003.

von Rad, Gerhard. "The Origin of the Concept of the Day of Yahweh." *Journal of Semitic Studies* 4 (1959): 97–108.

Watai, Yoko. "The Monuments of the Neo-Babylonian Kings as an Indication for Their Presence in the Western Territories of Their Empire." In *The Reach of the Assyrian and Babylonian Empires: Case Studies in Eastern and Western Peripheries*. Studia Chaburensia 8, 149–65. Edited by Shuichi Hasegawa and Karen Radner. Wiesbaden: Harrassowitz, 2020.

Watson, Wilfred G. E. *Classical Hebrew Poetry: A Guide to its Techniques*, JSOTSup 26. Sheffield: JSOT, 1984.

Webb, William J. and Gordon K. Oeste, *Bloody Brutal and Barbaric? Wrestling with Troubling War Texts*. Downers Grove, IL: IVP Academic, 2019.

Weima, Jeffrey A. D. *1–2 Thessalonians*. BECNT. Grand Rapids: Baker Academic, 2014.

Weiss Meir. "The Origin of the 'Day of the Lord' Reconsidered." *HUCA* 37 (1966): 29–71.

Welch, Eric Lee. "The Roots of Anger: An Economic Perspective on Zephaniah's Oracle Against the Philistines." *VT* 63 (2013): 471–85.

Wendland, E. "The Drama of Zephaniah. A Literary-Structural Analysis of a Proclamatory Prophetic Text." *Journal for Semitics* 16/1 (2007): 22–67.

_______. and David J. Clark. "Zephaniah: Anatomy and Physiology of a Dramatic Prophetic Text." *Journal of Translation and Textlinguistics* 16 (2003): 1–44.

Werse, Nicholas R. "Of Gods and Kings: The Case for Reading 'Milcom' in Zephaniah 1:5b." *VT* 68 (2018): 505–13.

_______. "Realigning the Cosmos: The Intertextual Image of Judgment and Restoration in Zephaniah." *JSOT* 45 (1) (2020): 111–27.

_______. "Reconsidering the Problematic Tripartite Structure of Zephaniah." *ZAW* 130 (4) (2018): 571–85.

Westermann, Claus. *Basic Forms of Prophetic Speech*. Translated by H. C. White. Philadelphia: Westminster Press, 1967.

Whybray, R. N. *Isaiah 40–66*. NCB. Grand Rapids, William B. Eerdmans, 1981.

Wiggins, Steve A. "Yahweh: The God of Sun?" *JSOT* 71 (1996): 89–106.

Wildberger, Hans. *Isaiah 13–27: A Commentary.* Continental Commentary. Translated by Thomas H. Trapp. Minneapolis: Fortress, 1997.

Wilson, Robert R. *Prophecy and Society in Ancient Israel*. Minneapolis: Fortress, 1980.

Zalcman, Lawrence. "Ambiguity and Assonance at Zephaniah II 4." *VT* 36, 3 (1986): 365–71.

NAME INDEX

G

H

I

J

K

L

M

N

O

P

R

SCRIPTURE INDEX

GENESIS

EXODUS

LEVITICUS

NUMBERS

RUTH

1 SAMUEL

2 SAMUEL

1 KINGS

2 KINGS

1 CHRONICLES

2 CHRONICLES

LAMENTATIONS

EZEKIEL

HAGGAI

ZECHARIAH

MALACHI

MATTHEW